Frontiers in Economic History

Economic historians have contributed to the development of economics in a variety of ways, combining theory with quantitative methods, constructing new databases, promoting interdisciplinary approaches to historical topics, and using history as a lens to examine the long-term development of the economy. Frontiers in Economic History publishes manuscripts that push the frontiers of research in economic history in order to better explain past economic experiences and to understand how, why and when economic change occurs. Books in this series will highlight the value of economic history in shedding light on the ways in which economic factors influence growth as well as social and political developments. This series aims to establish a new standard of quality in the field while offering a global discussion forum toward a unified approach in the social sciences.

John Sedgwick
Editor

Towards a Comparative Economic History of Cinema, 1930–1970

Springer

Editor
John Sedgwick
Oxford Brookes University
Oxford, UK

ISSN 2662-9771 ISSN 2662-978X (electronic)
Frontiers in Economic History
ISBN 978-3-031-05769-4 ISBN 978-3-031-05770-0 (eBook)
https://doi.org/10.1007/978-3-031-05770-0

This Springer imprint is published by the registered company Springer Nature Switzerland AG
The registered company address is: Gewerbestrasse 11, 6330 Cham, Switzerland

Preface

Over many years I have associated with film historians worldwide who have been involved in collecting and analysing source materials that reflect the experience of going to the cinema, the choices that audiences made and the cinemas in which they sat. From this base, other questions emerge connected to how a stock of films flows to a set of cinemas in a timely fashion: a process of diffusion that is deliberate and framed by the circumstances of time and place.

The scholars featured in this book have made significant contributions to developing this discourse. I am grateful for their patience, especially when, in a few cases, we started far apart. With their students in mind, I conceived the idea for the book; something that gained impetus after COVID-19 prevented me from taking up an invitation from Konrad Klejsa to teach and research Polish film history at the University of Lodz. I had intended to develop a methodological approach to the film industry in Poland during the 1930s based upon what would have been, for me, unknown source materials. Primarily, I wanted to show that the Polish film industry could be examined by following films on their non-random journey from their initial release. This is my starting point for film industries everywhere.

My academic background is in economic history. I was fortunate to study for a master's degree at Birkbeck College, London University, in the early 1980s, taking courses with Eric Hobsbawm, Roderick Floud, Pat Thane and Ben Fine. The material nature of what economic historians investigate and how it shapes landscapes, environments, lives and consciousness struck a chord. In searching for a dissertation topic, my friend Bernard Hrusa Marlow suggested looking at the early British film industry, which I did periodising the study from 1896 to 1908. From the trade journal *The Kinematograph and Lantern Monthly,* I learned that films were sold by their length, at first 6d per foot, reducing to 4d per foot in 1906. For an economic historian, this is essential information, suggesting producers and consumers considered films a homogeneous commodity. This state didn't last. It became clear that entrepreneurs were dynamically changing the business environment during these embryonic years, searching for innovations that earned them money. At the tail end of my study, film studios began to consciously differentiate their film products by extending their length and announcing acting inputs. They were also looking for ways to restrict supply, given the burgeoning second-hand market that was developing.

The motives of film business executives and owners are not very complicated. The quest for business advantage is measured ultimately in terms of profitability, and in this pursuit, owners' behaviour is not always transparent or truthful. In a newly emerging market, the danger of opportunism is mistrust, leading to markets that do not function very well. Accordingly, trade associations were formed, supply chain procedures codified, and miscreant behaviour punished. As films became longer and differentiated, audiences became more selective, developing preferences. Ultimately, consumers sanction those products put on the market. They do not pay if the entertainment is not good. Thus, equilibrium is formed, integrating the numerous acts of coordination entailed in film production with the judgements formed by substantial but unknown and fleeting audiences.

In this light, it is possible to understand the processes and procedures of the ten national markets investigated in the book. Two chapters are dedicated to the film business behind the Iron Curtain around the time of the death of Joseph Stalin, in which the behaviour of industry executives is politically constrained by ideological imperatives of a type not experienced by their Western counterparts. Nevertheless, while it is necessary to be more guarded about our findings in these two contexts, diffusion patterns emerge like those found in the capitalist world.

The analytical framework proposed in these national studies provides a base for investigating popular taste and the aesthetics evident in the films seen by many in each population. The contributors take various approaches—ranging from the close reading of the popular movies of the day and their mise-en-scene to archival investigations concerning government policy connected to the business of film production, distribution and exhibition. The purpose is to stimulate scholars starting a research career in cinema to broaden their investigations to include the materiality of cinema. A second objective is to demonstrate to economic history researchers that the subject is not confined to determinants of economic growth and development but also manifestations of human activity connected to prosaic and day-to-day that have cultural undertones.

As well as the contributors, I would like to say something about colleagues I worked with at an institution variously called the Polytechnic of North London, University of North London, and London Metropolitan University. Over many years they provided unwavering support for the Norman Stang research seminar I led and, through many conversations, candid criticism of the framework I was developing. Mike Pokorny brought an acute statistical eye to many investigations. I shared a room with Photis Lysandrou for 20 years, from whom I learned about the DNA of commodity production. Also, to Stuart Archbold, John Curran and Bob Morgan, I would like to express my thanks. I also should express my gratitude to Rob Rawlinson, who read and commented on the chapter on methods.

Finally, I should like to pay tribute to the late Karel Dibbets. At the University of Amsterdam, he developed an extraordinary database of everyday cinema in the Netherlands during the twentieth century before the German invasion in 1940. Karel was a pioneer scholar and a lovely man. It is in his memory that I should like to dedicate the book.

Derbyshire, UK John Sedgwick

Contents

Introduction: 'Millions of People Every Day'—Cinema as Part of the Quotidian of Life 1
John Sedgwick

Managing Risk in the Film Business—Key Concepts and Methods 19
John Sedgwick

How Did the Department of Justice Get It so Wrong? Philadelphia 1935–1936: The Stanley Warner Chain, Competitive Practices and Consumer Welfare 45
F. Andrew Hanssen and John Sedgwick

Comparative Film Popularity in Three English Cities—Bolton, Brighton, and Portsmouth: An Exercise in POPSTAT Methodology 65
John Sedgwick

Popular Films in Stockholm During the 1930s: A Presentation and Discussion of the Pioneering Work of Leif Furhammar 87
Åsa Jernudd and John Sedgwick

Dutch Films in the Mid-1930s Dutch Market: A Characteristics Approach to Film Popularity 143
Clara Pafort Overduin

Unravelling Australia's 'Infamous "Contract" System': Evidence from Adelaide, 1942–1943 185
Dylan Walker and Mike Walsh

Film Exhibition, Distribution and Popularity in German-Occupied Belgium (1940–1944): Brussels, Antwerp and Liege 217
Roel Vande Winkel and John Sedgwick

Five Italian Cities: Comparative Analysis of Cinema Types, Film Circulation and Relative Popularity in the Mid-1950s 249
Daniela Treveri Gennari and John Sedgwick

Cinemagoers Should '...learn from progressive movies, again and again'. Cinemagoing in Czechoslovakia, 1949–1952 281
Pavel Skopal, Terézia Porubčanská, and John Sedgwick

'It Seems to Me that the Most Popular Films in the West Are Very Harmful to Us': Film Popularity in Poland During the years of 'High Stalinisation' 307
Konrad Klejsa and John Sedgwick

Americanisation in Reverse? Hollywood Films, International Influences, and US Audiences, 1946–1965 339
Peter Miskell

Correction to: Film Exhibition, Distribution and Popularity in German-Occupied Belgium (1940–1944): Brussels, Antwerp and Liege C1
Roel Vande Winkel and John Sedgwick

Editor and Contributors

About the Editor

Sedgwick John is a visiting professor in the Faculty of Technology, Design and Environment, Oxford Brookes University. He researches the economic history of cinema and is particularly interested in the ontological characteristics of film as a commodity. He created the POPSTAT Index of Film Popularity as a proxy for box-office returns. This tool provides a means of reflecting audience preferences and monitoring the distribution process. His research has focused on American, Australian, British, Dutch, Italian and international markets during the 1930s and 1950/1960s. He has written a monograph, edited an anthology and published articles in *Business History, Cinema Journal, Economic History Review, Explorations in Economic History, Enterprise and Society, Film History, Historical Journal of Film, Radio and Television, Journal of Applied Statistics, Journal of Cultural Economics, Journal of Economic History* and *Journal of Transnational Cinema.*

Contributors

Gennari Daniela Treveri Oxford Brookes University, Oxford, UK

Hanssen F. Andrew Clemson University, Clemson, SC, USA

Jernudd Åsa The School of Humanities, Education and Social Sciences, Örebro University, Örebro, Sweden

Klejsa Konrad University of Lodz, Lodz, Poland

Miskell Peter Henley Business School, University of Reading, Reading, UK

Overduin Clara Pafort Department of Media and Culture Studies & Institute for Cultural Inquiry (ICON), Utrecht University, Utrecht, The Netherlands

Porubčanská Terézia Department of Film Studies and Audiovisual Culture, Masaryk University, Brno, Czech Republic

Sedgwick John Faculty of Technology, Design and Environment, Oxford Brookes University, Oxford, UK

Skopal Pavel Department of Film Studies and Audiovisual Culture, Masaryk University, Brno, Czech Republic

Walker Dylan Adelaide, SA, Australia

Walsh Mike Flinders University, Adelaide, SA, Australia

Winkel Roel Vande KU Leuven and LUCA School of Arts, Schaerbeek, Belgium

Introduction: 'Millions of People Every Day'—Cinema as Part of the Quotidian of Life

John Sedgwick

Abstract Cinema is a way of life during the period covered by this book in large parts of the world. Central to it is the transaction between an exhibitor and a customer and the mechanism whereby a stock of films-as-commodities flowed among a set of cinemas through time and place. The flow was calculated and deliberate, making popular movies much less scarce than unpopular ones. Economic rationality is apparent: exhibitors and distributors in capitalist economies maximised their returns by adjusting supply to reflect audience preferences once revealed. Each transaction generated filmgoing data, from which patterns emerged, sometimes challenging accepted wisdom concerning the popularity of films or how they were circulated. The book aims to show what can be achieved by bringing simple empirical methods to bear on the history of cinema. It also seeks to encourage scholars to develop studies of their own, allowing audiences to speak for themselves through the choices they made—a method built upon microfoundations.

> There must be millions of people every day who find entertainment, perhaps amusement, certainly relaxation, in this great new institution (cinema), entirely unknown to any previous generation.[1]

Although cinema was a small industry in terms of its contribution to national wealth, its importance lies in its appeal to people everywhere for much of the twentieth century. In Great Britain in 1934, three-quarters of all paid-for admissions to entertainment events were spent at the cinema, with audiences that year close to a billion, yet this constituted only one-hundredth of consumer expenditure for the nation.[2] These high attendances, amounting to 19.2 trips to the cinema per capita, partly resulted from cheapness. George Orwell in 1937 wrote of unemployed men in the North of England being able to afford the price of admission to get out of the cold

[1] Rowson (1936, p. 68).

[2] Sedgwick (2000, p. 42).

J. Sedgwick (✉)
Oxford Brookes University, Oxford, England
e-mail: sedgwicj52@gmail.com

J. Sedgwick (ed.), *Towards a Comparative Economic History of Cinema, 1930–1970*, Frontiers in Economic History, https://doi.org/10.1007/978-3-031-05770-0_1

of a winter's afternoon.[3] The out-of-work men probably weren't too fussy about what films they went to see. However, the evidence from those cinemas ledgers that have survived indicates that choices were made, from which it can be supposed that preferences were manifest in those choices. Cinema was an essential aspect of civil society for those in work and out, particularly young adults and women.[4]

This book addresses the industrial organisation of cinema, involving competition between producers, distributors, and exhibitors to attract audiences. It does so across various nations, most of whose inhabitants enjoy relatively high living standards. It examines the part that producers and distributors played in the supply of films and brings attention to those films that audiences regarded as exceptional.

Furthermore, it will contribute to the comparative institutional knowledge of economies, consumers, and culture. Central is the transaction between an exhibitor and a customer, which gives rise to a mechanism whereby a flow of films passes through a stock of cinemas. A series of national case studies are developed from such microfoundations, derived from unique datasets based upon these transactions. The flow of films is deliberate—making popular movies much less scarce than unpopular ones. Economic rationality is apparent: one in which exhibitors and distributors maximised their returns by dynamically adjusting supply to reflect audience preferences better, once revealed.

The most popular movies in the national markets featured in the book are identified through the systematic collection of cinema programming information or film revenues in trade magazines. The results are often surprising, drawing attention to little known films. As Miskell has shown, even Hollywood, with its evident superiority of resources, talent, and business networks, was only partially able to overcome a prevailing 'liability of foreignness'—the willingness of populations everywhere to watch films with which they could identify.[5]

Patterns emerge from these microfoundations, which often challenge accepted wisdom about the popularity of films or how they were circulated and screened. It brings to the table robust evidence that can be challenged. Filmgoing was part of the quotidian of life for a sizeable proportion of the world's population during our time frame. The book aims to show what can be achieved by bringing simple empirical methods to the history of cinema. It also seeks to encourage scholars to develop studies of their own, in which national histories can be told from the bottom upwards.

Thus, this book is intended for scholars interested in films that audiences liked and how they circulated. This interest might be what film popularity tells us about societies in the past—about choices made or how film selection was mediated. It might also be about the qualities of popular films at junctures in history and how these might have changed over the years. It might be about how film consumer

[3] Orwell (1962, p. 72).

[4] Fowler (1995, p. 110), McKibbin (1998, p. 421).

[5] Miskell (2016, p. 20).

tastes differed from place to place: not simply nation to nation, but region to region, province to province, city to city, or town to town. It might be about the cultural divide between the popular and artistic taste, or between mediums, say, film and television.

1 Film as a Commodity

Chapter 1 of Karl Marx's Das Capital, Volume 1, opens with statements about commodity production.

> The wealth of societies in which the capitalist mode of production prevails appears as an immense collection of commodities...The commodity is, first of all, an external object, a thing which, through its qualities, satisfies human needs of whatever kind, ... whether they arise, for example, from the stomach, or the imagination, makes no difference.[6]

For Marx, commodity production distinguishes the modern world—it encapsulates the capitalist mode of production and differentiates it from earlier production systems. In his famous conceptual depiction of the process of capitalism, M-C-M^1, in which M = Money and C = Commodity, Marx maintains that commodities come into being because money has been advanced in the form of capital, with the object that more money (profit) might be made. Implicit in this process are prices—how commodities are exchanged and revenues generated. In this tradition, Photis Lysandrou develops a two-space theory of the commodity. While commodities take on heterogeneous forms, they are traded in what he terms a homogenised commodity space: a space in which disparate commodity objects are stripped of their actual properties and stand in relation to one another by means of the socially determined prices they carry (Lysandrou, 2019).[7]

Films are such commodities, generally appreciated for their aesthetic and emotional qualities. They entail a producer/distributor/exhibitor who seeks the desired effect (profit) from exchanging the item-as-commodity with a purchaser seeking an affected desire (such as to be entertained) at an acceptable price.[8]

As a type, movies differ from other commodities, such as theatre, motor cars, or potatoes, in how they are supplied and used—what Ben Fine and Ellen Leopold have termed a *system of provision*. They write:

> ... different commodities or groups of commodities (are) distinctly structured by the chain or system of provision that unites a particular pattern of production with a particular pattern of consumption (in) ways in which each is moderated by the connections between them.[9]

---

6 Marx (1976, p. 125).

7 Lysandrou uses the centrality of Marx's conception to explain globalisation and the role played by finance in this.

8 See Sedgwick (2000, p. 8).

9 Fine and Leopold (1993, p. 4).

From Fine and Leopold, we learn that the characteristics of film as a commodity are derived from the particular practices of production, distribution, exhibition, and consumption, framing the behaviour of agents engaged in delivering or consuming movies. This applies throughout its history, from the embryonic period when entrepreneurs had to discover how to make money from the sale of moving pictures to today and online delivery.

The salient characteristics are proposed. No two films are identical. They can be reproduced infinitely at marginal costs much lower than the cost of production. They are also non-rival, in that one person's consumption does not diminish the prospect of another person making the same choice. Even so, during the decades of this study, audiences were excluded from consumption if they were unwilling or unable to pay the price of cinema admission. For their part, consumers rarely revisited films and, in urban settings, have a wide array of films from which to choose. In combination, these qualities make movies different from other cultural products, such as records, books, and live performances and give form to how the film industry developed historically within a capitalist framework.

Given that all films are unique, the central dichotomy of the economics of cinema is that consumers cannot know beforehand fully whether they will like a movie. According to Arthur De Vany and David Walls, they must discover '...what they like'.[10] In not knowing how to please filmgoers, film producers necessarily entertain risk. Filmgoers make choices from the set of films before them. Film producers make choices about what films to make. Through their decisions, filmgoers sanction those made by producers or not. The outcome of their respective activities is a rank order that reflects consumer preferences. The prevalence of uncertainty and the strategies adopted to overcome it are at the heart of this book.

Thus, an ontology is proposed, in which the material circumstances of supply and the immaterial nature of consumption are intimately interwoven:

Supply/Provision:

- Films are unique—no two film products are the same.
- They have no physical properties.
- They are infinitely reproducible at relatively low costs.
- They can be re-sized for screens of different dimensions.
- The physical means of producing film images deteriorates slowly—today, digitally, not at all.
- Consumers can be excluded from consumption—films are not public goods.
- Revenues can be generated from admission to cinemas, from selling broadcasting rights to television, DVD sales, and digital transfer.
- Finally, films are non-diminishable in consumption, meaning that the act of consumption by consumer *A* does not impact the stock available for consumers *B* to *Z*. They are *non-rival*.

Demand/Consumption:

[10] De Vany and Walls (1996, p. 1493).

- Consumers enjoy narratives entailing moving images which they consume cognitively as immaterial entities.
- Consumers are willing to allocate time away from other competing uses to consume them and pay for the pleasure.
- In consumption, consumers experience rapidly diminishing marginal utility—the pleasure they derive from each subsequent viewing of a film declines dramatically.
- Novelty, as a rule, is preferred to repeat consumption, even though this entails risk. Most people watch films just once.

These commodity characteristics ground the book. They are inherent in each case study, showing how the film business adapted to what Frederick Hayek termed '…the knowledge of the particular circumstances of time and place'.[11] Despite these characteristics being universal, the scale of production and consumption differed. For instance, take the highly socially stratified society of the Netherlands during the 1930s, when the Dutch did not go to the cinema very much, compared to the British.[12]

Why was this? A mixture of cultural and institutional arguments emerges. Jan De Vries developed the 'breadwinner-homemaker household' concept. He depicts the Dutch as sober homely people who acquired a market and non-market goods and services through the household division of labour that improved its members' material and moral welfare.[13] Furthermore, the social silos to which families typically belonged perceived cinema as a corrupting influence, making it a more conscionable activity for audiences. A third factor might be that the Dutch film trade body (NBB) determined the regulations of both exhibition and distribution sectors. This monopoly situation allowed them to impose restrictive practices and charge higher prices.

2 Hollywood

John Izod is in no doubt about the motives of agents supplying, distributing, and exhibiting movies. He prefaces his book on Hollywood and the box office with a statement:

> Profits have always, from the earliest days, been the primary objective of the American film industry …This is not to say that all American features do make profit – but almost all are intended to do so.[14]

By the 1930s, entertainment films could be watched worldwide, although they were not produced worldwide. The reach of films was primarily the consequence of the ambition of Hollywood's distributors to get their products circulated to as many markets as was feasible. The other side of this coin is the demand from populations everywhere for motion pictures: a demand that transcended the potential disruption

---

[11] Hayek (1945, p. 521).

[12] Sedgwick et al. (2012).

[13] De Vries (2008).

[14] Izod (1998, p. ix).

and expense associated with the 'coming of sound'.[15] The level of demand enticed local entrepreneurs to finance the building of cinemas, in many cases allowing the Hollywood distributors to play a leading role in organising the local framework of film distribution across the globe.

Krystin Thompson has shown that before the emergence of the Hollywood studios, most American companies based their European and world selling operations in London. Britain was attractive to American companies for three reasons: first, until 1915, there was no tariff on film imports; second, Britain was America's biggest foreign market, with American films taking a 50–60 per cent market share in the years immediately before 1914, and thirdly, the British shipping system was pervasive and 'British business people had knowledge of international commerce and could cope with the different currencies, languages and other special problems involved'.[16] The breakdown in European production and international business occasioned by the First World War gave the newly formed Hollywood studios Universal, Loew's, Fox and Paramount/Famous Players Lasky the opportunity to set up global networks, selling directly into foreign markets.[17]

By 1930, The Film Daily Yearbook (FDYB) of 1931 reports that MGM had offices in the following countries: Algeria, Argentina, Australia, Austria, Belgium, Brazil, Chile, China, Colombia, Costa Rica, Cuba, Czechoslovakia, Denmark, Dutch West Indies, Egypt, Finland, France, Germany, Great Britain, Guatemala, Greece, Holland, Hungary, India, Italy, Japan, Yugoslavia, Korea, Mexico, Morocco, New Zealand, Nicaragua, Norway, Palestine, Panama, Philippine Islands, Poland, Porto Rico, Portugal, Romania, Spain, Straits Settlements, Sweden, Switzerland, and Turkey. In addition to these, Paramount had offices in Bolivia, Estonia, Latvia, Lithuania, Peru, Tunisia, and Uruguay. In addition, Universal Studios was present in Venezuela and Warner Bros. in Japan. United Artists was also widely represented across these territories. Much less so, RKO (newly formed) and Columbia, and in the case of Fox, not at all; preferring to employ either one of their fellow Hollywood distributors or local agencies.[18]

Outside of the United States in the 1930s, film production in Czechoslovakia, France, Germany, Great Britain, Italy, Japan, Spain, and the USSR was geared mainly to their respective domestic markets. The Japanese and the Soviet markets were essentially closed. In the remainder, Hollywood films took a substantial market share. France, Great Britain, and Spain had a considerable presence in their respective imperial markets. German films circulated widely in bordering states.

In 1930, the world economy was entering into a sustained recession, bringing about massive levels of unemployment and hardship across the globe, reversing the growth in international trade that followed the end of the First World War. During

[15] 'By 1930 the potential thorny issue of sound—both in terms of language and projection—has been overcome.' Film Daily Yearbook (FDYB), (1931, p. 1001).

[16] Thompson (1985, p. 2).

[17] Thompson (1985, pp. 71–73).

[18] FDYB (1931, pp. 1052–56).

1932 and 1933, trade volumes had fallen below 1913 levels.[19] While filmgoing declined during the early 1930s, this falls likely to have been most significant among the poorest in society, judging by the closure of cinemas.[20]

By 1970 much of the world economy had enjoyed unprecedented growth for 25 years. Among the wealthiest capitalist nations, the State had become a key player in the economy, both in those industries nationalised after the Second World War and the through the general provision of social welfare. Coupled with more-or-less full employment, the growth of real wages over these years ensured a general sense of well-being. Of course, by this date, cinema was declining everywhere as television brought various entertainment and news information into the home. It was no longer central to the way of life as it had once been. By 1965 admissions to the cinema in Great Britain were five times lower than the peak of 1.635 billion recorded in 1946. Elsewhere in Europe, audiences peaked some ten years later, in the mid-1950s. In the United States, attendances halved from their 1946 peak, with box office falling by two-thirds in real terms by 1965, while recreational expenditure doubled in real terms.[21]

3 Industrial Organisation

The industrial organisation of the film industry during the period under investigation can be dated back to the revenue-maximising strategy pioneered by Adolf Zuckor in the early 1910s. Understanding that the capital embodied in film products could not be put to alternative uses and therefore had no alternative value, Zuckor realised that the film business should be entirely focused on diffusing films to as many consumers as possible. In modern economics speak, the costs of production and exhibition were sunk. Given *sunk costs*, it follows that popular films should be made less scarce than less popular films. The most popular movies should be ubiquitous and circulated to every locality subject to two conditions. The first is that exhibitors generated revenues that exceeded the rental fee cost. The second is that the rental fee charged by the distributor more than covers the costs involved to get the film to the exhibitor. Where rental prices could not be met, movies were not shown. This condition presents a limit to the reach of any film—a limit to its distribution.

Zuckor (along with four other producers) established a vertically integrated link between his production company *Famous Players,* the distributor *Paramount* and its fledgling cinema chains to achieve this end. In this way, Zuckor could ensure that his films were widely diffused by controlling the supply chain. However, Paramount's

[19] Federico and Junguito (2018).

[20] Variety (2 August 1932) ran the headline '6500 Dark Theatres'. See Balio (1993, ch. 2).

[21] Film Distributor's Society https://www.launchingfilms.com/research-databank/uk-cinema-admissions; Sedgwick (2002); Tables H873, H374, Historical Statistics of the United States, Colonial Times to 1975 https://www.census.gov/library/publications/1975/compendia/hist_stats_colonial-1970.html.

draconian insistence on blind block booking led other exhibition chains to resist and form a rival distribution network (First National). All the leading studios, distributors, and exhibitors moved towards vertical integration during the late 1910s and early 1920s.[22] The last part in this jigsaw was the contractual flexibility for cinemas under contract to a specific distributor to screen films handled by rival distributors—significant for the revenue potential of films in high demand.[23]

The final aspect of the revenue-maximising process was separating cinemas into hierarchical categories based upon their earning capacities in conjunction with limiting the life cycle of films to no more than 15 months.[24] The practice of charging different prices for the same product is known in economics as *price discrimination*. Clearly, the longer a film spends in higher-order cinemas, the greater the box-office revenue. A second condition for maximum revenue generation entails the reach of a movie—that is, the number and dispersion of cinemas screening it during its life in circulation across cinema runs and localities.

The separation of cinemas allowed distributors to stagger the diffusion process by placing time intervals between cinema categories known as cinema runs—first-run, second-run, etc. These intervals were managed and sealed: that is, a second-run cinema couldn't screen a film while it was still being screened in one or more first-run cinemas, and so on. The process of film circulation can thus be described as one in which a stock of new films flowed through a stock of cinemas in a pre-arranged but adaptable fashion—a flow which took them from box-office rich to box-office poor cinemas in response to consumer demand.

Thus, a highly flexible coordination mechanism developed by which films, once produced, were distributed as far and wide as was financially viable. The circulation of any single movie terminated once exhibitors, given a set of fixed and operational costs, could not raise sufficient box-office revenue to meet the threshold rental payment/price demanded by distributors. Hence, distribution economics assured that popular films received many more billings than films to which audiences were less attracted. Consumers got to see what, on average, they liked, and it is thus, coupled with the ubiquity of filmgoing in general, that makes filmgoing such a good indicator of social taste.

For instance, in 1935, in the large industrial town of Bolton in North England, with a population of 180,000, the Hollywood operetta *One Night of Love* was screened on ten separate occasions in one of the 18 cinemas that advertised daily programmes in the *Bolton Evening News*.[25] This phenomenon of the most popular films coming around time and again, well within 12 months, before exhausting their local audience was not a one-off but rather a regular aspect of urban cinema everywhere.

Price discrimination practices allowed distributors to exploit the willingness-to-pay of audiences, capturing what economists term *consumer surplus*. That is, they were able to seal off that section of the audience willing to pay higher prices to

---

[22] Izod (1998).

[23] Hanssen (2000, 2002).

[24] Greenwald (1950).

[25] Sedgwick (2000, p. 104).

see a particular film sooner rather than later. Other sections of the population were required to wait for it to appear later, in a less well-accoutred cinema that charged lower prices.

This system became institutionalised in the United States during the 1920s. Its genesis laid the foundation for substantial new investment in the industry as rival vertically integrated companies competed with one another in a rapidly expanding domestic and international market. Of course, the films themselves were at the centre of this industrial ferment with their peculiar embodiment of characteristics, including stars. Together they attracted audiences *en masse* but differentially, giving shape and point to the industrial infrastructure that emerged. Movies were the source of the revenues generated and the risks incurred. Scaling the industry to meet rising consumer demand took the form of fewer films, each of which, on average, cost more to make and circulated more extensively. During the 1920s, film costs soared as producers sought to release films that were qualitatively superior to the products of rival studios. With each studio doing the same, competition escalated quality.[26]

To get films made, distributed, and screened widely, a highly specialised division of labour was developed that crudely could be broken down into artistic, business, financial, and technical parts. Mainly, this division of labour was coordinated by firms, the largest of which were vertically integrated, traversing the supply-side functions of production, distribution, and exhibition. By the late 1920s, the Hollywood *Majors*—Fox, MGM, Paramount, RKO, and Warner Bros. supplemented production and distribution functions with substantial cinema chains acquired during the last half of the decade. In Europe, other vertically integrated firms emerged—British International Pictures and Gaumont British in Great Britain. However, most firms in the industry specialised in aspects of the division of labour—they supplied wigs, or specialist film cameras, or stuntmen or women, or owned, or managed a single cinema, or two, or a small geographically concentrated chain of cinemas. In some cases, individuals with unique talents marketed themselves, working from contract to contract with different studios—the American actor Barbara Stanwyck is a case in point. Indeed, it is rewarding to investigate the Year Books issued by film industry trade journals to get an idea of the extensiveness of the suppliers of film equipment and services.

The film industry is ultimately described by the configuration of firms—large and small that are competitively juxtaposed. At any moment in time, its contours are the consequences of strategic decisions made and risks incurred. For instance, one can imagine the supply of elocution services increased dramatically with the 'coming of sound'. Ronald Coase wrote an influential paper in which he maintained that the extent of the firm was determined by the costs and risk entailed in obtaining necessary goods and services from the market.[27] The market mechanism was not frictionless. He argued that under certain conditions, supplying these goods and services internally, under the single authority canopy of the firm, would enhance coordination efficiency and lessen the costs of using the market. Oliver Williamson and Douglass North later

[26] Bakker (2008, 2012).

[27] Coase (1937).

developed these ideas, respectively, to examine the strategic aspect of firm decision-making under uncertainty and, at a societal level, the costs to trade occasioned by institutional arrangements.[28]

By 1930, the industry can be best considered a mature oligopoly dominated by a few vertically integrated firms in which production distribution and exhibition operations were coordinated.[29] Geared to maximising revenue and mitigating risk, film studios produced portfolios of films ranging in cost. Before release, studios didn't know which films in their annual portfolios would generate revenues that exceeded their combined production and distribution costs. Before viewing these films, consumers didn't know which would yield them the greatest pleasure. They could only evaluate their choice, and hence experience, after the event.[30] The purpose of the portfolio for the Hollywood producer/distributor was to balance these risks.[31] Indeed, during the 1930s, had the *major* studios produced big-budget films only, they would have gone out of business. Only the constant positive earnings of the middle budget films of the portfolios kept them profitable, reflected in the much lower values of the *Gini coefficient* (a measure of inequality) during the era compared to the post-Second World War period beyond.[32] Indeed, as a characterisation, popular cinema during the 1930s in the United States was broad-based.

4 Measures of Popularity

Critical to the account of film popularity is knowledge of the box office. The book promotes three tools that allow historical audiences to speak for themselves through their filmgoing decision-making. Box-office statistics account for the comparative performance of films, their studios, stars, and directors. If detailed enough, they allow for comparative assessment of different audiences in different places. Of course, implicit in this line of investigation are the tastes and preferences of consumers and, through this portal, what they reveal about broader society. Unfortunately, because third parties systematically collected box-office receipts—how else would distributors obtain the rental payments specified in their contracts with exhibitors?—for the period 1930 to 1970, they are not easy to find. In their absence, based upon an estimate of the relative earning capacity of cinemas, the *POPSTAT Index of Film Popularity* was developed as a proxy.[33]

Recognising that not all films are similarly popular, the RelPOP method was introduced to compare taste differences between Northern and Southern cities in Italy during the 1950s and 60s. This comparative tool uses the revenue (POPSTAT)

[28] Williamson (1975), North (1990).

[29] Gomery (1992), Izod (1998).

[30] Sedgwick (2000, 2007), Sedgwick and Pokorny (2010).

[31] Sedgwick and Pokorny (1998), Pokorny and Sedgwick (2012).

[32] Pokorny and Sedgwick (2010).

[33] Sedgwick (2000).

statistical distribution to gauge the actual to median box-office ratio of each film in circulation and to compare these between localities.[34]

Noting that not all Hollywood films were equally received in foreign markets, Peter Miskell has developed a third method to analyse the performance of Hollywood films in international markets, building upon earlier work.[35] In giving form to the strategic thinking behind Hollywood's global sales effort, Miskell developed an analytical tool he terms the *International Orientation Index* to show how deliberate Hollywood was, and of course still is, in attracting large overseas markets for its products. Based on four factors entailing aspects of film scenarios and four describing the ethnic origins of the primary talent engaged (first and second stars, director, and screenwriter), Miskell scores over 1200 Hollywood films released between 1921 and 1951 and associates these with their respective performances in foreign markets.[36]

5 Audience Behaviour

Audience behaviour is perceived as a discursive practice in which taste regimes emerge through the intermediation of audiences and the objects of their interest. This means that filmgoers talk to one another about their film experiences. In doing this, they pass on their evaluations of films (recently) seen and, in return, hear those of others. In conjunction with other sources of information such as reviews, advertising and promotions, and previous experience, this exchange allows filmgoers to assess new film releases and form expectations. By constantly repeating this process, filmgoers develop tastes and order them as preferences—they discover what they like. In keeping with this framework of thinking, Arsel and Bean (2013, p. 900) maintain:

> ...a taste regime propagates a shared understanding of aesthetic order that shapes the ways people use objects and deploy the meanings associated with the material.[37]

While film consumption is personal, discursive interaction in the search for meaning(s) is social. In profiling the popularity of films in circulation within selected urban settings, contours of film consumer taste emerge, differing according to time and place.

Thus, it is conjectured that consumers, through personal experience, have a good idea of what they like, which they bring to the decision of which film to go next and see. However, and fundamentally, they do not have a complete conception of the films in their decision set. Thus, for instance, the possibility exists that their evaluation of their film of choice ends in disappointment and the realisation that the wrong choice has been made. Hence, what is being proposed is a range of possible experiences around an expectation that is not fully formed, bounded by the twin states of loss and

[34] Sedgwick et al. (2019).

[35] Thompson (1985), Jarvie (1992), Vasey (1997), Glancy (1999).

[36] Miskell (2016).

[37] Arsel and Bean (2013, p. 900).

gain—loss when the experience is disappointing, causing consumers to wish they made a different choice. In contrast, gain can result in something akin to ecstasy.

The process just described rests upon microfoundations. While it may be obvious, it is worth saying that decision-making always takes place before action, be it the film producer raising finance to make a film or the consumer's decision of what movie to watch tonight. The choices made by countless consumers in the various countries covered in this book are central to the approach taken in this book.

Felin, Foss, Heimeriks, and Madsen define microfoundations formally as follows:

> . . . theoretical explanation, supported by empirical examination, of a phenomenon located at analytical level N at time t (N_t). In the simplest sense, a baseline micro-foundation for level N_t lies at level N-1 at time t-1, where the time dimension reflects a temporal ordering of relationships with phenomena at level N-1 predating phenomena at level N. Constituent actors, processes, and/or structures, at level N-1_{t-1} may interact, or operate alone, to influence phenomena at level N_t. Moreover, actors, processes, and/or structures at level N-$1_{(t-1)}$ also may moderate or mediate influences of phenomena located at level N_t or at higher levels (e.g. N+$1_{(t+1)}$ to N+$n_{(t+n)}$).[38]

The approach adopted in this book entails investigating the film choices made by witting filmgoers. Its sources are mainly the advertisements and listings of local newspapers but also include the box-office records of local cinemas, studio ledgers, and national-based collections of statistics. Still, the work is cognisant of the institutional context and constraints in which those decisions were made—in 1953–4 Czech and Polish filmgoers could not include new films from the West in their choice sets. Nevertheless, in all case studies included, film consumer choices lead to social outcomes, in that distributors and exhibitors respond to taste preferences coalescing around particular films and make these more readily available. Simultaneously, such films are talked about—they enter a general social discourse.

6 Chapters in the Book

The book is a collaborative effort in which I have commissioned prominent film historians to produce a series of histories set in the countries where they are experts. Each chapter is based upon a national dataset, either created or discovered by the authors. I am responsible entirely for three chapters, including this Introduction. Chapter 2 "Managing Risk in the Film Business—Key Concepts and Methods" introduces a series of economics concepts and analytical tools used throughout the book, while Chapter 4 "Comparative Film Popularity in Three English Cities—Bolton, Brighton, and Portsmouth: An Exercise in POPSTAT Methodology" applies POPSTAT and RelPOP methods to investigate differences in film popularity in three English cities in the 1930s.

---

[38] Foss et al. (2012, 1355). See also Felin et al. (2015, Table 1).

Clara Pafort Overduin, Peter Miskell, and Dylan Walker and Mike Walsh contribute three chapters. In Chapter 6 "Dutch Films in the Mid-1930s Dutch Market: A Characteristics Approach to Film Popularity", Pafort Overduin revisits her work on the Dutch Industry during the 1930s, investigating the characteristics profile of 16 Dutch films released during the middle years of the decade and analyses the tastes of the home audience for these films across 22 Dutch cities and towns. The final chapter (Chapter 12 "Americanisation in Reverse? Hollywood Films, International Influences, and US Audiences, 1946–1965") has Miskell extending the International Orientation Index that he developed in 2016 to the US post-war home market, finding top-ranking films became more international in scope during the late 1950s and early 1960s in response to the changing nature of the home market. In contrast, Walker and Walsh (in Chapter 7 "Unravelling Australia's 'Infamous "Contract" System'. Evidence from Adelaide, 1942–1943") focus on the city, suburbs, and immediate hinterland of Adelaide, in South Australia, arguing that the Australian market was far from being a slavish outpost of the Hollywood empire.

Throughout the book, the run-clearance system of diffusion stands as the standard model by which films were distributed in the United States and elsewhere. Evidence about industry trade practices given to the 1936 Congressional Hearing on 'Compulsory Block Booking' and 'Blind Selling' provides the backdrop to Andrew Hanssen and my examination of industry economics in Chapter 3 "How did the Department of Justice Get it so Wrong? Philadelphia 1935–1936: The Stanley Warner Chain, Competitive Practices and Consumer Welfare". Using weekly box-office records of cinemas belonging to the Warner Bros. organisation operating in Philadelphia, from 1935–36, we investigate the diffusion mechanism process as films passed through this chain of cinemas.

English-speaking Australia and Great Britain experienced very high levels of import penetration from Hollywood—75 per cent in Great Britain during the 1930s and higher in 1940s Australia. Evidence from non-English speaking countries suggests that Hollywood distributors had a much less dominant position in European countries (outside the UK).

From a pioneering quantitative investigation into the film industry by Leif Fulhammar, we learn that Sweden during the 1930s, with a population of a little over six million, had intensive production studios and an extensive network of cinemas whose screens were shared between domestic and Hollywood productions. In Chapter 5 "Popular Films in Stockholm During the 1930s: A Presentation and Discussion of the Pioneering Work of Leif Furhammar", Åsa Jernudd and I recount Fulhammar's methods and replicate, where possible, his estimations and interpret his findings. Not only did Sweden have a substantial film industry, but domestic films were genuinely popular with Swedish audiences, as were the MGM films of Greta Garbo.

Like the Netherlands, Belgium had a small domestic industry. Unlike Sweden and The Netherlands, the country was separated by language. During the German Occupation (1940–44), the cultural divide between Dutch and French speakers was exacerbated (1940–44). In Chapter 8 "Film Exhibition, Distribution and Popularity in German-Occupied Belgium (1940–1944): Brussels, Antwerp and Liege", Roel

Vande Winkel and I show that while Dutch-speaking Flanders was considered ripe for Germanisation, the French-speaking Walloons predominantly watched films made in occupied France. Using cinema programming data in conjunction with archive sources, we examine the moviegoing preferences of audiences in Antwerp, Brussels, and Liege. Film preferences are shown to be binary, divided along cultural lines, as was the thorny practice of subtitles and dubbing.

European cinema was divided across the Iron Curtain in the post-war years, with the widespread diffusion of television occurring in the late 1950s and early 1960s. In Western Europe, domestic producers made films that attracted local audiences but were not screened widely outside their national boundaries, although there is evidence of French and Italian films being popular in Poland and the Soviet Union.[39] Of course, Western European markets were shared with Hollywood studios, whose distribution arms could still secure the best cinemas in the major cities to premiere their big-budget attractions.

This was certainly the case in Italy. In 1954 there was no shortage of films for audiences to choose between, as will become apparent in Chapter 9 "Five Italian Cities: Comparative Analysis of Cinema Types, Film Circulation and Relative Popularity in the Mid-1950s", in which Daniela Treveri Gennari and I examine film circulation and diffusion practices in five Italian cities, categorising the cinemas in which they appeared into one of four types. In addition, industry box-office data is used to profile film popularity in each city, comparing preferences through the RelPOP tool.

Behind the Iron Curtain, in contrast, a relative shortage of new films during the early 1950s required distributors to circulate films of past vintages, while new movies were given broad distribution. Two chapters are devoted to cinema under Communist rule, where newly released Hollywood films were banned. In Chapters 10 and 11 "Cinemagoers Should '…Learn from Progressive Movies, Again and Again': Cinemagoing in Czechoslovakia, 1949–52" and "'It Seems to Me that the Most Popular Films in the West are Very Harmful to Us': Film popularity in Poland During the Years of 'High Stalinisation'", Pavel Skopal and Terezia Porubcanska and I and Konrad Klejsa and I demonstrate how important the Communist Authorities in Czechoslovakia and Poland considered the film industry during the years of 'High Stalinism'—Stalin died in 1953. Attention is drawn to the dichotomy between the lofty ambition to create a new type of film audience and peoples' aspirations to be entertained, taking place within a context of unwavering official support to the Soviet Union and fellow People's Republics. Although new Soviet films were especially privileged, they were scarce.[40] In Poland, the shortfall of new Soviet films led the State to issue import licences to some highly vetted films from Western Europe. The Czechoslovakian authorities were better situated to supply their cinemas with home-produced films. Nevertheless, a characteristic feature of the film programmes was the presence of vintage cinema. Movies from the Eastern bloc had much longer shelf lives than their Western Counterparts.

---

[39] Knight (2018), Klejsa and Miller-Klejsa (2021).

[40] Knight (2018).

Using POPSTAT methods, cinema programming evidence from the cities of Brno and Cracow indicate that audiences went to see some films in large numbers. Popularity was an essential factor in determining a film's circulation, leading to differences between city, industrial, and rural audiences. One finding of note is the availability and popularity of western European films—primarily French and Italian—in Poland but not Czechoslovakia.

7 Conclusion

The book's time frame is bounded by the 'coming of sound' (*circa* 1929) and the demise of the tiered distribution system and subsequent replacement by saturation release in the 1970s. For most of the period, films were screened in cinemas. To give some scale of film turnover, at the high point of film popularity in the United States, the 1946/7 trade publication *International Motion Picture Almanac* reported that 15 million film shipments were made internally between exchanges and cinemas in 1946. As television diffused, consumers were offered an alternative medium of moving visual entertainment, an aspect of which was past films. The cinema remained the venue for seeing new movies. Television allowed audiences to watch old films in their living rooms.

In his book reflecting on historical method, Eric Hobsbawm wrote:

> I strongly defend the view that what historians investigate is real. The point from which they must start, however far from it they may end, is the fundamental, and for them, absolutely central distinction between establishable fact and fiction, between historical statements based on evidence and those which are not.[41]

I take this statement to mean that it is the job of historians to concern themselves with marshalling factual and contextual evidence to support and rescue the past from incompleteness. By implication, depictions of history can be shown to be false by presenting different, better, and contradictory historical evidence. The evidence being marshalled in this book rescues the decisions made by countless filmgoers, bringing into view the films they chose to watch from a set determined by filmmakers, distributors, exhibitors, and the authorities.[42] These choices had meaning.

This book is presented as a series of case studies. Each examines popular filmgoing in the context of national cinema and, where the data permits, contains intra-national and, or international comparisons. Taken together, the case studies—Australia, Belgium, Germany, Czechoslovakia, Great Britain, Italy, the Netherlands, Poland, Sweden, and the United States, evoke Douglass North's stricture about historical differences between cultures:

---

[41] Hobsbawm (1997, p. viii).

[42] Eagleton (2021).

> It is simply impossible to make sense out of history ...without recognising the central role that subjective preferences play in the context of formal institutional constraints that allow us to express our convictions at zero or very little cost. Ideas, organised ideologies, and even religious zealotry play major roles in shaping societies and economies (1990, pp. 43–4).

For North, formal institutional frameworks include political, legal, and economic rules. The more efficient institutions are, the lower the costs to society of information gathering, social monitoring and enforcement and expressing subjective preferences. Further, it is easier for organisations to harness and transform resources at scale. All of this takes place within a context of social norms, independent of formal constraints (state control). It is these that set cultures apart. Thus, although formal institutional arrangements and living standards in the Netherlands and Great Britain were similar during the 1930s, Dutch and British filmgoers experienced different informal institutional contexts. When deciding whether to go to the cinema, the British did in massive numbers while the Dutch did not.

References

Online Datasets

Federico, Giovanni; Tena Junguito, Antonio, 2018, "Federico-Tena World Trade Historical Database: World Trade", https://doi.org/10.21950/JKZFDP, e-cienciaDatos, V.

Film Distributor's Society https://www.launchingfilms.com/research-databank/uk-cinema-admissions; Tables H873, H374, Historical Statistics of the United States, Colonial Times to 1975 https://www.census.gov/library/publications/1975/compendia/hist_stats_colonial-1970.html

Articles and Books

Arsel, Z., & Bean, J. (2013). Taste regimes and market-mediated practice. *Journal of Consumer Research, 39*, 899–917.

Bakker, G. (2008). *Entertainment industrialised: The emergence of the international Film Industry, 1890–1940*. Cambridge University Press.

Bakker, G. (2012). How motion pictures industrialised entertainment. *Journal of Economic History, 72*(4), 1036–1063.

Balio, T. (1993). *Grand design: Hollywood as a modern business enterprise*. University of California Press.

Coase, R. (1937). The nature of the firm. *Economica, 4*, 386–405.

De Vany, A., & Walls, W. (1996). Bose-Einstein dynamics and adaptive contracting in the motion picture industry. *Economic Journal, 106*, 1493–1514.

De Vries, J. (2008). *The industrious revolution: Consumer behaviour and the household economy, 1650 to the present*. Cambridge University Press.

Eagleton, T. (2021). The Marxist and the Messiah. *London Review of Books, 43*(17), 27–28.

Fowler, D. (1995). *The first teenagers: The lifestyle of young wage-earners in interwar Britain*. Routledge.

Felin, T., Foss, N., Heimeriks, K., & Madsen, T. (2012). Microfoundations of routines and capabilities: Individuals, processes, and structure. *Journal of Management Studies, 49*, 1351–1374.
Felin, T., Foss, N., & Ployhart, R. (2015). The microfoundations movement in strategy and organisation theory. *The Academy of Management Annals, 9*(1), 575–632. https://doi.org/10.1080/19416520.2015.1007651
Fine, B., & Leopold, E. (1993). *The World of Consumption.* Routledge.
Glancy, H. M. (1999). *When Hollywood loved Britain.* Manchester University Press.
Greenwald, W. (1950). *The motion picture industry: An economic study of the history and practices of a business* [PhD dissertation, New York University].
Gomery, D. (1992). *Shared pleasures: A history of movie presentation in the United States.* BFI.
Hanssen, F. (2000). The block booking of films re-examined. *Journal of Law and Economics, 43*, 395–426.
Hanssen, F. (2002). Revenue-sharing in movie exhibition and the arrival of sound. *Economic Inquiry, 40*, 380–402.
Hayek, F. (1945). The use of knowledge in society. *American Economic Review, 35*(4), 519–530.
Hobsbawm, E. (1997). *On history.* Weidenfeld and Nicolson.
Izod, J. (1998). *Hollywood and the box office.* Macmillan.
Jarvie, I. (1992). *Hollywood's overseas campaign: The North Atlantic movie trade, 1920–1950.* Cambridge University Press.
Jurca, C., & Sedgwick, J. (2014). The film's the thing: Moviegoing in Philadelphia, 1935–36. *Film History, 26*(4), 58–83.
Klejsa, K., & Miller-Klejsa, A. (2021). Almost as good as Soviet cinema: Reception of Italian neorealism in Poland: 1946–56. *Journal of Italian Cinema & Media Studies, 9*(3), 367–384. https://doi.org/10.1386/jicms_00082_1
Knight., C. (2018). Nelli Morozova on Censors, Censorship and the Soviet Film Famine, 1948–52. *Slavonic and East European Review, 96*(4), 704–30.
Lysandrou., P. (2019). *Commodity.* Routledge.
Marx, K. (1976). *Capital* (Vol. 1). Penguin Books.
McKibbin, R. (1998). *Classes and cultures: England, 1918–1951: A study of a democratic society.* Oxford University Press.
Miskell, P. (2016). International films and international markets: The globalisation of Hollywood entertainment, circa. 1921–1951. *Media History, 22*(2), 174–200.
Miskell, P., & Nicoli, M. (2016). From outsiders to insiders? Strategies and practices of American film distributors in postwar Italy. *Enterprise and Society, 17*(3), 546–590.
North, D. (1990). *Institutions, institutional change and economic performance.* Cambridge University Press.
Orwell, G. (1962). *The road to Wigan Pier.* Penguin Books.
Pokorny, M., & Sedgwick, J. (2010). Profitability trends in Hollywood: 1929 to 1999. *Economic History Review, 63*, 56–84.
Pokorny, M., & Sedgwick, J. (2012). The financial and economic risks of film production. In M. Hjort (Ed.), *Film and risk* (pp. 181–196). Wayne University Press.
Rowson, S. (1936). A statistical survey of the cinema industry in Great Britain in 1934. *Journal of the Royal Statistical Society, 99*, 67–129.
Sedgwick, J. (2000). *Popular filmgoing in 1930s Britain: A choice of pleasures.* Exeter University Press.
Sedgwick, J. (2002). Product differentiation at the movies: Hollywood, 1946–65. *Journal of Economic History, 62*, 676–704.
Sedgwick, J. (2007). A Shacklean approach to the demand for movies. In M. Bianchi (Ed.), *The evolution of consumption: Theories and practice* (pp. 77–92). Elsevier.
Sedgwick, J., Miskell, P., & Nicoli, M. (2019). The market for films in postwar Italy: Evidence for both national and regional patterns of taste. *Enterprise & Society, 20*, 199–228.
Sedgwick, J., Pafort-Overduin, C., & Boter, J. (2012). Explanations for the restrained development of the Dutch cinema market in the 1930s. *Enterprise and Society, 13*, 634–671.

Sedgwick, J., & Pokorny, M. (1998). The risk environment of film-making: Warners in the interwar period. *Explorations in Economic History, 35*, 196–220.

Sedgwick, J., & Pokorny, M. (2005). The film business in the US and Britain during the 1930s. *Economic History Review, 58*, 79–112.

Sedgwick, J., & Pokorny, M. (2010). Consumers as risk takers: Evidence from the film industry during the 1930s. *Business History, 52*, 74–99.

Thompson, K. (1985). *Exporting entertainment: America in the world film market, 1907–1934*. BFI.

Vasey, R. (1997). *The world according to Hollywood, 1918–1939*. Exeter University Press.

Williamson, O. (1975). *Markets and hierarchies*. Free Press.

John Sedgwick is a visiting Professor in the Faculty of Technology, Design and Environment, Oxford Brookes University. He researches the economic history of cinema and is particularly interested in the ontological characteristics of film as a commodity. He created the POPSTAT Index of Film Popularity as a proxy for box-office returns. This tool provides a means of reflecting audience preferences and monitoring the distribution process. His research has focused on American, Australian, British, Dutch, Italian and international markets during the 1930s and 1950/60s. He has written a monograph, edited an anthology and published articles in *Business History, Cinema Journal, Economic History Review, Explorations in Economic History, Enterprise and Society, Film History, Historical Journal of Film, Radio and Television, Journal of Applied Statistics, Journal of Cultural Economics, Journal of Economic History, and Journal of Transnational Cinema*.

Managing Risk in the Film Business—Key Concepts and Methods

John Sedgwick

Abstract Box office is a measure of film popularity—the films people choose from an array made available for public consumption. While producer risk is a well-documented concept, commonly encapsulated in the so-called 'nobody knows' principle, consumer risk is less well-understood. Both are discussed. The POPSTAT method by which box office is estimated from programming data in the absence of archive evidence is also covered in this chapter. Its derivative RelPOP is used to make a comparative analysis of film popularity. Attention is also given to the International Orientation Index developed by Peter Miskell to explain the relative attractiveness of Hollywood movies in foreign markets. In addition, the importance of trade journals as a source of information and data and microeconomic concepts central to the investigation of industry behaviour are explained.

This chapter introduces the reader to economic and methodological concepts applied throughout the book. Behind these is the central idea that the risks commonly understood to characterise film production derive from consumer behaviour. That is, film consumers also take risks, each having a personal history of making mistakes—selecting films they dislike. During the years covered by this investigation, audiences living in urban settings consistently faced an array of movies from which to choose. These films stood against one another in a zero-sum competition—the relative gains of some films were at the expense of others as regular consumers made choices, realising favourites in the process. Exceptionally, notable movies emerged that attracted huge audiences, including those who only occasionally went to the cinema. Such films became hits earning many multiples more revenue than the median film.

The systematic distribution of films from box-office rich to box-office poor cinemas over time suggests that sections of the audience preferred to see films earlier after their release rather than later and were prepared and able to pay higher admission prices for this. It is also an indicator that films travelled widely in search of additional revenue, even if this entailed short-period screenings. Implicit in this process

J. Sedgwick (✉)
Oxford Brookes University, Oxford, UK
e-mail: sedgwicj52@gmail.com

J. Sedgwick (ed.), *Towards a Comparative Economic History of Cinema, 1930–1970*, Frontiers in Economic History, https://doi.org/10.1007/978-3-031-05770-0_2

of popular movies travelling everywhere is that social class—even poverty—was not a barrier to consumption.

Unfortunately, detailed box-office returns are scarce. The POPSTAT method was developed to address this lacuna. POPSTAT and its derivative for measuring relative popularity between localities (RelPOP) are explained in this chapter, as is the International Orientation Index developed by Peter Miskell to explain Hollywood's reach in foreign markets.

1 Trade Journals as Sources of Data

The evidence presented in this book is mainly derived from local daily newspapers and trade journals. Daily newspapers commonly carry a mixture of programme listings and advertisements. Datasets are created from the systematic collection of these over a period. Trade journals, in contrast, are weekly, bi-weekly, or monthly industry-based publications typically providing wide-ranging intelligence about industry matters. They provide an essential source for researchers wanting to understand the material concerns of the day. They vary in scope from country to country and offer a guide to all matters that preoccupied industry practitioners, particularly on the exhibition side of the business. Hence, they covered:

- domestic regulations—trade and legal restrictions to trade, safety, censorship, and official publications,
- new film registrations and releases, first-run programming,
- industry and finance—box-office and industry reports, mergers and take-overs, newly formed companies, stock exchange valuations,
- production—schedules, finance and personnel news, including stars, directors, and other talents,
- listings of cinemas, and their location, seating capacity and pricing,
- distribution and exhibition matters—issues to do with relations between renters and between them and exhibitors about access to films and the financial terms of that access, as well as the showman's angle—how to best market particular films in local communities,
- foreign films and their agents in domestic markets,
- foreign markets, including size, growth, and regulations about imports.

The weekly publications of trade journals were often supplemented by a Yearbook, in which annual releases of films, together with their actors and directors, were listed. They also contained all manner of reports and statistics. For instance, in Great Britain, *Kine Weekly* was supported by the *Kinematograph Yearbook* and the United States *Film Daily* by the *Film Daily Yearbook*. Distinctively, the weekly journal *Variety* was not supported by a Yearbook but rather dedicated the second weekly edition in January of each year to a similar purpose. Such publications are an excellent way to understand the film market—both domestic and international.

2 Vertical Product Differentiation

Each film is unique. Analytically, films can be placed along a horizontal continuum based on their characteristics profile. Depending upon this profile, they can be positioned near similar (near neighbour) films, distant from dissimilar (non-neighbour) films. Genres can be thought of in these terms, in which film clusters entailing killing, terror, and horror are at the opposite end of the spectrum to, say, romantic comedies and musicals. Niche audiences are attracted to specific film genres and their near neighbours, while others are not. Economists refer to the distinction between types as horizontal product differentiation.[1]

In the first chapter of the book, the concept of price discrimination was introduced—the idea that distributors could sell the same product to different sets of customers willing to pay different prices. During the period covered by this study, the organisation of the cinema sector was predicated on the idea that some consumers were willing to pay more to see films early in their life cycle in higher-order cinemas rather than wait for them to appear later at less-salubrious lower-order cinemas. The scale of cinema attendances, particularly in the years before the rapid diffusion of television, suggests that lower-order cinema prices were not much of a barrier to filmgoing but that profitability required sections of the audience to pay higher prices.

A second pricing characteristic was that cinemas did not change prices according to the films on their programmes, irrespective of their popularity. The consequence of invariant prices was that consumers could not mitigate against weak expectations of what they perceived to be a low-quality film by paying a lower price, causing them to stay away. Conversely, the fact that queuing was commonplace suggests that consumers reaped additional benefits from those films for which expectations were high—they would have been prepared to pay more. In the first case, it required lower prices to attract larger audiences, but in the second, higher prices to reduce queuing and turn customers away.

This uniform pricing strategy implies that consumers' perception of quality alone determined their choices, given the plentiful array of films they had access to. In such circumstances, a few movies could appear superior in almost every respect to all others for many consumers. Evidence for this can be found in the small number of extant box-office ledgers of cinemas, showing that when charging the same admission price, different films attracted different-sized audiences. When this practice is replicated throughout the population of cinemas in a locality/territory, these qualitative differences are compounded, giving rise to a highly skewed statistical distribution of revenues. While most films generate revenues that gravitate around a median value, a few *hit* films earn many times this. Such films are said to be *vertically differentiated*. They give the statistical distribution of revenues its long right tail, illustrated later in the chapter in Fig. 4.

Thus, vertical product differentiation prevails when qualitative differences exist between two products in a family of products so that one product can be shown to be

[1] For a discussion of *product differentiation* applied to the film industry, see Sedgwick (2002) and Sedgwick et al. (2019, pp. 202–203).

qualitatively better than another. Gerben Bakker has argued that Hollywood's ascendency as a film centre during the mid-to-late 1910s was founded on the escalation of quality associated with the product innovation of feature films.[2] In the context of intense competition between rivals in the rapidly expanding North American market during the years of the First World War, coupled with the curtailed supply of European film production, average budgets for film production in the US rose considerably above those of their European counterparts. During these years, the collective superiority of Hollywood films gave them a dominant position in world markets.

Yet, while films on average may appear technically superior, film history is littered with examples of expensively made films performing relatively poorly at the box office. Ultimately consumers play the leading role in judging quality, and their tastes may differ locality to locality and territory to territory. Their judgement at the box office collectively determines the rank order of films, from the most to the least successful. The primary position taken by Hollywood in world film markets required audiences everywhere to sanction and validate their quality.

3 Consumer Risk: Theory and Evidence

The introductory chapter argued that newly released films belong to a particular family of commodities for which consumer expectations are incompletely formed. Before watching movies, consumers cannot fully imagine the richness and complexity of new film images, narratives, and sounds. Economists refer to this commodity category as *experience goods*.[3] In addition, a common feature of film consumption behaviour over the history of filmgoing, at least since the emergence of feature films in the 1910s, is that consumers mostly watch movies just once, suggesting an unquenchable thirst for novelty. Understanding risk as the downside difference between expectations and experience, consumers prefer the potential risks of consuming new films to the known pleasures of repeat viewing.

Film consumption behaviour differs from other experience goods such as restaurant meals, hotel accommodation, or holiday destinations. For these types of experience goods, consumers conduct experiments in which they benchmark a new experience against a favourite, frequently reverting to it.[4] In contrast, while filmgoers develop a bank of film experiences, in which a small number of exceptional films stand out, they rarely re-consume favourites, preferring the chance prospect of the novel against repeat experience.[5]

[2] Bakker (2008).

[3] Nelson (1970, 1974).

[4] Ratner et al. (1999).

[5] Of course, it was in the interests of producers and distributors to remove films from the market as soon as consumers tired of them, effectively ending their lives as commodities, since films of vintage would stand in direct competition with new films released. The practice of re-releasing past

The idea that consumers take risks has been known in the film business for a long time. However, the first effort to measure systematically film consumer behaviour occurred only in the 1940s. One of the pioneers of audience research during this decade, Leo Handel, mused:

> The interrelation of the expectancy level and audience appeal of a picture is a familiar criterion with every moviegoer. A movie visit may be undertaken with the anticipation of seeing an outstanding picture. If the film in question is one of an average audience appeal, however, the discrepancy between the high expectation and the moderate enjoyment may result in disappointment and, possibly, dislike of the picture. Had the same moviegoer been under the impression that the picture he was about to see was not very good he might enjoy it considerably, due to the fact that the picture appeal was higher than the anticipated enjoyment.[6]

Consider experienced film consumers choosing from newly released films. The films in their choice set offer a mixture of complex sensory and aesthetic experiences, requiring them to use their imagination to map out the pleasure terrain associated with each. It is conjectured that this is done by recourse to personal cognitive banks of film experience acquired over time, enabling them to judge the likelihood and strength of pleasure from new releases.

They do this in a discursive environment involving pre-and post-release advertising and promotional activity and pre-and post-release word-of-mouth between filmgoers. The busyness of information around some films may be highly charged and all-reaching. For others, it may arouse high-interest levels only among specific niche viewers. Accordingly, film expectations are subjectively held. They can be strong or weak and shared by many or a few.

Finally, film consumers know from previous filmgoing that they make mistakes and choose the wrong film, leading to disappointment. From these events, let us suppose they form a cognitive possibility matrix that fits new movies according to the strength of imagined expectations and the range of possible outcomes. Such a matrix is suggested in Table 1, in which the prospect of loss and gain presents a calculus entailed in the film decision-making process. In this cognitive construct, preferences are formed and ranked. A film offering the prospect of higher levels of imagined pleasure/satisfaction will be preferred to one offering less at the same margin of risk. Film choice, then, is not a random process, although it is fraught with uncertainty, with experience only a partial guide to film quality.

Consider the four films, A, B, C, and D, depicted in Table 1. Suppose these films are recent releases, falling into a regular film consumer's choice set. Also, suppose that all four are seen. The prospect of watching Films A and B generates high expectations. However, having watched them, only Film A meets or possibly surpasses those expectations, while Film B disappoints.

---

films become common in the United States during the Second World War owing to film shortages. During the 1950s, the practice continued but was always limited to a small number of special films. The market was never awash with films of vintage, as was the case in the market for classical music recordings.

[6] Handel (1950, p. 70). For a fuller contribution of Handel's contribution to film consumer behaviour see Bakker (2003) and Sedgwick and Pokorny (2010).

Table 1 Film choice possibility matrix

Outcomes		
Expectations	High	Low
High	**Film A**	**Film B**
	Expectations met, possibly surpassed	Unexpected and surprising loss
Low	**Film C**	**Film D**
	Unexpected and surprising gain	Expectations met, perhaps not even that

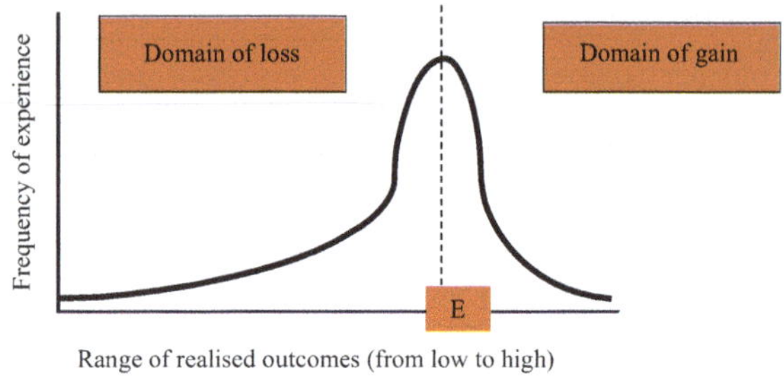

Fig. 1 Imagined film expectation of Film Z, set against a personal bank of memorised experience of filmgoing

Conversely, on release, both Films C and D represent low pleasure domains in the filmgoer's mind. Once seen, Film D confirms those expectations. In contrast, Film C is surprisingly good, bringing the unexpected pleasure referred to by Handel. Realistically, it might be considered unlikely that a filmgoer would choose to watch films with low expectations. However, if we suppose that filmgoing is a regular part of social intercourse, there might be reasons other than personal taste that motivate consumers. The net outcomes conjectured in Table 1 range from gain (Film C), through to neutral (Films A and D), through to loss (Film B).

The possibility matrix suggests the asymmetrical curve depicted in Fig. 1, which quantifies and profiles risk-taking. The curve represents the frequency with which the filmgoer has experienced and stored various levels of pleasure from previous film choices. In effect, it depicts a personal record of film risk. The asymmetry results from consumers choosing films mostly because they hold high expectations. As this curve is formed from memory, it is, of course, subject to the caveats associated with the reliability of memory, the subject in recent years of a burgeoning literature of oral cinema history.[7] It indeed should not be regarded as a probability distribution in which the probabilities associated with each experience sum to one. Better to consider the curve as a loose formulation of the store of experience that services the consumers' intuition about what film to watch next.

Consider a hypothetical Film Z. Let point E in Fig. 1 represent a filmgoer's expectation concerning this film, selected from a choice set and not yet seen. E is located towards the high end of the range of outcome possibilities and supposes

[7] See for instance, Kuhn (2002) and Treveri Gennari (2015).

that the consumer is motivated by films that generate high expectations and that this behaviour is normal. The weight of the frequency distribution depicted in Fig. 1 falls around the vertical dotted line. That is, the film consumer knows from experience that a good proportion of films chosen have resulted in a close match between expectations and outcomes—where expectations have been more or less met. However, this person also knows that the choice of Film Z is not without risk because a sizeable proportion of experiences exceed or fall short of what was hoped for, resulting in an unexpected gain or surprising loss. These states of gain and loss are depicted, respectively, by the right and left tails of the distribution. In both cases, it is conjectured that extreme states are rare. Nevertheless, the filmgoer is conscious of having made decisions that have ended in substantial disappointment.

Of course, each consumer will have a different filmgoing experience profile, reflecting, among other things, their filmgoing history, personality, attitude to novelty and risk, openness to peer pressure and particular social circumstances. So, for instance, a flatter curve would suggest a more adventurous attitude to filmgoing, in which outcomes are more randomly spread between loss and gain. In contrast, a steeper, more peaked curve will reflect consumers who have an obvious demarcation between what they like and what they do not like, thereby restricting their choice set, resulting in lower levels of loss and gain away from the expectation benchmark.[8]

Until this point, the discussion has been conducted mainly regarding a representative consumer who has developed a taste for certain films. As suggested, film consumption has a social dimension to it. The work of Arsel and Bean is significant in this respect.[9] They open their paper with a quotation by Antoine Hennion that is worth repeating:

> Taste is not an attribute, it is not a property (of a thing or of a person), it is an activity. You have to do something in order to listen to music, drink a wine, appreciate an object. Tastes are not given or determined, and their objects are not either; one has to make them appear together, through repeated experiments, progressively adjusted.[10]

Taste then is a dynamic consequence of what it is to live, from what people do and how they react to and store the experience of doing them. Accordingly, it comes from decisions that have been taken and impacts decisions yet to be made. Zeynep Arsel and Jonathan Bean introduce a concept that they call a *taste regime*, constituted by the social networks people keep and influencers they adopt. In the case of film, a taste regime could comprise the unformal word-of-mouth which emerges as part of everyday social intercourse, to more formal presentations of information and reviews found on niche media platforms, to membership of film clubs, all of which are interactive. For Arsel and Bean:

> ...little attention has been paid to how individuals convert taste into practice. We argue that taste, as well as the practical knowledge and action through which it is performed..., is

[8] These ideas are developed in Sedgwick (2000, 2007).

[9] Arsel and Bean (2013).

[10] Hennion (2007, p. 101).

> neither purely agentic nor completely un-conscious and conditioned but rather is a form of reflexivity bounded by socio-culturally constituted practice.[11]

Enrico Moretti has examined the social dimension of film consumer knowledge. He uses market-level data to test a model in which the diffusion of information is affected by perceived surprises in quality. For Moretti, quality is subjective: consumers have priors (their tastes) on quality (genre, actors, directors, ratings, budgets) and receive information from other consumers. He writes,

> I define social learning as a situation where consumers in week *t* update their prior on feedback from others who have seen the movie in previous weeks. The model predicts better or worse box-office sales dynamics depending on whether a movie's underlying quality is better or worse than peoples' expectations. Social learning should make successful movies more successful and unsuccessful movies less successful. Without social learning, there is no updating of individual expectations and therefore no divergence in sales over time – no surprises.[12]

Although individuals are influenced differently, many share the same or similar influencers, all of which, including tastes, change over time. These influences are present at the point of decision, with the subsequent drama played out as consumers discover whether their expectations have been realised. Furthermore, Moretti found that relative to expectations (based on the number of opening screens), films that produce disappointing revenues relative to expectations during the first week of release continue to do so over the remainder of their life cycle. The implication for studios is dramatic depending on whether a positive or negative information cascade is generated. 'Two products of similar quality may have vastly different demand, in the long run, depending on whether the initial set of potential consumers happens to like the product or not'.[13]

To summarise, consumer risk is thus central to understanding the film business. However, it is far from the deterministic process of knowing what is liked and purchasing it. Indeed, the nature of film as a commodity implies that consumers cannot fully imagine the experience they are likely to have by choosing, say, **Film Z**. Indeed, in searching for novelty, consumers seek an unknowable attribute that may be, or not, unlocked through the consumption experience. In this, they know that in the past, they have been disappointed by films that offered more than delivered but occasionally are delighted by the unforeseen pleasure of a movie that unexpectedly connects with them—such films, experienced rarely, are likely to impact strongly on taste. Therefore, consumers cannot know with certainty what they are looking for. For filmmakers, this constitutes both opportunity and risk. The opportunity is to influence the tastes of consumers aesthetically and in sufficient numbers to make profits. The risk is that although producers may invest considerable sums of money in trying to do this, they regularly fail, with Moretti suggesting that the information cascade generated by films may be randomly generated.

---

[11] Arsel and Bean (2013, p. 901).

[12] Moretti (2011, p. 2). See also Ginsburgh and Weyers (1999).

[13] Moretti (2011, p. 1).

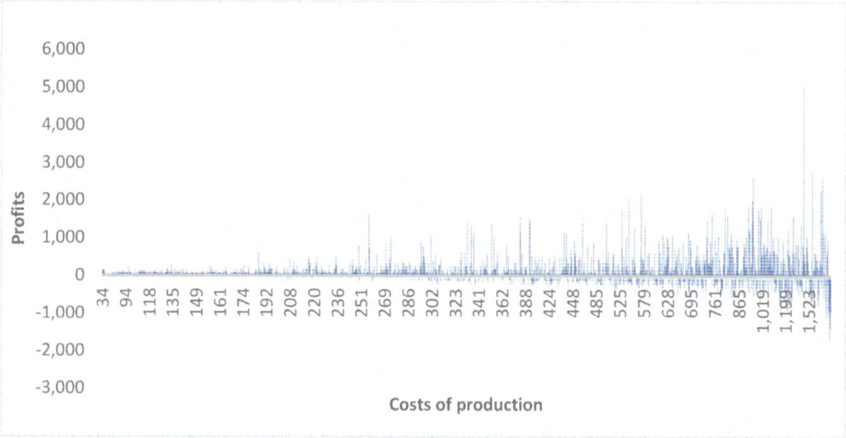

Fig. 2 The profitability of the 1796 films released by MGM, RKO, and Warner Bros. during the seasons 1929–1930 and 1941–1942 ($000s) in 1929 prices (*Sources* The Eddie Mannix [MGM], C.J. Trevlin [RKO] and William Schaefer Ledgers [WB])

4 Producer Risk in Hollywood

Evidence of the nature of producer risk is visualised in Fig. 2, depicting the profits of all 1,796 films produced by MGM, RKO, and Warner Bros. studios during the 1930s, set against production costs.[14] This data was discovered in three ledgers by Mark Glancy (Eddie Mannix [MGM], William Schaefer [Warner Bros.]), and Richard Jewell (C.J. Trevlin [RKO]).[15] Figure 2 shows a tendency for profits to rise with costs. However, it also indicates that losses increase with costs, implying that the variance in profitability does so as well, to the extent that no predictive value can be ascribed to the relationship between the two. Indeed, the profits of the seven most expensive films were all negative, with the 1937 MGM film *Conquest* losing near to $1,600,000, although costing over $3.3 million to make (all in 1929 prices). On its initial release, *The Wizard of Oz* (MGM, 1939) ran a close second in terms of loss-making. In contrast, the two most profitable films, again made by MGM, cost half as much to make and yet generated profits of over $5 million (*Mrs Minerva*) and $2,765,000 (*San Francisco*).[16]

During the 1930s, the major studios financed, produced, and distributed their annual releases, meaning they were fully exposed to downside risk. Given the degree of performance variance, they necessarily adopted a portfolio management approach, aiming to maximise the return on the portfolio rather than individual films. Evidence

[14] This calculation includes both domestic and foreign rental incomes. For the method of estimating distribution costs for films from the Warner Bros. studio see Pokorny and Sedgwick (2010, Appendix).

[15] Glancy (1992, 1995) and Jewell (1994).

[16] Sedgwick and Pokorny (2005, pp. 98–103).

indicates that the studios planned the overall annual production budget to include specific numbers of different category films. The consistent positive returns of the middle-budget films, with middle-ranking stars, evident in Fig. 2, allowed them to survive the economic downturn during the 1930s.[17]

However, the strategic response of the studios to the variability of profitability just described did not last.[18] As the bottom fell out of the cinema market during the 1950s, 60s, and 70s, studio exposure to film investments was diluted, with the studios attracting finance from various sources. This strategic change was coupled with a shift in focus from the portfolio to the individual film as the studios scaled back production: they became associated with many fewer annual releases, each designed to be screened across multiple platforms and profitable. In the light of these changes, the recent trend towards sequels as a strategy for mitigating risk can be understood.[19]

Consequently, the framework of loss and gain that characterises film consumption also represents film production. Consumption risk begets production risk. In both cases, expectations are pivotal. Larger budgets, entailing star acting and directorial inputs, coupled with greater promotional activity, raise expectations for producers and consumers alike—producers because of the need for profitability; consumers because they are subject to intense promotional activity. The films depicted below the break-even line in Fig. 2 indicate that during the 1930s, consumers were not sufficiently interested in certain big-budget films, disappointing the expectations of their producers.

Film rental data for the 1930s are described in Table 2. The weight of the distribution falls among the lowest decile of earnings, with the most popular film earning 15 times more rental income than the median film. Annual figures simply replicate the pattern of inequality found in Table 2.

This type of statistical distribution has characterised the film industry since the emergence of feature films during the 1910s. It can be considered an empirical regularity and indicates that 'hit' films stand as giants in relation to the median film. De Vany and Wall's (1996) work on the statistical properties of long tails that characterise the film industry remains an essential reference in the literature.[20]

The material base for these statistical properties is twofold. The first is the ability of distribution to circulate films far and wide, and the second is the clustering of tastes around particular films, making them stand out. A few movies in any season enjoy extreme and far-reaching popularity with consumers.

[17] Sedgwick and Pokorny (1998) and Pokorny and Sedgwick (2001).

[18] See Pokorny and Sedgwick (2010) for a long history of the profitability of Hollywood studios; and Pokorny et al. (2019) for an account of the significance of sequels to studio profitability in recent times.

[19] Pokorny et al. (2019).

[20] See also various chapters in De Vany (2004).

Table 2 US rental earnings: descriptive statistics of the 1,796 films released by MGM, RKO, and Warner Bros. during the seasons 1929–1930 and 1941–1942 ($000s) in 1929 prices

Statistic	Value
Mean	607.50
Standard Error	13.09
Median	414.27
Mode	263.72
Standard Deviation	554.93
Coefficient of Variation	0.91
Sample Variance	307,943.42
Kurtosis	14.23
Skewness	2.87
Range	5884.80
Minimum	66.83
Maximum	5951.63
Sum	1,091,061.53
Count	1796

Sources The Eddie Mannix (MGM), C.J. Trevlin (RKO) and William Schaefer Ledgers

5 The Reach of Hollywood

Table 2 is based on the North American domestic market. Yet, as was outlined in the Introduction, Hollywood films were ubiquitous: they were found almost everywhere in which a functioning market economy was in operation. Under the heading 'Big Foreign Film Coin', the American trade journal *Variety* in November 1934 reported on potential rental earnings from 52 countries. These are listed in Table 3. The article conjectured that an outstanding film could expect to earn over two million dollars in foreign markets—twice that of the domestic market—and hypothesised each country's contribution, assuming each of the 38,936 cinemas recorded in the table had an account with a Hollywood distributor. The accompanying article maintained that '…films of the right type can gross more than the wrong type' and goes on to describe five 'wrong type' films—'highly sophisticated'; the so-called 'walking and talking pictures'; '…pictures which depend on dialogue alone for motivation'; 'the purely American type of picture'; and finally, 'farce' comedies.[21]

Table 3 brings into stark relief the scope of filmgoing practices from around the globe during the mid-1930s. Madison's GDP per capita figures (column 2) for Australasia and European states provide an interesting point of departure. National material well-being measured by GDP is an essential part of the story of the extensiveness of cinema culture in these more affluent societies, but not all of it. Indeed, although positive, the correlation coefficient for the two variables in Fig. 3 is not strong ($r = 0.55$).

[21] *Variety*, 6 November 1934.

Table 3 Foreign market possibilities

Country	(1) Population	(2) (Madison) GDP per capita 1934 ($US)	(3) No. of cinemas	(4) Gross revenue possibilities ($US)
United Kingdom	4,61,59,445	5,608	4,950	6,75,000
France	4,18,34,923	4,192	3,900	3,50,000
Germany	6,46,00,000	3,858	4,000	3,00,000
Italy	4,11,45,041	2,894	2,500	2,25,000
Czecho-Slovakia	1,47,26,158	2,443	2,024	90,000
Spain-Portugal	2,94,21,706	2,381	2,850	85,000
Australasia	79,60,886	5,005	1,385	80,000
Argentine	1,88,35,727		1,985	45,000
Japan	9,17,93,681		1,669	40,000
China	46,23,87,000		250	37,000
Brazil	4,02,72,650		1,125	30,000
Belgium	81,29,405	4,624	650	25,000
Hungary	86,83,740	2,370	633	20,000
India	35,15,00,000		675	17,000
Sweden	61,41,571	3,991	1,100	15,000
Austria	67,26,113	2,852	850	15,000
Poland	3,19,27,773	1,593	752	15,000
South Africa	82,50,000		360	15,000
Switzerland	40,82,511	5,952	310	15,000
Philippines	1,20,82,366		300	12,500
Roumania	1,81,76,757	1,182	350	10,000
Holland	78,32,175	4,805	255	10,000
Panama/Jamaica/Central America	63,79,478		164	10,000
Dutch East Indies	6,07,31,025		108	8,000
Egypt	1,44,93,000		89	8,000
Straights Settlement	11,12,850		45	8,000
Cuba	37,17,767		400	7,800
Siam	1,19,40,000		19	7,500
Mexico	1,65,27,766		701	7,000
Norway	28,09,564	3,638	220	6,500
Porto Rico	26,68,335		121	6,500
Denmark	25,50,656	5,402	300	5,000

(continued)

Table 3 (continued)

Country	(1) Population	(2) (Madison) GDP per capita 1934 ($US)	(3) No. of cinemas	(4) Gross revenue possibilities ($US)
Greece	63,15,000	2,418	100	5,000
Jugo-Slavia	1,39,30,918	1,173	338	4,000
Baltic States	54,10,033		275	4,000
Finland	36,34,040	2,988	200	4,000
Bulgaria	59,44,000	1,309	109	4,000
Peru	62,37,000		100	4,000
Turkey	1,36,60,275		80	3,000
Columbia	78,51,000		385	2,500
Venezuela	32,50,000		134	2,250
Indo-China	2,03,51,000		50	2,250
Trinidad	9,05,468		22	2,000
Bermuda	27,789		9	1,500
Bolivia	30,14,069		25	1,000
Ecuador	25,00,000		22	1,000
Persia	1,00,00,000		30	800
Iraq	33,00,000		9	600
Haiti	25,50,699		8	175

Source Variety, 6 November 1934; Maddison (2001, Appendix A)
Note Columns 1, 3, and 4 are taken from the original

The difference in cinemagoing between Great Britain and the Netherlands (Holland) is a feature of the scatter diagram presented in Fig. 3. Attention is drawn to the divide between European cultures in which doctrinaire Protestantism was, or had been, a dominant influence and those it had not, including Great Britain. If Germany, with its mixed religious affiliation, is included in this group, then all those more affluent countries on or above the line in Fig. 3 had well-established and developed national film industries, with which Hollywood needed to compete in the respective home markets.[22]

Figure 3 also draws attention to how relatively ingrained cinemagoing had become in the English-speaking world. Table 3 indicates that a third of all potential foreign earnings were in the British and Australasian markets during the 1930s. At that time, over 90 % of Australians classified themselves as belonging to the British race.[23] Mark Glancy has described how Hollywood tailor-made films to appeal to British

[22] Of those below the line only Sweden had a substantial film production sector during the the 1930s.

[23] Commonwealth Bureau of Census and Statistics (1936), found in *The Official yearbook of the Commonwealth of Australia.*

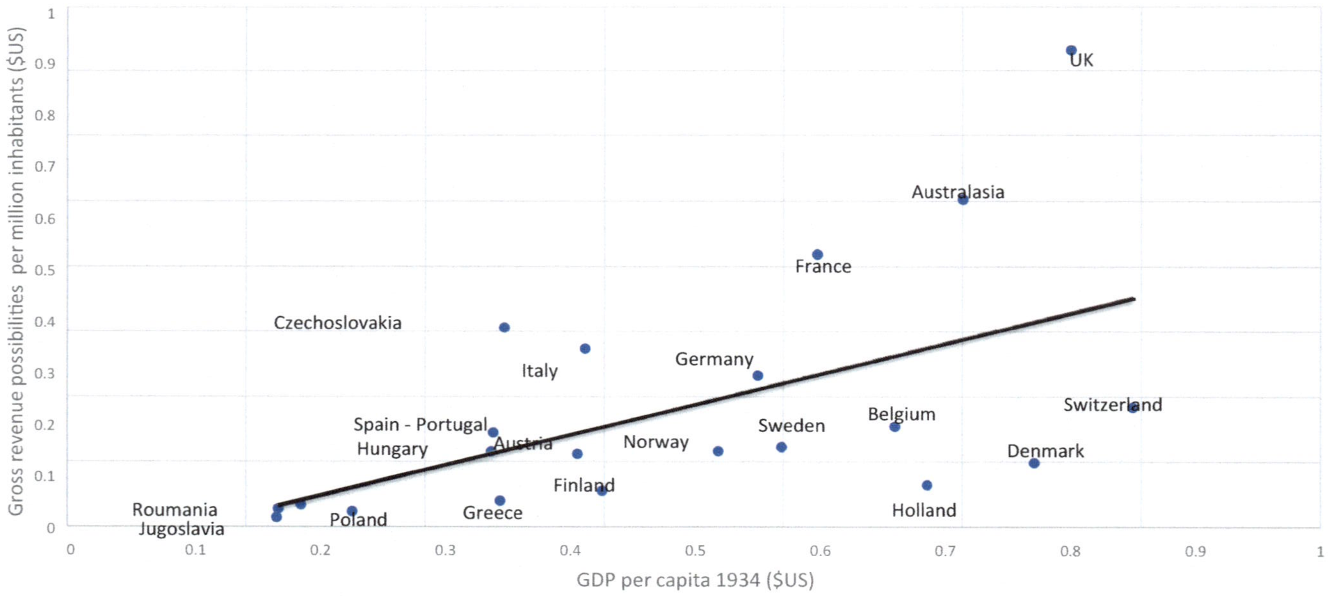

Fig. 3 Scatter of selected national GDP per capita and Gross revenue possibilities per million population for American film producers and distributors (*Source* Table 2, Maddison [2001, Appendix A])

audiences; Ruth Vasey, how Hollywood shaped national stereotypes according to the significance of respective market possibilities; and Ian Jarvie, how involved the State Department became in promoting Hollywood in international markets.[24]

6 International Orientation Index

Using the foreign revenue entries of 1,219 films recorded in the Mannix, Schaefer and Trevlin ledgers, Peter Miskell (2016) has taken an empirical approach to Hollywood's dominant position in world film markets, 1921–1951. Observing that considerable variance characterises the performance of films in foreign markets, Miskell looks to three explanatory factors: higher production costs; the extent of studios' distribution networks measured by the number of territories in which they ran distribution offices; and the attractiveness of films to foreign audiences. This last factor is measured by what he terms an International Orientation score that comprises two parts: each film is scored for its scenario (setting, character 1, character 2, and the national origin of the source text) and the national origins of the embodied artistic resources (director, writer, actor 1, and actor 2). Films such as *Queen Christina* (1934), starring Greta Garbo, and *Roman Holiday* (1954), starring Audrey Hepburn, generated exceptionally high International Orientation scores.

Miskell divides the period of his study into five periods: the silent (1921–1928), early talkies (1929–1932), the 1930s (1933–1938), the Second World War (1939–1945), and post-war (1956–1950)—and finds significant changes in the explanatory powers of the three factors in his model, with the size of networks being of greater importance in the silent and early talkie years; years during which the International Orientation of films was less important. From the 1930s, the latter became significant, suggesting that the Hollywood studios could mitigate the cultural barriers that emerged because of the 'coming of sound' by emphasising the cultural appeal of its films through their subject material and the talent embodied in them. However, Miskell adds the caveat that by taking these films, exhibitors in foreign territories could be bound by block booking contracts to screen other films less attractive to local audiences.

Two other findings are of importance. First, Miskell identifies threshold effects in the case of production costs and the number of foreign distribution offices. Positive returns to scale can be identified initially, but these taper off once a threshold is reached. Secondly, he draws attention to the poor performance of genres in his model. Drawing on the genre categorisation found in the Catalogue of the American Film Institute, he finds that genre effects, for the most part, are statistically insignificant across all five periods. Furthermore, when they appear significant for a period, they are negative.

Concluding, Miskell writes:

[24] Glancy (1999), Vasey (1997), and Jarvie (1992).

> The production of international films for international audiences appears to have been an effective strategy by which US film companies were able to retain their position in foreign markets after the coming of sound, but the success of this strategy was closely bound up with the activities of their foreign distribution subsidiaries. Without a strong network of distribution offices, the global appeal of Hollywood's most internationally oriented films could not be effectively exploited; for the distribution offices themselves, the task of selling American films in foreign markets was greatly aided by the availability of these internationally oriented pictures.[25]

7 POPSTAT

POPSTAT is now over 25 years old. As a method, it was developed to retrospectively assess the relative popularity of films when historical box-office data is missing. The first iteration was developed from the weekly programming records of 80 British city first-run cinemas screened in 1934 and published in the trade magazine *Kinematograph Weekly*. It brought attention to a new type of evidence about what films people paid to watch in large numbers.[26] It, therefore, enabled film historians to be able to say, unambiguously, that for whatever reason, ***Film Y*** was more popular with a particular audience than ***Film X***, often reversing established opinions. The article later led to a book in which the temporal span of the investigation was extended to 1932–1937.[27]

A criticism levelled at the British study concerns the truncated nature of the sample: notably, that the sample set of cinemas is taken from the upper tier of the film distribution process, leaving unexplored the diffusion process beyond—to lower-order cinemas in each of the respective cities. Two small cities with around 200,000 inhabitants were selected to address this issue—one in the North of England (Bolton) and one in the South (Brighton). In both, the object was to capture the complete life and death dynamics of film circulation in either locality during 1934–1935. The local studies were based upon the film programmes of those cinemas that were advertised in their local daily newspaper. As a result of Sue Harper's discovery of a first-run cinema box-office ledger in the naval city of Portsmouth, the third collection of film programmes was undertaken, this time for the year 1934 only.[28] The comparative analysis of filmgoing in the three cities is the subject of Chapter "ComparativeFilmPopularityinThreeEnglishCities—Bolton,Brighton,andPortsmouth:AnExerciseinPOPSTATMethodology".

---

[25] Miskell (2016, pp. 20–21).

[26] Sedgwick (1994). *Kinematograph Weekly* published a column 'Showing Next Week'. For the week commencing 5 March 1934 the cities of London (13 cinemas), Birmingham (5), Bradford (2), Bristol (9), Cardiff (5), Edinburgh (8), Glasgow (10), Leeds (7), Liverpool (7), Newcastle (5), and Sheffield (7) were represented. Unfortunately, the coverage of cities and cinemas is not always consistent. For instance, in the 5 March issue the first-run cinemas of Manchester are missing. Where this happens, the programmes were found in advertisements in local evening newspapers.

[27] Sedgwick (2000).

[28] Harper (2004) and Sedgwick (2006).

In each of the three local studies and the national study, a POPSTAT Index of Film Popularity was created, ranking films screened from first to last annually. In the case of the three local studies, the programming data was derived from advertisements found in the three respective daily newspapers—*Bolton Evening News*, *Brighton Evening Argus*, and *Portsmouth Evening News.*

Specifically, the POPSTAT methods require researchers to collect information about the films being screened, the cinemas where they are being screened, whether they are being screened as single or double bill entertainment, and, finally, the run length at each cinema. Formally, the method can be presented as:

$$POPSTAT_{it} = \sum_{j=1}^{n} a_{jt} \times b_{ijt} \times l_{ijt} \tag{1}$$

where $i = ith$ film,
$t =$ the period of the investigation,
$j = jth$ cinema, of which there were n in the population,
$a =$ the cinema weight,
$b =$ The billing status of a film, typically 1.0 if single billed or 0.5 if double billed,
$l =$ length of run.
The Greek letter Σ represents the operation of summing.

The formula can be read as follows: the *POPSTAT* value of the *ith* film in period t is derived by summing the respective products of the cinema weight (a), its billing status (b) and the length of run (l), at each *jth* cinema at which it is screened.

Cinema weights are a vital element in the formulation of POPSTAT. Without them, analytically, cinemas would be equivalents: it would not be possible to discriminate between them based on their size or revenue earning capabilities. For instance, programming data is available for 32 cinemas in Warsaw in 1925 from three daily newspapers *Kurier Poranny*, *Nasz Przegląd*, and *Kurier Warszawski*. However, pricing and seating information are not available. Accordingly, an assessment of popularity can only be performed on the number of screenings received by a film. The list of Top 10 movies by weighted screen days shown in Warsaw in 1925 is given in Table 4.[29]

Of course, this is valuable information. Drilling down into the dataset reveals the cinemas where each film appeared, giving form to the extant distribution and exhibition system. For instance, the 3-h long French film *Koenigsmark* that heads the list in Table 4 opened at two cinemas, the Rococo and Światowid, on 7 January 1925, playing for six and five weeks, respectively, before proceeding to the Tombola cinema on 18 April for a second run. *Koenigsmark* wasn't screened in any of the remaining 29 cinemas in the cinema dataset, presumably being distributed to lower-order cinemas later—cinemas that did not advertise in either of the three daily papers. Thus, outside the 32 cinemas, there is no record of diffusion. The dataset is, thus,

[29] From data collected by Karina Pryt and her team at Goethe University, Frankfurt, kindly shared with the author.

Table 4 Top 10 films by screening days screened in Warsaw in 1925

Rank	Film title in Poland	Days	Days weighted
1	Koenigsmark	81	81
2	Nibelungi	66	66
3	Dzwonnik z Notre Dame	56	56
4	Iwonka	55	55
5	Matka	47	47
6	Golgota uczciwej kobiety	42	42
7	Królowa Saba	42	42
8	Scaramouche	42	42
9	Brzdąc	62	40
10	Biała siostra (W ogniu Wezuwiusza)	35	35
11	Cud wilków	35	35
12	Arabka	32	32
13	Dorota Vernon	32	32
14	Tragedia domu Habsburgów	32	32
15	Tragedia w Lourdes	32	32
16	Czarna Lu	31	31
17	Mały Lord	31	31
18	Rywale	31	31
19	Demon morza	32	30.5
20	Ósmy cud świata (Wystawa w Wembley)	48	28

Source Kurier Poranny, *Nasz Przegląd*, and *Kurier Warszawski*
Note These films are listed by their marketed titles. Billing weights are 1 = single billing, 0.5 where the film appears as double billings

imperfect. Nevertheless, even though it is severely truncated as a sample of extant cinemas operating in 1925 (the number of extant cinemas is not known), it provides some qualified grounds for making comparative popularity statements in the manner shown in Table 4.

The sample cinema set also provides a means of understanding the cinema hierarchy in Warsaw at that time. For instance, it is possible to empirically separate the 32 cinemas into distinct categories by taking, say, the Top 20 films and investigating which cinemas each premiered, and then each that received them in the second run, etc. Profiling cinemas in this way will identify those that exclusively premiere the most popular films, those that take these films in the second run, and so forth, including, of course, those cinemas that do not screen Top 20 movies at all.[30] Patterns of diffusion are likely to be idiosyncratic, reflecting local circumstances and practice, providing a sound basis for comparative analysis.

The discussion is predicated upon the absence of complete information about audience size. Indeed, in the case of Warsaw in 1925, knowledge of the population of cinemas in operation is scarce. In establishing measures of national film popularity in the British study, only first-run cinemas were observed in selected cities. In the Warsaw study, only those cinemas that advertised in one of three daily newspapers. In both cases, the samples were truncated. They represent the upper levels of cinemas in a hierarchy. For the film choices observed in these cinemas to be representative, they would need to be replicated in cinemas not included in the selection. As argued earlier, the purpose of the three small English city studies was that they encompassed the whole population of cinemas. Accordingly, it is possible to ask whether the patterns of filmgoing observed in Bolton, Brighton, and Portsmouth reflect those established in the national study.

Roderick Floud sums up the issues facing the historian as follows:

> In sampling, we make a selection of cases from our data. We want to reduce the amount of data with which we have to deal, without greatly reducing the accuracy of the results we derive from the data. Our object therefore is that any conclusion we reach on the basis of our study of a selection of cases should be the same as the conclusion we would have reached if we had been able to study all of the cases. In other words, we want the sample to provide us with a good estimate of the true result…Our aim is always the same: to find a sample that will allow us to make a good estimate of the characteristics in which we are interested.[31]

As we have learned, in her investigation of filmgoing in the Netherlands in the mid-1930s, Clara Pafort-Overduin (2012) drew upon the film programmes of 22 different Dutch cities/towns between 1934 and 1936. Her surprising results show the Dutch film *De Jantjes* was the most popular film in 13 of the 22 locations over the three years, including the cities of Den Haag (The Hague), Groningen, Haarlem, Rotterdam, and Utrecht, and was second-placed in Amsterdam and Eindhoven.[32] In an extension of this work, the question was asked about why the Dutch didn't go to the cinema very often. The answer was anything but simple, rooted in a complex combination of business, cultural, economic, and institutional factors.[33]

In contrast, Joseph Garncarz draws upon a single sample of 52 cinemas located in central Berlin and its suburbs, whose programmes were advertised daily in the *Berliner Morgenpost*, to derive a national estimate of film popularity for the whole of the Nazi era, 1933–1945.[34] Garncarz justifies his choice of sample on three grounds: that the Berlin population comprised people from throughout Germany; that Berlin

---

[30] This is done in Chapter "Film Exhibition, Distribution and Popularity in German-Occupied Belgium (1940–1944): Brussels, Antwerp and Liege", with regards to the post-war Italian film industry.

[31] Floud (1979, p. 170).

[32] Pafort-Overduin (2012).

[33] Sedgwick et al. (2012).

[34] Joseph Garncarz (2020).

audiences contributed approximately a fifth of German box office; and, finally, that the sample included all types of cinema from premiere cinemas located in the city centre to neighbourhood cinemas in the districts.

Pafort-Overduin uses a version of POPSTAT in which cinema weights are given by seating capacity only. Garncarz uses an altogether more elaborate form of calculation. Not only does he derive cinemas weights from seating capacity and prices, but he also uses information about daily and monthly cinema usage (attendances) to weigh these. So, in terms of differentiating cinemas, Garncarz fine-tunes the methods employed to establish film popularity in the three small English cities. For him, it is not sufficient to argue that a film screened at a single cinema will generate the same cinema weight, irrespective of whether that film playing was the most or least popular at that cinema. From historical sources, knowing that film attendances on average varied according to the day of the week and month of the year, he restricts equivalence to the condition that films generate the same weight only if they are screened on, say, a Tuesday in December. Knowledge of differences in average daily attendances and average monthly attendances enables him to interpolate an additional weight—what he terms 'visitor frequency'—into the POPSTAT formula. As will become apparent in a later chapter, the Swedish scholar Leif Furhammar does the same.

Garncatz's ability to corroborate his results is somewhat limited, relying on a sample of 1,250 cinema owners in the 1930/31 season who were asked to rank the five most popular films in their respective cinemas. These results were aggregated and reported in the 25 May 1931 edition of the trade journal *Film Kurier*. Although conducted before the Nazi period, Garncarz trialled his method on 35 of the 52 cinemas in his Berlin sample and found a positive correlation of 0.47 between the votes for the most popular 35 films identified by the managers and their respective POPSTAT scores. He also found this a marginal improvement on the result generated by the conventional POPSTAT method, with lower variance. Garncarz calls his method 'Optimised POPSTAT'. He then compares his optimised results with annual ticket sales of the three most popular films between 1932 and 1933, extended to nine movies from 1938 and finds much higher correlations.

Both scholars use POPSTAT to establish an empirical base to estimate the relative size of cinema markets and audiences' preferences. Pafort Overduin's extended sample allows her to investigate intra-locality, inter-locality, and national film popularity, while Garncarz is concerned with single national popularity characteristics. The establishment of a POPSTAT Index of film popularity allows more comprehensive questions to be asked. For instance, Garncarz seeks to understand the preferences of Jewish filmgoers and whether these were substantially different for non-Jewish Germans during the Nazi period, while, as we learn in a later chapter, Pafort Overduin is fascinated by the tastes expressed by Dutch filmgoers. She is particularly interested in the qualities of three popular films—what are known as 'Jordaanfilms'—including *De Jantjes,* that depict in a light-hearted way the quotidian of life in the Netherlands at the time.

8 Comparative Analysis—RelPOP

Thus, the POPSTAT method establishes a numerical ranking of films according to their popularity within a locality and, implicitly, a means of comparing the popularity of films across populations of cinemas sited in different localities. Although adaptable to the circumstances of time and place and associated data constraints, it requires the researcher to compare like with like, making explicit procedures and constraints.

One major issue in assessing intra-locality film popularity is distinguishing between the ordinal and cardinal nature of POPSTAT Index values. Specifically, the rank order of films established by a POPSTAT Index will only imperfectly reflect differences in POPSTAT values because of the highly skewed nature of the POPSTAT Index distribution, which shows an ever-diminishing marginal POPSTAT value associated with rank. Derived from the British national study for 1934, this is evident in Fig. 4. The slope of the POPSTAT curve declines as rank order diminishes, becoming shallower along its length. Thus, a rank change from 1 to 2 represents a considerably more significant change in POPSTAT values than the shift from 99 to 100, which in turn is larger than 499–500. For this reason, the cardinal values of a POPSTAT distribution are preferred to ordinal values of rank when analysing film popularity, allowing us to understand how much more popular any one film is in relation to any other film; thus, by implication, all other films.

For the same reason, averaging the ranked performance of a movie in different localities does not adequately capture differences in respective performance. Take, for example, the popularity of the 1934 British film *Sing as We Go*, starring Lancashire-born Gracie Fields, in the three small cities of Bolton, Brighton and Portsmouth. Measured by its respective POPSTAT Index values, the film was the major attraction of the year in Bolton (Rank = 1) but performed less well in the cities of Brighton (15th) and Portsmouth (48th).[35] The arithmetic mean of these three ranks is $(1 + 15 + 48)/3 = 21.33$. The variance in rank is marked, suggesting that the film divided filmgoers across the country.

Further difficulties arise using rank order since the population of films screened differs in size between localities, meaning that a particular rank will reflect different levels of relative popularity. Hypothetically, if in locality A 200 films are screened and locality B just 20, a film ranked 20th in either has a different comparative meaning. For instance, in the chapter 'Five Italian Cities', Treveri Gennari and I count 731 and 598 films screened at least once in January 1954 in Rome and Milan, while in the same month, only 188 films were screened in Bari (Table 3). However, given the disproportionate size of the cinema markets in the two cities, averaging film popularity metrics—box office, POPSTAT, or the number of screenings—for the same set of films in the two cities will simply reflect the difference in the size of respective markets. Some form of standardisation is required. Otherwise, the mean will be biased in favour of the largest.

[35] The POPSTAT values are based on attributing equal billing weights (0.5) to each film sharing a double bill programme.

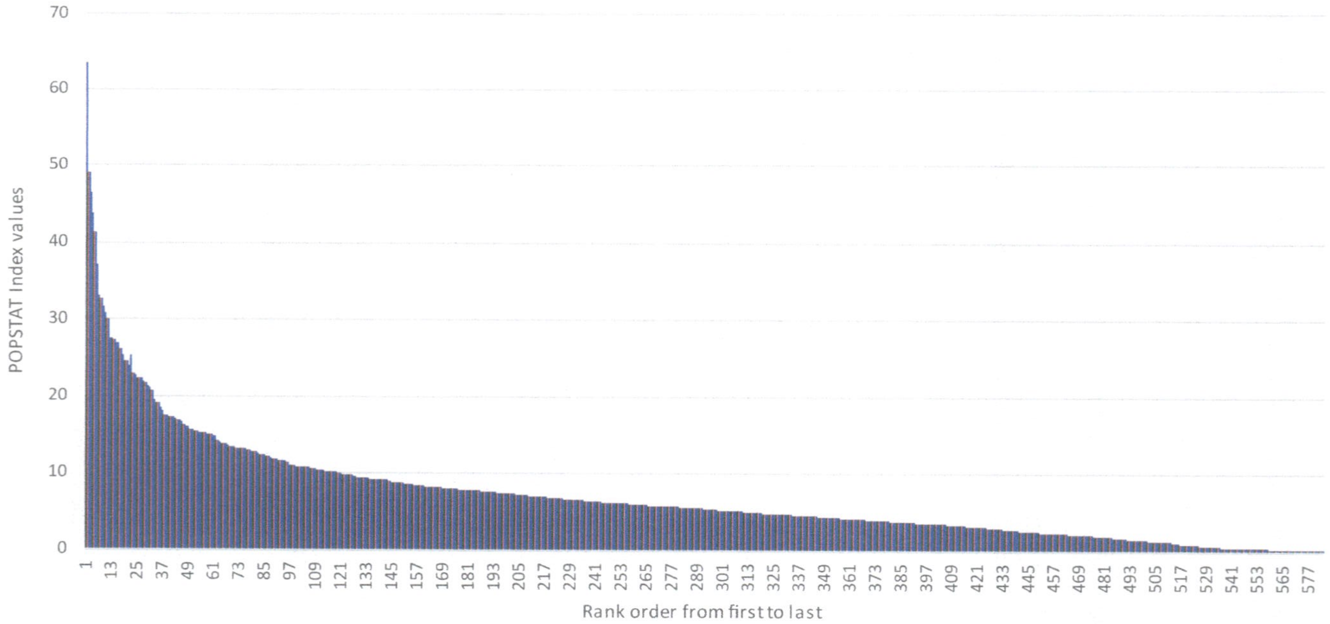

Fig. 4 The slope of the POPSTAT-Rank curve for the 574 films released in Great Britain screened at least once in the truncated sample of London West-End and provincial city cinemas in 1934 (*Source Kinematograph Weekly*, Sedgwick [2000])

Assume that POPSTAT is the metric. One way of proceeding is to express the POPSTAT Index values of those films that flow through a distinct population of cinemas during a period as proportions of the median value. I term this method RelPOP. It gives rise to a relative measure of popularity: one that standardises each of the various local populations of films being compared around a value representing the film that lies in the middle when ranked from first to last.[36] A RelPOP Index thus allows a researcher to make statements such as the films starring Actor X are very much more popular among audiences in locality *Loc1* than *Loc2*, or that *Film X* was more popular among audiences in *Loc2* than *Loc1*, even though *Loc2* has a smaller population and in absolute terms, fewer audiences attended the film. Implicit in these statements and the method that allows them to be made is the consideration that each locality in a study is equivalent, irrespective of size. Through RelPOP, it is possible to compare the relative popularities of films and their stars when screened in unequally sized cities, regions, or (more problematically) countries.[37]

RelPOP takes the general form:

$$RelPOP_i = \sum_{loc=1}^{n} \frac{BO_i}{BO_m} \div n \tag{2}$$

where, *RelPOP* = Relative Popularity,
i = *ith* film,
m = median value,
loc = locality,
n = number of localities,
BO_i = Box office of the ith film, or appropriate proxy such as POPSTAT, in each locality,
BO_m = Box office of the median film, or POPSTAT, in each locality.

Formally, the relative popularity of any particular film (the *ith* film) in a population of films can be expressed as a quotient of its actual popularity (measured by its box office or a proxy, such as POPSTAT) and the median of that population. Accordingly, a RelPOP value of 5 for a hit film indicates that it is five times more popular than the median film: a RelPOP value of 0.5 marks a film that is only half as popular as the median film. Across several localities, the relative popularity of a movie is given by the arithmetic mean of the localised RelPOP values. Measures of variance (such as the coefficient of variation) can then be used to identify films that performed consistently in various markets and those that did not.

In the research on the Italian film market between 1957 and 1966, where the concept was introduced, the RelPOP method showed the films of the comic actor,

[36] One film if the population is an odd number, two films (averaged) in the case of an even numbered population.

[37] RelPOP was first introduced in Sedgwick et al. (2019) when analysing actual box-office data gathered by an Italian trade body for the Italian film market, 1957–1966.

Totò, to be very much more popular among audiences in the southern cities of Naples and Bari than in Rome or the Northern cities of Milan and Turin.

9 Conclusion

In this chapter, economic and methodological ideas have been advanced that are central to the dynamics of films in market economies. Each informs the other. The object is twofold: first, to lay down an analytical base for the remainder of the book; and secondly, to outline tools that researchers might use in developing empirical research projects, entailing the investigation of films in circulation at a time and a place.

For this author, the evolution of filmgoers' preferences for certain films and the tastes that govern their choices, in conjunction with the mode of diffusion that responds to these choices across nations with different ideologies at different times, is intriguing. Each chapter draws upon a distinct dataset, identifying the films audiences most preferred and how these circulated. The POPSTAT method is used to examine:

- three English cities in the 1930s,
- 22 towns and cities in the Netherlands (Pafort-Overduin) during the same decade,
- the reach of films from the city centre of Adelaide out to the suburbs and beyond into the hinterland of South Australia during the Second World War (Walker and Walsh),
- the binary separation of the Belgium market under the Germany Occupation (with Vande Winkel),
- Film popularity in Brno, Czechoslovakia (with Porubčanská and Skopal) and Cracow, Poland (with Klejsa), during the early 1950s.

  Detailed business ledgers are called upon in the study of Philadelphia during the 1930s (with Hanssen), while trade journal records enable Miskell to investigate the changing nature of Hollywood film during the post-war era. The five-city study of Italy in 1954 (with Treveri Gennari) draws upon film programming datasets, as does the study of Furhammar's methods to establish an index of popular films in 1930s Sweden (with Jernudd).

What appears to be always the case everywhere is that audiences select what they want to see from a body of films determined by combinations of producer, distributor, and State agency. At the same time, the distribution system operationalises these choices reflecting the popularity of the movies chosen.

References

Arsel, Z., & Bean, J. (2013). Taste regimes and market-mediated practice. *Journal of Consumer Research, 39*, 899–917.

Bakker, G. (2003). Building knowledge about the consumer: The emergence of market research in the motion picture industry. *Business History, 45*, 101–127.
Bakker, G. (2008). *Entertainment industrialised: The emergence of the international film industry, 1890–1940*. Cambridge University Press.
De Vany, A. (2004). *Hollywood economics: How extreme uncertainty shapes the film industry*. Routledge.
De Vany, A., & Walls, W. (1996). Bose-Einstein dynamics and adaptive contracting in the motion picture industry. *Economic Journal, 106*, 1493–1514.
Floud, R. (1979). *An introduction to quantitative methods for historians* (2nd ed.). Methuen.
Garncarz, J. (2020). *Begeisterte zuschauer : Über die filmpräferenzen der Deutschen in der NS-Zeit*. Herbert von Halem.
Ginsburgh, V., & Weyers, S. (1999). On the perceived quality of movies. *Journal of Cultural Economics, 23*, 269–283.
Glancy, H. M. (1992). MGM film grosses, 1924–1948: The Eddie Mannix ledger. *Historical Journal of Film, Radio and Television, 12*, 127–144.
Glancy, H. M. (1995). Warner Bros. film grosses, 1921–1951: The William Schaefer ledger. *Historical Journal of Film, Radio and Television, 15*, 55–74.
Glancy, H. M. (1999). *When Hollywood loved Britain*. Manchester University Press.
Handel, L. (1950). *Hollywood looks at its audience*. University of Illinois Press.
Harper, S. (2004). A lower middle-class taste-community in the 1930s: Admissions figures at the Regent cinema, Portsmouth, UK. *Historical Journal of Film, Radio and Television, 24*, 565–587.
Hennion, A. (2007). Those things that hold us together: Taste and sociology. *Cultural Sociology, 1*, 97–114.
Jarvie, I. (1992). *Hollywood's overseas campaign: The North Atlantic movie trade, 1920 1950*. Cambridge University Press.
Jewell, R. (1994). RKO film grosses, 1929–1951: The C.J Trevlin Ledger. *Historical Journal of Film, Radio and Television, 14*, 37–51.
Kuhn, A. (2002). *An everyday magic: Cinema and cultural memory*. I.B. Tauris
Maddison, A. (2001). *The world economy: A millennial perspective*. Development Centre Studies, OECD Publishing. https://doi.org/10.1787/9789264189980-en
Miskell, P. (2016). International films and international markets: The globalisation of Hollywood entertainment, C.1921–1951. *Media History, 22*(2), 174–200.
Moretti, E. (2011). Social learning and peer effects in consumption: Evidence from movie sales. *Review of Economic Studies, 78*, 356–393.
Nelson, P. (1970). Information and consumer behavior. *Journal of Political Economy, 78*, 311–329.
Nelson, P. (1974). Advertising as information. *Journal of Political Economy, 82*, 729–745.
Pafort-Overduin, C. (2012). *Hollandse films met een Hollands hart. Nationale identiteit en de Jordaanfilms, 1934–1936*. University of Utrecht.
Pokorny, M., & Sedgwick, J. (2001). Stardom and the profitability of filmmaking: Warner Bros. in the 1930s. *Journal of Cultural Economics, 25*, 157–184.
Pokorny, M., & Sedgwick, J. (2010). Profitability trends in Hollywood: 1929 to 1999. *Economic History Review, 63*, 56–84.
Pokorny, M., Miskell, P., & Sedgwick, J. (2019). Managing uncertainty in creative industries: Film sequels and Hollywood's profitability, 1988–2015. *Competition and Change, 23*, 23–46.
Ratner, R., Kahn, B., & Kahneman, D. (1999). Choosing less-preferred experiences for the sake of variety. *Journal of Consumer Research, 26*, 1–15.
Sedgwick, J. (1994). The market for feature films in Britain in 1934: A viable national cinema. *Historical Journal of Film Radio and Television, 14*, 5–36.
Sedgwick, J. (2000). *Filmgoing in 1930s Britain: A choice of pleasures*. Exeter University Press.
Sedgwick, J. (2002). Product differentiation at the movies: Hollywood, 1946–65. *Journal of Economic History, 62*, 676–704.
Sedgwick, J. (2006). Cinemagoing in Portsmouth during the 1930s. *Cinema Journal, 46*, 52–85.

Sedgwick, J. (2007). A Shacklean approach to the demand for movies. In M. Bianchi (Ed.), *The evolution of consumption: Theories and practice* (pp. 77–92). Elsevier.
Sedgwick, J., Miskell, P., & Nicoli, M. (2019). The market for films in postwar Italy: Evidence for both national and regional patterns of taste. *Enterprise & Society, 20*, 199–228.
Sedgwick, J., Pafort-Overduin, C., & Boter, J. (2012). Explanations for the restrained development of the Dutch cinema market in the 1930s. *Enterprise and Society, 13*, 634–671.
Sedgwick, J., & Pokorny, M. (1998). The risk environment of film-making: Warners in the inter-war period. *Explorations in Economic History, 35*, 196–220.
Sedgwick, J., & Pokorny, M. (2005). The film business in the US and Britain during the 1930s. *Economic History Review, 58*, 79–112.
Sedgwick, J., & Pokorny, M. (2010). Consumers as risk takers: Evidence from the film industry during the 1930s. *Business History, 52*, 74–99.
Treveri Gennari, D. (2015). "If you have seen it, you cannot forget!" Film consumption and memories of cinemagoing in 1950s Rome. *Historical Journal of Film Radio and Television, 35*, 53–74.
Vasey, R. (1997). *The world according to Hollywood, 1918–1939*. Exeter University Press.

John Sedgwick is a visiting Professor in the Faculty of Technology, Design and Environment, Oxford Brookes University. He researches the economic history of cinema and is particularly interested in the ontological characteristics of film as a commodity. He created the POPSTAT Index of Film Popularity as a proxy for box-office returns. This tool provides a means of reflecting audience preferences and monitoring the distribution process. His research has focused on American, Australian, British, Dutch, Italian and international markets during the 1930s and 1950/60s. He has written a monograph, edited an anthology and published articles in *Business History, Cinema Journal, Economic History Review, Explorations in Economic History, Enterprise and Society, Film History, Historical Journal of Film, Radio and Television, Journal of Applied Statistics, Journal of Cultural Economics, Journal of Economic History, and Journal of Transnational Cinema.*

How Did the Department of Justice Get It so Wrong? Philadelphia 1935–1936: The Stanley Warner Chain, Competitive Practices and Consumer Welfare

F. Andrew Hanssen and John Sedgwick

Abstract From their pursuit of the Motion Picture Industry, the Department of Justice had a poor concept of the economics peculiar to the film industry outlined in the previous chapter. They failed to appreciate that scheduling a film's distribution (how many screens? how much time?) necessarily occurs before its popularity is known, requiring that the distribution and exhibition relationship must necessarily exhibit substantial post-contractual flexibility if the market works efficiently. Philadelphia was an exhibition stronghold for Warner Bros. In our investigation of the programming of its cinemas in the mid-1930s and the box-office returns that accrued, we find no evidence of monopoly practice in the first run. That is to say that as exhibitors Warner Bros. screened major attractions produced by other studios as a matter of standard practice. As a rule, films were screened for as long as a threshold number of customers bought tickets.

By most measures, the U.S. motion picture industry of the first half of the twentieth century was an unlikely candidate for antitrust prosecution. The industry was far from concentrated. For example, in 1938, when the *Paramount* antitrust case was filed by the United States Department of Justice (USDOJ), more than 700 feature films were released by more than 200 different companies. Seven of the eight studios commonly referred to as 'majors' (Columbia, Fox, MGM, Paramount, RKO, Universal, and Warner Brothers) each released thirty or more feature films (the exception was United Artists, a distributor of the movies of affiliated independent producers, which released 19).[1] Eleven other companies released ten or more feature

[1] Five studios—MGM, Paramount, RKO, Twentieth Century Fox (prior to 1935, Fox) and Warner Bros. were fully vertically integrated with substantial production, distribution and exhibition operations. Columbia, Universal and United Artists were partially vertically integrated—they did not run large cinema chains (Gomery, 2005).

F. A. Hanssen
Clemson University, Clemson, SC, USA

J. Sedgwick (✉)
Oxford Brookes University, Oxford, UK
e-mail: sedgwicj52@gmail.com

J. Sedgwick (ed.), *Towards a Comparative Economic History of Cinema, 1930–1970*, Frontiers in Economic History, https://doi.org/10.1007/978-3-031-05770-0_3

films that year. The four-firm concentration ratio is under 50 per cent, and the Herfindahl–Hirschman Index (HHI) is low.[2] Indeed, even if one excludes all film production except for releases by the eight majors (all of whom were *Paramount* defendants), the resulting HHI is still only 1329, well within the 'competitive' range. Of the approximately 15,000 cinemas operating nationwide, less than 20 per cent were owned by the vertically integrated 'major' studios, albeit these would tend to be located in major city downtown areas, have a larger capacity, and charge higher prices.[3] From a population of 127 million, Americans made 2.233 billion visits to the cinema in 1935, constituting an arithmetic mean of over 17 trips per head. They paid on average 25 cents per admission.[4] With one seat per 12 people, cinemagoing in the United States was more accessible than anywhere else in the world. Films and film stars were wildly popular and by far the most popular spectator activity, absorbing over one-fifth of all personal consumption expenditure.[5]

Yet, from the late teens through the 1940s, U.S. antitrust authorities pursued the motion picture industry with a Javert-like vigour, launching two major antitrust suits as well as making several lesser charges.[6] In 1948, the United States Supreme Court decided the *Paramount* case in the Department of Justice's favour, leading to consent decrees that effectively dismembered the industry, forcing the 'major' studios to divest themselves of their cinema chains.

It can be argued that, in effect, the Supreme Court ended an industrial structure that was in the process of becoming economically untenable, as post-war audiences increasingly stayed away from the cinema.[7] Nevertheless, they persisted, begging the question, why? What was it about motion pictures that aroused such hostility among the antitrust authorities? The answer appears to lie in the many distinctive practices that characterised vertical relationships in the film industry. Block booking, which

---

[2] Our source for film releases is Internet Movie Data Base (IMDB); see Hanssen (2020) and Hanssen and Raskovich (forthcoming) for a discussion of the IMDB's pros and cons. The HHI is a widely used measure of industry concentration calculated by summing the squared market shares of the competitors in a market. Including the largest 50 producers (the typical antitrust approach) the 1938 HHI is only 648. Using box-office data from national first-run cinemas, published weekly in the trade paper Variety, Sedgwick and Pokorny (2005) calculated the HHI to be 1260 for the middle years of the decade. According to the USDOJ's horizontal merger guidelines a market with an HHI of less than 1500 is considered to be 'competitive' while markets in which the HHI is between 1,500 and 2,500 points are 'moderately concentrated', and markets in which the HHI is in excess of 2,500 points are 'highly concentrated'. See https://www.justice.gov/atr/horizontal-merger-guidelines-08192010#5c.

[3] Huettig (1985, p. 6).

[4] Conant (1960) Table 1, from Department of Commerce Publications.

[5] Historical Statistics of the United States, Series H 878–893. Personal Consumption Expenditures.

[6] In re *Famous Players-Lasky Corp.*, 11 F.T.C. 187 (1927), the Federal Trade Commission attacked famous Player Lasky's (shortly to be renamed Paramount) use of block booking. The case was decided against the industry, but given the devastating effects of the Great Depression, was never enforced. In 1938, The USDOJ launched the case that culminated in *United States v. Paramount Pictures*, 334 U.S. 131, 140 (1948); the eight 'major' producer-distributors were charged with conspiring to limit competition through various vertical practices (including block booking).

[7] Sedgwick (2002).

involved exhibitors contracting for multiple films simultaneously, attracted particular attention—why should cinemas be forced to take a producer's bad movies along with its good ones?

In addition, films were sold 'blind'—exhibitors were required to book films before they had been released, making it impossible for them to judge film quality. Furthermore, formula deals (which specified revenue-sharing percentages based on a film's anticipated national gross rather than its performance in the specific theatre) and master agreements (which applied the same licensing terms to multiple theatres in a chain) were believed to favour large chains over independent houses. The system of runs, clearance and zoning through which films were distributed to cinemas was interpreted as price discriminating at best and anti-competitive foreclosure at worst.[8] The direct ownership of cinemas was said to facilitate collusion between the 'major' studios, blocking market entry.

Yet 'unusual' need not mean 'anti-competitive', and the years since have not been kind to the arguments made by the *Paramount* prosecutors. Far from forcing exhibitors to take films they did not want, Hanssen presents evidence that block booking was flexibly applied.[9] Industrially, it served primarily as a low-cost means of selling a product that cinemas purchased in large amounts—cinemas of the day were commonly screening double bill twice-weekly change programmes, requiring 208 films per year. Kenney and Klein argue that selling films 'blind' produced substantial savings on inventory costs—the alternative being that of keeping finished films in a vault for a year or so after booking.[10] De Vany and Eckert argue that formula deals and master agreements allowed motion picture companies to reduce contracting costs to the benefit of all parties (including consumers).[11] They also maintain that the system of runs, clearance and zoning was a solution to the problem of allocating film prints across screens to maximise their use. Sedgwick and Pokorny demonstrate the extent to which the exhibition wings of the 'majors' screened the popular films of their rivals.[12]

[8] A run was a designation that determined the order in which cinemas received new releases: first run first, second run second and so forth. A large city might have as many as a dozen run classifications, with the largest most central cinemas receiving the films first and smallest cinemas in smallest neighbourhoods receiving the films last. The 'clearance' was the period between runs; for example, two weeks might have to pass following the end of a first run before a second-run cinema could begin its showings. The 'zone' was the geographic area for which each run was defined. See, for example Huettig (1985) for a description.

[9] Hanssen (2000).

[10] Kenney and Klein (1983).

[11] De Vany and Eckert (1991).

[12] Sedgwick and Pokorny (2005).

Furthermore, vertical integration of film production and distribution with exhibition serves several efficiency-enhancing purposes. These include promoting post-release flexibility in run length,[13] avoiding double marginalisation,[14] and strengthening incentives to invest in actors under contract.[15] As a coda, in 2020, the USDOJ vacated the *Paramount* consent decrees after years of investigation.[16] The ostensibly anti-competitive booking practices may once again be engaged in legally.

How did the prosecutors get it so wrong? The fundamental problem was that neither the antitrust authorities nor the courts made any serious attempt to understand the film industry's unique challenges.[17] Every motion picture is different, and only by exhibiting a film to a paying audience can the otherwise unpredictable demand for it be revealed (see the introductory chapter). But by then, most costs related to production and distribution are sunk. In other words, one must invest nearly the total cost of a motion picture before one can determine whether it is a hit or a flop.

Moreover, the scheduling of a film's distribution (how many screens? how much time?) necessarily occurs before its popularity is known. The distribution and exhibition relationship must therefore exhibit substantial post-contractual flexibility. But the more flexible contracts are, the greater the possibility of *ex-post* opportunism on the part of exhibitors. The practices that evolved in the first half of the twentieth century—and eviscerated by the *Paramount* decision—were direct responses to this trade-off and captured in Stuart Head's testimony to a House of Representative sub-committee on the industry in 1935, in his capacity as President of Fox Films.[18]

1 Philadelphia Dataset

An examination is conducted into competitive characteristics of the film business based upon the passage of 326 films through 23 cinemas located in Philadelphia, screened at least once across 33 weeks, between week-ending 16 November 1935

---

[13] Hanssen (2010).

[14] Gil (2015).

[15] Hanssen and Raskovich (2020).

[16] The document is available at https://www.justice.gov/atr/page/file/1302816/download. The USDOJ's stated intention is 'to terminate the Decrees effective immediately, except for a two-year sunset period on the Decree's provision's banning block booking and circuit dealing' (page 1).

[17] For example, the U.S. District Court, the appeal of whose judgement would bring abaout the definitive 1948 Supreme Court decision, stated in its written opinion that 'It is argued that the steps we have proposed would involve an interference with commercial practices that are generally acceptable and a hazardous attempt on the part of judges – unfamiliar with the details of the business – to remodel its delicate adjustments which have hitherto provided the public with what is a new and great art'. But the court then followed immediately with, "But we see nothing ruinous about the remedies proposed" (*U.S. v. Paramount Pictures*, Inc., 66 F. Supp. 323, 357 S.D.N.Y. 1946). Because they did not understand the nature of the challenges facing the film industry, how could they possibly know what might be ruinous?

[18] Hearing before a Subcommittee of the Committee on Interstate and Foreign Commerce, House of Representatives (1936).

and 28 June 1936. To capture the programming history of these films in the sample set of cinemas, films ending their life cycle at the beginning of this period, such as MGM's *China Seas,* are traced back to their premiere—in this case, at the Stanley Theatre on Saturday 17 August 1935. Conversely, films premiered towards the end of the 33 weeks, such as MGM's *Fury*, which opened at the Stanley for a two-week run on Saturday 13 June 1936, last appeared in a sample cinema (Imperial, 60th Street) on 1 September 1936. Our principal source is the daily operational record of these cinemas recorded on Film Billing Sheets, supplemented by the weekly records found on Continuation Sheets, both held in the Warner Bros. Archives at the University of Southern California. From the Archive records, it is apparent that neither industry-standard practices of double billing nor run-clearance were operational in Philadelphia.

The dataset has been examined twice previously. Sedgwick and Pokorny investigate the system of movie circulation from a revenue maximising standpoint.[19] In contrast, Jurca and Sedgwick emphasise the historical detail of filmgoing in Philadelphia at the time. Attention is drawn to the unequal appeal of different films to audiences.[20]

After New York and Boston, the Philadelphia exchange area constituted the third-largest market in North America in the mid-1930s, generating over six per cent of overall sales revenue.[21] The cinemas in the dataset were all owned by Warner Bros, which held a dominant position among exhibitors in Pennsylvania State, with 66 cinemas located in Philadelphia, out of a total population of under 200 cinemas.[22] Other 'major' studio combines were barely represented in the city, but concentrated elsewhere in the country: the patchwork pattern was a result of the respective cinema acquisition policies practised by the 'majors' during the 1920s, with Fox dominant in Los Angeles and San Francisco; MGM in New York and Washington; Publix/Paramount in Buffalo, Chicago, Detroit and Minneapolis and RKO in Cincinnati and Denver.[23] However, regional dominance did not mean exclusivity and monopoly. In each regional case, the dominant 'major' exhibition chain screened the films of rivals, cooperating with distributors to ensure that: (a) exhibitors were not short of film product, (b) films of quality were widely distributed and (c) box-office and therefore film rentals were maximised.[24] The reason why the respective vertically integrated combines did not use their apparent monopoly power to screen only films from their in-house production wing was, of course, not altruism, but rather the self-interested need to fill their cinemas and avoid the potential tit-for-tat

[19] Sedgwick and Pokorny (2012).

[20] Jurca and Sedgwick (2014). Many thanks to Cathy Jurca for scrutinising the dataset.

[21] Film Daily Yearbook (1936, p. 835).

[22] The cinema's located in Philadelphia and part of the Warner Bros. Circuit are derived from the *Motion Picture Herald* (1935–1936, p. 1003). The number of operating cinemas in Philadelphia are listed in Film Daily Yearbook (1936, pp. 942–943) and include three cinemas in Germantown.

[23] Gomery (1992).

[24] Sedgwick and Pokorny (2005).

behaviour of their rivals in other areas of the country where they were not so strongly represented.

Table 1 lists the Top 20 films (by box-office) screened in the Stanley Warner chain during the study period. It identifies the three first-run cinemas at which they were premiered for extended runs of more than one week—the 3,009-seater Stanley, where, according to *Variety*, admission prices ranged from 40 to 55 cents; the 2,400-seater Boyd (prices 40–55 cents) and the 1,416-seater Aldine (40–65 cents). These admission prices can be contrasted to the national average given in the *Motion Picture Almanac* as 20.5 cents in 1935, rising to 22 cents in 1936.[25]

These films flow out in time and space through multiple cinemas as they move from the first to second to third and fourth run. It is notable that during their life cycle in the city, they appear at between 13 and 18 cinemas, suggesting similar diffusion trajectories. However, since box-office revenues declined by more than a half between the films ranked first and twentieth, quite different levels of business. However, perhaps as interesting as the statistics associated with the Top 20 movies are those associated with the remaining films. Although the most popular films stand as giants compared to the median, by themselves, they were unable to meet film demand, constituting just over 20 per cent of screening days and generating 30 per cent of the box-office of the sample of 23 cinemas used in this study. The film business required more than 'hit' films to meet demand, with audiences demonstrating an appetite for a wide variety of films outside of the Top 20 when screened in cinemas other than the first run. Furthermore, a film did not have to be a hit to be profitable.

Listed in Table 2, the 23 cinemas constitute a truncated sample of the population of over 60 cinemas owned and managed by Warner Bros in Philadelphia.[26] It includes all first and second-run cinemas in the chain, but only a fraction (approximately 25 per cent) of third and fourth-run cinemas. Accordingly, the contribution of lower-order cinemas to the discussion and analysis of the diffusion process, including the aggregation of box-office and screening days, is under-represented. Table 2 demonstrates that different films perform differently at the same cinema. Organised by mean earnings per film, the coefficient of variation (column 11) shows the extent of the variation in film earnings at each cinema, suggesting that audiences made choices irrespective of the cinema they attended. Films mattered![27] For instance, of the 36 movies that premiered at the Stanley during the 45 weeks—17 August 1935 to 24 June 1936—the most popular film was MGM's *Mutiny on the Bounty*, which was screened for 19 days continuously generating a box-office of $54,940, at a mean of

[25] Admission prices for the Stanley are taken from *Variety*, 4 December 1935: 10. Average prices are taken from 'Pertinent Statistics', *Motion Picture Almanac*, 1936–1937, p. 6. The *Film Daily Yearbook* (1936, p. 39) puts the average admission price higher at 25 cents for 1935. See Jurca and Sedgwick (2014) for a general discussion of the sample set of cinemas. The cinema characteristics depicted in Table 1 of this work are restricted to the central 33 weeks and not the period extension which informs the discussion here, leading to some differences in the statistics presented.

[26] The Weekly Capitulation sheets found in the Warner Bros. Archive lists these cinemas under the corporate identities of the Stanley Company of America, Lindy Amusement Company and Warner Bros. Theatres.

[27] Jurca and Sedgwick (2014).

Table 1 Top 20 films screened at the sample set of Stanley Warner Cinemas, 1935–1936

Rank	(1) Film	(2) Studio	(3) Screening days	(4) Box office revenue ($)	(5) Opening cinema	(6) Length of opening run (days)	(7) Number of cinemas
1	Top Hat	RKO	95	97,344	Stanley	12	17
2	Follow The Fleet	RKO	93	88,011	Stanley	15	17
3	Mutiny On The Bounty	MGM	69	80,827	Stanley	19	15
4	Rose Marie	MGM	85	73,780	Boyd	14	17
5	Mr Deeds Goes to Town	Columbia	89	73,584	Stanley	14	18
6	Magnificent Obsession	Universal	80	66,325	Boyd	14	17
7	These Three	Goldwyn	80	60,427	Aldine	21	16
8	Show Boat	Universal	82	60,157	Stanley	14	16
9	Broadway Melody Of 1936	MGM	69	57,980	Stanley	12	17
10	Night At The Opera	MGM	63.5	54,028	Stanley	9	15
11	Small Town Girl	MGM	75	51,222	Boyd	14	16
12	Tale Of Two Cities	MGM	50	51,206	Boyd	16	13
13	Story of Louis Pasteur	Warner Bros	66	49,738	Boyd	9	16
14	Little Lord Fauntleroy	Selznic	73	48,984	Aldine	23	15
15	Captain Blood	Warner Bros	66	46,629	Stanley	11	15
16	Strike Me Pink	Goldwyn	66	45,899	Aldine	21	13
17	Dark Angel	Goldwyn	57	45,320	Aldine	18	14
18	Wife Vs Secretary	MGM	53	44,959	Stanley	14	13
19	Barbary Coast	Goldwyn	62	44,759	Aldine	18	15
20	Petticoat Fever	MGM	65	43,860	Boyd	14	16
118	Rose of Rancho	Paramount	26	11,487	Stanley	7	11

(continued)

Table 1 (continued)

Rank	(1) Film	(2) Studio	(3) Screening days	(4) Box office revenue ($)	(5) Opening cinema	(6) Length of opening run (days)	(7) Number of cinemas
164	Devil's Squadron	Columbia	18	5,745	Stanton	7	7

Source Film Billing Sheets and Recapitulation Film Billing Sheets, Warner Bros Archive
Notes To be counted, films need to have been screened at least once during the 33 weeks week-ending 16 November 1935 and 28 June 1936. The films ranked 118 and 164 respectively represent the mean and median values of the 326-film population

$2,892 per day. Contrast this with the $1,819 garnered from a four-day screening at the same cinema of the least successful film, Paramount's *Coronado.*

The median film box-office for the 36 films screened during the period was $9,824, more than five times less than *Mutiny on the Bounty*, a measure of inequality of film earnings reflected by the very high coefficient of variation of 0.84. Only notable films kept cinema full. Cinemas like the Stanley were built to garner the maximum possible revenue from 'hit' films. The problem for its owners was that not all movies were equally attractive, meaning that lesser attractions resulted in empty seats and, in the Stanley case, lowered earnings per seat per day (column 8) to below that of the other first-run houses.

Contrast the Stanley with the 1,042-seater Imperial on 2nd Street. Between 28 October 1935 and 30 August 1936, 242 of the 326 films in the population of films screened at least once in the sample set of cinemas during the 33 weeks were screened at this cinema, 206 of which for just one day, with only one film (*Top Hat*) screened for three days. However, the most popular film at the Imperial box-office was not *Top Hat* but *Littlest Rebel* (Fox), starring Shirly Temple. Screened for two days (23–24 February 1936)—the film earned $396, more than three times the Imperial's mean box-office of $153. Some 241 places below this in ranked popularity was the 1933 film *The Bowery* (20th Century/United Artists), starring Wallace Beery, which was screened for one day on 11 May 1936, generating just $45 at the box-office. During this study, *The Bowery* appeared at one other cinema—The Family (30 April)—indicating that two and half years after its original release, the film was still doing the rounds of lower-order cinemas.

The most popular films screened at the Imperial on 2nd Street were near to, or at the end of, their circulation history in Philadelphia. For instance, all Top 10 films listed in Table 1, except for *Top Hat*, were screened for two days but were not necessarily as popular with Imperial audiences, with *Mr. Deeds Goes to Town* ranked 31st, *Broadway Melody of 1936*, 33rd, *Show Boat* 43rd, *Magnificent Obsession* 53rd, *These Three* 63rd and *Rose Marie* 67th. However, such was the tightness of the statistical distribution around these ranks, with the six films separated by just $54 (Mr. Deeds $254 to Rose Marie $200), that little significance should be attributed to these rankings. Differences could easily be accounted for by, say, a change in local weather conditions. Column 8 suggests that even with the rapid turnover of films, earnings per seat per day were low, a statistic shared by many lower-tier cinemas.

Table 2 Characteristics of the sample set of 23 cinemas, 1935–1936

(1) Cinemas	(2) No. of films screened	(3) Seating capacity	(4) Cinema status	(5) No. of days between first and last film	(6) Sum of total earnings ($)	(7) Daily earnings ($)	(8) Earnings per seat per day (cents)	(9) Mean earnings per film ($)	(10) Standard deviation	(11) Coefficient of variation
Stanley	36	3009	Ist	307.5	510,715	1,660.86	0.55	14,186.53	11,914.01	0.84
Aldine*	22	1416	Ist	284	290,122	1,021.56	0.72	13,187.37	8,456.38	0.64
Boyd	35	2338	Ist	303	442,026	1,458.83	0.62	12,629.31	8,259.76	0.65
Earle	44	2750	Variety	280.5	550,058	1,960.99	0.71	12,501.32	5,122.42	0.41
Stanton	34	1486	1st/2nd	279	183,823	658.86	0.44	5,406.56	4,206.37	0.78
Palace	44	1100	2nd	294	184,190	626.50	0.57	4,186.15	1,234.98	0.30
Orpheum	47	1693	2nd	309	150,178	486.01	0.29	3,195.28	1,176.56	0.37
Keith's	41	2300	1st/2nd	299	129,829	434.21	0.19	3,166.57	2,160.12	0.68
Karlton	37	1005	1st/2nd	278	115,467	415.35	0.41	3,120.74	3,927.21	1.26
State	75	3059	2nd	296	179,918	607.83	0.20	2,398.90	1,492.35	0.62
Victoria	62	987	3rd	284	127,931	450.46	0.46	2,063.41	1,135.53	0.55
Logan	76	1924	3rd	292.5	141,076	482.31	0.25	1,856.27	1,157.44	0.62
Strand	87	1690	3rd	301	103,475	343.77	0.20	1,189.37	594.41	0.50
Kent	139	1910	3rd	290.5	140,942	485.17	0.25	1,013.97	565.79	0.56
Park	146	1735	3rd	296.5	116,022	391.30	0.23	794.67	461.56	0.58
Oxford	107	1600	3rd	252	79,409	315.12	0.20	742.14	554.25	0.75
Fairmount	152	1344	4th	290	84,803	292.43	0.22	557.92	305.69	0.55
Family	236	547	4th	282	107,210	380.18	0.70	454.28	161.05	0.35

(continued)

Table 2 (continued)

(1) Cinemas	(2) No. of films screened	(3) Seating capacity	(4) Cinema status	(5) No. of days between first and last film	(6) Sum of total earnings ($)	(7) Daily earnings ($)	(8) Earnings per seat per day (cents)	(9) Mean earnings per film ($)	(10) Standard deviation	(11) Coefficient of variation
Imperial 60th St.	179	1474	4th	298	56,983	191.22	0.13	318.34	208.53	0.66
Holme	178	1364	4th	295	55,814	189.20	0.14	313.56	226.24	0.72
Grange	148	499	4th	280	45,691	163.18	0.33	308.73	195.30	0.63
Harrowgate	216	1150	4th	289	43,985	152.20	0.13	203.64	138.34	0.68
Imperial 2nd St.	242	1040	4th	279	37,260	133.55	0.13	153.97	83.05	0.54

Note Unless 33 weeks is specified in column heading, figures include all screenings of the relevant films
Source Film Billing Sheets and Recapitulation Film Billing Sheets, Warner Bros Archive
Note The table is based on box-office records of 326 films screened at least once during 33 weeks between week-endings 16 November 1935 and 28 June. It differs from Table 1 presented in Jurca and Sedgwick (2014), in that it accounts for the screening of films outside of the 33 week-period, reflected in the uneven number of days in which the 326 films were in circulation in the 23 cinemas (col. 5)
* The Aldine closed over summers; its last playdate was June 20, 1936

Table 2 points to the significance of that section of the audience watching films in first-run cinemas rather than waiting until they were circulated out to less expensive cinemas. Leo Handel describes that portion of the audience that made choices between films as 'selective'—the type of filmgoer that undertakes risk. Without this type of filmgoer, it is not possible to understand industry-specific structures and arrangements designed to attenuate the uncertainty of not knowing how film consumers will respond to films newly released onto the market.[28] However, as manifest in the coefficient of variation column in Table 2, it was not just in the upper tiers of venues where audiences made choices. Put differently, in urban settings, film choice permeated the exhibition sector, making the sociology of the audiences and the choices they made such an exciting aspect of cinema studies.

2 Competitive Analysis

The competitive environment enveloping film was dynamic and intense, making those films that people wanted to watch less scarce—run times were adjusted to let more popular movies screen for longer, with less popular films taken off more quickly. It involved the sale of numerous unique products moving between cinemas during a short commercial life, garnering as much revenue as their distributors could manage before moving on until there were no more cinemas to move on to. High revenues accrued to the distributors of these comparatively rare 'hit' films, for which demand filled the cinemas, and they took advantage of this by charging higher rental prices. The weekly billing sheets show first- and second-run cinemas operated contracts with the distributor, giving each party a percentage stake in the box-office. The first-run Stanley Theatre, for instance, paid a 25 per cent rental on box-office for most films, rising to 30 per cent for a small number of exceptionally attractive films, such as *Mutiny on the Bounty* and *Follow the Fleet* (reducing to 20 per cent for the second week of the run). But even for such giants, these gains were fleeting as audiences sated themselves and moved on for the next extraordinary experience. Once films had passed into the third and fourth runs, the more likely it was that they were contracted for a flat sum, reducing the producer's transaction costs (no need to monitor attendance) while giving the exhibitor the maximum incentive to exploit them.

The skill for the exhibitor was that of scheduling films from a time-dependent limited pool that would attract as many filmgoers as possible. When making their choices, filmgoers needed to know what these films were about and where they were being screened. A few movies attracted exceptionally high numbers of paying consumers, the consequence of which was, as we have seen, the considerable inequality of revenue streams.

[28] Handel (1950, pp. 100, 153). See Sedgwick and Pokorny (2012) for a discussion of Handel's contribution. For a general discussion of the risk environment that characterised the film business, see Pokorny and Sedgwick (2012).

In this study, it is only possible to get a partial view of distribution. Table 3 records the market share performance of the eight leading distributors, each primarily geared for distributing in-house productions and maximising returns. Of the 326 films screened during the period, 283 were distributed by them, taking 95 of the Top 100 berths and over 95 per cent of screening days and box-office in both Top 100 and Total films categories. The argument developed in connection to Table 1 that the strong presence of Warner Bros. in the exhibition sector in Philadelphia did not translate into privileging in-house films above the very popular productions of rival studios is reinforced. However, it is evident that beyond the most popular movies, as differences in box-office narrow, in-house films become more prominent. But ownership did not lead to the excluding films from the other studios at lower levels of film popularity. Thus, while Warner Bros. occupied none of the top 10 film berths and only three of the Top 25, 11 of the subsequent 25 films were in-house productions. Altogether, Warner Bros. distributed 25 of the Top 100 films, five more than market leader MGM. Nevertheless, 23 of the 48 films it handled during these months did not get a Top 100 berth.

The absence of films from the Fox organisation from the Top 50 column in Table 3 is noteworthy, with just two of their movies finding their way into the Top 100. The explanation for this is that as a distributor, Fox supplied major in-house studio releases to the first-run 2,457-seater Fox cinema. These films were not screened in first-run Warner Bros. cinemas in the city, and this absence was sufficient to minimise Fox's presence in Table 3.[29] For instance, as already mentioned, the film *Littlest Rebel* starring Shirly Temple—one of Fox's major stars—was the most popular film screened at Imperial, 2nd Street during the period of this study. It also appeared at the 2nd-run Palace for seven days, and a stack of 3rd and 4th-run cinemas—Oxford, Holme, Park and Fairmount (three days), Harrowgate, along with Imperial, 2nd Street (two days) and Family (one day). Yet this exposure was sufficiently only for the film to be ranked 119th. This pattern repeats itself for many other 20th Fox releases. The Victoria cinema doubled up with the Palace as an entry point into the Stanley Warner chain after an initial run in the first-run Fox cinema.

3 Quality Competition

Competition in the film industry pivots upon consumers' conception of quality. Although films are horizontally differentiated in that each is different and can be placed for their short lives along a continuum of films concurrently in circulation based upon the similarity or otherwise of their characteristics, they are also vertically differentiated in that some movies are regarded in almost all aspects as being superior by all/most consumers. Across industries, it is normal for qualitatively superior products to be sold at higher prices, reflecting a combination of higher costs of production

[29] In 1935 Fox studios became rebranded as 20th Century Fox, following the takeover of 20th Century films (Gomery, 2005).

Table 3 Producer/Distributor shares in the sample of 23 Warner Bros. cinemas

(1) Distributor	(2) No. top 10 films	(3) No. top 25 films	(4) No. top 50 films	(5) No. top 100 films	(6) Total films screened	(7) Top 100 films screening days	(8) Total screenings days	(9) Top 100 films box-office ($)	(10) Total box-office ($)	(11) Market Share
Columbia	1	2	3	5	29	260	429	180,510	260,016	0.07
Fox	0	0	0	2	33	86	501	41,046	183,360	0.05
MGM	4	10	13	20	43	980	1,320	754,804	875,738	0.23
Paramount	0	0	4	17	56	595	1,038	347,895	509,846	0.13
RKO	2	2	5	9	36	404	695	336,968	437,625	0.11
UA	1	6	8	11	19	605	692	402,213	433,002	0.11
Universal	2	2	2	6	19	245	383	196,768	237,900	0.06
Warners	0	3	14	25	48	1,089	1,328	649,769	762,057	0.20
Total for 8 studios	10	25	49	95	283	4,263	6,384	2,909,973	3,699,544	0.95
Total for all studios	10	25	50	100	326	4,343	6,660	3,016,586	3,876,932	1

Source Film billing sheets and recapitulation film billing sheets, Warner Bros archive

incurred by producers and a willingness to pay on the part of consumers. Paying more raises the threshold level of satisfaction required to compensate a consumer. In this way, the product is rationed because, depending on the measure of demand elasticity at the margin, (some/many) consumers will not be willing to pay the higher price. For the seller, it becomes a matter of judgement whether the additional revenue raised by higher prices is sufficient to offset the decline in revenue caused by fewer consumers.

In the case of the film industry, knowledge of the quality embodied in a film can only be had *ex-post*—after it has been screened. Furthermore, it is commonly not used again once acquired because consumers prefer new movie experiences, causing the short-lived duration of films in cinemas. Consider the effect of this behaviour on differential pricing? Paying higher prices to see films about which audiences shared high-quality expectations would impact the calculus of whether to see a movie or not. Film consumers know from experience that they make mistakes, adding to the general churn of uncertainty. For this reason, in-house differential pricing was and is not a standard industrial practice.[30] A further consideration is that in a revenue-sharing arrangement, the incentives of distributor and exhibitor diverge—independent exhibitors would like to charge a low price for films since they keep less than 100 per cent of the revenue generated, but charge high prices for concessions, keeping 100 per cent of the revenue.

To reiterate, because of the ill-defined nature of quality *ex-ante*, exhibitors do not charge higher prices for more expensively made films, even though these are expected to be more popular *ex-ante* (why else spend more on them?). In the minds of consumers, (a) production values associated with higher costs and quality are not always concomitant, and (b) continuous price changes matching different production costs aggravate the risk environment experienced by consumers. Rather than raise prices, box-office is maximised by keeping films on a screen until a threshold level of earnings is breached. Before saturation release—from the mid-1970s onwards—films circulated from box-office rich to box-office poor cinemas. In this way, consumers not prepared to pay admission prices in upper order cinemas could wait until movies filtered down through time to cinemas lower in the hierarchy.

From this discussion of film industry characteristics, it follows that if 'quality' governs, and box-office reflects choice, then box-office also reflects 'quality'. However, this is not a concept of 'quality' based upon exclusive values, although it can be argued that the cinematic qualities of the most popular films found in Table 1 are fine indeed, but rather a set of commonly shared aesthetic and cultural values across the population.[31] Given invariant pricing, it can further be supposed that 'consumer surplus'—a measure of welfare in which the utility enjoyed by consumers for a film exceeds what they pay to watch it—is greater the larger the box-office. That is, if a consumer was prepared to pay 40 cents to watch *Rose of Rancho* at the Stanley, how much more satisfaction did they derive from watching *Top Hat* for the same price at the same cinema. Accordingly, it can be argued that box-office is both a measure of quality and use-value.

---

[30] Orbach and Einav (2007).

[31] Arsel and Bean (2013).

To illustrate, consider Fig. 1, where the cumulative revenue curves of the most popular ten films screened in the sample set of cinemas during the period under investigation are depicted.[32] These films are joined by those ranked 30th, 50th, 90th and 163rd (the median movie).[33] Following the argument developed in the previous paragraph, the vertical axis represents a quality index. An immediate observation is the extensive reach of the ten most popular films, with the first eight screened between 80 and 96 days in the sample set of 23 cinemas. The comparison with lower-ranking films becomes increasingly marked. When contrasted with the 163 films that fell below the median movie, the difference in performance is dramatic, with the Top 10 films standing as giants compared to the lower half of the revenue distribution.

A second observation is that the slopes of the cumulative revenue curves of the most popular films are concave, reflecting a rapid increase in earnings during the early stages of their life cycles, coinciding with their appearance in their respective first-run cinema. They then taper off as films move to multiple second-run and third-run cinemas, flattening further as they reach the end of their life cycles in the fourth run. The pattern described contrasts with the 50th, 90th and median ranked films, which show flatter and shorter slopes. The curve of the 90th film lies below the 50th, and the median film below that: these films were not screened for very long and did not pass through the entire system of runs.

A third observation is that some curves overlap those of films above them, indicating different box-office trajectories. Take, for instance, *Mutiny on the Bounty*, which outperforms both *Top Hat* and *Follow the Fleet during its first run*. All three were premiered at the Stanley cinema, with *Mutiny on the Bounty* held over for a third week, while the two Astaire-Rogers musicals only achieved a second week's billing. However, from the end of its run at the Stanley, the growth in the revenue stream of *Mutiny on the Bounty* is lower than the two musicals. On the 46th day, the *Top Hat* curve crosses the *Mutiny* curve. It looks likely that the *Follow the Fleet* curve would have done the same had *Mutiny's* run in the sample set of Philadelphia cinemas continued beyond the 70th screening day. Something similar happens between the 6th and 10th ranked films (Magnificent Obsession to Night at the Opera) and beyond, where the cumulative revenue curves of these near-ranked films are interwoven. The trajectory of these curves tells us something potentially interesting about which films appeal most to what type of audience (wealthy first-run versus poorer lower-run).

The different pace of film revenue accumulation adds a degree of ambiguity to the discussion concerning 'quality'. All things being equal, the principle that consumers always prefer qualitatively better products requires qualification. Putting the case of *Mutiny on the Bounty* on the side for the moment, the cumulative revenue curves suggest that in the minds of filmgoers in Philadelphia during our period, *Top Hat* >

[32] This aspect of the discussion is influenced by De Vany and Walls (1996).

[33] As the population of 326 films is an even number, the 163rd (*Public Menace*—Columbia) has been taken to represent the median.

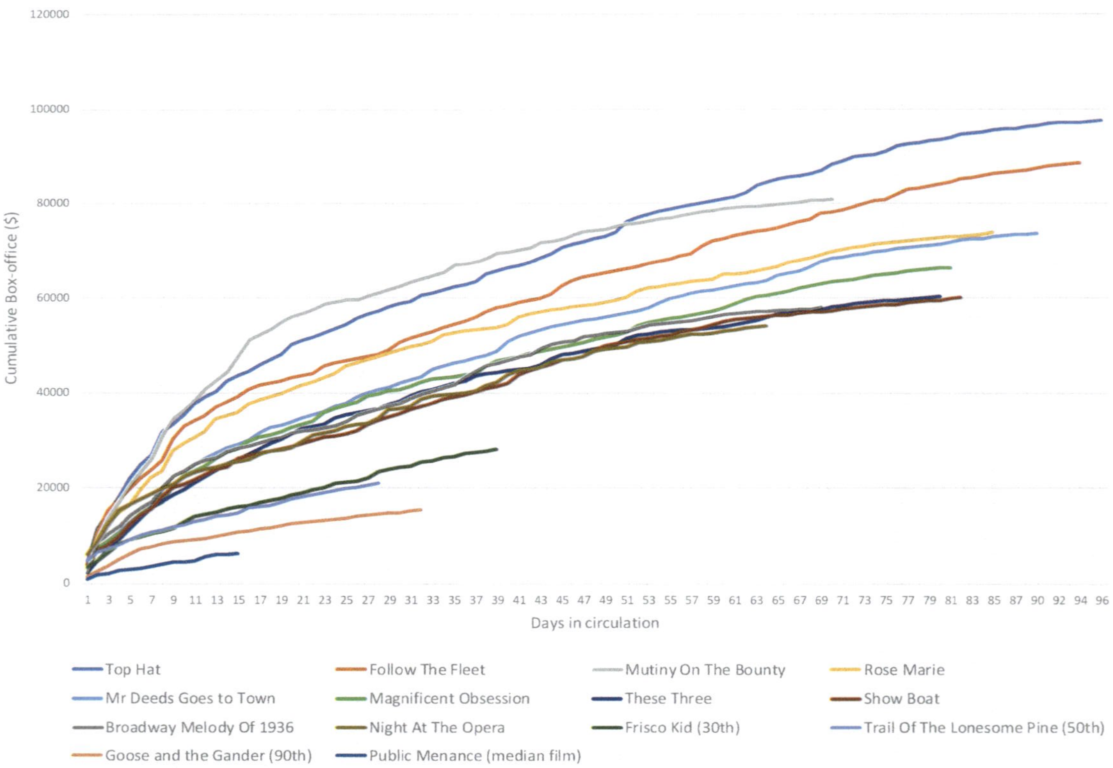

Fig. 1 Cumulative revenue flow of Top 10, 30th, 50th, 90th and median films. (Read the key from left to right)

Follow the Fleet > *Rose Marie* > *Mr. Deeds Goes to Town*.[34] However, it is more challenging to place *Mutiny on the Bounty*. At the Stanley, it was the most popular film during our period. However, the curve's flattening suggests that the film became less attractive to audiences in the third and fourth run.[35] When cumulative revenue curves change gradient, although not a surprising finding, it makes statements such as Film X > Film Y > Film Z problematic. What can be said more confidently is that films in Band A (say, the Top 10) > Band B (rank 11–50) > Band C (rank 51–100) > Bank D (rank 101 to the median film 163). In general, audiences share broad conceptions of quality. Occasionally, they share exhilarating experiences and create feedback loops that culminate in a 'must-see' imperative. When such dynamics happen, hits are born.

4 Discussion and Conclusion

Industrial concentration in the film industry during the 1930s was low and, the life cycles of films were short—12 to 15 months—with films typically earning the bulk of their revenues during the period following immediately after their release.[36] New releases were intensely circulated to towns and cities during the first six months of their lives, including abroad. During the remainder of their life cycle, they were found on the furthest reaches of the market before their inevitable extinction. In the 1930s, the practice of re-releasing films was not commonplace. During the 33 weeks of this study, 326 films circulated among 23 first to fourth-run cinemas owned and controlled by the city's foremost retailer—the Stanley Warner chain. In terms of days, the most popular films were in circulation among these cinemas for less than half of this period; the least popular, of which there were many, for hardly any time at all. Thus, even when a film achieved unusually high popularity, it lasted only weeks before being replaced by another movie around which tastes across the collective audience subsequently coalesced. The manifestation of popularity did not lead to higher admission prices. Neither did it result in restricted supply—indeed quite the opposite, although, unlike today, the release was managed to exploit price discrimination advantages.

Competition based upon the qualitative differences of films as perceived by audiences is central to understanding the industry-specific arrangements that emerged to attenuate the peculiar nature of risk that characterised the film industry during the

[34] Such was the short-lived life of even the most popular films, distributors were able to schedule major releases so as to avoid direct head-to-head competition, with major releases premiered between September and March.

[35] Divisions in the audiences based upon age, class, culture, ethnicity, gender, location and other factors likely account for differences in the taste for films as they move through the hierarchy of cinemas.

[36] Greenwald (1950) Table VI-2; and *Variety*, 2 October 1935, p. 7: 'Write off pix in 15 Mos. Cream Income in 39 weeks.'

1930s.[37] Some producers were better able to produce 'hit' films than others. MGM stands out in this respect in this study, even though it neither owned nor controlled cinemas in the city. But this was not a handicap because all distributors and exhibitors cooperated to enable filmgoers to enjoy the films they wanted to see. They did so not from altruism but from self-interest. It would have been foolhardy for the Stanley Warner chain to have given space to in-house productions at the expense of far more popular films made by rival studios. The idea of the Astaire-Rogers sequence of films not being screened in the city's upper-tier cinemas because they were produced by a rival studio (RKO) went against the spirit of making money. The logic of the system ensured that this did not happen.

In conclusion, audiences were given a rich array of films from which to choose. Choices were made, leading to certain films achieving extremely high levels of popularity. The argument that the most successful films raised the welfare of audiences is compelling. That these films were made available to the Stanley Warner chain by rival organisations is explained by the near-monopoly position of the chain in programming upper-tier cinemas. They needed to be screened at these cinemas to maximise their revenue potential. At the same time, it is the case that the Stanley Warner circuit privileged films from its in-house production wing, but only after the most popular movies from rival studios had been screened. To do otherwise would have been to deny itself maximising revenue opportunities.

The economic model used by the Department of Justice to accuse the vertically integrated film businesses (collectively known as Hollywood) of restrictive monopoly practices is flawed in that it failed to address the nature of risk peculiar to the industry.

References

Official Documents and Data Sources

'Hearing before a Subcommittee of the Committee on Interstate and Foreign Commerce, House of Representatives, Seventy Fourth Congress, on Bill to Prohibit and to Prevent the Trade Practices Known as 'Compulsory Block-Booking' and 'Blind Selling' in the Leasing of Motion Picture Films in Interstate and Foreign Commerce (Washington D.C., 1936).

Historical Statistics of the United States, Colonial Times to 1975. https://www.census.gov/library/publications/1975/compendia/hist_stats_colonial-1970.html

Bibilography

Arsel, Z., & Bean, J. (2013). Taste regimes and market-mediated practice. *Journal of Consumer Research, 39*, 899–917.

[37] Fine and Leonard (1993) theorise vertical linkages in the supply chain, mediated dynamically by one another in what they term a 'system of provision'.

Coase, R. (1937). The nature of the firm. *Economica, 4*(386), 405.
Conant, M. (1960). *Antitrust in the motion picture industry.* University of California Press.
De Vany, A. (2004). *Hollywood economics: How extreme uncertainty shapes the film industry.* Routledge.
De Vany, A., & Eckert, R. (1991). Motion picture antitrust: The Paramount cases revisited. *Research in Law and Economics, 14*, 51–112.
De Vany, A., & Walls, W. (1996). Bose-Einstein dynamics and adaptive contracting in the motion picture industry. *Economic Journal, 106*, 1493–1514.
Fine, B., & Leopold, E. (1993). *The world of consumption.* Routledge.
Gil, R. (2015). Does vertical integration decrease prices? Evidence from the Paramount antitrust case of 1948. *American Economic Journal: Economic Policy, 7*, 162–191.
Gomery, D. (1992). *Shared pleasures: A history of movie presentation in the United States.* BFI.
Gomery, D. (2005). *The Hollywood studio system: A history.* BFI.
Greenwald, W. (1950). *The motion picture industry: An economic study of the history and practices of a business* [PhD dissertation, New York University].
Handel, L. (1950). *Hollywood looks at its audience.* University of Illinois Press.
Hanssen, F. A. (2000). The block booking of films re-examined. *Journal of Law and Economics, 43*, 395–426.
Hanssen, F. A. (2002). Revenue-sharing in movie exhibition and the arrival of sound. *Economic Inquiry, 40*, 380–402.
Hanssen, F. A. (2010). Vertical integration during the Hollywood studio era. *The Journal of Law and Economics, 53*(3), 519–543.
Hanssen, F. A. (2020). "What's wrong with the way i talk?" The effect of sound motion pictures on actor careers. *Economic Inquiry, 58*, 474–495.
Hanssen, F. A., & Raskovich, A. (2020). Does vertical integration spur investment? Casting actors to discover stars during the Hollywood studio era. *Journal of Law and Economics, 63*, 631–666.
Huettig, M. (1985). Economic control of the motion picture industry. In T. Balio (Ed.), *The American film industry* (pp. 285–310). University of Wisconsin Press.
Jurca, C., & Sedgwick, J. (2014). The film's the thing: Moviegoing in Philadelphia, 1935–36. *Film History, 26*(4), 58–83.
Kenney, R. W., & Klein, B. (1983). The economics of block booking. *The Journal of Law and Economics, 26*(3), 497–540.
Orbach, B., & Einav, L. (2007). Uniform prices for differentiated goods: The case of the movie-theater industry. *International Review of Law and Economics, 27*(2), 129–153.
Pokorny, M., & Sedgwick, J. (2012). The financial and economic risks of film production. In M. Hjort (Ed.), *Film and risk* (pp. 181–196). Wayne University Press.
Sedgwick, J. (2002). Product differentiation at the movies: Hollywood, 1946–65. *Journal of Economic History, 62*, 676–704.
Sedgwick, J., & Pokorny, M. (1998). The risk environment of filmmaking: Warners in the inter-war period. *Explorations in Economic History, 35*, 196–220.
Sedgwick, J., & Pokorny, M. (2005). The film business in the U.S. and Britain during the 1930s. *Economic History Review, 58*, 79–112.
Sedgwick, J., & Pokorny, M. (2010). Consumers as risk takers: Evidence from the film industry during the 1930s. *Business History, 52*, 74–99.
Sedgwick, J., & Pokorny, M. (2012). Film consumer decision-making: The Philadelphia story, 1935–36. *Journal of Consumer Culture, 12*, 323–346.

F. Andrew Hanssen is a Professor of Economics at Clemson University. His research areas include law and economics, political economy, and industrial organisation. He has published more than forty articles and book chapters. He is an associate editor of the *International Review of Law and Economics and the Cambridge Elements in Law, Economics and Politics* and is on the editorial board of *Social Science Quarterly.* He was a visiting fellow at the Ostrom Workshop at Indiana University and the Hoover Institution at Stanford University. He spent the 2007-08 academic year as a visiting economist at the Antitrust Division of the U.S. Department of Justice. Andrew received his PhD from the University of Chicago.

John Sedgwick is a visiting Professor in the Faculty of Technology, Design and Environment, Oxford Brookes University. He researches the economic history of cinema and is particularly interested in the ontological characteristics of film as a commodity. He created the POPSTAT Index of Film Popularity as a proxy for box-office returns. This tool provides a means of reflecting audience preferences and monitoring the distribution process. His research has focused on American, Australian, British, Dutch, Italian and international markets during the 1930s and 1950/60s. He has written a monograph, edited an anthology and published articles in Business History, Cinema Journal, Economic History Review, Explorations in Economic History, Enterprise and Society, Film History, Historical Journal of Film, Radio and Television, Journal of Applied Statistics, Journal of Cultural Economics, Journal of Economic History, and Journal of Transnational Cinema.

Comparative Film Popularity in Three English Cities—Bolton, Brighton, and Portsmouth: An Exercise in POPSTAT Methodology

John Sedgwick

Abstract For 1934, film popularity (POPSTAT) statistics of three small English cities, Bolton, Brighton, and Portsmouth, are derived from daily local newspapers and used to investigate audience preferences. Box-office information for the Regent cinema, Portsmouth, is used to corroborate the POPSTAT Index values of those films screened during the year. A high correlation between the two is found. Comparisons between the POPSTAT charts are conducted using the RelPOP method, and differences in preferences are found for some British films. At the same time, many Hollywood productions are similarly popular across the three cities.

In his pathbreaking *The Age of the Dream Palace*, Jeffrey Richards sets the context of filmgoing in 1930s Great Britain thoroughly and imaginatively, depicting a country in thrall to the cinema. Drawing upon published contemporary sources, he writes:

> All the evidence, then, indicates that in Britain in the Thirties cinemagoing was regular and habitual, assuming a dominant role in the leisure of the working classes and in the life of the young and an increasingly important part in middle class leisure.[1]

Outside of the United States, the film market in Great Britain was more extensive than in any other country.[2] Indeed, according to the data published in *Variety* in 1934 and presented in Table 3 of Chapter "Managing Risk in the Film Business—Key Concepts and Methods", the revenue potential of the British market was more than twice that of France and Germany combined. The dominant players in this market were the American film studios and their in-house distributors, which held the largest share of the domestic market, alongside the major British exhibitors, whose chains of first run cinemas were found in the cities and large and medium provincial towns.[3]

[1] Richards (1984, p. 18).

[2] For other accounts of the British filmgoing culture see McKibbin (1998, Ch. 11) and Sedgwick (2000, Ch. 2).

[3] At this time, distributors were commonly referred to as renters in the UK.

J. Sedgwick (✉)
Oxford Brookes University, Oxford, UK
e-mail: sedgwicj52@gmail.com

J. Sedgwick (ed.), *Towards a Comparative Economic History of Cinema, 1930–1970*, Frontiers in Economic History, https://doi.org/10.1007/978-3-031-05770-0_4

British production had expanded considerably from the introduction of exhibitor and renter quotas in the 1927 Cinematograph Act. American distributors were forced to either acquire film products from British producers or make the films on British soil to fulfil their quota obligation. Neither of these options was attractive to them since the production wings of their parent organisations in Hollywood produced more than enough output for them to handle. Any significant investment in filmmaking in Great Britain on their part would lead to the production of films that would compete directly with in-house productions made in Hollywood. By and large, their strategy was one of damage limitation, resulting in the production of cheaply made inferior films that became known as 'quota quickies'. United Artists was an exception to this practice, becoming the distributor of bigger budget films made by London Films and British and Dominion. Later in the decade, RKO became involved with a few notable Herbert Wilcox productions—*Victoria the Great*, *The Rat* and *Sixty Glorious Years*. Following the new Cinematograph Act in 1938, MGM embarked on two British big-budget features—*A Yank at Oxford* and *The Citadel*, followed in 1939 by *Goodbye Mr Chips*. It also invested in and acquired the distribution rights to several major films made by Gaumont British—*The Lady Vanishes*, *Climbing High* and *Ask a Policeman*.[4]

Undoubtedly the principal beneficiaries of the 1927 Act were the two British vertically integrated (producer/distributor/and exhibitor) combines, Gaumont British (GB) and British International Pictures (BIP) and three production studios, Associated Talking Pictures, British and Dominions, and London Films. Because the Act compelled distributors and exhibitors to take an increasing quota of British films, but audiences were not obligated to watch them, the Cinematographic Act incentivised British producers to make films of a calibre attractive to audiences. Essentially, it changed British producers' risk environment, encouraging them to invest in filmmaking and associated organisations. As I was able to show in *Popular Filmgoing in 1930s Britain*, between 1932 and 1937, the principal British studios took a 17% share in the British market, producing 84 of the 300 Top 50 films over the six years. In contrast, the major Hollywood studios took a two-thirds share (66.25%), with 186 of their movies achieving a Top 50 status.[5] Compared to the market shares of other film-producing European nations such as Germany, France, Czechoslovakia, and Sweden, this is a weak performance.[6] Nevertheless, given the shared language with the United States and the deficient performance of the British film production in the late 1920s, the 1927 Act undoubtedly was a game-changer.

The purpose of this chapter is to examine and compare film popularity statistics of three small English cities, Bolton (population of approximately 180,000), Brighton (200,000), and Portsmouth (250,000) and to investigate differences in audience preferences.[7] Three types of information are used to prepare these statistics. The first is the daily newspapers carrying newspaper adverts and listings of film programmes;

[4] Low (1985, pp. 267–270).

[5] Sedgwick (2000, Table 4.4). Concerning risk, see the discussion on pp. 51–54.

[6] Garncarz (2015).

[7] These population figures are those given in the Kine Yearbooks of 1935 and 1936.

respectively, the *Bolton Evening News*, *Brighton Evening Argus*, and *Portsmouth Evening News*. In each case, programming information is extensive, providing reliable daily records of what was offered at cinemas across each city. The second type of information comes from trade sources. The publishers of the journal *Kinematograph Weekly* also produced *Yearbooks*, which, akin to the *Film Daily Yearbook* in the United States, published industry-wide information including detailed lists of urban cinemas in their localities, including, as a rule, seating capacity, prices of admission, the number of daily screenings, changes in the programme, and information about cinema facilities such as the presence of a café and availability of car parking. Finally, actual box-office recorded by the Regent cinema in Portsmouth is used to evaluate the POPSTAT method.

1 City and Cinema Characteristics

Knowledge of admission prices and the seating capacity of cinemas allows a distinction to be made between cinemas based on their revenue potential. Analytically, cinemas can be shown to be treated as non-equivalent. The measurement of film popularity is affected by the cinemas at which films are screened, with large first-run cinemas contributing more to the measure than smaller third-run cinemas. Each of the three city populations of cinemas and the movies they screened is comparable, comprehensive, and distinctive, allowing comparisons to be made.

From over 650 million Entertainment Duty returns for 1934, Simon Rowson, in his monumental study of filmgoing in Great Britain, estimated that the mean price of cinema admission in Great Britain in 1934 was 10.25d. He showed that approximately 2/3 of filmgoers paid less than this.[8] From this evidence, the minimum and maximum cinema prices published in the Kine Year Books are similarly weighted to give the average admission prices found in Tables 1 and 2. Cinemagoing in Bolton was considerably cheaper than in Brighton and Portsmouth and the country as a whole. While Bolton screened fewer films, a consequence of the first-run cinemas running single-bill programmes as a rule, in terms of value, the cinema market in Brighton was twice the size of Bolton and over a third larger than Portsmouth—a consequence of significantly higher admission prices. Nevertheless, it is interesting to note that the ratio of cinemas to the population in the three urban areas is comparable and close to Simon Rowson's estimate that, on average, there was one cinema for every 10,600 persons in Britain in 1934—a statistic leading him to declare:

> It would be difficult to quote another figure more eloquent of the hold that the cinema now has on the masses of the population … the modern institution is one of the sociological wonders of the century.[9]

---

[8] Rowson (1936) found that 43% of admissions paid 7d or less, with another 37% paying no more than 12d.

[9] Rowson (1936, p. 76).

Table 1 Characteristics of cinemas in three small British cities in 1934

	(1) Cinemas	(2) Population per cinema	(3) Aggregate seating	(4) Mean seating	(5) Mean weighted price (d)	(6) Potential revenue (£)	(7) Films Screened in 1934
Bolton	17	10,588	20,392	1,200	7.53	651	682
Brighton	18	11,111	20,970	1,165	13.54	1,304	841
Portsmouth	21	11,905	22,980	1,094	10.11	1,002	824

Source Kine Yearbook, 1934
Notes In the UK, before 1971, the Imperial, pre-decimal, measurement of money divided pounds sterling (£) into shillings (s) and pence (d). There were 20 shillings to the pound and 12 (old) pence to every shilling, meaning £1 = 240d. In keeping with Rowson (1936), the price statistic per cinema is given by the sum (Minimum price × 2/3) + (Maximum price × 1/3). These are then averaged across the population of cinemas

A likely explanation for the differences in these prices is to be found in the regional disparities in unemployment. Lancashire was particularly hard hit by the demise of the cotton industry during the inter-war period, even if the areas that specialised in weaving, of which Bolton was one, were less affected than the spinning areas around Oldham.[10] From data published in the Ministry of Labour Gazette in 1938, Nick Crafts (produces two tables in which regional patterns of long-term unemployment are detailed). While in the North of England (Northern, Northeast, and Northwest), long-term unemployment relief applications rose from 19.6 to 25.0% of the adult male population between 1932 and 1938. The comparable figures for the Southeast are 3.8 and 6.6%. Furthermore, in 1938 the average duration of long-term unemployment in the Northwest was 40.8 months, contrasted with 17 months in the Southeast.[11]

For purposes of comparing film popularity, cinema weights (shown in Table 2) are calculated separately for each of the three cities, reflecting their independence from one another as markets. Each city is treated analytically as a sealed entity. Film consumers in Bolton did not travel either to Portsmouth or Brighton to watch a film of their choice; neither did consumers from Brighton and Portsmouth in respect of the other two cities. From these premises, it is possible to state that film consumers in one city exhibited a particular taste, not replicated in the other two cities, for specific films or stars.

2 Cinema, Billing, and Monthly Weights

As explained in Chapter "Managing Risk in the Film Business—Key Concepts and Methods", Managing Risk, cinema weights reflect the revenue potential of each cinema (price × seating capacity) in a population of cinemas. They are obtained by

[10] Daniels and Jewkes (1928).

[11] Crafts (1987: Tables 2 and 3).

Table 2 Cinema characteristics of Bolton, Brighton, and Portsmouth in the mid-1930s

Bolton Cinemas	(1) Seating capacity	(2) Lowest price (d)	(3) Highest price (d)	(4) Weighted price (d)	(5) Revenue potential (£)	(6) Cinema weight
Belle	580	4	9	5.67	13.69	0.36
Capitol	1642	7	18	10.67	72.98	1.91
Carlton	1000	4	12	6.67	27.78	0.73
Crompton	1200	3	15	7.00	35.00	0.91
Embassy	600	6	12	8.00	20.00	0.52
Gem	1050	4	12	6.67	29.17	0.76
Hippodrome	1086	6	16	9.33	42.23	1.10
Majestic	1913	4	12	6.67	53.14	1.39
Palace	1021	4	7	5.00	21.27	0.56
Palladium	1238	4	12	6.67	34.39	0.90
Plaza	650	4	9	5.67	15.35	0.40
Queens	1480	6	18	10.00	61.67	1.61
Regal	2380	4	9	5.67	56.19	1.47
Regent	944	6	15	9.00	35.40	0.93
Rialto	1147	6	12	8.00	38.23	1.00
Royal	761	5	12	7.33	23.25	0.61
Theatre Royal	1700	6	18	10.00	70.83	1.85
				mean = 7.53	mean = 38.27	mean = 1.00
Brighton Cinemas						
Academy	1000	12	24	16.00	66.67	0.92
Astoria	2000	12	30	18.00	150.00	2.07
Cinema de Luxe	529	9	24	14.00	30.86	0.43
Court	1200	6	24	12.00	60.00	0.83
Duke of York's	1000	7	24	12.67	52.78	0.73
Granada	1592	7	24	12.67	84.02	1.16
Grand	1140	6	16	9.33	44.33	0.61
King's Cliff	370	4	9	5.67	8.74	0.12
Lido	2137	7	24	12.67	112.79	1.56
Odeon (Kemp Town)	958	6	18	10.00	39.92	0.55
Odeon	1200	12	28	17.33	86.67	1.20
Princes	550	6	24	12.00	27.50	0.38
Palladium	1200	12	28	17.33	86.67	1.20

(continued)

Table 2 (continued)

Bolton Cinemas	(1) Seating capacity	(2) Lowest price (d)	(3) Highest price (d)	(4) Weighted price (d)	(5) Revenue potential (£)	(6) Cinema weight
Regal	656	9	22	13.33	36.44	0.50
Regent	2020	12	42	22.00	185.17	2.56
Savoy	2630	12	30	18.00	197.25	2.72
Troxy	390	4	18	8.67	14.08	0.19
Tivoli	398	7	22	12.00	19.90	0.27
				mean = 10.11	mean = 72.43	mean = 1.00
Portsmouth Cinemas						
Apollo	1257	6	18	10.00	52.38	1.10
Arcade	504	5	12	7.33	15.40	0.32
Carlton	1294	7	18	10.67	57.51	1.21
Commodore	1000	7	18	10.67	44.44	0.93
Cosham/Waverley	545	4	22	10.00	22.71	0.48
Empire	574	7	15	9.67	23.12	0.48
Gaiety	1382	7	18	10.67	61.42	1.29
Majestic	1095	7	18	10.67	48.67	1.02
New Princes	1488	7	18	10.67	66.13	1.39
New Queen's	452	6	12	8.00	15.07	0.32
Palace	626	6	15	9.00	23.48	0.49
Plaza	1770	7	24	12.67	93.42	1.96
Regal	828	7	15	9.67	33.35	0.70
Regent	1972	7	24	12.67	104.08	2.18
Rialto	1250	7	15	9.67	50.35	1.06
Scala	743	7	24	12.67	39.21	0.82
Shaftesbury	1127	7	16	10.00	46.96	0.98
South Parade	496	4	18	8.67	17.91	0.38
Theatre Royal	1418	6	18	10.00	59.08	1.24
Tivoli	1752	9	15	11.00	80.30	1.68
Victoria	1407	3	18	8.00	46.90	0.98
				mean = 10.11	mean = 47.71	mean = 1.00

Sources *Bolton Evening News*, *Brighton Evening Argus* and *Portsmouth Evening News*
Note Admission prices are weighted as follows: Minimum price *2/3 + Maximum price *1/3

Table 3 Estimated average weekly cinema attendances during each month of 1934

	(1) Percentage of receipts from entertainment duty	(2) Estimated average weekly attendances	(3) Monthly weight
January	9.3	21.8	1.18
February	8.0	18.6	1.00
March	9.2	18.5	1.00
April	8.9	21.2	1.14
May	7.8	16.9	0.91
June	7.3	13.8	0.74
July	5.6	14.6	0.79
August	9.0	17.8	0.96
September	8.6	20.9	1.13
October	9.2	20.7	1.12
November	9.5	18.2	0.98
December	7.6	19.4	1.05
Mean	8.3	18.5	1

Source Rowson (1936, Table III)
Note Monthly Weights are based on column 2

dividing the revenue potential of each *jth* cinema by the average revenue potential of all cinemas in that population. Thus, cinema weights for each population of cinemas average 1.0. Table 2 shows that in each of the three cities, the cinema with the greatest box-office potential generates a cinema weight that is many times larger than the cinema with the lowest.

In addition, weights are also applied to the billing status of films—1.0 if a single feature, 0.5/0.5 if a double-bill programme with both films of equal standing in cinema adverts, and 0.8/0.2 if there is a clear difference in the attractions of two films on the same programme.

Finally, the seasonal nature of filmgoing is well known. For instance, Rowson lists the percentage of Entertainment Duty receipts attributable to each month of 1934 across the nation.[12] Table 3 shows that they range from 9.5% of the annual tax return in November to 5.6% in July, rebounding to 9% during the holiday month of August.[13] From Rowson's estimates of weekly attendances for the months of the year, weights have been calculated and shown in column 3 of the table.

The principal effect of adding monthly weights in the calculation of POPSTAT values is to exaggerate further the performance of the most popular films released during January, April, September, and October at the expense of movies released at

[12] Rowson (1936, Table III).

[13] Leif Furhammar (1990) and Joseph Garncarz (2020) include differences in monthly average attendances in their estimates of film popularity.

Table 4 Statistics of POPSAT Index for Portsmouth, 1934

Statistics	Values
Mean	1.37
Standard error	0.05
Median	0.70
Standard deviation	1.54
Coefficient of variation	1.12
Sample variance	2.36
Kurtosis	1.86
Skewness	1.50
Range	7.80
Minimum	0.02
Maximum	7.82
Sum	1127
Count	824

Source Portsmouth dataset

other times, especially during the summer. Thus, while the mean and median hardly change, the statistics of variance increase marginally.

These weights are applied to the films as they circulate. Accordingly, each screening of Film X at a particular cinema attracts a score, which, when multiplied by its length of run and billing status, and the month in which it is screened generates a POPSTAT value. These are then aggregated for all cinemas at which Film X is screened to create a locality specific POPSTAT value, which can then be compared with the POPSTAT values of all other films screened in the same locality during a given period. For example, Table 4 shows the descriptive statistics of the 1934 Portsmouth dataset. The inequality and skewed nature of the distribution are marked with the median film over ten times lower than the most popular—*It Happened One Night*.

3 Regent Cinema

Like all cinemas, the Regent, Portsmouth, kept a sales ledger recording weekly attendances and daily matinee and evening box-office revenue. Such documents are rare. Sales of tobacco, confectionery, and ices and receipts from its café are also included. The ledger is held by Portsmouth City Museum and Records Office and covers 1931–1948.[14] Figures 1 and 2 illustrate weekly box-office takings for 1934, during which 79 films were screened, comprising 25 single-bill programmes and 27

[14] See Harper (2004) and Sedgwick (2006) for a fuller discussion of the ledger and cinemagoing in Portsmouth in general.

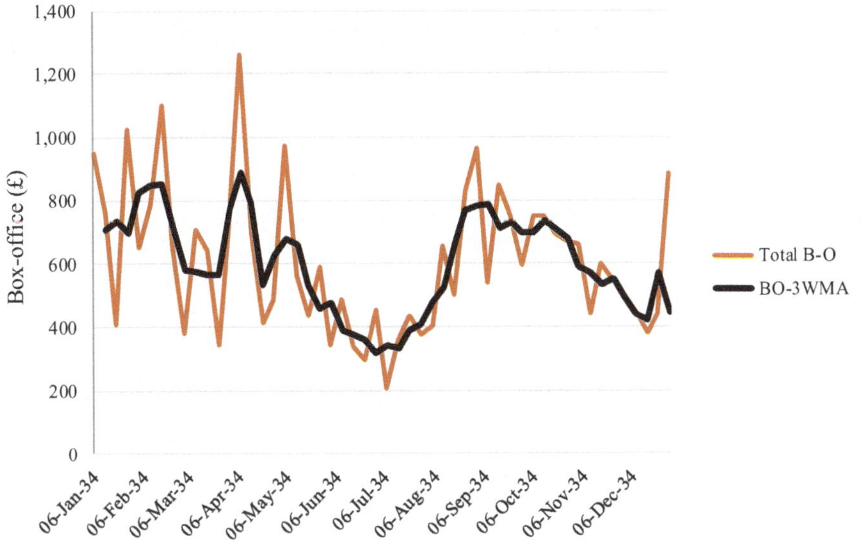

Fig. 1 Weekly changes in box-office (B-O) at the Regent in 1934 week and 3-week moving average (3WMA)

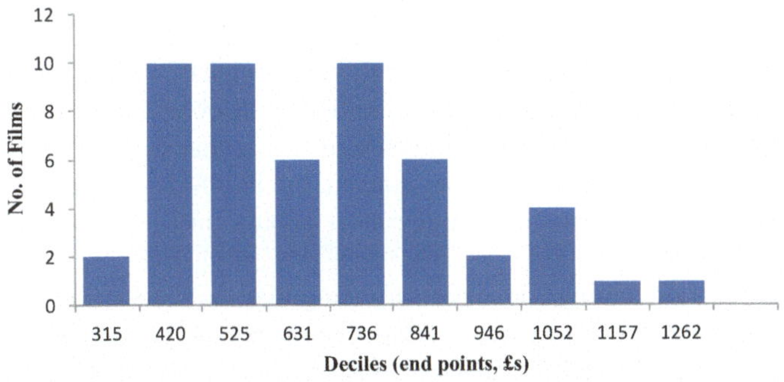

Fig. 2 Histogram of the frequency distribution of weekly box-office takings of the Regent in 1934

double-bill programmes. All films were screened for one week. The unevenness of the box-office line in Fig. 1 is a testament to the attractions of certain movies and the unattractive qualities of others. The 3-week moving average confirms the seasonal trend of filmgoing described by Rowson and depicted in Table 3, characterised by declining attendances through the Spring months up until July. They pick up, peaking in the late summer and early autumn and again in January and April.

The statistics reported in Table 5 indicate that the most popular film *Jack Ahoy!* screened in April 1934 as a single feature, generated over twice the mean and median weekly revenues. In contrast, the least popular single feature *All Men are Enemies*, screened in July, earned just over a third of either statistic. Similar evidence of this

Table 5 Weekly box-office statistics, Regent, 1934

Statistic	Value
Count	52
Mean	610.9
Variance	51,361.57
Standard Deviation	226.63
Coefficient of Variation	0.37
Minimum	209.63
Maximum	1,262.13
Range	1,052.5
Median	594.33
Sum	31,766.98
Skewness	0.68
Kurtosis	3.07

Source The Regent Ledger Portsmouth City Museum and Records Office

level of variability can be found in a comparative study of two premiere cinemas—the Empire, in London's West End and the Tuschinski, in central Amsterdam.[15]

The Regent ledger demonstrates that films are not equivalent, even when screened as single features at the same cinema in the same month. In contrast, the POPSTAT method implicitly assumes that they are. For this reason, the POPSTAT Index can only hope to approximate true box-office when applied to the population of films moving through a population of cinemas. The consequence is that by attributing a single weight to films screened at a particular cinema, the POPSTAT method will under-estimate the box-office generated by the most popular movies and over-estimate those of the least popular.

Given these shortcomings, it is not surprising that the association between the POPSTAT scores generated by the 79 films that opened at the Regent in 1934 and subsequently diffused to other cinemas in the city later is less than perfect. In my *Cinema Journal* article of 2006, I suggested a correlation statistic of 0.47, indicating a positive but not strong relationship between the box-office generated at the Regent and the subsequent POPSTAT Index values generated by those same films diffusing outwards to other cinemas in the population. However, a re-examination of the dataset showed that the Regent data in this calculation had not been adjusted to reflect that over half the programmes were double billed.

After applying the weights of 0.5/0.5, or 0.8/0.2 to films on these double-bill programmes, the adjusted Regent box-office values were then correlated with their POPSTAT Index values, derived from regressing POPSTAT Index values on Regent

[15] Sedgwick and Pafort-Overduin (2012).

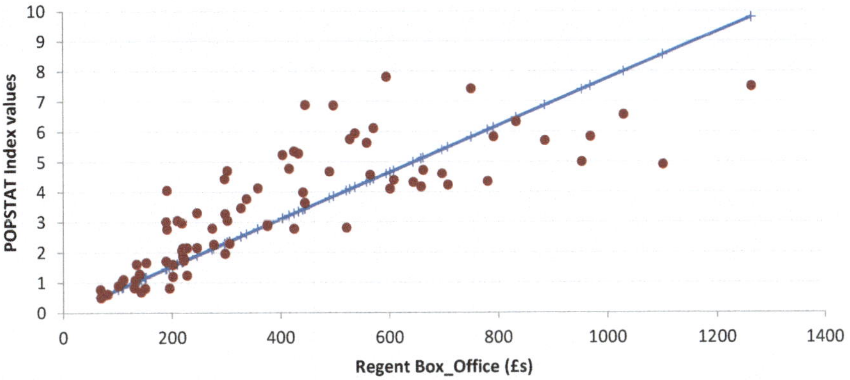

Fig. 3 Scatter of Portsmouth POPSTAT Index values on Regent box-office (79 films) in 1934 (*Source* The Regent Ledger Portsmouth City Museum and Records Office and *Portsmouth Evening News*. *Note* Software: StatPlus)

box-office, assuming a zero intercept.[16] A correlation coefficient of 0.94 measures the strength of association. The associated coefficient of determination (R^2) of 0.89 indicates that a measure of change in Regent box-office would explain almost nine-tenths of any subsequent change in POPSTAT. Films that were popular at the Regent were, as a rule, popular in the city as a whole.

Figure 3 shows a good fit, with the probability of it being a false result small. (The test results are reproduced in the Appendix to this chapter.) The spread of data points around the regression line Y = X appear evenly distributed about the trend line. The chart depicting the scatter of residual values in the Appendix suggests a degree of bias as predicted, with the top films generating lower and less successful films higher POPSTAT Index values than predicted by the model.

The statistical distribution of POPSTAT Index values in Bolton and Brighton shows similar characteristics to those in the Portsmouth data, as shown in Table 4. Each of the indices takes the form of a skewed frequency distribution with a long right tail, in which the median film is in the first or second decile. Once again, using Portsmouth to represent the three cities, the histogram in Fig. 4 shows the highly unequal frequency distribution of POPSTAT values for the 824 films screened in the city in 1934. Table 5 records the associate statistics.[17] Broken into decile classes, over half the observations fall into the first decile group—the mass of films did very little business. A small number of must-see movies populate the other end of the distribution. The last two deciles comprise ten films, with the top film—*It Happened One Night*—generating a POPSTAT Index value ten times that of the median film. The statistics of Bolton and Brighton reflect similar inequalities.

[16] POPSTAT values for all films screened in Portsmouth were calculated using the same billing weights.

[17] To maintain compatibility with the Bolton and Brighton datasets, billing weights are simply 1 for single features and 0.5 for films in a double bill.

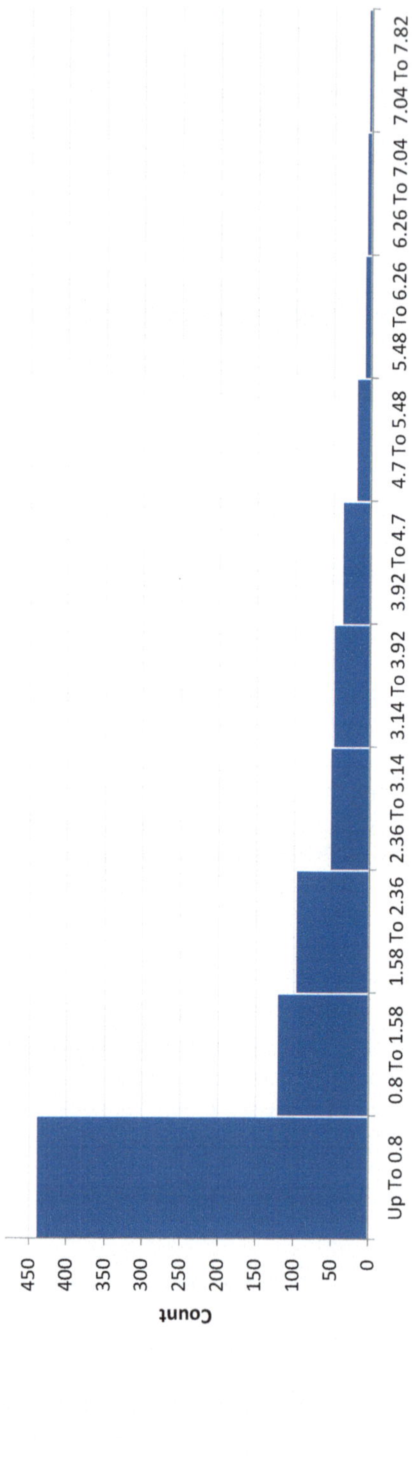

Fig. 4 Histogram (deciles) of the frequency distribution of POPSTAT Index values for Portsmouth, 1934 (Source *Portsmouth Evening News*)

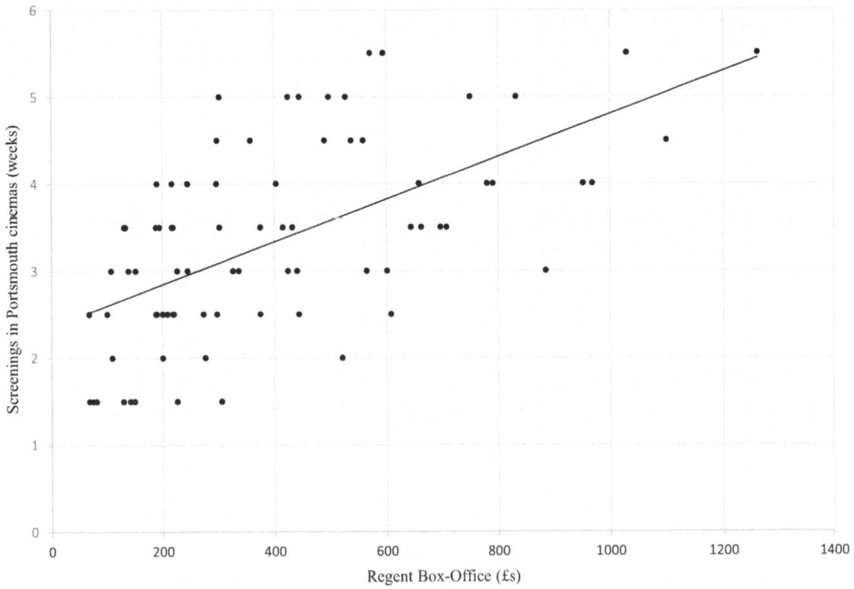

Fig. 5 Scatter of Regent box-office and screening weeks in the cinemas of Portsmouth

Compared with the box-office generated by the Regent cinema reported in Table 3 and Fig. 2, Fig. 4 shows the city-wide distribution of POPSTAT Index values to be much more unequal—contrast the skewness coefficient of 0.68 for the Regent, with that of 1.50 found in Table 4. The explanation for this is due to two factors. First, the Regent had access to a particular set of films because it was a first-run cinema owned by the vertically integrated Gaumont British organisation. This organisation ran 324 cinemas nationally in 1934.[18] The management of the Regent was allocated a film schedule that included the most popular films in circulation, comprising films marketed under the in-house brands of Gaumont British and Gainsborough and, except for Warner Bros., from the top Hollywood studios. Indeed, only four of the POPSTAT Top 20 films screened in Portsmouth in 1934 did not premiere at the Regent.

Secondly, given that the Regent had access to the most popular films, their relative success with Regent audiences would likely be replicated across subsequent cinema bookings, compounding differences with less popular movies. The most popular films populate the last two decile classes of the histogram in Fig. 4. While it is not always the case that films were equally popular across the range of cinemas at which they appeared, it can be seen in Fig. 5 that a broadly upward trend is evident in the relationship between the Regent box-office of the 79 films screened during 1934 and the number of weeks (in whole and half weeks) that these films appeared subsequently on other cinema screens in the city.

[18] Rowson (1936, p. 83).

4 Comparative Analysis

The film distribution system in Great Britain was highly centralised, based on the London offices of the major distribution companies in and around the Soho district of central London. Both major chains, Gaumont British and ABC, comprising respectively 324 and 200 cinemas in 1934, in conjunction with the major distributors, organised a programme of circuit releases, thereby ensuring that the same films were screened throughout their network of cinemas.[19] Furthermore, their size and geographical spread enabled them to book and schedule Hollywood big-budget productions to run in conjunction with their in-house product—respectively, Gaumont British and Gainsborough Films; and British International Films. Regarding the three cities of this study, the ABC ran three cinemas in Bolton (Capitol, Palladium, and Regal), two in Brighton (Savoy and Astoria), and two in Portsmouth (Victoria and Savoy). Gaumont British was not represented in Bolton but ran three cinemas in Brighton (Academy, Court, and Regent) and one in Portsmouth (Regent). These cinemas co-existed with smaller regional chains and independents for the most part. (Two other national cinema chains—Granada and Odeon, were at early stages in their development.)[20]

While distribution was coordinated from a London base, distributors were mindful that audience tastes throughout the country were not homogeneous. A simple way of measuring this is to count the number of days or screenings of a film in a locality. For instance, in 1934, the Gracie Fields vehicle *Love, Life and Laughter* appeared at 11 different cinemas in Brighton, 10 in Bolton, and 9 in Portsmouth, making it the most widely circulated film. However, a closer examination shows that around half of the film's screenings were on half weekly programmes at lower order cinemas, either as a single attraction or the main attraction on a double-bill programme. In Brighton, it was only screened on a shared billing; important information concerning the make-up of the audience attracted to the film. Consequently, in POPSTAT values, the film performs less well than other films programmed in fewer cinemas as single-bill attractions on weekly bookings in more prestigious cinemas.

Table 6 highlights similarities and differences in the popularity of the Top 20 'hit' films across the three cities.[21] Based on the 574 films screened at least once in all three cities, the table is ranked according to Mean RelPOP values (column 4).[22] Columns 1, 2, and 3 are formed by dividing the POPSTAT score of the films in the respective cities by the median POPSTAT value of each. From Table 6, it is evident that some movies are consistently popular across the three cities, while others vary: differences that are reflected in the magnitude of the coefficient of variation (column 6).

[19] Rowson (1936, p. 83).

[20] For a detailed account of the two organisations and their cinemas, see Eyles (1993, 1996).

[21] The table is particular to the three cities and differs substantially from that found in Sedgwick (2000, Appendix 3) for Great Britain in 1934.

[22] See Chapter "Introduction: 'Millions of People Every Day'—Cinema as Part of the Quotidian of Life", for an explanation of the RelPOP method.

Table 6 Comparative performance of the 20 most popular films in the three cities

Rank	Film	(1) Bolton RelPOP	(2) Brighton RelPOP	(3) Portsmouth RelPOP	(4) Mean RelPOP	(5) RelPOP Standard Deviation	(6) RelPOP Coefficient of Variation
1	Roman Scandals	5.13	6.26	5.55	5.65	0.47	0.08
2	House of Rothschild, The	5.13	4.89	6.17	5.40	0.55	0.10
3	It Happened One Night	4.39	4.42	7.20	5.34	1.32	0.25
4	Love Life and Laughter	6.51	3.58	5.60	5.23	1.22	0.23
5	Sing as We Go	6.76	3.56	4.29	4.87	1.37	0.28
6	Wonder Bar	3.97	3.67	6.28	4.64	1.16	0.25
7	Dinner at Eight	3.38	4.09	6.24	4.57	1.22	0.27
8	Little Women	2.93	5.47	5.17	4.53	1.13	0.25
9	Jew Süss	2.46	3.63	7.44	4.51	2.12	0.47
10	Barretts of Wimpole Street, The	3.92	3.37	5.85	4.38	1.06	0.24
11	Evergreen	2.89	3.18	6.92	4.33	1.84	0.42
12	Tugboat Annie	3.91	2.88	6.15	4.31	1.36	0.32
13	Queen Christina	3.67	4.49	4.66	4.28	0.43	0.10
14	Chu Chin Chow	2.34	3.13	7.33	4.27	2.19	0.51
15	Unfinished Symphony, The	2.48	3.18	7.10	4.25	2.03	0.48
16	Footlight Parade	4.89	2.18	5.11	4.06	1.33	0.33
17	Masquerader	3.98	4.15	3.94	4.03	0.09	0.02
18	Jack Ahoy!	2.18	2.66	6.86	3.90	2.10	0.54
19	Evensong	1.64	3.00	6.96	3.86	2.25	0.58
20	Cat and the Fiddle, The	3.23	2.15	6.14	3.84	1.68	0.44

Source *Bolton Evening News*, the *Brighton Argus,* and *Bolton Evening*

It is apparent from Table 6 that the most popular films were made either in Hollywood or in British studios in and around London.[23] It is also notable that British films were more unevenly received. Six of the eight films in the list generated coefficient of variation values near, or above, 0.5, while many of their Hollywood counterparts were consistently popular. Four films—*Roman Scandals*, *The House of Rothchild*, *Queen Christina*, and *The Masquerader*—recorded particularly low levels of variance.

In contrast, take the Gaumont British film *Jew Süss*—an '...historical drama concerning the rise and fall of an ambitious Jew in an 18th Century German court'.[24] The film circulated as a single-bill attraction in Portsmouth, playing for a week at the Regent, Plaza, and Theatre Royal cinemas and half weeks at the lower order cinemas, Regal, Scala, and Carlton. In Brighton, the film was also screened in six different cinemas, but on each occasion as part of a double-bill programme, the first three as single-week bookings (Regent, Lido, and Academy) and the latter three as half-week bookings (Tivoli, Odeon Kemp Town, and Court). Finally, in Bolton, *Jew Süss* secured three bookings as a single attraction, getting its premiere at the first-run Capital for a week, followed by half a week at the Regent and one night only at the Gem cinema. These observations suggest different levels of popular reception of this expensively made Gaumont British film. Also, when contrasted to the film *Love, Life and Laughter* starring Gracie Fields, the film had far fewer screenings in smaller neighbourhood cinemas. Another Gaumont British film *Jack Ahoy!*, a comedy starring Jack Hulbert, was the most popular film at the Regent in 1934, attracting just under 30,000 customers during its one-week billing, just under twice the audience that saw *It Happened One Night*. The film had a naval setting and so, perhaps not surprisingly in a maritime city, appeared at eight cinemas, the first three as single-bill attractions. In contrast, *Jack Ahoy!* received five cinema bookings in Brighton, none of which was a single-bill attraction. In Bolton, the film also appeared at five different cinemas, but even though it premiered as a single billing, it only had one whole week-long booking, the remainder of its run being half week bookings and, on one occasion, just a day.

A second Gracie Fields film appears in the Top 20 of Table 6—*Sing as We Go*. In Chapter "Introduction: 'Millions of People Every Day'—Cinema as Part of the Quotidian of Life", *Managing Risk*, attention was drawn to the disparity in the film's ranked position in the three English cities. Set in contemporary industrial Lancashire with location shots, *Sing as We Go* was tremendously popular among Bolton audiences, being screened on eight separate occasions during 1934, each time as a single-bill attraction. Very unusually, the film was held over for a second week at the Rialto after it premiered on 24/12/1934, with weekly bookings in three other cinemas. It was

[23] *Unfinished Symphony* was a joint Cine Allianz—Gaumont British joint production and shot in Vienna.

[24] Low (1985, pp. 141–142).

also screened at eight different cinemas in Brighton, but always as part of a double-bill programme and the last three bookings, only for half a week. The film appeared at five cinemas in Portsmouth, the first four bookings as week-long single-bill features.

Distinctive taste regimes coalesced around *Jack Ahoy!* and *Sing as We Go* in each locality. The subject matter of each was likely influential in this social behaviour, as was the star. Audiences in Bolton identified strongly with *Sing as We Go*, as did audiences in Portsmouth regarding *Jack Ahoy!*

5 Quality British Films

Seven British films and one joint Anglo-Austrian production are included in the Top 20 circulated in the three cities in 1934. Five of these were produced by the Gaumont British organisation, and the two in which Gracie Fields stars, by Associated Talking Pictures. Like many studies in this book show, film audiences were attracted by well-made films made by domestic producers about domestic subjects. Moreover, as Mark Glancy (1999) has shown, British subject material, particularly its history, was a rich source of inspiration for Hollywood, with Table 6 films showing two such films—*The House of Rothschild* and *The Barretts of Wimpole Street*.[25]

Using secondary sources, Richards, in his study of film and society, brought attention to the genuine popularity of British cinema during the 1930s.[26] From my national POPSTAT investigations of the programmes of first-run cinemas for the six years 1932 to 1937, I counted 98 (84 of which came from the top British studios) British films in the annual Top 50 listings across the six years.[27] However, the first evidence that well-made British films were genuinely popular with British audiences was contemporary, given by a Board of Trade Departmental Committee chaired by Lord Moyne in 1936, established to review the operation of the 1927 Cinematographic Act.[28] In his submission, Mr. R.D. Fennelly (an official at the Board of Trade) presented qualitative evidence collected by the exhibitor's trade body (Cinematographic Exhibitor' Association—CEA). It was based on ratings of new releases from 1933 to 1935 and presented as three annual tables in Appendix VII of the Report. Scoring was performed around the benchmark of 8.0 for what constituted a 'good film'. Categories were banded in quarter marks above and below 8 with an upper band of '8.75 and above' and a lower band of 'under 7'. Unfortunately, only British films were included in the three annual tables he presented.

The upper part of Table 7 represents evidence found in the Report (in the 1934 section of Appendix VII), indicating that a small number of studios produced the bulk of 'good' and 'very good' films. These were Associated Talking Pictures,

---

[25] Glancy (1999).

[26] Richards (1984).

[27] Sedgwick (2000, Table 4.4).

[28] Minutes of Evidence.

Table 7 Schedule of markings of quality British released in 1934 and Hollywood films released in 1935

Distributor	British producer(s)	Films	CEA Score: 8–8.5	CEA Score: 8.75 and over	Principal titles
Schedule of markings of films from the principal British Producers in 1934					
Associated British Film Distributors	Associated Talking Pictures (4) Phoenix (1) Wyndham (1)	6	2	1	*Sing As We Go Love, Life and Laughter, Death at Broadcasting House*
Gaumont British	Gaumont British, Gainsborough	23	16	5	*Jew Süss, Chin, Chin, Chow, Evergreen, Jack Ahoy!, Evensong, Cup of Kindness, Man of Aran, Pricess Charming, Man Who Knew Too Much, Unfinished Sympthony*
United Artists	London Films, British and Dominions	8	4	2	*Catherine the Great, Nell Gwyn, Private Life of Don Juan, Lilies of the Field,*
Wardour	British International Pictures	19	11	3	*Blossom Time, Red Wagon, Radio Parade of 1935, Those Were the Days*
Total of named British Studios		56	33	11	
Total of all British Studios		184	53	11	
Schedule of markings of films from the principal Hollywood producers in 1935					
Columbia	Columbia	41	14	2	
Fox	Fox	45	16	1	
MGM	MGM	43	34	5	
Paramount	Paramount	56	39	4	
Radio	RKO	45	22	2	
United Artists	Goldwyn, 20th Century	14	9	3	
Universal	Universal	44	14	1	

(continued)

Table 7 (continued)

Distributor	British producer(s)	Films	CEA Score: 8–8.5	CEA Score: 8.75 and over	Principal titles
Warner Bros. and First National	Warner Bros. and First National	47	39	2	

Source Evidence given separately by Mr. R.D. Fennelly, and Mr. T.H. Fligelstone and Mr. W.H. Fuller to the Departmental Committee of the Board of Trade chaired by Lord Moyne in 1936: respectively, First day, Tuesday 5 May 1935, Appendix VI; and Fourth Day, Tuesday 26 May 1935, Annex

Gaumont British and Gainsborough, London Films, British and Dominions, and British International Pictures.

While the films were not named, Appendix 3 of Sedgwick (2000) has been used to identify the likely films counted in Fennelly's table. This is supplemented in the lower section of Table 7 by evidence to the Moyne Committee provided by Mr. T.H. Fligelstone and W.H. Fuller of the CEA of the qualitative assessment of American studio productions released in Great Britain in 1935. While the years, and hence films covered, differ between the two sections, an idea of the qualitative competition facing British producers at the time can be had from the table. While MGM, Paramount and Warner Bros. dominate the quality market, Gaumont British stands alongside the other principal Hollywood studios as a quality film producer in terms of scale.

6 Conclusion

The fact that differences in film popularity exist is an empirical matter—the reason is cultural. In Europe, domestically produced films attracted audiences within borders but not across borders. Materially, there is no reason why films were not distributed across territories other than there was no market for them—matters of language, identity, and history result in differences in tastes between nationalities. Yet, unless the subject of banning orders by totalitarian regimes, Hollywood movies contributed significantly to the list of the most popular films in European territories, with the spoken word either dubbed or supplemented by subtitles. American films could engage audiences, even when customs and traditions differed. As Peter Miskell has shown, the Hollywood films popular with European audiences had cultural proximity to Europe, either in subject material or star and director inputs.[29] Examples are the two Top 20 films identified in Table 6 with British historical subject material—*The House of Rothchilds* and *The Barretts of Wimpole Street*. A further movie told the story of the abdication of a seventeenth century-European monarch—*Queen Christina* of Sweden.

[29] Miskell (2016).

Although a broader study than that conducted in this chapter would be necessary to examine systematically regional or class differences in taste in Great Britain, the purpose of this chapter is to show how the POPSTAT/RelPOP method allows researchers to formulate questions. Differences in the reception of films and the stars that appear in them can be investigated through the microfoundations of programming data.

Table 6 opens a window into civil society in three English cities in the middle of the 1930s in that it provides a guide to filmgoers' tastes. When the films listed in the table had reached these cities, they were two to three months beyond their initial premiere run in one of London's West End cinemas. It is apparent that while a small number of Hollywood productions were universally popular across the three cities, differences can be discerned in the popularity of others. Thus, two well-made British films, *Sing as We Go and Jack Ahoy!*, can be identified strongly with the respective populaces of Bolton and Portsmouth. The second of these seems to have had little traction in Bolton. In contrast, the two Gracie Fields films *Sing as We Go* and *Love* and *Life and Laughter* were screened in numerous lower order cinemas in Portsmouth and Brighton, suggesting social class and regional differences in audience preferences.

Appendix

Regression test results

Linear Regression						
Regression Statistics						
R	0.94					
R-square	0.89					
Adjusted R-square	0.89					
S	1.32					
N	79					
Column U = 7.77E-3 * Column P						
ANOVA						
	d.f	*SS*	*MS*	*F*	*p-level*	
Regression	1	1,111.53	1,111.53	640.41	0	
Residual	78.	135.38	1.74			
Total	79.	1,246.92				

(continued)

(continued)

	Coefficient	*Standard Error*	*LCL*	*UCL*	*t Stat*	*p-level*	*H0 (5%)*
Intercept	0						
Column P	7.77E-3	3.07E-4	7.15E-3	8.38E-3	25.31	0	*rejected*
T (5%)	1.99						
LCL—Lower value of a reliable interval (LCL)							
UCL—Upper value of a reliable interval (UCL)							

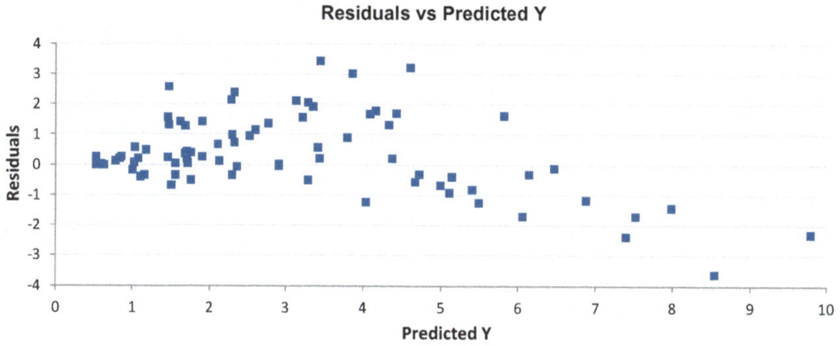

References

Crafts, N. (1987). Long-term unemployment in Britain in the 1930s. *Economic History Review, 40*(3).

Daniels, G., & Jewkes, J. (1928). The post-war depression in the Lancashire cotton industry. *Journal of the Royal Statistical Society, 91*(2), 153–206.

Eyles, A. (1993). *ABC: The first name in entertainment*. BFI.

Eyles, A. (1996). *Gaumont British cinemas*. BFI.

Furhammar, L. (1990). *Stockholmspublikens biopreferenser under 1930-talet: en undersökningsrapport*. Stockholm University Press.

Garncarz, J. (2015). *Wechselnde Vorlieben: Über die Filmpräferenzen der Europäer, 1896–1939*. Stoemfeld.

Garncarz, J. (2020). *Begeisterte Zuschauer : Über die Filmpräferenzen der Deutschen in der NS-Zeit*. Herbert von Halem.

Harper, S. (2004). A lower middle-class taste-community in the 1930s: Admissions figures at the Regent Cinema, Portsmouth, UK. *Historical Journal of Film, Radio and Television, 24*, 565–587.

Low, R. (1985). *Film making in 1930's Britain*. George Allen and Unwin.

McKibbin, R. (1998). *Classes and cultures: England, 1918–1951: A study of a democratic society*. Oxford University Press.

Miskell, P. (2016). International films and international markets: The globalisation of Hollywood entertainment, C.1921–1951. *Media History, 22*(2),174–200.

Richards, J. (1984). *The age of the dream palace*. Routledge.

Rowson, S. (1936). A statistical survey of the cinema industry in Great Britain in 1934. *Journal of the Royal Statistical Society, 99*, 67–129.
Sedgwick, J. (2000). *Filmgoing in 1930s Britain: A choice of pleasures*. Exeter University Press.
Sedgwick, J. (2006). Cinemagoing in Portsmouth during the 1930s. *Cinema Journal, 46*, 52–85.
Sedgwick, J., & Pafort-Overduin, C. (2012). Understanding audience behaviour through statistical evidence: London and Amsterdam in the mid-1930s. In I. Christie (Ed.), *Audiences* (pp. 96–110). Amsterdam.

John Sedgwick is a visiting Professor in the Faculty of Technology, Design and Environment, Oxford Brookes University. He researches the economic history of cinema and is particularly interested in the ontological characteristics of film as a commodity. He created the POPSTAT Index of Film Popularity as a proxy for box-office returns. This tool provides a means of reflecting audience preferences and monitoring the distribution process. His research has focused on American, Australian, British, Dutch, Italian and international markets during the 1930s and 1950/60s. He has written a monograph, edited an anthology and published articles in *Business History, Cinema Journal, Economic History Review, Explorations in Economic History, Enterprise and Society, Film History, Historical Journal of Film, Radio and Television, Journal of Applied Statistics, Journal of Cultural Economics, Journal of Economic History, and Journal of Transnational Cinema.*

Popular Films in Stockholm During the 1930s: A Presentation and Discussion of the Pioneering Work of Leif Furhammar

Åsa Jernudd and John Sedgwick

Abstract Leif Furhammar was an esteemed professor of Film Studies at the University of Stockholm. In 1990 he produced a report on filmgoing in Stockholm during the 1930s. The report is little known to film scholars, especially outside of Sweden. Furhammar takes a novel approach to investigate what films people watched by counting film programmes listed in a daily city newspaper. Using similar methods to POPSTAT, Furhammar produces charts of the annual best-attended films in Stockholm for the decade, including all Swedish movies released. His work introduced an entirely new type of evidence concerning film popularity. This chapter discusses his methods, replicates his results (where data permits), and analyses his findings.

In this chapter, attention is directed to a hitherto neglected treatise of Swedish film history, written in 1990 by Leif Furhammar and discovered in The Swedish Film Institute archive in the form of a report.[1] The study is important because it constitutes one of the few quantitative investigations of the film business conducted by a practising academic during the twentieth century. From various newspapers, trade journals and company sources, Furhammar developed a metric that enabled him to catalogue the most popular films watched by the population of Stockholm during the 1930s. We believe his methods and findings to be worthy of wider recognition and dissemination.

Leif Furhammar (1937–2015) was appointed as a professor in Film Studies at Stockholm University in 1977. Besides working in academia, his list of achievements includes work as a film and television critic, film censor and television producer.

[1] Furhammar (1990).

Åsa Jernudd and John Sedgwick, based upon a translation made by Åsa Jernudd.

Å. Jernudd
The School of Humanities, Education and Social Sciences, Örebro University, Örebro, Sweden
e-mail: Asa.Jernudd@oru.se

J. Sedgwick (✉)
Oxford Brookes University, Oxford, UK
e-mail: sedgwicj52@gmail.com

J. Sedgwick (ed.), *Towards a Comparative Economic History of Cinema, 1930–1970*, Frontiers in Economic History, https://doi.org/10.1007/978-3-031-05770-0_5

Furhammar was interested in film as a mass medium throughout his career, referring to its political and social influence as a 'social-psychological field of power'.[2] However, there was also another side to his work. He was an advocate for what we today call film literacy. He believed strongly that knowledge of film should be an integral component in school and youth education and should extend to the population at large. In the 1980s, Furhammar started writing what became the standard history of Swedish film—and cinema.[3] This work has an inclusive approach to its subject, yet one aspect is missing for the most part: the audience's perspective. The simple explanation for this is that there was no such body of research. When writing *Filmen i Sverige*, he decided to investigate the possibilities of knowing historically which films audiences preferred.[4]

Furhammar set himself the task to make sense of the undoubted growth in the popularity of filmgoing in Sweden during the 1930s. Following the impact of the Great Depression, the economy grew dramatically, with the index of industrial production rising from a low of 89 in 1932 to 152 by 1937 (1929 = 100).[5] He was particularly concerned to gather quantitative evidence to substantiate knowledge of those films that attracted audiences. From this evidence-based platform, he intended to question claims prevalent in Swedish film historiography, involving the considerable popularity of the so-called 'pilsnerfilms' or the enormous financial success of the film *Pensionat Paradiset*.

Furhammar recognised that he would need to overcome the absence of audience records to do this work. He tells us that before the mid-1960s, there was no central collection of audience data in Sweden and that '…film companies were very secretive about film revenues and attendance numbers'.[6]

Furhammar thus set himself the task of establishing a method that would allow him to rank all films released annually during the 1930s in terms of their popularity. Akin to POPSTAT, Furhammar created an index number scale based upon the circulation of films among Stockholm cinemas, which he termed the HB ('hypotetiskt besökstal'), which we translate as Hypothetical Audience (HA scale). Finding a source that gave him the film rental earnings of 25 films produced and (or) distributed by the small Swedish studio Wive, Furhammer estimated audience size. He then found a strong positive correlation between these and their corresponding HA-scale values. By interpolating the statistical relationship between the two to all films appearing on the HA scale, Furhammar created a Best Guess (BG-scale), from which he charted the popularity of films appearing in Stockholm during the decade.

Like POPSTAT, his analysis was built upon the process of film circulation and diffusion that was driven by box-office performance. New releases opened at 'suitable' cinemas, after which their performance at the box office determined their

---

[2] Furhammar (2015, p. 220).

[3] Furhammar (1991, 2003).

[4] Furhammar's methodological experiment, are presented and discussed in Furhammar (2003, pp. 133–135, 157–161).

[5] Feinstein, Temin and Toniolo (1997, Table 9.3).

[6] Furhammar (1990, p. 1).

circulation trajectory. They stayed a second week if they surpassed a predetermined threshold attendance figure. Their subsequent distribution to lower-order cinemas was dependent upon earlier ticket sales. Furhammar refers to this process as a life cycle—films are born and then die.

In this chapter, Furhammar's methods and findings are presented in detail. He starts his report with a detailed account of his methods and follows this by setting the context and analysing his findings. At the end of his report, Furhammar presents a series of annual popularity tables, in which all Swedish films and the most popular foreign films screened in Stockholm over the decade are ranked according to their respective HA and BG index values.[7] Furhammar distinguishes between Swedish and Foreign films and 'successful' films and less 'successful' films. He lists films annually in the Appendix to his work, referred to as the 'Big Table'. This chapter aims to explain the gist of his procedure for estimating the size of film audiences and review his findings. Wherever the data in his publication allows, his calculations are replicated, followed by a discussion of their significance. Finally, we present the annual Top 20 films from Furhammar's Big Table in the Appendix.

1 Context

The crisis of international capitalism, commonly known as the Great Depression, impacted Sweden and most, if not all, other European economies during the 1930s. Along with Great Britain, Sweden left the Gold Standard in 1931, with both Governments allowing their currencies to float. From July 1933, the Swedish Government and the other Scandinavian countries pegged their exchange rates to Sterling.[8] Unemployment in Sweden peaked in 1933, with industrial production falling by 11%. By 1933, the value of the export sector had contracted by two-thirds of its 1929 value.[9] During these years, the consumer prices index (CPI) had fallen by 7%, with wholesale prices falling even further (13%). However, with wages declining only by 5% during these years, those in work were substantially better off in 1933 than they had been in 1929.[10] In common with much of the developed world, industrial unemployment remained stubbornly high during the period of recovery, averaging at 16.8% between 1930 and 1938, some four percentage points higher than it had been during the previous decade.[11]

[7] In his report Furhammar delivers at length his procedure for estimating national audiences of films. However, as he doesn't present his findings, we limit ourselves in this chapter to his methods and findings applied to Stockholm audiences only.

[8] Straumann and Woitek (2009).

[9] Feinstein et al. (1997, Table 6.3).

[10] Fregert (2009).

[11] Feinstein et al. (1997, Table 7.1). Between 1921 and 1929 unemployment in Sweden was recorded at 14.2%.

Table 1 Number of cinema tickets sold (in thousands) in Stockholm

(1) Exhibition season	(2) Tickets sold (000s)	(3) Growth in ticket sales (per cent)	(4) Population of Stockholm	(5) Tickets per capita	(6) No. of Swedish films	(7) No. of foreign films	(8) Total films
1929–1930	7,650		486,184	16	9	322	331
1930–1931	7,906	3	502,215	16	23 (13)	275	298
1931–1932	7,815	−1	504,333	15	20 (15)	295	315
1932–1933	7,634	−2	519,711	15	25	253	278
1933–1934	7,532	−1	521,618	14	22 (20)	268	290
1934–1935	8,370	11	526,027	16	21 (20)	273	294
1935–1936	9,803	17	534,286	18	22 (21)	271	293
1936–1937	10,473	7	545,786	19	27	323	350
1937–1938	11,453	9	556,594	21	27 (25)	294	321
1938–1939:	12,386	8	570,771	22	27 (25)	304	331

Source Furhammar (1990, Tables 2 and 3); Statistisk Årsbok för Stockholms Stad, 1930–1940
Notes The population figures are given for the year the season begins. Figures in parenthesis show the number of new Swedish films on the Stockholm market produced by Swedish companies. The difference is explained by those films made outside of Sweden, staring Swedish actors. For instance, several Swedish sound films were made in the Joinville Studios, Paris (Furhammar, pp. 18–19)

2 The Stockholm Market

Drawn from official secondary data, Furhammar produces a series of tables and charts to describe the characteristics of the Stockholm cinema market during the 1930s. Furhammar points out that Swedish film production was at a low ebb in 1929, with no films premiered during the first half of the year—something that he claims was 'unique in the history of Swedish cinema'.[12] During the 1929–1930 season, the first two Swedish sound films (out of only nine films) were premiered, expanding rapidly to 19 films (out of 23) during the following 1930–1931 season, after which no commercial silent films were made.

Table 1 shows the annual number of cinema tickets sold and the number of films screened in Stockholm.[13] Over the decade, attendances grew by almost three quarters—well ahead of the city's population, with particularly strong growth noticeable from the 1934–1935 season onwards. Furhammar commented that attendances in the latter half of the decade were 'unprecedented' and from 1936 comparable on a *per capita* basis to those recorded in Great Britain.[14] Furthermore, the modest growth in ticket sales in the 1930–1931 season, followed by two seasons in which attendances fall, suggests that the 'coming of sound' had little impact initially.

[12] Furhammar (1990, p. 15).
[13] 'Statistisk Årsbok för Stockholms Stad,1930–40'.
[14] Furhammar (1990, p. 16). See Sedgwick (2000, Table 2.1).

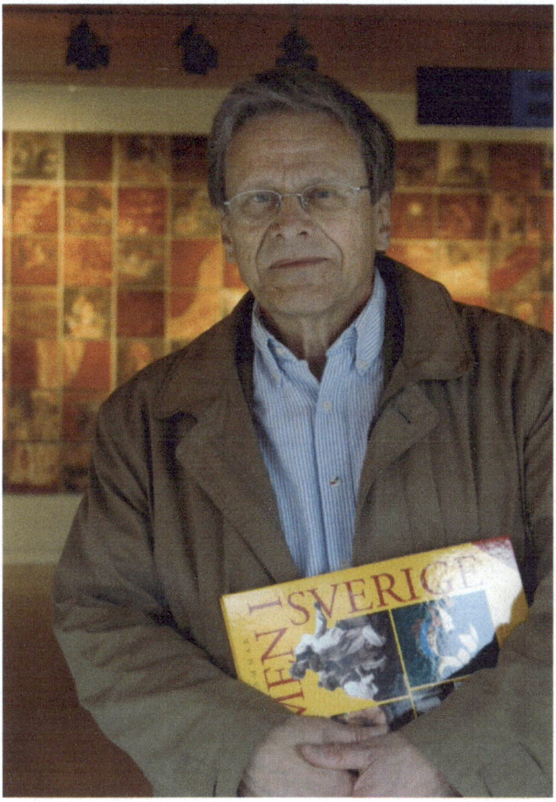

Fig. 1 Leif Furhammar (*Source* The Swedish Film Institute)

Furhammar used the HA-scale index to apportion attendances between Swedish and non-Swedish films, indicating that during the height of the Great Depression, Swedish audiences turned away from foreign films in favour of domestic productions. In conjunction, Fig. 1 and Table 1 suggest that during the first four seasons covered by the analysis, the relatively small number of Swedish films attracted more than one-third of the market share, with approximately ten times that number of foreign films making up the remainder. After that, the share in Stockholm remained around one-third, with Furhammar claiming it was higher in the rest of the country (Fig. 2).[15]

To study 'the structure of the audience' in greater depth, Furhammar investigated the concentration of audience preferences for the exhibition season 1934–1935, during which 8.37 million Stockholmers attended the screenings of 294 films. He found that the 'four most attractive films together accounted for one million visitors. The subsequent five films most popular films accounted for another million. The next six films drew the third million, nine the fourth, 11 the fifth, 18 the sixth, 37 the seventh, around 90 the eighth and around 115 accounted for the remainder (0.37

[15] The 1941 government report on cinema calculated the Swedish share of the total film rentals as 44, 37.4 and 37.2% respectively for the calendar years 1937–39 (SOU, 1942: 36, p. 15).

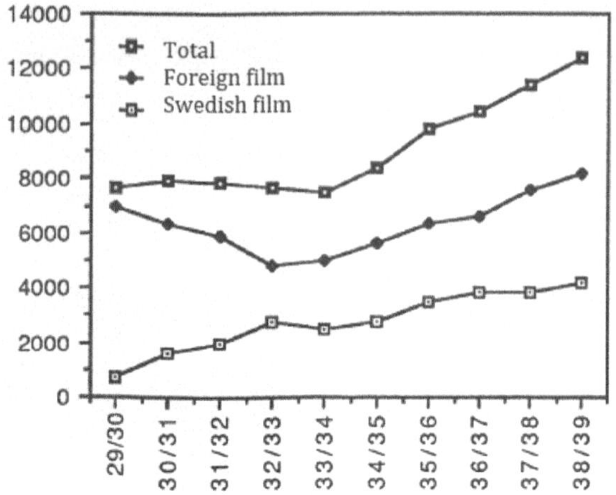

Fig. 2 Audience of Swedish and foreign film (000s) (*Source* Furhammar 1990, Fig. 4)

Table 2 The concentration of film popularity in Stockholm

(1) Exhibition Season	(2) Films accounting for 25% of box-office	(3) Films accounting for 50% of box-office	(4) Total films released
1930–1931	15	–	331
1931–1932	11	36	298
1932–1933	10	29	315
1933–1934	10	28	278
1934–1935	10	26	290
1935–1936	12	30	294
1936–1937	12	32	293
1937–1938	13	31	350
1938–1939	14	33	321

Source Furhammar (1990, Table 4)

million)'. In essence, Furhammar describes a 'long right tail' statistical distribution, so typical of filmgoing everywhere. He observes: 'We can conclude that a remarkably small share of the exhibited films attracted a very large share of the audience, and a remarkably large share of the exhibited films attracted a proportionally insignificant audience'. After ranking films (from the most to the least popular) annually, Table 2 demonstrates a recurring pattern across the decade, a phenomenon that he found surprising: writing in 1990, he had supposed that this empirical regularity, applied to more recent times only—for him, the 1970s and 1980s.[16]

The expanding market for movies was, of course, made possible by the growing provision of cinemas and cinema seats, in which the emergence of four major cinema

[16] Furhammar (1990, p. 20). Also, see for example, Reinholds (1987, p. 129).

Table 3 Cinema data for 1930, 1936 and 1939

	1930	1936	1939
Stockholm Cinemas	66	77[a]	102
Seats	29,880	35,022	48,620
Mean seating per cinema	453	455	474
Population per seat	263	295	260
AB Riteatrarna (cinemas)	0	9	11
AB Riteatrarna (seats)	0	4,553	7,003
AB Riteatrarna (mean seats)	0	506	637
AB Sandrew-Biograferna (cinemas)	3	10	16
AB Sandrew-Biograferna (seats)	1,669	6,081	10,430
AB Sandrew-Biograferna (mean seats)	556	608	652
AB Svensk Filmindustri (cinemas)	11	14	16
AB Svensk Filmindustri (seats)	9,035	10,516	12,674
AB Svensk Filmindustri (mean seats)	821		792
Europa Film, G. & P. Scheutz (cinemas)	0	0	2
Europa Film, G. & P. Scheutz (seats)	0	0	1377
Europa Film, G. & P. Scheutz (mean seats)	0	0	689

Sources Förteckning över Sveriges biografer: dessutom adress- och telefonuppgifter å ägare och föreståndare samt övriga upplysningar av intresse för facket, Sveriges biografägareförb., 1930; Förteckning över biografer, biografägare och biografföreståndare, Sveriges biografer, Sveriges biografägareförb., Stockholm, 1936; Förteckning över biografer, biografägare och biografföreståndare, Sveriges biografer, Sveriges biografägareförb., Stockholm, 1939

[a]Omits the Odéon for which no seating information is given in Sveriges biografägareförb and didn't advertise in *Dagens Nyheter* during the two weeks in September 1936 used for checking

chains—Svensk Filmindustri (AB Svensk Filmindustri), Sandrews (AB Sandrew-Biograferna), Europa Films and RI (AB Riteatrarna) cinemas—played a significant role. The oligopoly formed by these large chains in Stockholm remained until the 1980s. Furhammar explains: 'In the early 1930s, Svensk Filmindustri was the sole vertically integrated company. Sandrews began building its cinema chain at the end of the 1920s and in film production in the late 1930s. Europa Film started as a production company in 1931 and began adding cinemas in Stockholm from 1936. Finally, RI's first cinema opened in the 1920s and expanded rapidly in the 1930s but did not get involved in film production'.[17] Europa Film's role in the expansion of cinemas and seats in Stockholm in the 1930s was, however, modest in comparison with the other chains.

The extent of the concentration of cinema ownership is depicted in Table 3. It shows a marked increase in concentration during the decade, with the major chains' ownership of Stockholm cinemas rising from 17% in 1930 to near 50% by 1939.[18]

[17] Furhammar (1990, p. 21).

[18] See also Furhammar (1990, Figs. 6 and 7).

Because the cinemas in these chains were larger, the measure of seating concentration (seats managed by the major chains) is even more significant, growing significantly over the period from 36 to 65%. Another notable feature of Table 3 is the increase in the supply of seats in response to increasing ticket sales (see Table 1).

3 Method for Establishing Film Popularity Statistics

The primary source for establishing film popularity statistics in Furhammar's report is the entertainment section of the Stockholm based daily newspaper *Dagens Nyheter*, in which the screenings at Stockholm cinemas were listed. Expecting films to be screened for a week with a change of programmes on Mondays, Furhammar drew upon cinema programmes listed in the Monday editions of the newspaper throughout the decade—replaced by Tuesday, when Monday was a public holiday. Over the decade, the 520 weekly listings of films screened in Stockholm cinemas entailed making 30,000 programme entries. For each film, a table was constructed charting its circulation among those cinemas.

Furhammar distinguished between cinemas based on their seating capacity but did not tell us how many cinemas are used or how representative they are.[19] Checking those cinemas that advertised in *Dagens Nyheter* in two weeks of September of each year against the listing of Stockholm cinemas found in the two trade journals for 1930, 1936, and 1939 shows that the newspaper carried the programmes of 47 of the 66 cinemas in 1930, a proportion rising to 75 from 77 in 1936 and 90 of 102 in 1939. The numbers for the years of this study are presented in Table 4. This examination of the advertisements found in *Dagens Nyheter* confirms that Monday was the preferred day for change of film programme for most cinemas. No double bills were offered to audiences in the weeks checked.

During a typical week in the 1930s, Stockholm cinemas screened twice daily evening programmes.[20] Knowledge of the seating capacity of cinemas and the times of screenings for each cinema allowed Furhammar to calculate the number of seats available (AS) for each film during its time in circulation. A central problem for him was how seating occupancy changed between the months. He writes: 'As a general rule, attendances were constant during the period September to March, declined steadily after March to reach the lowest point in June and July, after which it successively would rise again and reach its seasonal norm. Mid-December would show a dip, explained by Christmas activities and holiday closure at cinemas'.

[19] This information is available for the years 1930, 1936, 1937 and 1939 in two trade papers - *Förteckning över Sveriges Biografägare och Biografer* (published by the Film Owners Association - Filmägarnas Kontrollförening u.p.a.) and in *Förteckning över Biografer, Biografägare och Biografföreståndare*, (published by the Swedish Cinema Owners Association - Sveriges Biografägareförbund). Cinema expert Olle Waltå assisted in this exercise.

[20] Exceptions to this pattern, such as Christmas and Easter, were negligible. Most cinemas also screened matinées. If the censor permitted, the evening programme would typically also be screened as a matinée.

Table 4 The number of Stockholm cinemas that advertised feature film programmes in *Dagens Nyheter*

Year (September)	Cinemas that advertised (from total no. of cinemas)	Seating capacity of cinemas that advertised	Cinemas that changed program on other days than Mondays
1929	49		10
1930	47 (from 66)	22,469	8
1931	58		
1932	61		7
1933	65		
1934	66		18
1935	70		
1936	75 (from 77)	35,446	7
1937	81		
1938	85		15
1939	90 (from 102)	45,924	

Source Dagens Nyheter, from a sample taken on the first Monday in September to the Sunday of the second week in September for 1929, 1930, 1932, 1934, 1936, 1938 and the first two Mondays of September 1931, 1933, 1935, 1937 and 1939; *Förteckning över Sveriges biografer: dessutom adress- och telefonuppgifter å ägare och föreståndare samt övriga upplysningar av intresse för facket*, Sveriges biografägareförb, 1930; *Förteckning över biografer, biografägare och biograf-föreståndare*, Sveriges biografer, Sveriges biografägareförb., Stockholm, 1936; *Förteckning över biografer, biografägare och biografföreståndare*, Sveriges Biografer, Sveriges biografägareförb, Stockholm, 1939

Furhammar tackled this problem by calling upon the Entertainment Tax returns of cinemas. Published in the 'Statistical Yearbook of the City of Stockholm', this information gave him monthly information on ticket sales.[21] By dividing the total number of cinema visits by the total number of available cinema seats, Furhammar obtained a measure of average monthly seat occupancy in Stockholm—what is termed 'Seating Capacity Norm Coefficient' (SONC).[22]

Over the decade, this amounted to 120 monthly seat occupancy norms, with the monthly norm varying between 16% (June 1934) and 57% (October 1938). During the high season (September to March), SONC was constantly above 40%.[23] When applied to individual films, Furhammar explains: 'The seating occupancy norm coefficient (SONC) indicates the percentage of seats a film would have occupied, given it had drawn an audience that corresponded to the period average'.

[21] 'Statistisk Årsbok för Stockholms Stad - 1905–1971', publicerad av Stockholms Stads statistiska kontor / Statistical year-book of Stockholm- 1905–1971', published by Stockholm Office of Statistics.

https://sok.stadsarkivet.stockholm.se/Databas/statistik-arsbok-1904-2006/Visa/skatter/879?sidindex=2&ar=1939. Accessed 2021/04/06.

[22] Furhammar used the term 'normalbeläggningskoefficient' (NK).

[23] See Furhammar (1990, Fig. 5).

For most films, the calculation of SONC does not present any problems. Difficulties arose in those cases in which a film was screened across several months. He writes: 'For example, a few films that opened at cinemas during the summer stayed on the repertoire into the autumn. As the seating occupancy curve rises steeply from July to September, it cannot be ruled out that the calculations are uncertain in these cases and offer interpolation problems. Christmas caused a similar short-term uncertainty (for films screened) in December'.[24]

The two information sets—SONC in conjunction with AS—allow Furhammar to estimate attendances generated by films while circulating through Stockholm's cinemas. In this method, all cinema seats, irrespective of cinema, are treated as equivalents, with each weighted by the average monthly capacity utilisation of cinema seats. Furhammar terms this product the 'hypothetical attendance number' (HA): '...the HA scale is the basis from which we consider and make qualified guesses about the actual audience figures'.[25]

$$\text{HA Index}_{it} = \sum_{j=1}^{n} \text{seating capacity (AS)}_j \times \text{capacity utilization (SONC)}_{jt}$$

where HA = estimate of attendances
$i = i$th film
$t =$ months of circulation
$j = j$th cinema in a population of n cinemas.

In contrast to the POPSTAT method, which serves as a proxy index of box-office revenue, Furhammar's concern is estimating actual attendances. However, like POPSTAT, the HA-Index cannot distinguish between the popularity of different films screened at the same cinema. It is worth quoting his full justification of the method: 'It should be pretty obvious that the HA scale does not correspond in absolute numbers to real audience figures, since the assumption of normal seat occupancy is not valid for all films... However, the motivation behind considering normal seating occupancy in this context is that there is reason to assume that the deviation of the hypothetical visitor numbers from the real is both consistent and systematic. Suppose the programming principles presented earlier hold. In that case, we can assume that films that disappear quickly from the repertoire (films with low AS value) had a real seating occupancy number below the norm for the short time they were in circulation. Similarly, films with lengthy bookings at several cinemas with high AS values are likely to have had a higher real seating occupancy number compared to the norm'.[26]

Thus, similarly to POPSTAT, the HA-Index will systematically overestimate the popularity of films with low circulation levels and underestimate the popularity of those that achieve high circulation levels. Because most films vary little from the

---

[24] Furhammar (1990, p. 4).

[25] Furhammar (1990, p. 4).

[26] Furhammar (1990, p. 5).

average, Furhammar thought that the HA scale's values should correlate positively and strongly with actual attendance figures.

In his search to find data that would allow him to test the accuracy of the HA-Index against particular films, Furhammar came upon the business records of the small Swedish film producer and distributor Wive, whose account ledger for the 1930s is preserved in the Swedish Film Institute Library.[27] The register records the film rental incomes generated by nine in-house productions made by the company and 16 foreign films it handled in its capacity as a distributor. These are listed in Table 5.[28] A significant problem for Furhammar was converting the rental earnings accrued by these films into estimates of attendances. He was concerned that '…film rentals are not an immediate expression of audience size'.[29] His method was to deduce the proportion of box office absorbed by film rentals.[30] He used this to estimate box-office values, which he then converted to audience numbers, knowing that each admission contributed SK1.0 to the box office.[31]

Thus, Furhammar creates two independent statistical series. The first is based upon rental earnings of 25 films that Wive either produced or distributed (column 6), from which he deduced audience numbers (column 8). The circulation histories of these films in Stockholm cinemas are the second in the form of their HA-Index scores (column 9). Using a univariate model to regress the estimated audience for the 25 Wive films on their HA-Index values, Furhammar found a good fit. The results of his analysis are found in Table 6 and depicted in Fig. 3 (Table 7).

These show a high correlation coefficient (*R*) and a correspondingly high coefficient of determination (*R* Square), with intercept and slope coefficients statistically significant at the 95% level. Using Furhammar's words: 'The regression analysis shows that the correlation is very high between the estimated audience and the HA-values, indicating that the HA-scale has high validity as a measure of the attractiveness of the Wive films screened in Stockholm'.[32] Two pages later, he wrote: 'The high correlation between the HA scale and the Wive films' results for Stockholm, probably can be explained by a direct causal relationship of the kind suggested in

[27] Wive Film, Uncatalogued Archive, The Swedish Film Institute Library.

[28] Eleven films distributed by Wive with an HA value below 15 are excluded from the table and subsequent analysis '… so as not to impose undue weight in the upcoming regression analysis (a misrepresentation due to a so-called statistical floor effect). The material thus becomes regrettably small, but it is what is available.' Furhammar (1990, p. 7).

[29] Furhammar (1990, p. 5).

[30] Furhammar's method for establishing rental percentages was based on the distribution of Wive's first feature *Pettersson & Bendel* (1933) from which he interpolated differences between rental rates in Stockholm and the rest of the country, and then differences between the four categories of film—A, B, C, D.

[31] The average price of cinema admissions during the 1930s was SK1.10, of which 10 ore was contributed to entertainment duty.

[32] Furhammar (1990, p. 8).

Table 5 Wive films are used to estimate audience size and hypothetical number of cinema visits (HA)

(1) Film category	(2) Source title	(3) Original title	(4) Release date Sweden	(5) Imdb ID	(6) Rental revenues (SK)	(7) Film rent (%)	(8) Estimated audience (000s)	(9) HA-Index
A	Pettersson & Bendel	Pettersson & Bendel	21-08-1933	24,442	66,318	31.0	215	120
B	Anderssonskans Kalle	Anderssonskans Kalle	15-08-1934	24,829	54,210	28.5	190	115
B	Sången om den eldröda blomman	Sången om den eldröda blomman	12-11-1934	25,854	30,149	28.5	105	90
B	Flickornas Alfred	Flickornas Alfred	23-08-1935	26,366	27,773	28.5	95	85
B	Vi går landsvägen	Vi går landsvägen	01-11-1937	29,732	28,057	28.5	100	90
C	På solsidan	På solsidan	03-02-1936	28,151	44,972	26.0	175	105
C	Släkten är värst	Släkten är värst	27-07-1936	28,268	41,661	26.0	160	95
C	65, 66 och jag	65, 66 och jag	23-11-1936	27,248	58,829	26.0	225	145
C	Bara en trumpetare	Bara en trumpetare	26-08-1938	29,896	44,242	26.0	170	105
D	Alarm på Medelhavet	Alerte en Méditerranée	26-12-1938	190,961	30,489	23.5	130	90
D	Den stora illusionen	La grande illusion	04-10-1937	28,950	18,732	23.5	80	65
D	Port Arthur	Port Arthur	01-02-1937	28,128	17,115	23.5	75	55
D	Jean från Paris	La belle équipe	02-08-1937	27,342	6,542	23.5	30	40
D	På falskt pass	Au service du tsar	16-04-1937	165,095	7,328	23.5	30	35
D	Den döde tar till flykten	Break the News	30-04-1938	29,944	9,755	23.5	40	35
D	Den skyldige	Le coupable	11-10-1937	201,542	11,117	23.5	45	30

(continued)

Table 5 (continued)

(1) Film category	(2) Source title	(3) Original title	(4) Release date Sweden	(5) Imdb ID	(6) Rental revenues (SK)	(7) Film rent (%)	(8) Estimated audience (000s)	(9) HA-Index
D	Sovvagnskonduktören	Der Schlafwagenkontrolleur	08-05-1937	130,240	3,469	23.5	15	25
D	En glad vagabond	The Beloved Vagabond	05-10-1936	27,347	3,066	23.5	15	20
D	Kejsaren av Kalifornien	Der Kaiser von Kalifornien	30-09-1936	27,834	5,130	23.5	20	20
D	På fjället i storm[a]	Die weiße Hölle vom Piz Palü	15-10-1936	20,570	5,407	23.5	25	20
D	Vem är mr Flow	Mister Flow	12-11-1938	27,997	3,719	23.5	15	20
D	Bland bålde riddersmän	When Knights Were Bold	12-01-1937	28,495	1,976	23.5	10	15
D	Lucrecia Borgia	Lucrèce Borgia	24-10-1936	26,660	2,685	23.5	10	15
D	Kampen om Matterhorn	Der Berg ruft!	07-03-1938	28,620	2,571	23.5	10	15
D	Mitt andra jag	Carrefour	16-01-1939	29,972	3,110	23.5	15	15

Source Furhammar (1990, Table 1)

[a] *På fjället i storm* is a rerelease of a Leni Riefenstahl film released initially by SF in December 1930 with the title *Lavinen*

Table 6 Regression equation of the estimated attendances of the 25 Wive films (*Y*) and their HA-Index values (*X*)

Adjusted *R* Square	0.951843902			
Standard Error	15.81806121			
Observations	25			
	Coefficients	*Standard Error*	*t Stat*	*P-value*
Intercept	−20.14634386	5.577265731	−3.612225924	0.001465479
X Variable 1	1.708981977	0.078382186	21.80319351	7.30652E-17

the introduction: both variables fall back on the same real basis, which is the real numbers of audience attendance'.[33]

Having satisfied himself that HA index values adequately reflect the estimates of visits for Wive films, Furhammar, extrapolates the regression equation values found in Table 6 to all films screened in Stockholm cinemas during the 1930s. He terms the dependent variable 'Best guess' (BG) and explains 'Best guess' (BG) of a film's results in terms of audience size in Stockholm follows from the results of the analysis above according to the regression formula: BG = HA × 1.7–20, in which BG calculates best guess of attendance (in thousands) of a film screened in Stockholm during its 'normal' life cycle (not counting matinées, later re-circulations or re-openings of the film)'.

Furhammar was aware of the methodological problems associated with estimating audience size from the rental income returns of such a small number of films. 'If my assumptions about the rental tariffs' proportional relationship with the distribution revenues are incorrect or are not dimensioned correctly, the regression between the HA scale and the actual audience figures will have a systematic flaw independent of the high correlation. If this is the case, the effects of such misrepresentation will imply that the audience numbers in the higher register of the scale are overestimated'.[34]

Despite his concerns about the validity of the assumptions made concerning rental incomes, Furhammar speculated that the national attendance figures for 28 Wive films could be used to extend the analysis to the whole country.[35] He uses the same methods, making different assumptions about rental categories and establishes a high correlation coefficient between national attendances and HA-Values. He conducts the same exercise using 49 SF films and brings the two analyses together, finding robust correlation coefficients (R and R^2).

Furhammar terms his national analysis, as 'secondary'. He was sufficiently doubtful about the SF source material, scaling issues and the assumptions behind the conversion of rental incomes into attendances for him to deliberately restrict his analysis to the Stockholm market only.

[33] Furhammar (1990, p. 10). On page 8 he recognises the possibility that some films might have been 'milked'—kept on the screen even when the audience size was insufficient to warrant this. About this, he argues that there is no way of knowing whether the practice took place or not.

[34] Furhammar (1990, p. 9).

[35] In the source document, three Wive films had national rental figures only.

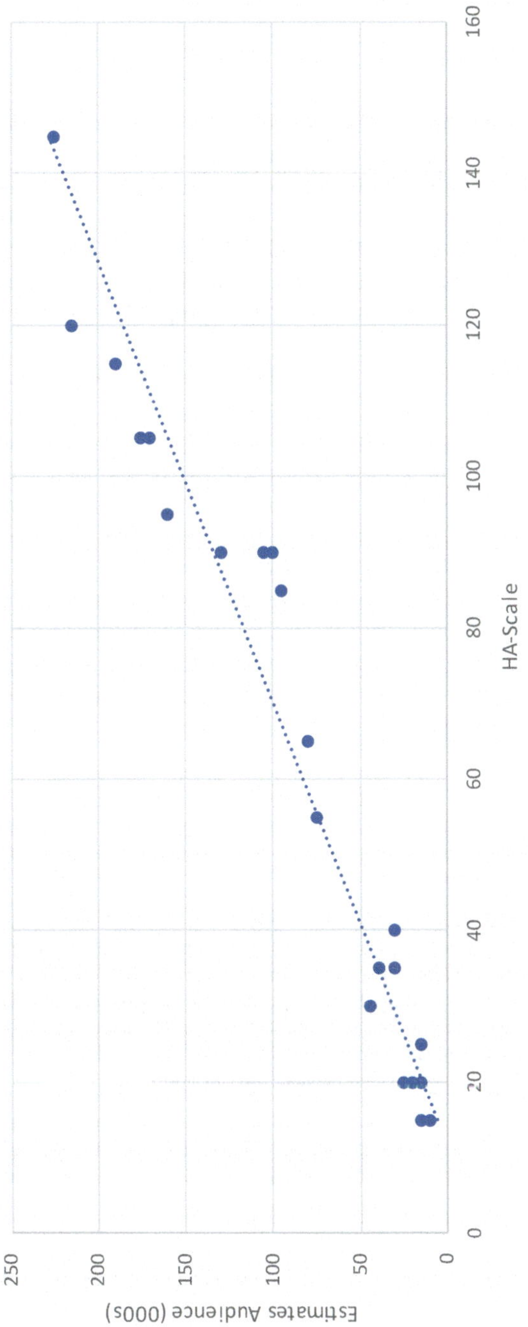

Fig. 3 Scatter and line of best fit

4 Findings

4.1 General

Furhammar's results are reproduced in annual tables found in the Appendix at the end of his report. As mentioned in the introduction, we term this the 'Big Table'. He restricted the population of films to those that generated an HA-Index value of at least 60 (estimated audience size [BG] = 80,000), causing a truncated distribution of 364 films, of which 173 were Swedish (47%) and 142 from Hollywood (39%).[36] Given the number of foreign films released in Stockholm during the decade, depicted in Table 1, Swedish film production represents a small proportion of the film population (7.6%).

Concerned that his results were biased, Furhammar cautions about taking the annual rank order of films too literally. Instead, he argues the tables should be read broadly as a general indication of the order of popularity. 'There is no doubt that *Söder om landsvägen* (1936) (*South of the Highway*), *Kalle på spången* (1939) (*Charlie the Innkeeper*) and *Snövit* (1938) (*Snow White and the Seven Dwarfs*) drew the three largest audiences in Stockholm during the 1930s. There is also no doubt as to the complete failure of, for example, *Bleka greven* (1937) and *Tystnadens hus* (1933) (*House of Silence*)'. He also advises readers against drawing inferences from preferences revealed by the popularity charts, arguing: 'Audience's preferences never appear in "pure" form. Clear overlays including effective marketing, geographic access, and other secondary factors need consideration'.[37] Neither is the audience a homogeneous entity, writing:

> The Stockholm audience was, of course, composed of groups of audiences – actually individuals – with different tastes and preferences. The results produced in the report are not the equivalent of a uniform average Swedish ideology. In several cases, unusually large audience segments have come together to show an interest in particular films, which subsequently become great audience successes.
>
> It is likely that the social structure (in terms of class) would be reflected in the pattern of preferences, if indeed there were instruments available to analyse the results through such categories. Furthermore, it is plausible that several of the popular comedies, which were overall moderate successes, could have had a strong attraction among working-class families and could have performed well in this audience segment, while perceived as too vulgar to attract the middle-class audience.[38] Other films have surely fared well among intellectuals, while not in other audience segments, and hence were economic failures.
>
> A few smaller audience segments have obviously been extremely faithful to their special preferences and have thus contributed by keeping specific genre films in the cinema repertoire. Westerns and horror films were rarely huge audience successes, yet loyal audience segments

[36] The discrepancy between the number of Swedish films found in the Big Table (236) and the sum of the numbers found in Table 1, is explained by the inclusion of the releases of the incomplete 1939 season in the Big Table.

[37] Furhammar (1990, p. 14).

[38] 'folkliga lustspel'.

were large enough to sustain their existence in cinemas specialised in the exhibition of genre films.

Shirley Temple is a good example of how particular audience segments behaved in ways that can lead to confusion in the interpretation of results. Around ten films starring Shirley Temple premiered in cinemas in Stockholm in the 1930s, yet none of the films attracted a sizeable audience. They (probably) attracted a faithful family audience that was not large enough to elevate any of the films to a top position. Yet, taken together, the Shirley Temple films had an unparalleled audience. This example can be compared with her slightly older teenage star colleague Deanna Durbin, who obviously addressed a broader age range of Stockholmers for whom, although she played in fewer films, appeared to be a bigger star.'[39]

4.2 Successful Films

Furhammar identifies 93 foreign films and 40 Swedish films as the decade's most 'successful' films based on the HA-BG method.[40] However, in arriving at this listing, he adopts separate inclusion criteria for foreign and domestic productions. Regarding foreign films, he sets the threshold that a film must attract at least 1.25% of the estimated Stockholm yearly audience. However, he maintains if this criterion were applied to Swedish films, it would result in a couple of seasons in which no Swedish films were represented. To get around this problem, Furhammar used what he termed a three-step 'qualifying scale': '...in the seasons with a total audience in Stockholm of up to 8 million, films with BG values of at least 195 are counted as successful; in the seasons with a total audience of 8–12 million, a successful film is one for which the BG value is equal to or larger than 200; and in seasons with a total audience of more than 12 million, the qualifying limit is set at BG $\geq$ 205. He argued that this progression follows naturally from the distribution of the data itself'.[41]

His dual method does not always produce coherent results. Foreign films classified by Furhammar as 'successful' may have attracted a smaller audience than domestic films not meeting the criteria. For instance, in the 1935–6 season, the 'successful' Astaire-Rogers film *Top Hat* generated HA-BG values of 95 and 140 (140,000), respectively. In that year, seven Swedish-made films have higher index scores but are not classified in the 'Big Table' as 'successful'—they are not presented in an upper-case format.

For this reason, we do not follow Furhammar's listing of 'successful' films but rather adapt the 'Big Table' by identifying the annual Top 20 movies when measured by their HA-BG Index values, irrespective of their national origins.[42] These films,

---

[39] Furhammar (1990, pp. 14–15).

[40] He denotes these by presenting them in upper case letters in the Big Table. The count of Swedish 'Successful' films differs quite dramatically from their Top 20 representation, with Furhammar awarding this accolade to a mere 40 films, whereas 130 Swedish films are listed in the annual Top 20 tables. Conversely, Hollywood productions move in the other direction but only marginally, from 71 'successes' to 66 Top 20 films'.

[41] Furhammar (1990, p. 23).

[42] In the case of the 1929–30 season, this amounted to 19 films only.

Table 7 Annual Top 20 characteristics by nationality

	Denmark			France		
(1) Year	(2) Films	(3) Aggregated HA-Index	(4) Market share	(5) Films	(6) Aggregated HA-Index	(7) Market share
1929	1	65	0.05			
1930	1	60	0.04			
1931	1	70	0.04			
1932			0			
1933			0			
1934			0	1	90	0.04
1935			0	1	120	0.05
1936			0			
1937	1	120	0.05			
1938			0	2	235	0.10
1939			0			
Totals	4	315	0.01	4	445	0.02

(continued)

Table 7 (continued)

Germany			Sweden		
(8) Films	(9) Aggregated HA-Index	(10) Market share	(11) Films	(12) Aggregated HA-Index	(13) Market share
1	65	0.05	8	485	0.34
			9	810	0.48
4	340	0.18	11	1,145	0.61
1	80	0.04	12	1,355	0.64
2	200	0.10	13	1,405	0.67
			13	1,470	0.66
			13	1,615	0.72
			14	1,790	0.72
			10	1,225	0.46
1	120	0.05	13	1,730	0.71
			14	1,720	0.77
9	805	0.03	130	14,750	0.63

(continued)

Table 7 (continued)

United Kingdom			United States				
(14) Films	(15) Aggregated HA-Index	(16) Market share	(17) Films	(18) Aggregated HA-Index	(19) Market share	(20) Total films	(21) Total H-A Index
1	30	0.02	8	770	0.54	19	1,415
			10	815	0.48	20	1,685
			4	335	0.18	20	1,890
			7	675	0.32	20	2,110
			5	480	0.23	20	2,085
			6	770	0.34	19	2,240
1	95	0.04	5	540	0.24	19	2,250
			6	700	0.28	20	2,490
			9	1,300	0.49	20	2,645
1	110	0.05	3	480	0.20	18	2,440
3	290	0.13	3	215	0.10	20	2,225
6	525	0.02	66	7080	0.30	215	23,475

Source Furhammar (1990, Appendix)
Note Only 19 films are listed in the Appendix for the 1929–1930 season

listed in the Appendix to this chapter, are the 'hits' of their respective seasons—movies that circulated more intensely and were screened for longer runs. Based on the separation of these films into national categories, Table 7 demonstrates the dominant position of Swedish cinema, taking a three-fifths share of the expanding Top 20 market over the 11 years 1929–1939, broadly rising annually and culminating in a 77% share in 1939. The United States follows with approximately a one-third share, varying dramatically over the last three years. Other European countries make a marginal contribution to the listings of popular films.

Given the much smaller body of Swedish film releases and Furhammar's claim that no films were made in Sweden during the first half of 1929, the apparent popularity of Swedish films appears remarkable.[43] Contrasting this success with the ubiquity of the Hollywood product, Furhammar claims that 'The Swedish repertoire offered an entirely different set of attractions'.[44]

From the Top 20 listings, Table 8 identifies the seven production companies that generated aggregate HA-Index scores of 1,000 or more. The annual sum of HA-Index values (column 1) shows a steady growth throughout the 1930s, keeping with the sale of tickets shown in Table 1. In Table 8, three companies overshadow 'hit' production—the vertically integrated Swedish companies Svensk Filmindustri and Europafilm, and the Hollywood giant MGM, each of which accumulated more than 10% over the decade of the Top 20 market share. These are joined in the table by one other Hollywood producer (Paramount) and three Swedish producers, Ire, Minerva and Wive, each of which achieves shares between 4 and 6%.[45] They consistently take over 50% share of the Top 20 markets between them. It is interesting to note that none of the Swedish language films made in the Joinville studios in Paris by the Paramount company, referred to by Furhammar as the 'Joinville Films', feature in any of the Top 20 listings.

4.3 Audience Tastes

Furhammar's first observation about the list of foreign 'successful' films is that it radically differs from the movies commonly regarded as the period's masterpieces in established film historiography.[46] 'That the audiences' tastes differed from elite intellectuals and critics is not news and hardly sensational. It does, however, highlight a general reflection that values in the academic context rely on tradition and

[43] For instance, even with quota legislation in operation, British films achieved only a 24% market share in Great Britain during the years 1932–1937 (Sedgwick, 2000, Table 4.4).

[44] Furhammar (1990, p. 26).

[45] Minerva was a subsidiary production company to Svensk Filmindustri which formed in 1929 to restructure/reorganise inhouse production. It was disassembled in 1933 in a new company reorganisation that followed in the wake of the collapse of the business empire built by Ivar Kreuger.

[46] Szekeres (1984).

Table 8 Annual shares of the Top 20 markets by production studio

		Europa Film		Irefilm		Svensk Filmindustri		Wive		Minerva		MGM		Paramount	
Year	(1) Sum of HA-Index	(2) Aggregate HA-Index	(3) Total Films	(4) Aggregate HA-Index	(5) Total Films	(6) Aggregate HA-Index	(7) Total films	(8) Aggregate HA-Index	(9) Total Films	(10) Aggregate HA-Index	(11) Total Films	(12) Aggregate HA-Index	(13) Total Films	(14) Aggregate HA-Index	(15) Total Films
1929	1,415					330	4			95	2	320	4	270	2
1930	1,685									595	6	245	3	210	3
1931	1,890	160	2			100	1			695	6	65	1	185	2
1932	2,110	320	3							360	3	425	4	250	3
1933	2,085	205	2			615	5	120	1			80	1	185	2
1934	2,330	415	3			500	4	205	2			250	2	240	2
1935	2,370	380	3	260	2	355	3	105	1			210	2		
1936	2,490	345	2	230	2	405	3	240	2			430	3	90	1
1937	2,645	350	3	265	2	245	2	110	1			645	4		
1938	2,675	280	2	140	1	525	4	150	1			110	1		
1939	2,225	370	2	105	1	370	3	145	1			175	2	70	1
Total	23,920	2,825	22	1,000	8	3,445	29	1,075	9	1,745	17	2,955	27	1,500	16

Source Furhammar (1990, Appendix)
Note The market in 1939 (1939–1940) is limited because HA statistics are not collected beyond Christmas 1939, thus underrepresenting the popularity of films that extend into 1940 (Furhammar, 1990, 43)

narrow insight. There are likely masterpieces among the forgotten successful films that deserve a re-evaluation.[47]

However, it worried Furhammar that of the 160 films identified by *Film Facts* as the most successful in The North American market, only 60 generated HA-Index scores of 60 and above (BG audiences of 80,000 or more).[48] He gave examples of the Astaire-Rogers musicals made during the 1930s, of which only *Top Hat* made an annual Top 20. Similarly, just two of Shirley Temple films—*Little Colonel* and *Sunny Side Up*—were included in the Big Table, and neither of these made a Top 20 cut. Finally, none of the Bette Davis films released by Warner Bros./First National featured in the Big Table.

In his chapter in this book, Peter Miskell shows that those Hollywood films with a marked foreign orientation did better in international markets than in the US domestic market. His thesis is indeed illustrated by the success of the films of Greta Garbo in the Stockholm market; all 14 MGM productions in which she starred during the 1930s took Top 20 berths, many of which had central European settings.

Furhammar provides evidence of differences between the tastes of Stockholm and American audiences by examining popular directors and male and female stars. Table 9 lists directors of annual Top 20 films ranked by aggregate HA-Index scores. Employing the threshold of at least three Top 20 films, the list is dominated by Swedish directors. Notably, many more famous Hollywood directors lie in the bottom half of the list.

A similar exercise is carried out for the top-ranking stars. Comprising the top 20 stars of Top 20 films, Table 10 counts the number of appearances made by each as first or second-named star and the respective HA-Index values of the movies they appeared in. Swedish stars dominate the table. The HA-Index can be seen as a kind of power index. The most consistent performance is MGM's Swedish star Greta Garbo with 14 Top 20 lead appearances. The other five top berths in Table 9 comprised Swedish stars in Swedish productions.

The two other Hollywood stars featured in Table 10 are Maurice Chevalier and Jeanette MacDonald (whom Furhammar refers to as the '…brightest shining truly foreign film star'.[49] They share four films as co-stars (*Love Me Tonight, One Hour with You, The Love Parade, The Merry Widow*). Ranked by their HA-Index score, Hollywood stars listed immediately outside of the Top 20 are Gary Cooper (24th), Clark Gable (26th), Claudette Colbert (27th) and Charles Boyer (28th). Deanna Durbin, who appeared in three of Furhammar's 'successful' films and thought a bigger star than Shirley Temple, is ranked 38th. Of the female stars, Furhammar comments: 'It is striking to note that none of the film stars that were great attractions to the audience in Stockholm at the time, Greta Garbo, Jeanette MacDonald, and Deanna Durbin, had equivalent status in the USA'.

Switching perspective to those stars most popular in the United States, '…Shirley Temple was the greatest star of the 1930s in the USA, yet she was not as great an

---

[47] Furhammar (1990, p. 24).

[48] Steinberg (1990, pp. 17–19).

[49] Furhammar (1990, p. 25).

Table 9 The most successful directors, 1929–1939

Director	HA-Index (aggregate)	Films
Gustaf Molander	2,255	19
Schamyl Bauman	1,740	14
Sigurd Wallén	1,280	12
Gustaf Edgren	1,365	11
Ivar Johansson	905	9
Per-Axel Branner	795	8
Ragnar Arvedson	760	6
Weyler Hildebrand	730	6
Anders Henrikson	615	5
Clarence Brown	525	5
Ernst Lubitsch	510	5
Edvin Adolphson	395	4
Gösta Rodin	435	4
Robert Z Leonard	565	4
Cecil B DeMille	235	3
Emil A. Pehrsson	515	3
Frank Capra	310	3
Lau Lauritzen	195	3
Paul Merzbach	335	3
Rouben Mamoulian	300	3
Sölve Cederstrand	345	3

Source Furhammar (1990, Appendix)

attraction to the Stockholm audience. Neither was Joan Crawford, Marie Dressler, Sonia Heine, Mae West and Norma Shearer'.

Of the male stars, Furhammar comments: 'Neither Chevalier (who worked in Hollywood for most of the decade) nor Boyer was as attractive to an American audience.[50] Conversely, the great American stars Will Rogers and Wallace Beery were not of particular interest to Stockholm audiences. From the European film industry, only Robert Donat has more than one success towards the end of the period in two MGM British films—*The Citadel* and *Goodbye Mr Chips*'.[51]

In his discussion of Swedish stars, Furhammar comments: '...only a few of those listed had real marketable star status: Fridolf Rhudin (who died in 1935), Edvard Persson, Adolf Jahr and Elof Ahrle, among the men and of the women, only Tutta Rolf and Ingrid Bergman (whose fame came toward the end of the decade)'. However, the list does allow a comparison to be made between domestic and foreign stars. He continues: 'If you place Dagmar Ebbesen and Edvard Persson next to Jeanette

[50] See Steinberg, p. 57.

[51] Furhammar (1990, p. 25).

Table 10 The most successful stars, 1929–1939

Stars	Rank	(1) Star 1 Films	(2) Star 2 Films	(3) Staring films	(4) Sum of HA 1	(5) Sum of HA 2	(6) Total HA
Edvard Persson	1	9	2	11	1,410	245	1,655
Sigurd Wallén	2	9	6	15	955	630	1,585
Greta Garbo	3	14		14	1,415	0	1,415
Tutta Rolf	4	9	2	11	1,155	195	1,350
Adolf Jahr	5	10		10	1,285	0	1,285
Fridolf Rhudin	6	9		9	1,070	0	1,070
Jeanette MacDonald	7	3	5	8	410	580	990
Maurice Chevalier	8	8		8	820	0	820
Karin Swanström	9	4	3	7	390	365	755
Thor Modéen	10	5	2	7	485	235	720
Dagmar Ebbesen	11	2	4	6	210	495	705
Åke Söderblom	12	3		3	415	225	640
Ingrid Bergman	13	1	4	5	170	455	625
Gideon Wahlberg	14	2	3	5	245	360	605
Elof Ahrle	15	2	2	4	295	280	575
Edvin Adolphson	16	5	1	6	470	90	560
Bengt Djurberg	17	2		2	140	405	545
Gösta Ekman	18	3	1	4	360	140	500
Sture Lagerwall	19	3	1	4	355	140	495
Victor Sjöström	20	4		4	455	0	455

Source Furhammar (1990, Appendix)

Table 11 Genre categorisation of foreign 'Successful' films

Genre	Films
Musical, operetta, show, saga	30
Screwball comedy, farce	15
Action-adventure	14
Romantic melodrama	22
Fiction films in an exotic setting	12
Fiction films in an historical setting	22
Biopics	6
Unclassified	6
Total	127

Source Furhammar (1990, p. 26)
Note The hybrid nature of genre classification of the 93 'successful' films sums to 127 genre categorisations

MacDonald and Maurice Chevalier as symbols of the preferences of the Stockholm 1930s audiences, it is apparent that they represent essentially different kinds of attractions'.[52] Ebbesen and Persson represent a Swedish colloquial, gruff though good-hearted couple, while the foreign stars are symbols of a glamorous lifestyle in a fictitious other world (Fig. 4).

For Furhammar, Swedish films and the stars that appeared in them constituted a different type of film entertainment when compared with foreign films. He categorises the 93 foreign 'successful' films into seven categories: Musicals, Romantic Melodrama, Fiction Films in Historical Settings, Fiction Films in Exotic Settings, Screwball Comedies and Action-Adventure Films. His breakdown is shown in Table 11. Based on this genre analysis Furhammar contends that of foreign films, audiences favoured those that offered escapism 'to fictional worlds far removed from any form of psychological realism, whether distant in time, place or living conditions'.[53] In an analysis of the 40 domestic 'successful' films of the period using the same genre categories, Furhammar shows that their attraction, on the contrary, relied on cultural proximity. All but one of the films were comedies specific to domestic audiences and markedly different from films made outside of Sweden.[54] An exception to this was *Valfångare*, released as a drama in November 1939.[55]

[52] Furhammar (1990, p. 27).

[53] Furhammar (1990, p. 26).

[54] Furhammar (1990, p. 28) makes a special note of Swedish military farces as sub-genre, of which six out of ten were 'successful'. There was no equivalent genre or sub-genre among the foreign films.

[55] *Valfångare* was in many ways an exceptional film. It was Svensk Filmindustri's most expensive 1930s production, due to a series of unexpected events during production. It became one of the company's largest economic failures. The total box office revenues didn't match up to the expectations, despite optimistic figures from its initial weeks on the repertoire in Stockholm. It is possible that the film is an example of 'milking', which would explain its high HA-values. It is also possible that it was a success in Stockholm and not in the countryside.

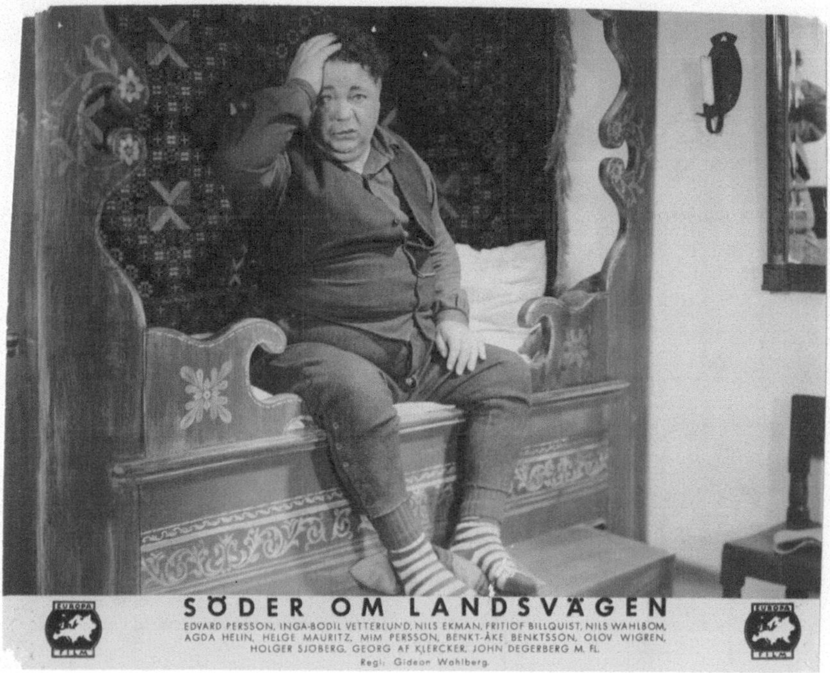

Fig. 4 Edvard Persson in a still from *Söder om landsvägen* (1936) (*South of the highway*) (*Source* The Swedish Film Institute Stills and Posters Archive)

Film historian Tytti Soila suggests a strong affiliation between the 'exceptionally popular' outdoor summer stage tradition of vaudeville, comedy and humorous plays, and the Swedish films of the 1930s.[56] A stage play that had been successful in the parks could be transposed to film with the crew intact.[57] Furthermore, accomplished performers in the vaudeville tradition were recruited from the provinces to act in films anchored in specific regional and often rural settings. Two of the most successful stars based upon Annual Top 20 films of the 1930s, Edvard Persson and Fridolf Rhudin, are prominent examples.

It was common for actors and actresses to play the same roles throughout their careers.[58] Dagmar Ebbesen is a good example. In 1921 Ebbesen was offered the lead role as a maid in the stage comedy, *Hemslavinnor*, at a theatre in Stockholm. The play became a huge success, and Ebbesen played the maid Christiane on stage in more than 500 performances and three adaptations for cinema—in 1923, 1933 and 1944. She was cast in similar roles on stage and in films; her legacy thus became

---

56 Soila (1998, p. 202). As with Furhammar (1990, 2003), Soila doesn't consider differences over time. For an analysis of different forms of comedy and thematic changes in the Swedish films of the 1930s, see Qvist (1995a, 1995b).

57 Qvist (1995a, p. 81).

58 Soila (1998, p. 168).

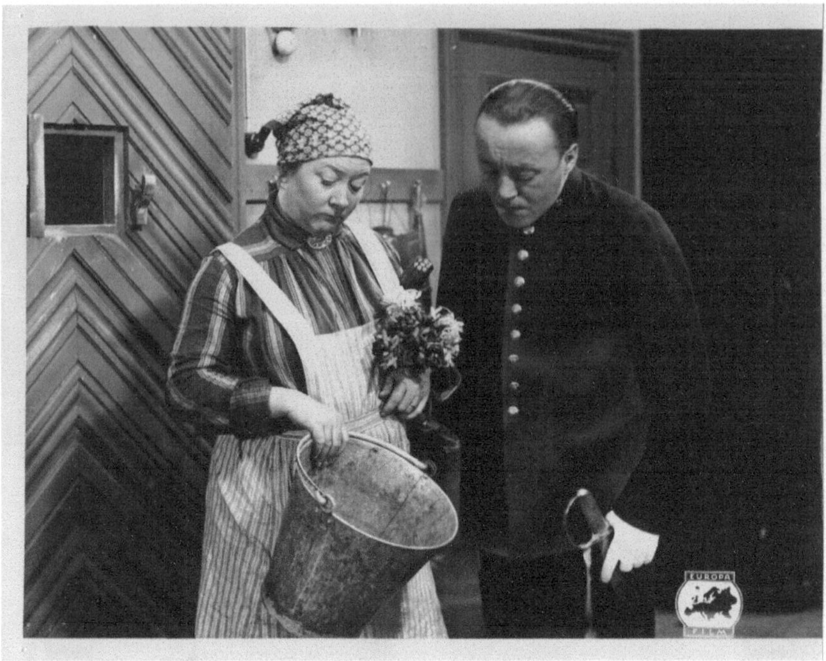

Fig. 5 Dagmar Ebbesen and Fridolf Rhudin in a still from *Hemliga Svensson* (1933) (*Source* The Swedish Film Institute Stills and Posters Archive)

associated with a stern yet righteous housekeeper or maid. Fridolf Rhudin, Edvard Persson and Sigurd Wallén were likewise type cast (Fig. 5).[59]

However, of the top male performers, Adolf Jahr's screen persona differs from the others in being less conformist. Jahr personified an athletic, polite and gentlemanly ideal, often carrying an air of elegance and romance. However, he could cross class boundaries, performing in alternative roles with apparent ease.[60] Also worth noting in this context, the high-ranking female actress, Tutta Rolf, is second only to Greta Garbo in audience popularity. Rolf came to Sweden from Norway in the early

[59] Soila describes Rhudin's onscreen persona thus: 'In his films Rhudin plays the part of an innocent country boy who is harassed by other, more clever types. It is always Rhudin who wins the game, however, through his cheerful manner (and sense of humour).' Persson's film persona was constructed as a jovial and reassuring patriarch with an 'impressive physique and just the right mixture of local patriotic conservatism and sentimentality.' Soila (1998, p. 202). Sigurd Wallén often played a man-of-the-people, shrewd yet kind-hearted. In history books he is mentioned predominantly for his political films with Social democratic (or more leftist) sympathies. Among the top-ranking successful actors of the decade, Sigurd Wallén stands out as he is also ranked as one of the most successful film directors of the 1930s. His significance in the industry has yet to be explored.

[60] Qvist, Per Olof, 'Adolf Jahr', Svensk Filmdatabas. Accessed 2021/04/09.

1930s. She played 'dashing young-girl roles' in which she transgressed conventional gender expectations, breaking with the domestic industry's stereotypical portrayal of women.[61]

5 Discussion

In 1998, film scholars Tytti Soila, Astrid Söderbergh Widding and Gunnar Iversen reflected on research about national film production in the Nordic countries. Historical overviews have been written mainly in a masterpiece tradition, they contend, with a focus of interest on periods in which great directors and stars came to the fore.[62] For this reason, the films of the 1930s are largely overlooked and are heavily critiqued for their popularism.[63]

Qvist has published the most comprehensive study of Swedish cinema of the 1930s. In *Folkhemmets bilder: Modernisering, motstånd och mentalitet i den svenska 30-talsfilmen*, Qvist claims that the mentality represented in the movies of the 1930s is a clue to understanding the transformation of Sweden into a modern welfare state and the foundation of the new ideal society (the *folkhem*). Furthermore, Qvist challenges a set of related propositions about the period's cinema put forth by Leif Furhammar in two early publications.[64] Qvist contests the idea that production quality was lower than in any other period in Swedish cinema history. For him, the domestic industry could be accurately described as a 'Klondike period'.[65]

Qvist argues that ambivalence towards modernisation permeates these films. On the one hand, most films have a 'strong tendency' to 'preach a gospel of order and discipline', harmonising with the ideological ambitions of organised worker movements that dominated political discourse.[66] On the other hand, a more disrespectful

61 Soila (1998, p. 168).

62 Soila (1998, pp. 5–6).

63 Contemporary and popular accounts of 1930s Swedish cinema include Bornebusch (1935), Björklund (1945), Schildt (1970), and Rodin (1976). An overview of the representation of Jews and other ethnic outsiders in Swedish film devotes a chapter to the pervasive occurrence of negative stereotypical representations of Jewish characters in the films of the 1930s. The most "heavy-handed caricatures" are found in *Trötte Teodor* (Edgren, 1931), *Söderkåkar* (Hildebrand, 1932), *Kära släkten* (Molander, 1933) and *Pettersson & Bendel* (Branner, 1933), all of which are among the top-ranking films of their season. In the second half of the decade the depiction of Jewish characters is more nuanced (Wright, 1998). The films of Edvard Persson and his persona are analysed in Jerselius (1987). An investigation of speech, translation, and cultural identity in the reception of the 'Joinville films', shows how the Swedish language version of *Marius* (Korda, 1931) is integrated into the domestic entertainment culture, and how it strikes a balance between the foreign and the local (Rossholm, 2006). Taking a broader, cultural approach, a doctoral dissertation explores interfaces at which film, visual culture and commercial publicity merged in 1930s Stockholm (Habel, 2002).

64 Furhammar (1979, 1983).

65 Qvist (1995, pp. 13–14).

66 Qvist (1995, p. 23).

attitude with roots in a rural, working-class culture also prevailed. Qvist proposes that the aesthetics of disrespect towards social democratic hegemonic values provoked critics and scholars such as Furhammar, who mistook the aesthetics for an expression of poor quality and bad taste.[67]

Though Qvist acknowledges Furhammar's audience study in his monograph, it has little impact on his analysis, shaped by the total corpus of films of the period. Soila's feminist study of 1930s Swedish films, on the contrary, demonstrates how the results of Furhammar's report can be used to produce innovative research. From a selection of 63 Swedish movies with an HA-value of 115 and above, Soila creates a taxonomy of female stereotypes to analyse their ideological function in the diegetic social sphere of the film. She approaches audience preferences, combining quantitative content analysis with post-structuralist analysis. For Soila, the most popular movies represent a dominant patriarchal discourse. Yet, she also discerns what she terms 'harassed discourses' in which women are troubled by, and develop resistance to, societal expectations.[68]

In their overview of Nordic national Cinemas, Soila, Söderbergh Widding, and Iversen contended that 'popularity is an important criterion in discussing national cinema'.[69] Yet, drawing on secondary sources to construct the respective while interconnected histories, the grounds for assessing the popularity of films remains vague.

6 Conclusion

Furhammar developed a set of quantitative tools, which he used as a platform to conduct 'qualitative research operations'.[70] He sought to investigate film popularity empirically rather than accept established cannons of authority on the subject. In doing this, he turned the 'normal' research perspective of Film Studies on its head, prioritising the choices of the film audiences within a specific national-historical production context rather than film production decisions. In this way, Furhammar's report offers a means to assess the 'national' film culture at large in Stockholm in the 1930s.[71] His approach, concerns, methods and findings deserve greater recognition. He worked from the premise that audiences made free choices between films. While

[67] Ibid. Soila (1998, p. 178).

[68] In two films, *Intermezzo* (Gustaf Molander, 1936) and *En kvinnas ansik*te (*A Woman's Face*, Gustaf Molander, 1938) the leading female characters, both played by Ingrid Bergman, couldn't be easily categorised, and are therefore granted a closer analysis as representatives of, what Soila coins, a 'harassed discourse'. Soila (1991).

[69] Soila (1998, p. 6).

[70] Furhammar (1990, p. 14).

[71] Higson (1989). Accessed October 29, 2021. https://search-ebscohost-com.db.ub.oru.se/login.aspx?direct=true&db=fah&AN=BFLI910762630069680&site=ehost-live.

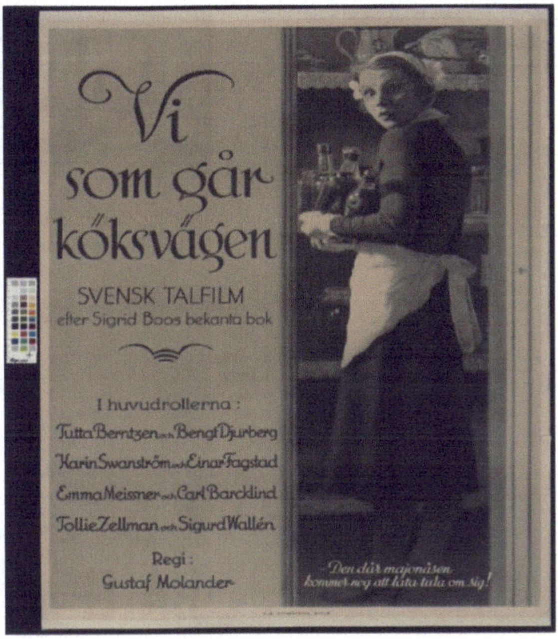

Fig. 6 Poster, *Vi som går köksvägen* (1933) (*Source* The Swedish Film Institute Stills and Posters Archive)

recognising that these could be influenced by advertising, peer group pressure and other social pressures, he nevertheless believed that audience size was the best gauge of film preferences. His methods were elaborate and thorough, and they have been replicated and confirmed in this chapter where the data allowed it.

While his approach to the most popular films—what he termed 'successes'—is not altogether transparent, his annual listings in what we term the 'Big Table' found at the end of his report provided sufficient information for these authors to construct an alternative listing. At the end of this chapter, we produce annual Top 20 tables based simply upon the size of the estimated audience. Reflectively, Furhammar divided the preferences of Stockholm audiences into two parts. Regarding 'successful' foreign films, '…the Stockholm audience in the 1930s preferred films that offer escapism into attractive fictional worlds with great psychological distance in terms of time, space or conditions-of-life'.[72] 'In contrast (he writes), 'domestic escapism was closer to contemporary life'. Domesticity was central to the 40 'successful' films made in Sweden, in which work and occupation drove character development (in almost all); alcohol consumption (in at least half); and the centrality of the family (in half) (Figs. 6, 7, 8, and 9).[73]

---

[72] Furhammar (1990, p. 26).

[73] Furhammar (1990, p. 28).

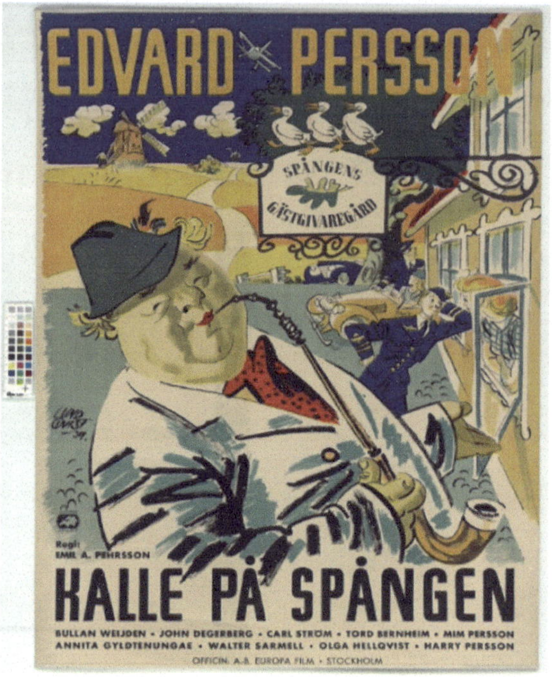

Fig. 7 Poster, *Kalle på spången* (1939) (*Source* The Swedish Film Institute Stills and Posters Archive)

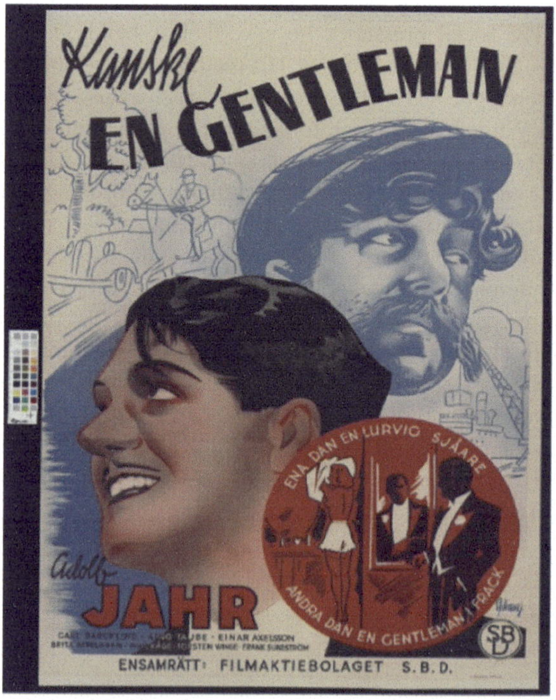

Fig. 8 Poster, *Kanske en gentleman* (1935) (*Source* The Swedish Film Institute Stills and Posters Archive)

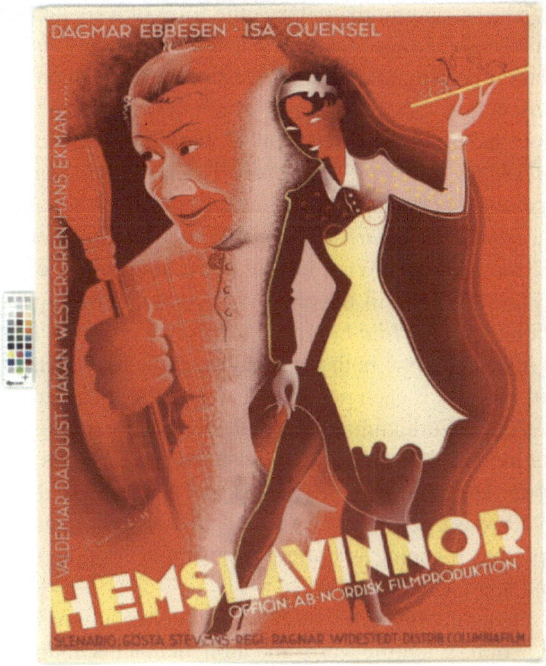

Fig. 9 Poster, *Hemslavinnor* (1933) (*Source* The Swedish Film Institute Stills and Posters Archive)

Of these, Furhammar identifies two recurring motifs, which, while not having 'the more solid contours of genre, do have a strange thematic consistency'. The first, he writes '…concerns community and social cohesion, usually with a core group in the lower middle class or below, yet which take place at several levels simultaneously: male bonding, family cohesion, neighbourhood loyalty, professional community, fraternisation within class boundaries, and regional and national affinity are key terms that continuously recur. It's about solidarity in the face of threats toward social cohesion, economic security, friendship, and honour. Yet it is also about a striving to expand social networks, about caring and collective responsibility, all of it woven into the undisciplined structure of popular comedy'.[74] Of the 34 Swedish successful films released from the autumn of 1932, at least 13 belonged to this motif group (not counting the group-oriented military comedies). For Furhammar, this concentration can be viewed as a response to the social crisis brought about by the collapse of the Kreuger industrial and financial empire in 1932.[75]

[74] Furhammar (1990, p. 29).

[75] Furhammar refers to these films as 'folkhemsidealiserande filmer'. 'Folkhemmet' is a term coined by Social Democrat (later two-time Prime Minister) Per Albin Hansson in a radio speech in 1928. The term was used by the Social Democratic Party to refer to their vision of an ideal welfare society (an inclusive peoples' home) governed by neutrality and reformist social corporatism.

The second motif '...takes the form of a social experiment with radical lifestyle changes or swaps—mainly but not exclusively regarding transgressions of social class. The critical dramatic question in these films is: What happens if you place a person in a social context to which they are alien? Can the spoiled upper-class girl from the city manage the toil of working in service in the countryside (*Vi som går köksvägen*, (*Servant's Entrance*))? Can the docker become a socialite (*Kanske en gentleman*, (*Perhaps a Gentleman*))? Can the low-born become king (*Karl Fredrik regerar*, (*Karl Fredrik Reigns*))? What happens when a bourgeois becomes Bolshevik (*Ryska snuvan*)? What happens if a man must do a women's job (*Herr husassistenten*)? What will happen if the company manager and the caretaker swap place (*Landstormens lilla Lotta*)?' Furhammar contends that the answer to these questions is affirmative, '...both the higher and the lower classes fare well in their new roles, but it is best if each person remains in the social group where they belong'.[76]

Again, Furhammar finds evidence of this among the most popular Swedish films, stating that 17 of the 40 Swedish successful films have this motif at their dramatic core. The motif also makes sense from a social-psychological perspective. The 1930s was a period when social class transgressions and social emancipation seemed possible, for some as a future opportunity, for others perhaps as a source of insecurity and approaching threat.

In summarising his research and contribution, Furhammar personally was sceptical of its scientific worth and thought that his findings better represented the general order of popularity and that not too much attention should be given to minor differences in the ranked order of films per se. The reason for this lies in the degree of measuring error that results from treating films screened at a particular cinema during one specific month as equivalents—of equal attractiveness. Clearly, this is not the case. Like POPSTAT, his method implicitly creates relative weights for all cinemas—in his case, based upon their respective seating capacities. Unlike POPSTAT, his method does not require him to tackle the thorny issue of cinema prices since audience size, rather than box office, is his preferred measure. That is, two cinemas in Stockholm with the same seating capacity will have identical weights, irrespective of their place in the cinema hierarchy—whether first or last run. He judged his method as too imprecise and questioned whether its utility was worth the effort entailed. This chapter serves to applaud the pioneering contribution that Furhammar made to audience research. It serves as a foundation for much historical research undertaken in recent years concerned with popular cinema.

[76] Furhammar (1990, p. 30).

Appendix: Annual Top 20 Films

Rank	HA-score	BG-score	Swedish title in Furhammar's list	Original title (Imdb)	IMDB id	Principal nationality	Principal production company	Distribution company	Director	Star 1	Star 2
1929–1930 season											
1	145	225	Prinsgemålen	The Love Parade	tt0020112	USA	Paramount		Ernst Lubitsch	Maurice Chevalier	Jeanette MacDonald
2	135	210	Säg det i toner	Säg det i toner	tt0020473	Sweden	AB Svensk Filmindustri	AB Svensk Filmindustri	J. Julius	Elisabeth Frisk	Håkan Westergren
3	125	195	Paris, Paris	Innocents of Paris	tt0020026	USA	Paramount		Richard Walace	Maurice Chevalier	
4	120	185	Konstgjorda Svensson	Konstgjorda Svensson	tt0020068	Sweden	AB Svensk Filmindustri	AB Svensk Filmindustri	Gustaf Edgren	Fridolf Rhudin	Brita Appelgren
5	105	160	Rio Rita	Rio Rita	tt0020332	USA	RKO		Luther Reed	Bebe Daniels	John Boles
6	105	160	Gröna hatten	A Woman of Affairs	tt0019591	USA	MGM	Metro	Clarence Brown	Greta Garbo	John Gilbert
7	85	125	Söderhavets sång	The Pagan	tt0020253	USA	MGM	Metro	WS Van Dyke	Ramon Navaro	Renee Adoree
8	75	110	Mannen med järnmasken	The Iron Mask	tt0020030	USA	Elton Corporation	United Artists	Allan Dwan	Belle Bennett	Marguerite De La Motte
9	70	100	Bleka grevens bröllop	Spite Marriage	tt0020442	USA	MGM	Metro	Edward Sedgwick	Buster Keaton	Dorothy Sebastian
10	65	90	Moster Malins millioner	Højt paa en Kvist	tt0123899	Denmark	A/S Dansk Filmindustri Palladium	National Film AB	Lau Lauritzen	Carl Schenstrøm	Harald Madsen

(continued)

(continued)

Rank	HA-score	BG-score	Swedish title in Furhammar's list	Original title (Imdb)	IMDB id	Principal nationality	Principal production company	Distribution company	Director	Star 1	Star 2
11	65	90	Dig har jag kär	Dich hab ich geliebt	tt0020675	Germany	Aafa		Rudolf Walther-Fein	Mady Chris	Walter Jankuhn
12	60	80	Norrlänningar	Norrlänningar	tt0021186	Sweden	Film AB Minerva	AB Svensk Filmindustri	Theodor Berthels	Elisabeth Frisk	Harry Ahlin
13	60	80	En kvinnas moral	The Single Standard	tt0020410	USA	MGM	Metro	John S Robertson	Greta Garbo	Nils Asther
14	45	55	Ville Andesons äventyr	Ville Andesons äventyr	tt0020554	Sweden	Filmfred Produktion	AB Fredrik Andersons Filmbyrå	Sigurd Wallén	Sune Holmqvist	Carl Hagman
15	45	55	Den starkaste	Den starkaste	tt0020450	Sweden	AB Svensk Filmindustri	AB Svensk Filmindustri	Alf Sjöberg	Bengt Djurberg	Anders Henrikson
16	35	40	Rågens rike	Rågens rike	tt0020352	Sweden	Tellus Film	AB Fribergs Filmbyrå	Ivar Johansson	Margit Manstad	Eric Laurent
17	35	40	Hjärtats triumf	Hjärtats triumf	tt0019990	Sweden	Film AB Minerva	AB Svensk Filmindustri	Gustaf Molander	Carl Brisson	Anna Lindahl
18	30	Not given	Fången 53	A Cottage on Dartmoor	tt0020793	UK	British Instructional Films	AB Svensk Filmindustri	Anthony Asquith	Uno Henning	Norah Baring
19	10	Not given	Farornas ö	Farornas ö	tt13194258	Sweden	Nordenskiöld-Film	AB Fribergs Filmbyrå	Sten Nordenskiöld		

(continued)

(continued)

Rank	HA-score	BG-score	Swedish title in Furhammar's list	Original title (Imdb)	IMDB id	Principal nationality	Principal production company	Distribution company	Director	Star 1	Star 2
1930–1931 season											
1	140	220	Kronans kavaljerer		tt0021034	Sweden	Film AB Minerva	AB Svensk Filmindustri	Gustaf Edgren	Fridolf Rhudin	Weyler Hildebrand
2	140	220	Stadens ljus	City Lights	tt0021749	USA	Charles Chaplin Film Corp	United Artists AB	Charles Chaplin	Charles Chaplin	Virginia Cherrill
3	105	160	Charlotte Löwensköld	Charlotte Löwensköld	tt0020755	Sweden	Film AB Minerva	AB Svensk Filmindustri	Gustaf Molander	Pauline Brunius	Gertrud Pålsson-Wettergren
4	105	160	Trader Horn	Trader Horn	tt0022495	USA	MGM	Metro	WS Van Dyke	Harry Carey	Edwina Booth
5	95	140	För hennes skull	For Her Sake	tt0020912	Sweden	Film AB Minerva	AB Svensk Filmindustri	Paul Merzbach	Gösta Ekman	Inga Tidblad
6	90	135	Markurells i Wadköping	Father and Son	tt0022126	Sweden	Film AB Minerva	AB Svensk Filmindustri	Victor Sjöström	Victor Sjöström	Pauline Brunius
7	85	125	Röda Dagen	The Red Day	tt0022334	Sweden	Film AB Minerva	AB Svensk Filmindustri	Gustaf Edgren	Sigurd Wallén	Dagmar Ebbesen
8	80	115	Fridas Visor	Frida's Songs	tt0020905	Sweden	Film AB Minerva	AB Svensk Filmindustri	Gustaf Molander	Elisabeth Frisk	Bengt Djurberg
9	80	115	Anna Christie	Anna Christie	tt0020641	USA	MGM	Metro	Clarence Brown	Greta Garbo	Charles Pickford
10	80	115	På västfronten intet nytt	All Quiet on the Western Front	tt0020629	USA	Universal	Universal	Lewis Milestone	Lew Ayres	Louis Wolheim

(continued)

(continued)

Rank	HA-score	BG-score	Swedish title in Furhammar's list	Original title (Imdb)	IMDB id	Principal nationality	Principal production company	Distribution company	Director	Star 1	Star 2
11	75	110	Flottans lilla fästmö	na	tt0020892	Sweden	Fredfilm	AB Svensk Filmindustri	Fredrik Andersson	Lars Egge	Inez Lundgren
12	75	110	Marocko	Morocco	tt0021156	USA	Paramount	Film AB Paramount	Josef von Sternberg	Gary Cooper	Marlene Deitrich
13	70	110	När rosorna slå ut	When Roses Bloom	tt0021194	Sweden	Les Studios Paramount	Film AB Paramount	Edvin Adolphson	Karin Swanström	Nils Wahlbom
14	70	110	Vi två	Vi tva	tt0021518	Sweden	Les Studios Paramount	Film AB Paramount	John W. Brunius	Edvin Adolphson	Margit Manstad
15	70	100	Sunny side up	Sunny Side Up	tt0020466	USA	Fox	Fox	David Butler	Janet Gaynor	Charles Farrell
16	70	100	Fötterna först	Feet First	tt0020876	USA	Harold Lloyd Productions	Film AB Paramount	Clyde Bruckman	Harold Lloyd	Barbera Kent
17	70	100	Charmören på lilla caféet	Playboy of Paris	tt0021261	USA	Paramount	Film AB Paramount	Ludwig Berger	Maurice Chevalier	Frances Dee
18	65	90	Monte Carlo	Monte Carlo	tt0021153	USA	Paramount	Film AB Paramount	Ernst Lubitsch	Jeanette MacDonald	Jacj Buchanan
19	60	80	Kyssen	The Kiss	tt0020062	USA	MGM	Metro	Jacques Feyder	Greta Garbo	Conrad Nagel
20	60	80	Flirt, funkis och fullträffar	na	tt0123895	Denmark	A/S Dansk Filmindustri Palladium	National-Film	Lau Lauritzen	Carl Schenstrøm	Harald Madsen

(continued)

(continued)

Rank	HA-score	BG-score	Swedish title in Furhammar's list	Original title (Imdb)	IMDB id	Principal nationality	Principal production company	Distribution company	Director	Star 1	Star 2
1931–1932 season											
1	135	210	Skepp ohoj!	na	tt0022393	Sweden	Film AB Minerva	AB Svensk Filmindustri	Gustaf Edgren	Fridolf Rhudin	
2	130	200	En kärleksnatt vid Öresund	na	tt0022041	Sweden	Svensk Ljudfilm	AB Svea Film	Sölve Cederstrand	Elisabeth Frisk	Bengt Djurberg
3	125	195	Trötte Teodor	Tired Theodore	tt0022508	Sweden	Film AB Minerva	AB Svensk Filmindustri	Gustaf Edgren	Valdemar Dalquist	Karin Swanström
4	125	195	Falska miljonären	The False Millionaire	tt0021848	Sweden	Film AB Minerva	AB Svensk Filmindustri	Paul Merzbach	Fridolf Rhudin	Zarah Leander
5	115	180	Svärmor kommer	na	tt0023542	Sweden	Film AB Minerva	AB Svensk Filmindustri	Paul Merzbach	Karin Swanström	Bullen Berglund
6	115	180	Wien dansar och ler	Congress Dances	tt0022034	Germany	UFA	AB Svensk Filmindustri	Eric Charell	Lilian Harvey	Willy Fritsch
7	110	165	Kärlek och landstorm	na	tt0022040	Sweden	AB Europa Film	AB Europa Film	John Lindlöf	Gideon Wahlberg	Gösta Gustafson
8	105	160	Leende löjtnanten	The Smiling Lieutenant	tt0022074	USA	Paramount	Film AB Paramount	Ernst Lubitsch	Maurice Chevalier	Claudette Colbert
9	100	150	Svarta rosor	Black Roses	tt0023541	Sweden	AB Svensk Filmindustri	AB Svensk Filmindustri	Gustaf Molander	Esther Roeck-Hansen	Einar Axelsson
10	100	150	Skepparkärlek	na	tt0022394	Sweden	Film AB Minerva	AB Fribergs Filmbyrå	Ivar Johansson	Weyler Hildebrand	Einar Fagstad

(continued)

(continued)

Rank	HA-score	BG-score	Swedish title in Furhammar's list	Original title (Imdb)	IMDB id	Principal nationality	Principal production company	Distribution company	Director	Star 1	Star 2
11	100	150	Kärlekskommando	Love's Command	tt0022072	Germany	Super-Film	Rosenbergs Filmbyrå AB	Geza von Bolvary	Dolly Haas	Gustav Fröhlich
12	95	140	Hans livs match	na	tt0022975	Sweden	Film AB Minerva	AB Svensk Filmindustri	Per-Axel Branner	Sigurd Wallén	Björn Berglund
13	85	125	Delicious	Delicious	tt0021793	USA	Fox	Fox	David Butler	Janet Gaynor	Charles Farrell
14	80	115	En timme med dig	One Hour with You	tt0023303	USA	Paramount	Film AB Paramount	Ernst Lubitsch	Maurice Chevalier	Jeanette MacDonald
15	70	100	På Petterssonskans pensionat	na	tt0125325	Denmark	A/S Dansk Filmindustri Palladium	National-Film	Lau Lauritzen	Carl Schenstrøm	Harald Madsen
16	65	90	Inspiration	Inspiration	tt0022001	USA	MGM	Metro	Clarence Brown	Greta Garbo	Robert Montgomery
17	65	90	En natt i Wien	A Bit of Love	tt0125014	Germany	H.M.-Film	Film AB Paramount	Max Neufeld	Lee Parry	Magda Schneider
18	60	80	Längtan till havet	na	tt0022098	Sweden	Les Studios Paramount	Film AB Paramount	John W. Brunius	Edvin Adolphson	Inga Tidblad
19	60	80	En natt i Monte Carlo	Bombs Over Monte Carlo	tt0021681	Germany	UFA	AB Svensk Filmindustri	Hanns Schwarz	Hans Albers	Anna Sten
20	50	65	Ett skepp kommer lastat	na	tt0023482	Sweden	AB Europa Film	AB Europa Film	Thure Alfe	Helle Winther	Nils Jacobsson

(continued)

(continued)

Rank	HA-score	BG-score	Swedish title in Furhammar's list	Original title (Imdb)	IMDB id	Principal nationality	Principal production company	Distribution company	Director	Star 1	Star 2
1932–1933 season											
1	195	310	Vi som går köksvägen	Servant's Entrance	tt0023658	Sweden	AB Bild & Ton	AB Svensk Filmindustri	Gustaf Molander	Tutta Rolf	Bengt Djurberg
2	150	235	Pojkarna på Storholmen	na	tt0023346	Sweden	Film AB Minerva	AB Svensk Filmindustri	Sigurd Wallén	Fridolf Rhudin	Sigurd Wallén
3	135	210	Söderkåkar	Shanty Town	tt0023547	Sweden	AB Europa Film	AB Europa Film	Weyler Hildebrand	Gideon Wahlberg	Edvard Persson
4	125	195	Tarzan	Tarzan the Ape Man	tt0023551	USA	MGM	Metro	W S Van Dyke	Johnny Weissmuller	Maureen O'Sullivan
5	115	180	Giftasvuxna döttrar	na	tt0024058	Sweden	AB Bild & Ton	AB Svensk Filmindustri	Sigurd Wallén	Sigurd Wallén	Karin Swanström
6	110	165	Värmlänningarna	The Varmlanders	tt0023664	Sweden	Film AB Minerva	AB Svensk Filmindustri	Gustaf Edgren	Annalisa Eriksson	Gösta Kjellertz
7	110	165	Muntra musikanter	na	tt0023246	Sweden	AB Europa Film	AB Europa Film	Theodor Berthels	Fridolf Rhudin	
8	110	165	Susan Lenox	Susan Lenox (Her Fall and Rise)	tt0022453	USA	MGM	Metro	Robert Z Leonard	Greta Garbo	Clark Gable
9	105	160	Hemslavinnor	na	tt0024106	Sweden	Nordisk Film A/S	Columbia Film AB	Ragnar Widestedt	Dagmar Ebbesen	Isa Quensel

(continued)

(continued)

Rank	HA-score	BG-score	Swedish title in Furhammar's list	Original title (Imdb)	IMDB id	Principal nationality	Principal production company	Distribution company	Director	Star 1	Star 2
10	105	160	Mata Hari	Mata Hari	tt0023196	USA	MGM	Metro	George Fitzmaurice	Greta Garbo	Ramon Novarro
11	100	150	Kärlek och kassabrist	Love and Deficit	tt0023105	Sweden	Film AB Minerva	AB Svensk Filmindustri	Gustaf Molander	Tutta Rolf	
12	95	140	Bomans pojke	na	tt0023824	Sweden	AB Centrum-Film	AB Fribergs Filmbyrå	Ivar Johansson	Bengt Djurberg	Birgit Tengroth
13	90	135	Modärna fruar	na	tt0023233	Sweden	Filmindustri AB Triumvir	Film AB Paramount	Edvin Adolphson	Margit Manstad	Edvin Adolphson
14	85	125	Blonda Venus	Blonde Venus	tt0022698	USA	Paramount	Film AB Paramount	Josef von Sternberg	Marlene Dietrich	
15	85	125	Grand Hotel	Grand Hotel	tt0022958	USA	MGM	Metro	Edmund Goulding	Greta Garbo	John Barrymore
16	85	125	I korsets tecken	The Sign of the Cross	tt0023470	USA	Paramount	Film AB Paramount	Cecil B DeMille	Fredric March	Claudette Colbert
17	80	115	Kiki	Kiki	tt0022026	Germany	Ondra-Lamac Films	Rosenbergs Filmbyrå AB	Carl Lamac	Anny Ondra	Hermann Thimig
18	80	115	Din för i kväll	Love Me Tonight	tt0023158	USA	Paramount	Film AB Paramount	Rouben Mamoulian	Maurice Chevalier	Jeanette MacDonald
19	75	110	Lyckans gullgossar	na	tt0023166	Sweden	AB Skandinavisk Produktion	AB Svensk Filmindustri	Sigurd Wallén	Sigurd Wallén	Tutta Rolf

(continued)

(continued)

Rank	HA-score	BG-score	Swedish title in Furhammar's list	Original title (Imdb)	IMDB id	Principal nationality	Principal production company	Distribution company	Director	Star 1	Star 2
20	75	110	Fridolf i lejonkulan	na	tt0024038	Sweden	AB Europa Film	AB Europa Film	Weyler Hildebrand	Fridolf Rhudin	Weyler Hildebrand
1933–1934 season											
1	145	225	Karl Fredrik Regerar	Karl Fredrik Reigns	tt0025341	Sweden	AB Svensk Filmindustri	AB Svensk Filmindustri	Gustaf Edgren	Sigurd Wallén	Dagmar Ebbesen
2	140	220	Kära släkten	Dear Relatives	tt0024233	Sweden	AB Svensk Filmindustri	AB Svensk Filmindustri	Gustaf Molander	Tutta Rolf	Gösta Ekman
3	140	220	Cavalcade	Cavalcade	tt0023876	USA	Fox	Fox	Frank Lloyd	Diana Wynyard	Clive Brook
4	125	195	På sångens vingar	Lover Divine	tt0024249	Germany	Cine-Allianz	AB Fribergs Filmbyrå	Willi Forst	Mártha Eggerth	Luise Ullrich
5	120	185	Pettersson & Bendel	na	tt0024442	Sweden	AB Wive	Film AB Warner Bros.-First National	Per-Axel Branner	Adolf Jahr	Semmy Friedmann
6	120	185	Atlantäventyret	Blind Passager	tt0024845	Sweden	AB Svensk Filmindustri	AB Svensk Filmindustri	Edvin Adolphson	Valdemar Dalquist	Birgit Tengroth
7	110	165	Hemliga Svensson	na	tt0024105	Sweden	AB Europa Film	AB Europa Film	Schamyl Bauman	Fridolf Rhudin	Edvard Persson
8	110	165	Djurgårdsnätter	na	tt0023954	Sweden	AB Svensk Talfilm	AB Europa Film	Gösta Rodin	Sture Lagervall	Ann Marie Brunius

(continued)

(continued)

Rank	HA-score	BG-score	Swedish title in Furhammar's list	Original title (Imdb)	IMDB id	Principal nationality	Principal production company	Distribution company	Director	Star 1	Star 2
9	105	160	Hälsingar	The People of Haelsingland	tt0024148	Sweden	AB Svensk Talfilm	AB Stockholms Filmcentral	Ivar Johansson	Inga Tidblad	Sten Lindgren
10	105	160	En stilla flirt	A Quiet Affair	tt0025832	Sweden	AB Svensk Filmindustri	AB Svensk Filmindustri	Gustaf Molander	Tutta Rolf	Margit Manstad
11	105	160	En natt i Smygeholm	na	tt0024374	Sweden	AB Svensk Filmindustri	AB Svensk Filmindustri	Sigurd Wallén	Adolf Jahr	Annalisa Ericson
12	100	150	Pappa opp i dagen	A Bedtime Story	tt0023787	USA	Paramount	Film AB Paramount	Norman Taurog	Maurice Chevalier	Helen Twelvetrees
13	95	140	Lördagskvällar	Saturday Nights	tt0024283	Sweden	AB Europa Film	AB Europa Film	Schamyl Bauman	Edvard Persson	Gideon Wahlberg
14	90	135	Två män om en änka	na	tt0024705	Sweden	John Lindlöf	Film AB Le Mat-MGM	John Lindlöf	Gösta Ekman	Martin Öhman
15	90	135	Uppsagd	na	tt0025936	Sweden	Film AB Imago	AB Fribergs Filmbyrå	Ivar Johansson	Sture Lagervall	Anne-Marie Brunius
16	85	125	Höga visan	The Song of Songs	tt0024598	USA	Paramount	Film AB Paramount	Rouben Mamoulian	Marlene Dietrich	Brian Aherne
17	80	115	Som du vill ha mig	As You Desire Me	tt0022641	USA	MGM	Metro	George Fitzmaurice	Greta Garbo	Melvyn Douglas
18	75	110	En sång till dig	A Song for You	tt0024253	Germany	Cine-Allianz	International	Joe May	Jan Kiepura	Jenny Jugo

(continued)

(continued)

Rank	HA-score	BG-score	Swedish title in Furhammar's list	Original title (Imdb)	IMDB id	Principal nationality	Principal production company	Distribution company	Director	Star 1	Star 2
19	75	110	Skandalen i Rom	Roman Scandals	tt0024507	USA	Goldwyn	United Artists AB	Frank Tuttle	Eddie Cantor	Ruth Etting
20	70	100	Farmors revolution	na	tt0024004	Sweden	Filmindustri AB Triumvir	Film AB Paramount	Per-Axel Branner	Hilda Borgström	Nils Wahlbom
1934–1935 season											
1	175	280	Den sjungande Venus	One Night of Love	tt0025601	USA	Columbia	Columbia Film AB	Victor Schertzinger	Grace Moore	Tullio Carminati
2	160	250	En bengalisk lansiär	The Lives of a Bengal Lancer	tt0026643	USA	Paramount	Film AB Paramount	Henry Hathaway	Gary Cooper	Franchot Tone
3	150	235	Ungkarlspappan	The Bachelor Father	tt0027160	Sweden	AB Svensk Filmindustri	AB Svensk Filmindustri	Gustaf Molander	Olof Winnerstrand	Birgit Tengroth
4	150	235	Kvinnorna kring Larsson	The Women Around Larsson	tt0025359	Sweden	AB Europa Film	AB Europa Film	Schamyl Bauman	Edvard Persson	Katie Rolfsen
5	135	210	Flickorna från Gamla Stan	The Girls from the Old Town	tt0025123	Sweden	AB Europa Film	AB Europa Film	Schamyl Bauman	Karin Ekelund	Birgit Rosengren
6	135	210	Christina	Queen Christina	tt0024481	USA	MGM	Metro	Rouben Mamoulian	Greta Garbo	John Gilbert
7	130	200	Tjocka släkten	Close Relations	tt0027114	Sweden	AB Europa Film	AB Europa Film	Sölve Cederstrand	Edvard Persson	Gideon Wahlberg
8	125	195	Swedenhielms	Swedenhielms	tt0027062	Sweden	AB Svensk Filmindustri	AB Svensk Filmindustri	Gustaf Molander	Gösta Ekman	Karin Swanström
9	120	185	Fasters millioner	na	tt0025102	Sweden	AB Svensk Filmindustri	AB Svensk Filmindustri	Gustaf Molander	Bullen Berglund	Tutta Rolf
10	115	180	Anderssonskans Kalle	Madam Anderssons Kalle	tt0025854	Sweden	AB Wive	Film AB Warner Bros.-First National	Sigurd Wallén	Björn Berglund	Tollie Zellman
11	115	180	Glada änkan	The Merry Widow	tt0025493	USA	MGM	Metro	Ernst Lubitsch	Maurice Chevalier	Jeanette MacDonald

(continued)

(continued)

Rank	HA-score	BG-score	Swedish title in Furhammar's list	Original title (Imdb)	IMDB id	Principal nationality	Principal production company	Distribution company	Director	Star 1	Star 2
12	105	160	Simon i Backabo	na	tt0025795	Sweden	AB Svensk Filmindustri	AB Svensk Filmindustri	Gustaf Edgren	Fridolf Rhudin	
13	105	160	Det hände en natt	It Happened One Night	tt0025316	USA	Columbia	Columbia Film AB	Frank Capra	Clark Gable	Claudette Colbert
14	95	140	Munkbrogreven	The Count of the Old Town	tt0026737	Sweden	AB Fribergs Filmbyrå	AB Svensk Filmindustri	Sigurd Wallén	Valdemar Dalquist	Sigurd Wallén
15	90	135	Sången om den eldröda blomman	Man's Way with Women	tt0025854	Sweden	AB Wive	Film AB Warner Bros.-First National	Per-Axel Branner	Edvin Adolphson	Inga Tidblad
16	90	135	La Bataille	The Battle	tt0025892	France	Gaumont British	National	Nicolas Farkas	Charles Boyer	Merle Oberon
17	85	125	Kungliga Johansson	na	tt0025357	Sweden	AB Svensk Talfilm	AB Stockholms Filmcentral	Sölve Cederstrand	Thor Modéen	Bullen Berglund
18	85	125	Pettersson, Sverige	na	tt0025650	Sweden	AB M-film	AB Fribergs Filmbyrå	Sigurd Wallén	Thor Modéen	Sigurd Wallén
19	85	125	Bränningar	Ocean Breakers	tt0026146	Sweden	Film AB Skandinavien	AB SBD	Ivar Johansson	Sten Lindgren	Ingrid Bergman
20	80	115	Kleopatra	Cleopatra	tt0024991	USA	Paramount	Film AB Paramount	Cecil B DeMille	Claudette Colbert	Warren William
1935–1936 season											
1	180	285	Samvetsömma Adolf	Conscientious Objector Adolf	tt0028215	Sweden	AB Svensk Talfilm	Svensk Talfilms Distributionsbyrå AB	Sigurd Wallén	Adolf Jahr	Karin Albihn
2	150	235	Kanske en gentleman	Perhaps a Gentleman	tt0026559	Sweden	AB Irefilm	AB Anglo Film	Tancred Ibsen	Adolf Jahr	
3	145	225	Valborgsmässoafton	Walpurgis Night	tt0027164	Sweden	AB Svensk Filmindustri	AB Svensk Filmindustri	Gustaf Edgren	Victor Sjöström	Lars Hanson

(continued)

(continued)

Rank	HA-score	BG-score	Swedish title in Furhammar's list	Original title (Imdb)	IMDB id	Principal nationality	Principal production company	Distribution company	Director	Star 1	Star 2
4	140	220	Smålänningar	na	tt0027016	Sweden	Triangelfilm	Svensk Talfilms Distributionsbyrå AB	Gösta Rodin	Sigurd Wallén	Thor Modéen
5	140	220	Moderna tider	Modern Times	tt0027977	USA	Charles Chaplin Film Corp	United Artists AB	Charles Chaplin	Charles Chaplin	Paulette Goddard
6	135	210	Larsson i andra giftet	Larsson's Second Marriage	tt0026604	Sweden	AB Europa Film	AB Europa Film	Schamyl Bauman	Edvard Persson	Gideon Wahlberg
7	125	195	Skärgårdsflirt	na	tt0027009	Sweden	AB Europa Film	AB Europa Film	Arne Bornebusch	Nils Lundell	Rut Holm
8	120	185	Raggen det är jag	na	tt0028155	Sweden	AB Europa Film	AB Europa Film	Schamyl Bauman	Isa Quensel	Nils Wahlbom
9	120	185	Mayerlingdramat	Mayerling	tt0027951	France	Nero Films	National	Anatole Litvak	Charles Boyer	Danielle Darrieux
10	115	180	Anna Karenina	Anna Karenina	tt0026071	USA	MGM	Metro	Clarence Brown	Greta Garbo	Frederick March
11	110	165	Bröllopsresan	na	tt0027403	Sweden	AB Svensk Filmindustri	AB Svensk Filmindustri	Gustaf Molander	Karin Swanström	Anne-Marie Brunius
12	110	165	Ä vi gifta	na	tt0028535	Sweden	AB Irefilm	AB Anglo Film	Ragnar Arvedson	Adolf Jahr	Nils Wahlbom
13	105	160	På solsidan	On the Sunny Side	tt0028151	Sweden	AB Wive	AB Wive	Gustaf Molander	Lars Hanson	Ingrid Bergman
14	100	150	Under falsk flagg	na	tt0027155	Sweden	AB Svensk Filmindustri	AB Svensk Filmindustri	Gustaf Molander	Tutta Rolf	Allan Bohlin
15	100	150	Ungdom av i dag	Youth of Today	tt0027159	Sweden	Skandinaviska Biograf AB	Film AB Paramount	Per-Axel Branner	Anne-Marie Brunius	Kotti Chave
16	95	140	Janssons frestelse	na	tt0027816	Sweden	Triangelfilm	Svensk Talfilms Distributionsbyrå AB	Gösta Rodin	Sigurd Wallén	Inga Tidblad

(continued)

(continued)

Rank	HA-score	BG-score	Swedish title in Furhammar's list	Original title (Imdb)	IMDB id	Principal nationality	Principal production company	Distribution company	Director	Star 1	Star 2
17	95	140	Top Hat	Top Hat	tt0027125	USA	RKO	RKO	Mark Sandrich	Fred Astaire	Ginger Rogers
18	95	140	Den brokiga vävnaden	The Painted Veil	tt0025617	USA	MGM	Metro	Richard Boleslavsky	Greta Garbo	Herbert Marshall
19	95	140	Älska mig evigt	Love Me Forever	tt0026654	USA	Columbia	Columbia Film AB	Victor Schertzinger	Grace Moore	Leo Carrillo
20	95	140	Övergiv mig icke	Escape Me Never	tt0026320	UK	British and Dominions	United Artists AB	Paul Czinner	Elisabeth Bergner	High Sinclair
1936–1937 season											
1	250	405	Söder om landsvägen	South of the Highway	tt0028339	Sweden	AB Europa Film	AB Europa Film	Gideon Wahlberg	Edvard Persson	Inga Bodil Vetterlund
2	160	250	Kameliadamen	Camille	tt0028683	USA	MGM	MGM	George Cukor	Greta Garbo	Robert Taylor
3	160	250	San Fransisco	San Francisco	tt0028216	USA	MGM	Metro	W S Van Dyke	Clark Gable	Jeanette MacDonald
4	145	225	Intermezzo	Interlude	tt0027796	Sweden	AB Svensk Filmindustri	AB Svensk Filmindustri	Gustaf Molander	Gösta Ekman	Ingrid Bergman
5	145	225	Ryska snuvan	na	tt0029506	Sweden	AB Svensk Filmindustri	AB Svensk Filmindustri	Gustaf Edgren	Åke Söderblom	Kirsten Heiberg
6	145	225	65, 66 och jag	65, 66, and Me	tt0027248	Sweden	AB Wive	AB Wive	Anders Henrikson	Katie Rolfsen	Elof Ahrle
7	140	220	Fröken blir piga	A Young Lady Becomes a Maid	tt0027649	Sweden	AB SBD	AB SBD	Ivar Johansson	Ernst Eklund	Marianne Löfgren
8	120	185	Stackars miljonärer	na	tt0028303	Sweden	AB Irefilm	AB Anglo Film	Ragnar Arvedson	Adolf Jahr	
9	120	185	Adolf Armstarke	Adolf Armstrong	tt0028553	Sweden	AB Svensk Talfilm	Svensk Talfilms Distributionsbyrå AB	Sigurd Wallén	Adolf Jahr	Weyler Hildebrand

(continued)

(continued)

Rank	HA-score	BG-score	Swedish title in Furhammar's list	Original title (Imdb)	IMDB id	Principal nationality	Principal production company	Distribution company	Director	Star 1	Star 2
10	115	180	Klart till drabbning	Cleared for Action	tt0029084	Sweden	AB Svensk Filmindustri	AB Svensk Filmindustri	Edvin Adolphson	Thor Modéen	Åke Söderblom
11	110	165	Annonsera!	It Pays to Advertise!	tt0027297	Sweden	AB Fribergs Filmbyrå	AB Fribergs Filmbyrå	Anders Henrikson	Thor Modéen	Åke Söderblom
12	110	165	Spöket på Bragehus	na	tt0028301	Sweden	AB Irefilm	AB Anglo Film	Ragnar Arvedson	Adolf Jahr	
13	110	165	Konflikt	Conflict	tt0029090	Sweden	AB Allians Film	Svensk Talfilms Distributionsbyrå AB	Per-Axel Branner	Lars Hanson	Sigurd Wallén
14	110	165	Den store Ziegfeld	The Great Ziegfeld	tt0027698	USA	MGM	Metro	Robert Z Leonard	William Powell	Myrna Loy
15	95	140	Släkten är värst	na	tt0028268	Sweden	AB Wive	AB Wive	Anders Henrikson	Karin Swanström	Thor Modéen
16	95	140	Kvartetten som sprängdes	na	tt0027857	Sweden	AB Europa Film	AB Europa Film	Arne Bornebusch	Carl Barcklind	Nils Lundell
17	90	135	Pensionat Paradiset	na	tt0029388	Sweden	Stockholm Film	AB Wive	Weyler Hildebrand	Thor Modéen	Calle Hagman
18	90	135	De tappra 600	The Charge of the Light Brigade	tt0027438	USA	Warner Bros	Film AB Warner Bros	Michael Curtiz	Errol Flynn	Olivia de Havilland
19	90	135	En gentleman kommer till sta'n	Mr. Deeds Goes to Town	tt0027996	USA	Columbia	Columbia Film AB	Frank Capra	Gary Cooper	Jean Arthur
20	90	135	Generalen dog i gryningen	The General Died at Dawn	tt0027664	USA	Paramount	Film AB Paramount	Lewis Milestone	Gary Cooper	Madeleine Carroll
1937–1938 season											
1	180	285	Senorita	The Firefly	tt0028873	USA	MGM	MGM	Robert Z Leonard	Jeanette MacDonald	Allan Jones
2	165	260	En gång i maj	Maytime	tt0029222	USA	MGM	MGM	Robert Z Leonard	Jeanette MacDonald	Nelson Eddy

(continued)

(continued)

Rank	HA-score	BG-score	Swedish title in Furhammar's list	Original title (Imdb)	IMDB id	Principal nationality	Principal production company	Distribution company	Director	Star 1	Star 2
3	160	250	Marie Walewska	Conquest	tt0028739	USA	MGM	MGM	Clarence Brown	Greta Garbo	Charles Boyer
4	160	250	100 man och 1 flicka	One Hundred Men and one Girl	tt0029347	USA	Universal	Universal	Henry Koster	Deanna Durbin	Adolphe Menjou
5	140	220	Milly, Maria och jag	na	tt0030452	Sweden	Nordisk Films Kompagni A/S	Svenska AB Nordisk Tonefilm	Eric Malmberg	Marguerite Viby	Ernst Eklund
6	140	220	Full i 17	Mad About Music	tt0030395	USA	Universal	Universal	Norman Taurog	Deanna Durbin	Herbert Marshall
7	140	220	Havets hjältar	Captains Courageous	tt0028691	USA	MGM	MGM	Victor Fleming	Freddie Bartholomew	Spencer Tracy
8	135	210	Än leva de gamla gudarna	Old Titans Are Still Here	tt0029822	Sweden	AB Europa Film	AB Europa Film	Schamyl Bauman	Edvard Persson	Dagmar Ebbesen
9	135	210	Sara lär sig folkvett	Sara Learns Manners	tt0029515	Sweden	AB Svensk Filmindustri	AB Svensk Filmindustri	Gustaf Molander	Tutta Rolf	Emma Meissner
10	135	210	Kamrater i vapenrocken	na	tt0030309	Sweden	AB Irefilm	Irefilms Distributionsbyrå AB	Schamyl Bauman	Sture Lagerwall	Elof Ahrle
11	130	200	En sjöman går iland	na	tt0029575	Sweden	AB Irefilm	Irefilms Distributionsbyrå AB	Ragnar Arvedson	Adolf Jahr	Birgit Rosengren
12	125	195	Fången på Zenda	The Prisoner of Zenda	tt0029442	USA	Selznic International Productions	United Artists AB	John Cromwell	Ronald Colman	Madeleine Carroll
13	120	185	Laila	En Saga	tt0029106	Denmark	Nordisk Films Kompagni A/S	Svenska AB Nordisk Tonefilm	George Schnéevoigt	Aino Taube	Åke Öhberg
14	115	180	Med folket för fosterlandet	With the People for the Fatherland	tt0030427	Sweden	AB SBD	AB Svensk Filmindustri /AB SBD	Sigurd Wallén	Sigurd Wallén	

(continued)

(continued)

Rank	HA-score	BG-score	Swedish title in Furhammar's list	Original title (Imdb)	IMDB id	Principal nationality	Principal production company	Distribution company	Director	Star 1	Star 2
15	115	180	Emile Zolas liv	The Life of Emile Zola	tt0029146	USA	Warner Bros	Film AB Warner Bros	John Ford	Paul Muni	Gale Sondergaard
16	115	180	Orkanen	The Hurricane	tt0029030	USA	Samuel Goldwyn Inc	United Artists AB	John Ford	Dorothy Lamour	Jon Hall
17	110	165	Storm över skären	na	tt0030799	Sweden	AB Europa Film	AB Europa Film	Ivar Johansson	Karin Ekelund	Sten Lindgren
18	110	165	John Ericsson	The Great John Ericsson	tt0029068	Sweden	AB Svensk Filmindustri	AB Svensk Filmindustri	Gustaf Edgren	Victor Sjöström	Sigurd Wallén
19	110	165	Den stora kärleken	na	tt0030797	Sweden	AB Wive	AB Wive	Anders Henrikson	Tutta Rolf	Håkan Westergren
20	105	160	Skicka hem nr 7	Send Home Number 7	tt0029576	Sweden	AB Europa Film	AB Europa Film	Schamyl Bauman	Dagmar Ebbesen	Carl Barcklind
1938–1939 season											
1	250	405	Snövit och de sju dvärgarna	Snow White and the Seven Dwarfs	tt0029583	USA	Walt Disney Productions	RKO Radio Films AB	Walt Disney	n/a	n/a
2	170	270	En kvinnas ansikte	A Woman's Face	tt0030337	Sweden	AB Svensk Filmindustri	AB Svensk Filmindustri	Gustaf Molander	Ingrid Bergman	Tore Svennberg,
3	150	235	Herr husassistenten	na	tt0031422	Sweden	AB Wive	AB Wive	Ragnar Arvedson	Elof Ahrle	Aino Taube
4	140	220	Skanör-Falsterbo	Skanor-Falsterbo	tt0031931	Sweden	AB Europa Film	AB Europa Film	Emil A. Pehrsson	Edvard Persson	Arthur Fischer
5	140	220	Karriär	Career	tt0030311	Sweden	AB Irefilm	Irefilms Distributionsbyrå AB	Schamyl Bauman	Signe Hasso	Sture Lagerwall
6	140	220	Kustens glada kavaljerer	Cavaliers, the Happy	tt0030336	Sweden	AB Europa Film	AB Europa Film	Ragnar Arvedson	Åke Söderblom	Karl-Arne Holmsten

(continued)

(continued)

Rank	HA-score	BG-score	Swedish title in Furhammar's list	Original title (Imdb)	IMDB id	Principal nationality	Principal production company	Distribution company	Director	Star 1	Star 2
7	140	220	På kryss med Albertina	Cruise in the Albertina	tt0030640	Sweden	AB Svensk Talfilm	Svensk Talfilms Distributionsbyrå AB	Per-Axel Branner	Adolf Jahr	Ulla Wikander
8	130	200	Baldevins bröllop	Baldwin's Wedding	tt0029893	Sweden	Olle Ekman	AB Europa Film	Emil A. Pehrsson	Edvard Persson	Dagmar Ebbesen
9	130	200	Efterlyst	na	tt0031263	Sweden	Produktion S. Bauman AB	AB Europa Film	Schamyl Bauman	Edvin Adolphson	Birgit Rosengren
10	125	195	Dimmornas kaj	Port of Shadows	tt0030643	France	Ciné-Alliance	Film AB Skandinavien	Marcel Carné	Jean Gabin	Michel Simon
11	120	185	Gubben kommer	na	tt0031396	Sweden	AB Svensk Filmindustri	AB Svensk Filmindustri	Per Lindberg	Victor Sjöström	Tora Teje
12	120	185	En enda natt	Only One Night	tt0031270	Sweden	AB Svensk Filmindustri	AB Svensk Filmindustri	Gustaf Molander	Edvin Adolphson	Ingrid Bergman
13	120	185	Rena rama sanningen	Nothing But the Truth	tt0031846	Sweden	AB Fribergs Filmbyrå	AB Fribergs Filmbyrå	Weyler Hildebrand	Håkan Westergren	Sickan Carlsson
14	120	185	Gummi	The Green Hell	tt0030315	Germany	UFA	AB Svensk Filmindustri	Eduard von Borsody	René Deltgen	Gustav Diessl
15	115	180	Dollar	Dollar	tt0030066	Sweden	AB Svensk Filmindustri	AB Svensk Filmindustri	Gustaf Molander	Tutta Rolf	Kotti Chave
16	115	180	Vi två	Vi Tvaa	tt0032097	Sweden	Terrafilms Produktions AB	AB Terrafilm	Schamyl Bauman	Sture Lagerwall	Signe Hasso
17	115	180	Robin Hoods äventyr	The Adventures of Robin Hood	tt0029843	USA	Warner Bros. Pictures Inc	Film AB Warner Bros.-First National	Michael Curtiz	Errol Flynn	Olivia de Havilland
18	115	180	Komedin om oss människor	You Can't Take It with You	tt0030993	USA	Columbia	Columbia Film AB	Frank Capra	Jean Arthur	James Stewart
19	110	165	Citadellet	The Citadel	tt0029995	UK	MGM	MGM	King Vidor	Robert Donat	Rosalind Russell
20	110	165	Gibraltar	It Happened in Gibraltar	tt0030180	France	Cine Alliance	Stockholms Filmcentral	Fédor Ozep	Viviane Romance	Roger Duchesne

(continued)

(continued)

Rank	HA-score	BG-score	Swedish title in Furhammar's list	Original title (Imdb)	IMDB id	Principal nationality	Principal production company	Distribution company	Director	Star 1	Star 2
1939–1940 season											
1	245	395	Kalle på spången	Charlie the Innkeeper	tt0031526	Sweden	AB Europa Film	AB Europa Film	Emil A. Pehrsson	Edvard Persson	
2	180	285	Landstormens lilla Lotta	na	tt0031553	Sweden	AB Fribergs Filmbyrå	AB Fribergs Filmbyrå	Weyler Hildebrand	Sickan Carlsson	Allan Bohlin
3	155	245	Valfångare	Whalers	tt0032089	Sweden	AB Svensk Filmindustri	AB Svensk Filmindustri	Anders Henrikson	Tutta Rolf	Allan Bohlin
4	145	225	Åh, en så'n grabb!	na	tt0032171	Sweden	AB Wive	AB Wive	Ivar Johansson	Elof Ahrle	
5	130	200	Kadettkamrater	Cadets Together	tt0031525	Sweden	AB Svensk Filmindustri	AB Svensk Filmindustri	Weyler Hildebrand	Åke Söderblom	Hans Ekman
6	130	200	Hennes lilla majestät	Her Little Majesty	tt0031416	Sweden	Terrafilms Produktions AB	AB Terrafilm	Schamyl Bauman	Sonja Wigert	Anders Henrikson
7	125	195	Frun till handa	The Servant Girl	tt0031351	Sweden	AB Europa Film	AB Europa Film	Gunnar Olsson	Britta Brunius	Karl-Arne Holmsten
8	105	160	I dag börjar livet	na	tt0031468	Sweden	Produktion S. Bauman AB	AB Sandrew-Bauman Film	Schamyl Bauman	Sture Lagerwall	Sonja Wigert
9	105	160	Midnattssolens son	na	tt0031646	Sweden	AB Irefilm	Irefilms Distributionsbyrå AB	Rolf Husberg	Per Henning Nutti	Anni Kuhmunen
10	105	160	Pygmalion	Pygmalion	tt0030637	UK	Pascal Film Productions Ltd	AB Svensk Filmindustri	Anthony Asquith	Leslie Howard	Wendy Hiller
11	105	160	Adjö, mr Chips	Goodbye, Mr. Chips	tt0031385	UK	MGM	MGM	Sam Wood	Robert Donat	Greer Garson
12	90	135	Sjöcharmörer	na	tt0031930	Sweden	Film AB Panorama	AB Fribergs Filmbyrå	Gösta Rodin	Sigurd Wallén	Emil Fjellström

(continued)

(continued)

Rank	HA-score	BG-score	Swedish title in Furhammar's list	Original title (Imdb)	IMDB id	Principal nationality	Principal production company	Distribution company	Director	Star 1	Star 2
13	85	125	Gläd dig i din ungdom	Rejoice While You're Young, Fellow Cadets	tt0031374	Sweden	AB Svensk Filmindustri	AB Svensk Filmindustri	Per Lindberg	Birgit Tengroth	Peter Höglund
14	80	115	Mot nya tider	Towards New Times	tt0031671	Sweden	AB Svensk Talfilm	Svensk Talfilms Distributionsbyrå AB	Sigurd Wallén	Victor Sjöström	Sigurd Wallén
15	80	115	De fyra fjädrarna	The Four Feathers	tt0031334	UK	London Film Productions	United Artists AB	Zoltan Korda	John Clements	Ralph Richardson
16	75	110	Melodin från Gamla Stan	na	tt0031637	Sweden	AB Svensk Talfilm	Svensk Talfilms Distributionsbyrå AB	Ragnar Frisk	Nils Poppe	Carl Reinholdz
17	75	110	Endast änglar ha vingar	Only Angels Have Wings	tt0031762	USA	Columbia Pictures	Columbia Film AB	Howard Hawks	Cary Grant	Jean Arthur
18	70	100	Rosor varje kväll	na	tt0031879	Sweden	Film AB Paramount	Film AB Paramount	Per-Axel Branner	Max Hansen	Siv Ericks
19	70	100	Union Pacific	Union Pacific	tt0032080	USA	Paramount	Film AB Paramount	Cecil B DeMille	Barbara Stanwyck	Joel McCrea
20	70	100	Fury	Fury	tt0027652	USA	MGM	MGM	Fritz Lang	Sylvia Sidney	Spencer Tracy

References

Björklund, C. J. (1945). *Kampen om filmen: en studie i filmens sociologi*. Sveriges skriftställare förbundets förlag.

Blomqvist, M. (2015). *Leif Furhammar har avlidit*. Minnesord publicerade på Svenska Filminstitutets hemsida, Nyheter om svensk film. https://www.filminstitutet.se/sv/nyheter/2015/leif-fur hammar/. 2015-11-02. Accessed 2020/08/05.

Bornebusch, A. (1935). *De lever ett rikt liv: filmdiktare*. Bonnier.

Feinstein, C., Temin, P., & Toniolo, G. (1997). *The European economy between the wars*. Oxford University Press.

Förteckning över Sveriges biografer: dessutom adress- och telefonuppgifter å ägare och föreståndare samt övriga upplysningar av intresse för facket. (1930). Stockholm, Sveriges biografägareförb.

Förteckning över biografer, biografägare och biografföreståndare. (1936). Stockholm, Sveriges biografer, Sveriges biografägareförb.

Förteckning över biografer, biografägare och biografföreståndare. (1939). Stockholm, Sveriges biografer, Sveriges biografägareförb.

Fregert, K. (2009). The Great Depression in Sweden as a wage coordination failure. *European Review of Economic History, 4*(3), 341–360.

Furhammar, L. (1979). Den svenska trettiotalsfilmen. In *Svensk filmografi 3 1930–1939*. Svenska filminstitutet: 9–23

Furhammar, L. (1983). En skamfläck för vår kultur. In *Kultur och värderingsförändringar*. Sekretariatet för framtidsstudier, Forskningsrådsnämnden (FRN)

Furhammar, L. (1990). Stockholmspublikens biopreferenser under 1930-talet: en undersökningsrapport. (The Stockholm Audience's Film Preferences in the 1930s: A report). Stockholm University.

Furhammar, L. (1991). *Filmen i Sverige: en historia i tio kapitel*. Wiken and Svenska Filminstitutet, Höganäs.

Furhammar, L. (1998). *Filmen i Sverige: en historia i tio kapitel* (2nd revised ed.). Bra böcker and Svenska Filminstitutet.

Furhammar, L. (2003). *Filmen i Sverige: en historia i tio kapitel och en fortsättning* (3rd revised ed.). Dialogos and Svenska filminstitutet.

Furhammar, L (2015). Egocentrisk betraktelse över tillkomsten av ett universitetsämne. In M. Hyvönen, P. Snickars, & P. Vesterlund (Eds.), *Massmedieproblem. Mediestudiets formering* (pp. 215–224) Mediehistoriskt arkiv, Lunds universitet.

Habel, Y. (2002). *Modern media, modern audiences: Mass media and social engineering in the 1930s Swedish welfare state*. Aura.

Higson, A. (1989). The concept of national cinema. *Screen, 30*, 36–46.

Jerselius, K. (1987). *Hotade reservat: spelfilmerna med Edvard Persson*. Diss. Stockholm: Univ. Uppsala.

Qvist, P. O. (1995a). *Folkhemmets bilder: modernisering, motstånd och mentalitet i den svenska 30-talsfilmen*. Lund, Arkiv Förlag.

Qvist, P. O. (1995b). The 1930s' Folklustspel and film farce. In M. Larsson & A. Marklund (Eds.), (2010), *Swedish film: An introduction and reader* (pp. 119–133). Nordic Academic Press.

Qvist, P. O. Adolf Jahr. Svensk Filmdatabas. Accessed 2021/04/09.

Reinholds, J. (1987). *Filmindustri 1900–1975: tekniska genombrott och produktion av fotografiska skådespel*. Reinholds.

Rodin, G. (1976). *Den svenska filmens glada 30-tal: en överlevandes minnen*. Nordisk bokindustri.

Rossholm, A. (2006). *Reproducing languages, translating bodies: Approaches to speech, translation and cultural identity in early European sound film*. Stockholm University.

Schildt, J. (1970). *Det pensionerade paradiset: anteckningar om svensk 30-talsfilm*. PAN/Norstedt.

Sedgwick, J. (2000). *Filmgoing in 1930s Britain: A choice of pleasures*. Exeter University Press.

Soila, T. (1991). *Kvinnors ansikte: Stereotyper och kvinnlig identitet i trettiotalets svenska filmmelodram*. University of Stockholm.

Soila, T. (1998). Sweden. In T. Soila, A. Söderbergh Widding, & G. Iversen (Eds.), *Nordic national cinemas* (pp. 142–188). Routledge.
SOU 1942: 36. Sverige. Ecklesiastikdepartementet (1942). Betänkande med förslag rörande statligt stöd åt svensk filmproduktion. Stockholm.
Statistisk Årsbok för Stockholms Stad - 1905–1971, publicerad av Stockholms Stads statistiska kontor / Statistical year-book of Stockholm- 1905–1971', published by Stockholm Office of Statistics. https://sok.stadsarkivet.stockholm.se/Databas/statistik-arsbok-1904-2006/Visa/skatter/879?sidindex=2&ar=1939. Accessed 2021/04/06.
Steinberg, C. (1990). *Film facts*.
Straumann, T., & Woitek, U. (2009). A pioneer of a new monetary policy? Sweden's price-level targeting of the 1930s revisited. *European Review of Economic History, 13*(2), 251–282.
Szekeres, P. (1984). *All-time great films*. Institute for Culture.
Wredlund, B., & Lindfors, R. (1983). *Långfilm I Sverige 3 1930–1939: fakta om 3,465 långfilmer godkända för visning eller censurförbjudna i Sverige 1930–1939*. Proprius Förlag.
Wright, R. (1998). *The visible wall: Jews and other ethnic outsiders in Swedish film*. Southern Illinois University Press.

Åsa Jernudd is an associate professor in Media and Communication Studies at Örebro University, with a Ph.D. in Film Studies from Stockholm University (2007). She has published in edited volumes and journals on the historical spaces of cinema exhibition in Sweden and the complexity of memories of cinemagoing. Currently (2019–2022), Åsa is the principal investigator of a research project about Swedish cinema audiences and exhibition in the 1950s and 1960s, funded by the Swedish National Research Council.

John Sedgwick is a visiting professor in the Faculty of Technology, Design and Environment, Oxford Brookes University. He researches the economic history of cinema and is particularly interested in the ontological characteristics of film as a commodity. He created the POPSTAT Index of Film Popularity as a proxy for box-office returns. This tool provides a means of reflecting audience preferences and monitoring the distribution process. His research has focused on American, Australian, British, Dutch, Italian and international markets during the 1930s and 1950/60s. He has written a monograph, edited an anthology and published articles in *Business History, Cinema Journal, Economic History Review, Explorations in Economic History, Enterprise and Society, Film History, Historical Journal of Film, Radio and Television, Journal of Applied Statistics, Journal of Cultural Economics, Journal of Economic History* and *Journal of Transnational Cinema*

Dutch Films in the Mid-1930s Dutch Market: A Characteristics Approach to Film Popularity

Clara Pafort Overduin

Abstract This chapter analyses the relationship between 17 Dutch films produced in 1934 and 1935 and their popularity with Dutch filmgoers. Starting from the concept of cultural nearness and appropriation, I have examined recurring character types, themes, and plot developments, arguing that those can reveal preferences for certain morals and values and thus shed light on aspects of Dutch culture. Audiences better appreciate films in which working-class characters take control over their future. This is especially the case in the movies starring Fientje de la Mar, in which a positive image of a successful, independent, and nonconformist woman is presented. In contrast, a popular male character was clumsy, not too bright, and not very handsome: a goodhearted working-class boy, like those characters played by Johan Kaart. Most plotlines revolve around newly formed romantic couples or married couples. Jealousy is the main obstacle they must overcome. Invariably, the emotional state is resolved by showing that partners were unjustly jealous. Coming from the wrong social class is a recurring obstacle as well. Crossing the borders between social classes to marry is acceptable when the transgressor is open, honest, and not pursuing financial gain. In most films, multiple plot lines show different couples. Movies that depict traditional relations are juxtaposed by highly popular films in which the main female protagonist refuses to commit herself to one man. A considerable amount of humour is created at the expense of bossy women and superior men from upper-class backgrounds. Such characters always come off badly, making it clear that their behaviour is not appreciated.

C. P. Overduin (✉)
Department of Media and Culture Studies & Institute for Cultural Inquiry (ICON), Utrecht University, Utrecht, The Netherlands
e-mail: c.pafort-overduin@uu.nl

J. Sedgwick (ed.), *Towards a Comparative Economic History of Cinema, 1930–1970*, Frontiers in Economic History, https://doi.org/10.1007/978-3-031-05770-0_6

> How can the same piece be shown many hundreds, even thousands of times in a row? Mystery. [...] A comparison of those plays gives even less insight into the essence of success. It only shows that the national psyche is clearly exerting its influence [...].[1]

Where films were made in Europe during the 1930s, they proved highly popular with home audiences, co-existing in the charts with more well-known Hollywood productions—particularly those films with a high International Orientation Index.[2] Undoubtedly, part of the reason for this is the spoken language, as well as the cultural proximity of those films to the lives led by the audiences. In two chapters in this book set during the 1930s, Swedish and British movies found favour with home audiences, but not with audiences in the other. This asymmetry was commonplace throughout Europe, with Hollywood proving the exception in all cases, where its products were not forbidden or heavily restricted.

Although with a comparable population to Sweden, the Netherlands did not have a history of film production on the same scale. Nevertheless, during the 1930s, Dutch films experienced a brief period of popularity.[3] Indeed between 1934 and 1936, they dominated the popularity charts (see Table 1): the first successes in 1934, led to a wave of 37 new Dutch films that ended with the German occupation in 1940. Having new Dutch-language movies on their screens was unusual for Dutch audiences. Yet, no matter how these films were praised for their accessibility, this did not guarantee a good reception. In other words, while having films spoken in the home language helped their popularity, it was not sufficient. The variation in the audience response to Dutch cinema is the subject of this chapter. How should we explain differences in their popularity?

I turn to the films themselves to find an answer. Not to evaluate and review them as it is usually done in critical approaches, but to understand the roles played by their characters and the response of Dutch audiences to them. As little as we know about movies and their relationship to their audiences and the societies in which they are shown, we cannot simply ignore some films are more popular than others and that this changes over time and space.[4] Based on the concept of cultural nearness, I contend that although we cannot establish a direct relationship, a correlation can be observed between film popularity and how dramatic conflict is handled and resolved. To do this, I analyse the characteristics of on-screen conflicts; what are they about, between whom, and how are they resolved.

To keep the investigation manageable, I focus on those Dutch films released in their home market between 1934 and 1936. This experiment in interpretation is intended as

---

[1] Hoe is het mogelijk eenzelfde stuk vele honderden, zelfs duizenden malen achtereen te vertoonen? Mysterie.[...] Een vergelijking van die stukken geeft nog minder Inzicht in het wezen van het succes. Slechts blijkt, dat de nationale psyche duidelijk haar invloed doet gelden [...] Van Gigch Jr. Mr. L. (1921). Van Gigch wrote this in response to the phenomenal success of the theatre play *De Jantjes*. (Bouber 1920).

[2] Miskell (2016). See Chaps. 1 and 12 for an explanation of the concept.

[3] See Sedgwick et al. (2012) for an account of the complexities of Dutch society in the mid-1930s and how this affected filmgoing.

[4] See for example a discussion of this fact in Jurca and Sedgwick (2014).

a starting point for a deeper investigation into differences in film characteristics and popularity in the Netherlands. Before turning to the film analysis, I briefly introduce the dataset and explain the method used to calculate popularity. This is followed by a discussion of the literature concerning the importance of cultural nearness in understanding film popularity, finally leading to an analysis of the films themselves.

1 The Dataset and Measuring the Popularity of Films

The dataset used to establish which films were popular in the Netherlands between 1934 and 1936 consists of programming information drawn from 144 cinemas in 22 cities and towns, varying in population from 781,645 (Amsterdam) to 6,944 (Zierikzee). Details of the sample can be found in Appendix 1 at the end of the chapter. The sample is comprehensive, covering a little over 40% of Dutch cinemas in that period. It comprises 26,059 programs (13,134 single bills and 6,462 double bills), involving 2,411 feature films.

Films are followed for 12 months after first appearing in the dataset for equity purposes, meaning that films that premiered after the first week of January 1936 were not included in the comparison, leaving 752 premiere movies to be included in the investigation. Of these, 17 were Dutch.

The calculation of the popularity (POPSTAT) and relative popularity (RelPOP) of films is based upon the methods developed by John Sedgwick but adjusted to reflect the inconsistent availability of price information.[5] POPSTAT for each film in each city is the product of the number of screenings, the weights of the cinemas where they are screened, and their billing status—1.0 if a single billing, 0.5 if a double billing.[6] The POPSTAT values of films screened in each city or town form an index. By expressing the POPSTAT value of each movie as a proportion of the median value of each, a standardised measure of popularity is established, which can be used for comparative purposes. Hence, if Film X in Utrecht has a RelPOP value of 3 while generating a value of 2 in Amsterdam, it is possible to say it is more popular in Utrecht even though it may have sold many more tickets in the larger city. Some films are more varied in their reception than others. While aggregating RelPOP values of films across the 22 cities and towns allows a ranking order of movies to be formed—see Table 1—, it will disguise the variance inherent in circulation. This is overcome by calculating the coefficient of variation.

The table shows the relatively high presence of eleven Dutch films in the top 30; nine films were of European origin (other than the Netherlands), and eight were

[5] See Chap. 1. Also see Sedgwick (2000, 2020a, b).

[6] Screenings provide a more accurate measure of supply than half-weeks or weeks, capturing better the intensity of circulation. Cinema weights are established by dividing the number of seats in a cinema by the average seating capacity of all cinemas in a locality. Thus, the mean weight for each of the 22 cities is 1.0.

Table 1 The 30 most popular films in 22 Dutch towns and cities, measured by RelPOP

Rank	Film	Country	Year	Director	Total ReLPOP	Mean RelPOP	Standard Deviation	Coefficient of variation	Towns and cities	Localities in which ranked first	Highest ranking	Lowest ranking
1	Jantjes, De	NL	1934	Jaap Speyer	170.34	8.13	4.25	0.52	22	12	1	13
2	Bleeke Bet	NL	1934	Alex Benno & Richard Oswald	104.05	5.29	3.29	0.62	21	2	1	61
3	Bright eyes	US	1934	David Butler	93.82	5.27	3.55	0.67	19	2	1	125
4	Meisje met den blauwen hoed, Het	NL	1934	Rudolf Meinert	92.30	4.62	2.46	0.53	21	1	1	182
5	Big van het regiment, De	NL	1935	Max Nosseck	88.90	4.11	1.97	0.48	22	1	1	126
6	Op hoop van zegen	NL	1934	Alex Benno	85.05	4.43	2.06	0.46	20	0	2	42
7	Malle gevallen	NL	1934	Jaap Speyer	82.13	4.60	2.33	0.51	19	0	2	155
8	Kribbebijter, De	NL	1935	Henry Koster & Ernst Winar	69.26	3.69	2.34	0.63	20	0	2	168
9	Little colonel, The	US	1935	David Butler	66.95	3.94	2.77	0.70	19	1	1	167
10	Maternelle, La	FR	1933	Jean Benoît-Lévy & Marie Epstein	62.14	3.50	2.49	0.71	20	0	2	192
11	Familie van mijn vrouw, De	NL	1935	Jaap Speyer	58.11	3.03	1.28	0.42	20	1	1	166

(continued)

Table 1 (continued)

Rank	Film	Country	Year	Director	Total ReLPOP	Mean RelPOP	Standard Deviation	Coefficient of variation	Towns and cities	Localities in which ranked first	Highest ranking	Lowest ranking
12	Lives of a Bengal Lancer, The	US	1935	Henry Hathaway	57.02	2.72	1.61	0.59	22	0	4	152
13	Suikerfreule	NL	1935	Haro van Peski	56.52	2.85	1.51	0.53	20	0	2	192
14	Episode	AT	1935	Walter Reisch	54.40	3.00	1.97	0.66	19	0	2	212
15	Mein Herz ruft nach dir	DE	1934	Carmine Gallone	53.76	3.28	1.93	0.59	18	0	8	209
16	Merry widow, The	US	1934	Ernst Lubitsch	52.41	2.75	1.51	0.55	20	0	2	209
17	Gold (1934)	DE	1934	Karl Hartl	51.98	2.94	1.84	0.62	19	0	5	210
18	Czardasfürstin, Die	DE	1934	Georg Jacoby	50.30	3.08	1.88	0.61	17	0	5	369
19	Stern fällt vom Himmel, Ein	AT	1934	Max Neufeld	50.11	3.11	2.37	0.76	18	0	6	210
20	Wenn du jung bist, gehört dir die Welt	DE	1934	Richard Oswald	48.23	3.21	3.72	1.16	19	1	1	511
21	One night of love	US	1934	Victor Schertzinger	47.61	2.80	1.72	0.61	17	0	7	164
22	Viktor und Viktoria	DE	1933	Reinhold Schünzel	47.39	2.63	1.21	0.46	18	0	2	130
23	Witte, De	BE	1934	Jan Vanderheyden	47.23	2.36	1.16	0.49	20	1	1	135

(continued)

Table 1 (continued)

Rank	Film	Country	Year	Director	Total ReLPOP	Mean RelPOP	Standard Deviation	Coefficient of variation	Towns and cities	Localities in which ranked first	Highest ranking	Lowest ranking
24	Queen Christina	US	1933	Rouben Mamoulian	46.53	2.59	1.50	0.58	18	0	8	77
25	Zigeunerbaron, Der	DE	1935	Karl Hartl	44.45	2.61	1.32	0.51	17	0	5	194
26	Vier Mullers, De	NL	1935	Rudolf Meinert	44.02	2.32	1.31	0.57	19	0	3	220
27	Op stap	NL	1935	Ernst Winar	44.01	2.10	1.23	0.59	21	0	3	337
28	Painted veil, The	US	1934	Richard Boleslawski	43.87	2.31	1.15	0.50	19	0	15	156
29	Maskerade	DE	1934	Willi Forst	43.75	2.19	1.23	0.56	20	0	9	362
30	Viva Villa	US	1934	Jack Conway & Howard Hawks & William A. Wellman	42.49	2.12	1.02	0.48	20	0	16	157

Source Dataset

produced in the USA. It can be observed that the Dutch films in the top 30 still show the least variation, ranging from 0.42 to 0.63. The only Belgium film in the list falls into the same range, while films from the USA showed a little more variation ranging from 0.48 to 0.70. Films from Germany and Austria showed the most variation with the coefficient of variation ranging from 0.46 to 1.16, although without the outlier *Wenn du jung bist, gehört dir die Welt*, the range would have been less—0.46–0.76. The explanation for differences in coefficient of variation values will be examined later in the chapter.

Here it is more important to ask about the reach of the films. We can expect that the most popular movies would reach most places, and indeed as Table 1 shows, they did. Each Top 30 film was shown in at least 17 of the 22 cities, rising to 18 where films arrived after the 12 months cut-off period. This occurred mainly in two small towns with only one cinema that commonly were at the bottom of the distribution network: Culemborg (a small town just east of the centre of the Netherlands) and Zierikzee (a small town in Zeeland, near the coast, in the south-west of the country). Furthermore, it is telling that Dutch films were less appreciated in two mining towns in the south-east of the Netherlands, close to the German border. In Geleen, four of the eleven Dutch films were not shown and in Heerlen, five. With an influx of German coalminers, the populations of both towns were more oriented towards their German neighbour, suggesting the fluidity of culture and the idea of cultural nearness.[7]

2 Cultural Nearness

Several earlier studies have explored the relationship between popularity and cultural nearness. The assumption is that films depicting cultural aspects of a society related to the audiences watching those films are more appreciated than films made in a non-related culture. For instance, Larry May accounts for the popularity of the Hollywood star Bud Rogers among working-class white Americans.[8] Evidence from the annual British Top 100 charts (1932–1937) suggests that his movies did not travel well, even in English-speaking countries, with films such as *County Chairman* attracting near to median POPSTAT values in 1935.[9] Garncarz included genres and their basic structures in his work on the popularity of Hollywood in Germany.[10] He shows that changing attitudes in German cinemagoing audiences coincides with changing popularity of particular genres. For example, in the late 1970s and early 1980s, young Germans appreciated the Hero/Spectacle movies, films that expressed values like purposefully taking control of things by oneself as personified by a hero who consistently achieved his goal. Garncarz contents that ‘the cultural affinity between the country of production and the country of export is a prerequisite for the exported

[7] Pafort-Overduin (2018).

[8] May (2000).

[9] Sedgwick (2000, Appendix).

[10] Garncarz (2015).

films to become popular in the other country.'[11] In his next book, Garncarz explores this hypothesis and shows that cultural affinity can account for differences in films popular in different European countries and within regions of one country.[12] He refers to Norbert Elias' concept of interdependency, in which community members create culture and language in an exchange process. Garncarz points out that this relationship exists between film audiences and film supply.[13] In other words, films are cultural constructs in their production and consumption.

Peter Miskell has shown that Hollywood films do better in foreign markets when they resonate culturally with their audiences. The variables he selects in his investigation are the nationality of the artistic talent (director, scriptwriter, and the two main actors), the geographical setting of the scenario, and the author of the source text.[14] Like Garncarz, he explains that cultural norms and values are reflected in cultural products and that these are most appreciated by audiences who belong to or associate with the cultural group being depicted. Reasoning from a European perspective, this would mean that Hollywood films with a solid European association are likely to be more attractive. A very preliminary test by Van Wissen et al. seems to confirm this. Hollywood films that were more foreign oriented were slightly more popular in the Netherlands than those that were not.[15] As discussed earlier; Table 1 supports this. Other than two Shirley Temple films, the remaining six Top 30 Hollywood films have a European or Imperial focus. However, more significantly, Dutch audiences preferred European films, particularly those made by Dutch filmmakers—the majority (22) of the films are European in origin, and half of these are Dutch. Most of the other European films are from neighbouring country Germany (7) or German spoken but produced in Austria (2).

More generally, the cultural proximity argument is supported by the demand and supply percentages in Dutch cinemas during 1934–1936. In the dataset described earlier, 55% of films marketed in the Netherlands emanate from Hollywood, garnering 46% of market demand measured by POPSTAT. In contrast, these proportions are reversed for German and Austrian films, which supply 25% but capture 30% of the market. For Dutch movies, this difference is even more striking, with the 2% of films supplied capturing an 11% share.[16]

These examples point to the importance of culture as one of the factors explaining popularity. Related to that is the way people learn to understand their environment. Psychological research has shown in a general sense that when a person processes

[11] Garncarz (2013, pp. 174–175). Translated by author. 'Die kulturelle Affinität zwischen dem Produktions- und dem Exportland ist die Voraussetzung dafür, dass die exportierten Filme im anderen Land Populär werden können.

[12] Garncarz (2015).

[13] Garncarz (2015, pp. 193–194).

[14] Miskell (2016).

[15] Wissen et al. (2021) The authors note that they did not collect information about all the categories Miskell discerns. Also the calculation of the popularity was solely based on the number of screening weeks of a film. The size of the cinema was not included.

[16] Pafort-Overduin (2012).

information, they try to relate it to earlier acquired knowledge through schemata—patterns developed to understand the world.[17] A similar approach is at work when someone watches a film. Gained from personal histories of filmgoing, spectators will 'consult' their schemata to understand the story in narratological terms (the narrative form and the style) and substantive terms such as the themes and the actions of the characters. When filmmakers work in the same production environment—like, for example, Hollywood—they will develop shared schemata about creating a film, reflected in the movie they make.[18] The same applies to the stories told and the morals and values reflected in them.

The process of creating a representation about a particular group—recognised and then repeated, is referred to by Willem Frijhoff as 'appropriation.'[19] Appropriation revolves around the adaptation of cultural assets and, consequently, is dynamic and constantly changing. Typically, there is always an interaction between the suppliers of a cultural product, such as a film, and an audience expressing positive or negative opinions about it. Positive reactions lead to higher product consumption (in the case of cinema, a higher box-office). Where film producers aim to reach as large an audience as possible, they will be tempted to repeat their success by telling a story in a similar form, using the same star or choosing a similar theme.

Recognisability is thus seen as an essential condition for a film's appreciation. Yet, the relationship between recognisability and popularity is neither simple nor straightforward. Too many movies with the same structure will be recognisable. They may also become tedious for audiences because they are predictable. This danger also applies to themes and their elaboration—too many films with the same theme will make them commonplace and less entertaining.[20] The challenge for filmmakers is to combine recognisability with surprise, catering to various audiences with different attitudes to cinematic risk.

In the absence of subsidies, film producers aim to generate positive returns for their investors. Consequently, they need to make films attractive for the largest possible audience. One way of doing this is by identifying trending currents in society. In the early days of Hollywood film, Paramount, for example, had teams at work looking for appealing stories and subjects in theatre plays, literature and newspapers and magazines.[21] A similar strategy was followed in the Netherlands, where producers also used successful plays and books as sources (Table 2). How the original pieces were adapted—what was added and removed—indicates the producer's expectation of the audience for whom the film was made. In turn, a movie's popularity is an indicator of audience taste, not just in terms of the narrative form and the style but

[17] Emmott and Alexander (2014).

[18] Bordwell (1989, 2007) Of the latter, see chapter 4 (pp. 135–150) for an example of how schemata can be used in an analysis.

[19] Frijhoff (2003).

[20] Thompson (1988).

[21] *Motion Picture Herald* (1933, June 3, p. 28).

Table 2 Sources of the 17 Dutch films released between 1934–1936

Rank RelPOP	Title	Source	Title source	Author source	Year source	Earlier success
1	*De Jantjes*	Play & silent film	*De Jantjes*	Herman Bouber	1920/1922	26 October 1921, 500 performances; 4 April 1922 600 performances;[a] no information about number of screenings of the silent film
2	*Bleeke Bet*	Play & silent film	*Bleeke Bet*	Herman Bouber	1917/1923	27 May 1918, 200 performances[b] no information about number of screenings of the silent film
4	*Het meisje met den blauwen hoed*	Novel	*Het meisje met den blauwen hoed*	Johan Fabricius	1927	novel was his breakthrough as writer for adults[c]
5	*De big van het regiment*	Novel	*Spionnage in het veldleger*	A. Roothaert	1933	thriller genre became popular in the 1930s[d]
6	*Op hoop van zegen*	Play & silent film	*Op Hoop van Zegen*	Herman Heijermans	1900/1918/1924	play 650 performances on 26 February 1918; 27 September 1919 700 performances;[e] the 1924 silent version was a German coproduction;[f] no information about number of screenings of the silent films

(continued)

Table 2 (continued)

Rank RelPOP	Title	Source	Title source	Author source	Year source	Earlier success
7	*Malle gevallen*	Novel & Play	*Malle gevallen*	Hans Martin	1913/1920	in 1920 adapted to a theaterplay by Hans Martin[g]
8	*De Kribbebijter*	Play	*Willis Frau*	Max Reimann & Otto Schwartz	1917	14 Februari 1920, 150 performances in the Netherlands; 10 August 1932 500 performances[h]
11	*De familie van mijn vrouw*	Play	*My Wife's Family*; also referred to as "*Een huis vol herrie*"	Hal Stephens & Harry B. Linton; also reworked by Alfred Duprez & A. Milo Bennet;	1905	premiere 4 December 1931, run until last week of April 1932[i]
13	*Suikerfreule*	Play	*Suikerfreule*	Henri van Wermeskerken	1917	5 March 1927 500 performances[j]
26	*De vier Mullers*	Play	*Schottenring*	Armin Friedman & Ludwig Nerz	1933	9 August 1934 200 performances[k]
27	*Op stap*	Original script			1935	
36	*Het Leven is niet zoo kwaad*	Original script			1935	
62	*Fientje Peters - Poste restante*	Novel	*Fientje Peters - Poste restante*	K.R. Neubert	unknown	
64	*Het mysterie van de Mondscheinsonate*	Novel	*Het mysterie van de Mondscheinsonate*	Willy Corsari	1934	successful writer; thriller genre became popular in the 1930s[l]

(continued)

Table 2 (continued)

Rank RelPOP	Title	Source	Title source	Author source	Year source	Earlier success
101	*Dood water*	Original script			1934	
175	*Willem van Oranje*	Original script			1934	
688	*Blokkade*	Original script			1934	

[a](1921, October 20). *Algemeen Handelsblad*, p. 8. https://resolver.kb.nl/resolve?urn=ddd:010655087:mpeg21:p008; (1922, April 4). *Algemeen Handelsblad*, p. 8. https://resolver.kb.nl/resolve?urn=ddd:010655215:mpeg21:p008

[b](1918, May 27). *Het nieuws van den dag*, p. 8. https://resolver.kb.nl/resolve?urn=MMKB15:000638048:mpeg21:p00008

[c]Vos, J. (2011) Johan Fabricius. In J. Van Coillie, W. Van der Pennen, J. Staal, H. Tromp (Eds.) *Lexicon van de jeugdliteratuur*. Groningen: Martinus Nijhoff. https://www.dbnl.org/tekst/coil001lexi01_01/lvdj00307.php

[d]Walch, F. (1996). *Roothaert: een biografie*. Baarn: De Prom

[e](1918, February 25). *De Telegraaf*, p. 3. https://resolver.kb.nl/resolve?urn=ddd:110549771:mpeg21:p003; (1919, September 27). *De Telegraaf*, p. 7. https://resolver.kb.nl/resolve?urn=ddd:110550798:mpeg21:p007

[f]Donaldson, G. (1997). *Of joy and sorrow. A filmography of Dutch silent fiction.* Amsterdam: Stichting Nederlands Filmmuseum

[g]Jong, A.M. (1920, December 4). Centraal Theater. Malle gevallen. *Het volk*, p. 4. https://resolver.kb.nl/resolve?urn=ddd:011081819:mpeg21:p004

[h](1921, February 5). *Algemeen Handelsblad*, p. 8. https://resolver.kb.nl/resolve?urn=ddd:010654606:mpeg21:p010; (1932, August 10). *Haagsche courant*, p. 8. https://resolver.kb.nl/resolve?urn=MMKB04:000146839:mpeg21:p007

[i](1931, December 2). *De Telegraaf*, p. 11. https://resolver.kb.nl/resolve?urn=ddd:110571094:mpeg21:p011; (1932, April 25). *Algemeen Handelsblad*, p. 12. https://resolver.kb.nl/resolve?urn=ddd:010662530:mpeg21:p012

[j](1927, March 02). *Algemeen Handelsblad*, p. 7. https://resolver.kb.nl/resolve?urn=ddd:010657990:mpeg21:p007

[k](1934, August 10). *Het Vaderland*, p. 4. https://resolver.kb.nl/resolve?urn=ddd:010015504:mpeg21:p012

[l]Nieuwe uitgaven. (1934, July 12). *Het Vaderland*, Avondblad, c.p. 1. https://resolver.kb.nl/resolve?urn=ddd:010015454:mpeg21:p009; Koning, J. (1934, April 18). Een nieuw boek van mevrouw Szekeley-Lulofs. *Haagsche Courant*, b.5.p. 3. https://resolver.kb.nl/resolve?urn=MMKB04:000148166:mpeg21:p019

also in dramatic content. As more films adopt similar themes, 'appropriation' occurs. This idea is at the core of the film analysis conducted in the remainder of the chapter. The goal of the analysis is not to point out 'unique' Dutch characteristics so much as to establish what representations recur, seemingly appreciated by the film-going audiences of the time and thus give us a glimpse into Dutch culture.

3 Method of Film Analysis

The analysis of the films is inspired by Keiko McDonald and her book on Japanese cinema. In the introduction, she calls her approach a combination of New Criticism, neo-formalism, and a cultural/historical analysis and explains that she discerns an internal and external perspective. The internal view is focused on the structure of the film and the function of its essential parts like the characters, symbols, setting, and events (hence the neo-formalist influence). The analysis is built on the protagonist's choices when confronted with a central problem and how the film prompts the protagonist to make such choices. Endings receive particular attention as it is here that the outcome of the main situation is presented.

In contrast, the external analysis focuses on the film's structure and its relation to its audience.[22] McDonald is concerned with the audience's point of view and whether it (dis)agrees with, (dis)likes, the choices made by the characters. She points to knowledge of cultural specificities needed to interpret a Japanese film 'in a meaningful way.'[23] In other words, she tries to bring films from a different culture closer by explaining its cultural norms and values.

Her work inspired me to concentrate on the developments of the plotlines and the outcome of the central conflicts and regard them as reflecting cultural norms and values. The underlying assumption is that Dutch filmmakers used the same schemata as their audiences: the choices created for individual storylines and character types resonate with what they believe will be appreciated by the target public. If specific themes are repeated in similar ways and attract a large audience, we may assume that they appeal to and say something about that audience's cultural values and norms.

I start by describing analysing the different plot lines and their outcome. The questions for research were: What is at stake? What are the character's semes and goals? And finally, which characters and goals prevail? Based on this, recurring characters and repeated themes and outcomes are identified.

17 Dutch films are included in the dataset that could be followed for the 12 months following their premiere. Since only a couple of fragments remain for the film *Blokkade*, 16 Dutch films are included in the content analysis. *Blokkade* is included in the sections that do not rely upon content analysis.

---

[22] McDonald (2006, p. 15).

[23] McDonald (2006, p. 14).

4 Appropriating Earlier Successes

Earlier successes are as significant to film producers as they are to audiences. As argued in the introduction, Dutch film producers, like their foreign counterparts, were looking for subjects and stars that would appeal to a large audience. There was no state support at the time, so every Dutch Guilder invested had to be earned back in the cinemas in which films were circulated.

Audiences also attempted to manage the risk they took when purchasing tickets since they had no sure way of knowing beforehand whether their decisions would pay off.[24] Choices were made using information from personal experiences, such as earlier acquired knowledge about a story or an actor, the opinions of friends and family with a similar taste, and the information provided by the marketing machines of the producers.

To investigate the choices made by producers, the source material of the 17 films is identified—whether each was based on a previously published source or an original script. I have investigated how celebrated and popular the original sources are to establish possible positive or negative influences on the popularity of the films (Table 2). Next to that, an overview of the actors and their earlier careers was created as one would expect that well-known actors had a greater appeal (Appendix 2).

Table 2 shows that of the eleven Dutch films that made up the 30 most popular films, eight were based on a popular theatrical predecessor. In the column 'earlier success,' an indication of the scale of popularity is given by the number of theatrical performances. The numbers are based on advertisements found in newspapers and articles in journals. When a play was very successful, it gained press coverage, including announcements when new milestones were reached. These repetitions of the same representations can be considered part of the process of 'appropriation' referred to earlier, suggesting that audiences recognised them as meaningful, leading to more visits. Such success encourages producers to re-use the representation, and a new cycle begins. In economic terms, it shows that film producers tried to manage their investment risk by relying on successful performances of past theatrical plays to forecast similar success at the cinema. Their choices were vindicated if judged by their cinematic popularity Table 2 illustrates the difference between films based on a popular play and those with an original script, with the latter located in the lower part of the table, starting with position 27 for *Op Stap*.

A similar pattern appears with the five films based on novels—two of which had already been on the market for some time and were widely known. The novel *Het meisje met de blauwe hoed* was published in 1927 and marked the breakthrough of author Johan Fabricius.[25] *Malle gevallen* by Hans Martin was first published in 1913 and was adapted to a theatre play in 1920. In contrast, the film *Fientje Peters—Poste Restante* was the Dutch version of the German UFA film *Hilde Petersen-Postlagernd*, based on the German novel of the same title by K.R. Neubert that had not been

[24] See Chap. 1.

[25] Vos (2011).

translated into Dutch. This factor probably partly explains the relatively limited popularity of this comedy.

Both *De Big van het regiment* and *Het mysterie van de Mondscheinsonate* can be associated with the popularity of the detective/thriller genre in the 1930s in the Netherlands.[26] Both were recent novels published one year before the film. Both authors were celebrated, even though the first of these was Anton Roothaert's debut novel (His second novel was published almost at the same time). Roothaert was praised for his new approach to the detective genre and his witty style and humour.[27] Willy Corsari, on the other hand, had already 13 titles to her name when *Het mysterie van de Mondscheinsonate* was published. Her books were widely read.[28] Accordingly, when it comes to the familiarity of the sources, the films do not seem to be far apart. Yet, they rank very differently: *De big* is in 5th place and '*Het mysterie*' in 64th. Here other factors were at play, which I will come back to in the analysis of plotlines. Before this, the role of the actors in the popularity of the films is discussed.

5 Famous Names and the Popularity of the Films

When the Dutch film wave took off in 1934, no feature film had been produced for four years. Indeed, after the bankruptcy of Filmfabriek Hollandia in 1923, the production side of the industry had been largely moribund.[29] Accordingly, film producers had no reservoir of film actors from which to draw. Appendix 2 lists the 85 actors that played leading parts or supporting roles in the 17 Dutch films and the number of films they appeared. Other columns provide details about the actors, including the actor's year of birth, their first appearance in theatre or film, and the number of years between the start of a career and the release of the first Dutch talking picture. Also added is the field or genre the actor was most known for in the theatre—operetta, revue, dance, film. The overview comprises well-established names, rising stars, and short-lived personalities.

Appendix 2 shows that producers and directors chose their actors from the theatre in general. Almost 57% (48) of the listed actors worked for theatre companies, with another six working for theatre companies but sometimes appearing in revues or operettas. Only three actors had an earlier career in film through working abroad. Most of the actors (49) had a career of over ten years before their first appearance in a Dutch sound movie. For as many as 30, this stretched for more than 20 years. The table also lists 13 new actors with no previous career.

[26] Ross (1986).

[27] Walch (1996).

[28] Koning (1934, April 18), *Het Vaderland* (1934, July 12).

[29] Bishoff (1986).

In most films, the cast was a mix of (very) experienced and less experienced actors. In general, actors with longer careers were more widely known than actors with shorter careers. However, this could differ, making it hard to conclude the effect of experience on film performance and reception. Combining an original script with unknown actors was not very beneficial, as can be told from the ranked position of *Dood Water* (101) and *Blokkade* (688). In *Dood Water*, only one of the main characters was played by a well-known actor—Jan Musch, whose stage career started in 1899 but took off in 1910. The other four main characters were new to the field or were hardly known in the Netherlands. Two of them had left for Germany around 1920 and appeared only once in the Netherlands in a theatre play—Theo de Maal in 1932 and Arnold Marlé in one year later. In *Blokkade*, a similar strategy was followed: Louis de Vries was by then a household name in the theatre, having been in the public eye continuously from 1903, two years after the start of his career. Jacques Reule had a lower profile, although he had also been around for a long time in the theatre, beginning in 1907. For the other two main actors, this was their first part.

Two other films with original scripts were *Op Stap* and *Het leven is niet zoo kwaad* were more popular, ranked, respectively, at 27 and 36. Both films used actors that had become popular since the beginning of the revival of Dutch cinema. *Het leven is niet zo kwaad* featured eight actors who, between them, appeared in eleven previous Dutch films. The cast of *Op Stap* boasted five actors who had featured in four Dutch films. Moreover, two of the leading actors, brother and sister Henriette and Louis Davids, were highly popular revue stars. Both films starred Fientje de La Mar who had been in the highly popular film *De Jantjes*. *Op Stap* was her third film and *Het leven is niet zoo kwaad* her fifth.

Undoubtedly, the degree of fame played a role, but that did not mean that well-known actors guaranteed success, as the example of *Willem van Oranje* illustrates. Although the cast boasted many big names from the theatre, the film did not resonate with Dutch audiences. The distributor and exhibitors will have been disappointed, having four copies of the film in circulation. Indeed, the take-up by exhibitors was so poor that after the first week following release was the only period during which this number of copies was in circulation. The film, about the life and death of the 'father' of the Dutch nation, was withdrawn from circulation 18 weeks after its premiere. Obviously, although big names can attract audiences during the first weeks after release, it is difficult to maintain high attendances when the film itself is unappealing. At the time, Dutch audiences preferred a melodramatic story about ordinary folks found in *De jantjes* over a political-historical drama about the birth of a nation depicted in *Willem van Oranje*.

6 The Role of Genre

Ten of the 17 Dutch films were comedies. Eight of these were ranked among the Top 30 most popular films. As is evident in Table 2, this did not mean that dramas per se ended up at the very bottom of the popularity scale—*Op Hoop van Zegen* was a big success, whereas *Dood Water* was not. The first was based on the phenomenal successful play by Herman Heyermans starring the famous Esther de Boer-van Rijk, who played the well-known central character Kniertje in an extended theatrical run and two film versions (1918 and 1934). Having lost her husband and two sons to the sea, Kniertje forces her youngest son to sign on as a fisherman. He then dies in a storm, and she speaks the famous words 'the fish has taken its toll' ('de vis wordt duur betaald'). Over the years, Esther de Boer-van Rijk had become the personification of Kniertje.

Based on an original script, *Dood* Water features actors who were not well-known. Nevertheless, it was presented as a prestigious art film at the 19th Venice Biennale in 1934. The famous Dutch Concertgebouw Orchestra conducted by Willem Mengelberg pompously underscored the very long animated introduction on how the land was won from the water. The film's tone was propagandistic and created a peculiar paradox by opposing two symbols showing the Dutch reign over the sea: the Volendammer fishermen, a famous national icon over the centuries, and the polders and dykes safeguarding the low countries from the North Sea. In a patronising way, the film shows that the fishermen had to accept the loss of their livelihood and life at sea, convert to farmers and embrace the newly reclaimed land as the new source of living. This combination did not resonate well with Dutch audiences as *Dood Water*, ranked at 101, was one of the least popular Dutch films at the time. *Willem van Oranje* ranked 175th, and the experimental thriller *Blokkade* (688th) was even less popular.

7 Transcending Genre: Song and Dance

The narrative structure of most Dutch films in the dataset, irrespective of genre, is enriched with characters that burst out in song and dance, commonly interrupting the plot but sometimes as part of the plot. Films in which this occurs are identified in Table 3. Even in dramatical stories like *Dood Water* and *Op Hoop van Zegen*, dance is shown as part of a way of living of the fishermen who spend spare time in the café where they dance. Dancing and singing, either doing it or watching it, is an integral part of the lives of Dutch film characters. Where this is done depends on the social class of the characters being portrayed—poor street singers entertain passers-by in the street; fishermen and sailors enjoy themselves in the café, soldiers and their commanders in their respective messes, the cabaret and revue are open to all, while the theatre is frequented mainly by middle or higher classes. The rich and famous are entertained by hired musicians at private parties in exclusive abodes.

Table 3 The genre of Dutch films and incidence of song and dance, 1934–1936

Rank RelPOP	Title	Genre
1	De Jantjes	Melodrama with song and dance
2	Bleeke Bet	Melodrama with song and dance
4	Het Meisje met den blauwen hoed	Comedy with song and dance
5	De big van het regiment	Comedy—espionage with song and dance
6	Op hoop van zegen	Drama
7	Malle gevallen	Comedy with song and dance
8	De Kribbebijter	Comedy
11	De familie van mijn vrouw	Comedy—burlesque -songs
13	Suikerfreule	Comedy—songs
26	De Vier Mullers	Comedy—songs
27	Op stap	Comedy—songs and dance
36	Het leven is niet zoo kwaad	Comedy—song and dance
62	Fientje Peters - Poste restante	Comedy—one song dance intermezzo
64	Het mysterie van de Mondscheinsonate	Detective, drama—song and dance but not much
101	Dood water	Drama
175	Willem van Oranje	Historical drama, biography
688	Blokkade	Experimental thriller

Source Dataset

Characters with lesser means bring their instruments and sing themselves. Singing together is part of the fun. In the private (music) rooms, the song is typically used to express the first declarations of love. The piano in the room facilitates advances between couples or, in contrast, causes greater distance between characters from different social statuses. In the songs, characters express love (either for a person or a place), kind-heartedness, a sense of humour and often an optimistic view on life. Other more negative feelings like sadness, lovesickness, or anger are seldom part of the songs in a Dutch film from that period.

8 Recurring Actors and Recurring Types of Characters

During the Dutch film boom, producers recast actors from the films that proved initially popular, a practice that led to several film stars emerging. *De Jantjes* was the start of many film careers. Almost all the actors who played significant roles reappeared in later films. This was especially the case with Fientje de la Mar and Johan Kaart, each cast for leading roles in five of the movies in the dataset. Aaf Bouber-ten Hoope also appeared in five films but, except for *Suikerfreule*, played smaller parts. It was not only the actors who became famous through their roles in *De Jantjes*; the characters they played also proved popular and would return in subsequent films, sometimes slightly adapted. This happened most clearly with Fientje de la Mar, Johan Kaart, Silvain Poons, and Henriette Davids, who all played similar characters in their subsequent films. These recurring characters are a clear example of the process of appropriation, providing insight into which cultural values and norms were recognisable by the Dutch audience.

By way of example, I will focus on Fientje de la Mar and Johan Kaart and the types of characters they played. From her first appearance in *De Jantjes*, Fientje de la Mar became associated with a female character in some way related to showbusiness, either as a glamorous revue star or as a local singer in the soldiers' canteen. The character has difficulties committing to one man but never really suffers as a consequence. Her first character, Jans (*De Jantjes*), openly cheats her boyfriend and explains to her friends that for as long as he cannot provide a good income, she will not commit to him but rather stay with her wealthy boyfriend, who she met at the cabaret. There is no punishment for her behaviour; on the contrary, she flourishes. This positive image of the nightclub is repeated in the storyline of her friend Greet. She is in a relationship with short-tempered sailor Dries. Their relationship is threatened by Aunt Piet, the owner of the neighbourhood café. Aunt Piet wants to help her son Leendert, who has a crush on Greet, by manipulating Dries into believing Greet has cheated on him. Following a knife attack on Dries, Leendert accidentally stabs himself. His mother declares that Dries stabbed her son, and Dries is imprisoned. Again, the nightclub turns out to be a place where a working-class girl like Greet can find help; in this case, from a lawyer to release her boyfriend from prison. However, instead of being grateful, her boyfriend then leaves her because he believes the false accusations about Greet being unfaithful while she was in the cabaret. Viewers know that this is not true; not only have they seen that Greet only searched for help in the cabaret, but they also saw that before her visit, Leendert tried to force himself upon her and that she was saved by her girlfriend, Jans. The truth comes out, and Dries must admit that he was wrong, after which the couple reunites. We are thus invited to have a favourable opinion of the cabaret as a safe place for working-class girls. In contrast, the traditional neighbourhood café is presented as a place of lies and manipulation.

As the character Ka in *Bleeke Bet*, Fientje again plays a working-class girl, this time a maid, who finds a way to a better future in the cabaret, where she is discovered as a singer. Drama is added to her character by giving her a secret and unfulfilled love for the boyfriend of her boss's daughter. She accepts the marriage proposal of her well-to-do boyfriend even though she does not love him, and he agrees to her career as a singer.

Fientje plays two different character types in her following two films: a lower-class girl (*De big van het regiment*) and a star persona (*Op Stap*). The two films premiered on the same date, so the audiences could literally choose between these two versions of Fientje. In *De big van het regiment*, she plays Fietje (note that her character's name only differs one letter from her real name), a singer in the soldiers' canteen. She is introduced as an independent woman whose heart beats for the whole company. She sings:

'Who has the right to say
she belongs to me?
My heart beats for the whole company!
I wouldn't know who to choose.
Whether I see Jan or Piet or any other sweetheart
I will never lose my heart to one of them.[30]

As expressed in the song, her opinion corresponds with her attitude towards her two suitors asking for her hand; she meets with both but does not commit herself to either.

In *Op Stap*, Fientje plays the megastar Bella Ramona. Like in *De Big van het regiment,* she is not impressed by any man begging for her hand, but her background has changed. There is no hint at a working-class background; she is a settled, respected, and powerful woman. As a cabaret star, she acts the same way as the men we saw earlier in *De Jantjes*: she helps others build a career and prevents a man from being imprisoned after being accused of fraud. Her selfless help is contrasted with the suspicion of a young woman who thinks Ramona has a crush on her boyfriend. The young woman has to admit that she was wrong, which again invites us to regard the cabaret as respectable.

The star personality is taken further in her next film *Het leven is niet zoo kwaad*, but some changes altered her image as an independent woman. Revue star Anita discovers a new male talent and bets with her producer that she can turn this hawker into a star. She wins and states that from now on, she will do things her way and not be tyrannised by him any longer. The producer then leaves. Her protégé does not appreciate her part in making him successful. He feels caged by her, and when he finds out about the bet, he feels deeply humiliated and decides to return to his job as a hawker. Anita is in pieces and concedes that her producer should take charge once again. In this case, the film reinforces negative connotations about the cabaret. The plot development shows that fame comes at the price of being forced into a role one does not want. The hawker is dominated by the star Anita and she, in turn, is dominated by her producer. While the hawker decides to break free, Anita conforms to the rules of her producer. This plot enlarges the dramatic aspect of her character at the expense of the image of strength and independence; she wants to free herself but must ultimately accept that she cannot if she wants to stay at the top.

Het leven is niet zoo kwaad was the lowest scoring of all her films. It seems that the recurring figure of the cabaret star had lost some of its appeal by altering her character from a strong and independent working-class girl to a wealthy star persona trapped in the clutches of fame, with a man in charge of her career.

The plotlines suggest that audiences preferred a working-class girl becoming a star instead of a story in which the negative aspects of being a star are foregrounded. Also, the plotline in which a woman can climb the social ladder is more appreciated than those in which they are punished for it. This is confirmed by the even lower scoring film *Het mysterie van de Mondscheinsonate*, a film in which Fientje does not appear, but the same negative plot development concerning cabaret and the female

[30] Translation by the author.

star is central. The plot revolves around solving the murder of Enrica, a former dancer who is now married to a rich husband. Longing to return to her life in the theatre, she plans to relaunch her career and meets secretly with her former dance partner. When her sister, who has been staying with her from before her marriage and does not want to return to a former life she regards as miserable, learns of her plans, she shoots her in a rage. Here there is not just a negative association with life as a performer but also with life as an ex-performer who has married a rich husband. Although this likely was one of the reasons for the low interest in this film, other factors played a role. There was a lack of established names in the cast, fitting the trend established earlier concerning the marketability of established stars. Furthermore, the story is at times difficult to follow.

In his autobiography, Johan Kaart remembers becoming famous overnight due to his role as Manus—nicknamed 'The Squinter' (De Schele)—in *De Jantjes*. Manus is a sailor who does not know how to handle his unfaithful girlfriend. Director Jaap Speyer had instructed him to squint in close-ups when De Schele was ridiculed by friends and crying when leaving for the Indonesian army.[31] This kind, naive and somewhat sheepish character that one could laugh at and feel sorry for became a recurring role for Kaart in his subsequent films. He explains that he was looking for a 'generally acceptable character,' (…) 'The average type of working-class boy, (…) who doesn't worry about anything, goes straight to his goal, the simple rough-diamond-type accepted everywhere.'[32] Speyer cast Kaart similarly again in his following two films, followed by other directors.

In *Malle Gevallen*, he is the odd man out when he and his friends go out courting. His two companions fall in love with a girl, but he is not part of the romantic plotline. Instead, his character functions as comic relief, interrupting the narrative flow. In *De Big van het regiment,* in which his character is involved in a minor romantic subplot, he is depicted as a blockhead, unable to win the girl's heart with whom he has fallen in love. Kaart has a bigger part in *De familie van mijn vrouw*. He plays Dr Nix, a junk-dealer—philosopher—veterinarian—English and French teacher—manicurist—podiatrist, obsessed with food. Throughout the film, his failed attempts to get a decent meal are the running gag. Dr Nix creates misunderstandings everywhere he goes preventing the real problem from being solved. The same structure is followed in *De vier Mullers*, where again, he appears as a sheepish and naive man who stubbornly is in pursuit of the discarded clothes of his rich distant relative. The scenes in which he tries to lay hands on the desired blue suit and fur coat function as a comic interlude in the narrative.

The fact that this character reappears several times suggests that the directors of those films expected Kaart in this specific role to enhance their appeal. His appearance likely contributed to their success as films Top-30 films. Considering appropriation, the way the plots develop invites sympathy with precisely this type of unpretentious, straightforward, not always very bright, working-class boy. The exaggeration of his stupidity, sometimes combined with stubbornness, creates humour, never malicious,

[31] Hielkema (1969, pp. 27, 82).

[32] Hielkema (1969, pp. 82–83).

rather compassionate. In other words, the film presents these traits as being positive, the character as a figure we can like.

Further support for this argument can be found in the way unsuccessful male figures from a higher class were represented. These were given negative traits such as vanity, smugness, and conceit to create a less friendly source of humour. The films do not invite us to like them. In *Malle Gevallen*, Kaart's character is contrasted with that of an admirer of one of the young women—a young man nicknamed 'The Leech' (De Klit), who is so full of himself that he ignores all her very outspoken rejections (she is already taken), asking her parents for her hand. His behaviour is punished when the three friends mercilessly fool him. We are invited to the same negative evaluation of the very big-headed, wealthy factory manager from *De Suikerfreule*, who is trying in vain to woo a young lady. He believes that he can do whatever he likes since his sister has the majority interest in the company and will protect him. He lacks responsibility, misbehaves, has gambling debts and drinks. His character is ridiculed in every possible way: he is vain, acts exaggeratedly, gets the wrong ideas, resulting in multiple misunderstandings. All these situations are humorous, but there is no sympathy for him. In the end, it feels as though he is getting what he deserves when his sister fires him.

A similar characterisation is created for the bosses who try to court female subordinates in the films *Het Leven, who is niet zoo kwaad* and *Fientje Peters*. In the first of these, the chief has a reputation among his secretaries: he invites every new secretary into his office, closes the curtains, and tries to persuade her to go out with him. Through exaggerated acting, the boss is meant to come across as funny. Still, at the same time, his acts are negatively commented upon by the other secretaries, thus creating a negative undertone. Like 'The Leech,' this boss is blind to the real feelings of the woman he pursues. At first, the secretary politely declines the honour, but when she suspects her boyfriend of cheating on her, she accepts the invitation hoping to make her boyfriend jealous. However, she regrets her decision, running away from the theatre and her manager during the date.

In *Fientje Peeters*, humour is created by contrasting an obsessive hotel manager who writes love poems to the beautiful new assistant of one of his guests and the manager's assistant who is madly in love with him, trying everything to get his attention. Only when he is rejected does he feel that he 'has no other choice' than to accept the intentions of his not particularly elegant assistant. His utterly negative attitude towards her when he takes her as his girlfriend is obnoxious and prevents sympathising with him. Instead, the film invites us to pity the assistant who gets the man she wanted but one who abhors her.

In Dutch films, characters who behave pompously are usually ridiculed and suffer defeat unless they repent and adopt a friendlier attitude towards their subordinates. This dramaturgical device is used repeatedly, pointing to an underlying conception of these types. It is not desirable to set oneself above others and be complacent. When confronted with this behaviour, one may resist and make clear that no one is more than another. Interpersonal relationships are always more important than money and financial gain. Fame receives a similar dramaturgical treatment. Time and again, it is made clear that fame is not worth pursuing because the price is an unhappy personal life. These representations and the emphasis on wealth and gender equality implicit in these plot developments may not have been exclusive to the Netherlands. Still, they are recognised as meaningful and repeated time and again in the Dutch films of that period. They are part of Dutch cultural identity.

9 Recurring Themes: Marriage

The formation of a new heterosexual couple or the sustenance of a married relationship are dominant themes of the Dutch films found in the analysis: the troubles and perils associated with both constitute either the main plot or a subplot of most of these movies. Overcoming them is the end goal of plotlines, constituting the denouement of the narrative. Only two films deviate from this, both featuring Fientje de la Mar. In *De Jantjes* and *De big van het regiment*, the subplot ends with a woman who explicitly decides not to commit to one man and instead has relationships with two. In both films, this subplot is contrasted with a traditional romantic couple, thus creating more versions of men-women relationships. In *De big van het regiment,* a third subplot is added that ridicules marriage and introduces the bossy wife dominating her meek husband as a source of humour. This exaggerated character reappears in *De Familie van mijn vrouw; De Suikerfreule;* and *Op Stap.* In these three films, the wife, in the end, relents, reinstalling the husband as head of the family, but probably only temporally. In *Malle Gevallen* the character of the bossy woman is also ridiculed. Here she is not put in a relationship but tries in vain to prevent her female students from flirting with the male students. The inclusion of several marriage/relationship versions in the narrative structure of these films provides an opportunity for audiences to consider alternatives to the singular dominant male-submissive female relationship.

In many films, jealousy creates a delay in the plot's denouement and forms the obstacle couples need to overcome before being formed or reunited. The implicit meaning that can be read into this is that jealousy is the biggest threat for partners, whether married, engaged, or newly formed. In most cases of suspected infidelity, it turns out that it had not happened. The cause for suspicion can be manifold, but the common outcome is that trust is undermined. It can arise from false accusations by a third party, the meddling of a parent in a relationship, the misunderstanding of a situation, and even a premeditated imitation of cheating to evoke jealousy and make them realise whom they love. All these plot lines end with the revelation of the truth, at which point the quarrelling couples forgive each other, laugh about it and reunite. When a third party deliberately spreads lies, this person is in some way punished and must show remorse. In other words, jealousy is the driving force of many actions and plays a big part in the development of the plot, but the resolution always shows that it is not a very constructive emotion.

The ending invariably shows that partners can and should trust each other. This is even confirmed in the plot lines concerning women involved in two relationships, as these are conducted openly. Her boyfriends or admirers know that she will not commit to any one of them. In other words, even the polyamorous woman can be trusted as she does not hide her actions. The ranking of the films suggests that the deliberate deception by one of the partners to make the other partner jealous is less appreciated by audiences than in those movies where this happens because of an external factor: *De Jantjes* and *Bleeke Bet* are ranked 1 and 3, whereas *Op Stap* is ranked 27th, and *Het Leven is niet zoo kwaad*, 36th. The film where the making-the-other-partner-jealous theme forms the main plot, *Fientje Peters*, ranks the lowest of the three—62nd. This was not the only possible reason for the low ranking, but the comparison with the other films suggests that it was at least part of the explanation.

Another important theme is the role of class in relationships. Especially in the comedies, this takes the shape of a conflict between parents and children, in which a parent tries to prevent a son or daughter from marrying into a lower-class family (*De Kribbebijter*). But the conflict can also be shaped the other way round, where a parent wants a son or daughter to marry up the social ladder instead of someone from their class (*Bleeke Bet*). In both situations, the obstacle to overcome is the parents' attitude towards other classes, and in all cases, the parents admit that they were wrong.

At first glance, the plot developments can affirm class differences or a crossing of the boundaries between classes. However, a closer analysis of what is accepted shows that ultimately, each social class acknowledges the same values: an acceptance of unpretentiousness as a virtue and, following from this, a choice of love over economic gain or social prestige. When this is not the message, like in *Het mysterie van de Mondscheinsonate* (ranked 64th), in which the main character is killed by her jealous sister to maintain her standard of living, or in *Dood Water* (rank 101st), where traditional fishermen's lives are sacrificed for the more lucrative trade of farming, the films are less popular. Invariably wealth is a corrupting influence. In comedies and melodramas, its influence is restrained in the resolution of conflict, following which a bright future and a happy life become possible. In a drama like *Op Hoop van Zegen*, the death of fishermen shows what can happen when the power of money has free rein. However, the shipowner is not punished in the end. Kniertje does not speak up against him, but instead, she accepts his charity. Although the film's message is implicitly highly political, the focus is on human suffering, which likely helped its widespread popularity.

Films in which characters from the upper class are ridiculed seemed to have been appreciated better than films with severe upper-class characters. In *Malle Gevallen* (ranked 7th), *De kribbebijter* (8th), and *De familie van mijn vrouw* (rank 11th), those characters act exaggeratedly; they have an affected speech, react outrageously in all kinds of situations, and are full of themselves. Again, *Het mysterie van de Mondscheinsonate* (rank 64) shows the opposite: the upper classes are not ridiculed, and all characters are treated seriously.

10 Conclusion

In most cases, we can conclude that Dutch film producers looked for proof of earlier successes in the theatre or literature. In particular, previous success in the theatre provided a good forecast for success in the cinema. Although an actor's reputation in the theatre did not automatically translate to film, Dutch films could bring fame. During the short period of two years, Dutch film stars emerged. The examples of Fientje de la Mar and Johan Kaart are discussed in the chapter, but there are more.

From the analysis of the films, it can be concluded that the great majority of plotlines revolve around newly formed romantic and married couples. This points to an almost obsessive interest in gender relations. In films other than dramas, there are at least two plotlines, each presenting the struggles of a different couple. The main problem new couples must overcome is jealousy, often related to a lack of trust. The resolution introduced in the plot development is that one should trust the other party. Going out or talking to another man/woman does not necessarily mean that a partner cannot be trusted. By creating such an outcome, the plotlines 'allow' men and women more freedom in their contacts and interactions with the opposite sex.

Another recurring theme is the initial rejection of a partner because of their social position. Here the borders between social classes can be crossed when true love is at play, but not when financial gain is the objective. Honest, open characters not pursuing any financial gain are the ones that triumph and can achieve marriage.

The case study of Fientje de la Mar pointed to an interest in a positive image of an independent, nonconformist female character. This character is shown in plot developments deviating from the conventional path to love. Still, this plot is always countered with one or more other plotlines in which a more traditional romantic couple is formed. Both storylines end well. This favourable treatment of modern and more traditional women's roles is essential in explaining the popularity of the actor's films.

The same thing happens in Johan Kaart's first three films. The characters he plays are part of a general plotline in which the traditional development of a young man pursuing love is not followed because he cannot gain the love of a woman. However, it seems that it is not the love interest but the comical effect of his character which is the main reason for his popularity.

This is further developed in his other two films. His character is not very handsome, not very bright, but goodhearted, one with whom viewers laugh and sympathise. Interestingly, during the period under investigation, no male Dutch star played strong male heroes like, for example, Clark Gable. None of the actors playing romantic leads of the period became stars like Johan Kaart, with Dutch audiences, seemingly, preferring the comical type of the guy-next-door. This is confirmed by analysing other male characters who fail to attract the woman they are after. Unpretentious, down-to-earth characters are treated more favourably in the plot developments, suggesting that film producers responded to a known preference among Dutch audiences.

The concepts of appropriation and cultural nearness turn out to be fruitful, facilitating a textual analysis of a batch of Dutch films released in 1934–1935, from which recurring types and plot developments are identified which producers believed would appeal to Dutch audiences. The first results suggest a relation between the kind of conflict encountered, the means of its resolution, and the popularity of a film—between content that depicts societal concerns and popularity. Analysis of this nature can thus shed a different light on how we should understand the appreciation of the films. Further research could address how these new findings relate to other discourses and other themes that circulated in Dutch society at the time.

This chapter analysis has focused on Dutch films. However, to better understand the preferences of Dutch audiences, foreign films should be included as well. What themes are presented, and what values and norms are propagated through the plot developments? How do popular foreign movies relate to popular Dutch films? The function of song and dance is a case in point. That song and dance has a presence in most Dutch films is an indicator of its importance to Dutch audiences. However, this phenomenon extends to foreign cinema, especially German movies. According to the critic I quoted at the opening of this chapter, the popularity of music in a play was an international phenomenon. In this respect, audiences were similar everywhere. But, as he added, each country did it differently.[33]

One final note I want to add is about the role of humour. Again, I only refer to this incidentally, but that most of the films are comedies deserves closer attention. In Dutch comedies, the main targets are bossy women, higher social classes, especially men who are full of themselves. Humour is created by exaggerated acting and the failure of the characters to exert power over other characters. The implication is that they should not think of themselves as better than other persons. Whether true or not, as a Dutch person, I can affirm that this is considered a typical Dutch characteristic. This example illustrates that in comedy, humour is created by a contradiction between what is expected and what happens, often taking the form of a transgression of certain norms and values.[34] To understand and appreciate the joke, it is necessary to know what these are, making this type of comedy challenging to translate to another culture. The implication is that comedy serves as a gateway to understanding cultural values and norms. In terms of our criticism, it can help to understand the 'national psyche.'

[33] Van Gigch Jr. Mr. L. (1921).

[34] Palmer (1987).

Appendix 1: Towns and Cities Appearing in the Dataset

Place	Inhabitants	Number of cinemas in place	Number of cinemas included in dataset*	Seating capacity
Alkmaar	30,467	6	6	2,566
Amsterdam	7,81,645	36	33	19,559
Apeldoorn	68,590	2	2	771
Culemborg	9,359	1	1	500
Den Haag	4,82,397	26	23	17,740
Dordrecht	60,131	2	2	1,002
Eindhoven	1,03,030	5	5	3,808
Geleen	14,289	1	1	900
Groningen	1,15,185	4	4	2,543
Haarlem	1,31,257	5	5	3,203
Heerlen	49,724	3	2	1,407
Leiden	73,612	5	5	2,199
Maastricht	65,929	3	3	2,450
Nijmegen	90,739	6	5	4,365
Rotterdam	5,95,448	23	22	17,100
‘s Hertogenbosch	46,212	4	4	3,098
Schiedam	61,845	3	3	1,614
Tiel	12,730	2	2	1,138
Tilburg	88,890	6	6	2,990
Utrecht	1,61,093	7	7	4,589
Zeist	29,691	2	2	1,050
Zierikzee	6,944	1	1	450

Source Dataset

Appendix 2

Actor	Film title 1	Film title 2	Film title 3	Film title 4	Film title 5	Films 1934–1935	Year of birth	Start career	Career before first Dutch sound film (years)	First silent film	Number of silent Dutch films	Career before film
Aaf Bouber-ten Hoope	De Jantjes	Bleeke Bet	Op hoop van zegen	De Suikerfreule	Het leven is niet zoo kwaad	5	1885	1902	32	1915	6	Theatre
Adolf Bouwmeester	De vier Mullers					1	1889	1907	28	no films	0	Theatre
Adolph Engers	Op Stap	De Big van het Regiment				2	1884	1912	23	1918	5	Theatre
Adolphe Hamburger	De familie van mijn vrouw					1	1898	1920	15	no films	0	Theatre
Adriaan van Hees	Malle Gevallen	Het leven is niet zoo kwaad				2	1910	1931	4	no films	0	Theatre
Adrienne Solser	Het Meisje met de Blauwe Hoed	De Suikerfreule	Het leven is niet zoo kwaad			3	1873	1883	51	1921	10	Variete
Ank van der Moer	Het mysterie van de Mondscheinsonate					1	1912	1932	3	no films	0	Theatre
Annie van Duyn	Malle Gevallen	De Suikerfreule				2	1915	1930	4	no films	0	Theatre
Annie Verhulst	Op hoop van Zegen	Het mysterie van de Mondscheinsonate				2	1895	1919	15	1931	1	Theatre & Operette

(continued)

(continued)

Actor	Film title 1	Film title 2	Film title 3	Film title 4	Film title 5	Films 1934–1935	Year of birth	Start career	Career before first Dutch sound film (years)	First silent film	Number of silent Dutch films	Career before film
Arnold Marlé	Dood Water					1	1887	1919	15	1919	0	Film (abroad) - German film actor - started his career in 1919 (9 films) in Netherlands September 1933 tour Kabale und Liebe (Schiller) Leopols Jessner group)
Betsy Ranucci-Beckman	Dood Water					1	1877	1897	37	no films	0	Theatre
Bill Benders	Het mysterie van de Mondscheinsonate					1	not known	1935	0	no films	0	No earlier career
Cees Laseur	Het leven is niet zoo kwaad					1	1899	1916	19	no films	0	Theatre
Chris Baay	De Kribbebijter					1	1904	1930	5	no films	0	Theatre
Cissy van Bennekom	De Jantjes	Op hoop van zegen	De familie van mijn vrouw	De vier Mullers		4	1911	1928	6	no films	0	Theatre

(continued)

(continued)

Actor	Film title 1	Film title 2	Film title 3	Film title 4	Film title 5	Films 1934–1935	Year of birth	Start career	Career before first Dutch sound film (years)	First silent film	Number of silent Dutch films	Career before film
Claire Clairy	Het mysterie van de Mondscheinsonate					1	1901	1932	3	no films	0	Operette - German actres - started her career in the Netherlands in 1932 (operette) fled in 1933 from Germany
Cor Hermus	Willem van Oranje	De Jantjes	Bleeke Bet	Fientje Peters, Poste restante		4	1889	1912	22	no films	0	Theatre - (acted in reprise of De Jantjes in 1924)
Cor Ruys	De Kribbebijter					1	1889	1905	30	1919	2	Theatre
Cor van der Lugt Melsert	Willem van Oranje					1	1882	1897	37	no films	0	Theatre - directed one silent film in 1927
Cor van der Lugt Melsert jr	Willem van Oranje					1	1907	1934	0	no films	0	No earlier career
Cruys Voorbergh	Willem van Oranje	De familie van mijn vrouw	De Big van het Regiment			3	1898	1918	16	no films	0	Theatre
Darja Collin	Het mysterie van de Mondscheinsonate					1	1902	1928	7	no films	0	Dance

(continued)

(continued)

Actor	Film title 1	Film title 2	Film title 3	Film title 4	Film title 5	Films 1934–1935	Year of birth	Start career	Career before first Dutch sound film (years)	First silent film	Number of silent Dutch films	Career before film
Dolly Bouwmeester	Fientje Peters, Poste restante					1	1913	1926	9	1931	2	Theatre & Operette
Dolly Mollinger	De Kribbebijter	Het leven is niet zoo kwaad				2	1911	1935	0	no films	0	No earlier career
Egon Karter	Het mysterie van de Mondscheinsonate					1	1911	1934	1	no films	0	Operette - Czech actor and singer - was part of the Fritz Hirschberg operette in 1934
Enny Meunier	Malle Gevallen	Het mysterie van de Mondscheinsonate				2	1912	1929	5		0	Theatre - 1933 advertisement film for Persil
Esther de Boer-Van Rijk	Op hoop van Zegen					1	1853	1873	61	1913	13	Theatre
Fie Carelsen	Malle Gevallen					1	1890	1907	27	1916	1	Theatre
Fientje Berghhegge	Fientje Peters, Poste restante					1	1913	1918	17	no films	0	Theatre
Fientje de la Mar	De Jantjes	Bleeke Bet	Op Stap	De Big van het Regiment	Het leven is niet zoo kwaad	5	1898	1915	19	no films	0	Operette & Theatre
Frits van Dongen	Op hoop van Zegen	Op Stap	De Big van het Regiment	De kribbebijter		4	1901	1926	8	no films	0	Theatre

(continued)

(continued)

Actor	Film title 1	Film title 2	Film title 3	Film title 4	Film title 5	Films 1934–1935	Year of birth	Start career	Career before first Dutch sound film (years)	First silent film	Number of silent Dutch films	Career before film
Gusta Chrispijn-Mulder	Malle Gevallen	Het Meisje met de Blauwe Hoed	De familie van mijn vrouw	De vier Mullers		4	1876	1893	41	no films	0	Theatre
Hans van Meerten	De Suikerfreule					1	1895	1921	14	no films	0	Theatre
Hansje Andriesen	De Big van het Regiment					1	1929	1935	0	no films	0	Child actor - No earlier career
Hein Harms	Het Meisje met de Blauwe Hoed					1	1863	1886	48	1933	0	Theatre - 1933 advertisement film for Persil
Helga Gogh	Dood Water					1	1912	1934	0	no films	0	No earlier career
Henriette Davids	De Jantjes	Op Stap	De Big van het Regiment			3	1888	1907	27	1906	7	Revue & Operette
Herman Tholen	Fientje Peters, Poste restante					1	1897	1916	19	no films	0	Cabaret & Singer
Hilde Alexander	Fientje Peters, Poste restante					1	1909	1935	0	no films	0	German actress - No earlier career
Jacques Reule	Blokkade					1	1879	1907	27	1918	2	Theatre
Jacques van Bijlevelt	De vier Mullers	De Big van het Regiment				2	1885	1911	24	1925	1	Opera & Operette
Jan Musch	Dood Water					1	1875	1899	35	1922	1	Theatre

(continued)

(continued)

Actor	Film title 1	Film title 2	Film title 3	Film title 4	Film title 5	Films 1934–1935	Year of birth	Start career	Career before first Dutch sound film (years)	First silent film	Number of silent Dutch films	Career before film
Jan van Ees	De Jantjes	Bleeke Bet	Op hoop van zegen	De Big van het Regiment		4	1896	1914	20	1920	2	Theatre
Jean Lemaire jr	Bleeke Bet					1	1906	1924	10	1921	2	Theatre
Jean Stapelveld	Fientje Peters, Poste restante					1	1887	1906	29	1921	1	Theatre
Johan Elsensohn	Bleeke Bet	De Suikerfreule				2	1884	1916	18	1922	6	Theatre
Johan Heesters	Bleeke Bet	De vier Mullers				2	1903	1920	14	1924	2	Operette & Revue
Johan Kaart jr	De Jantjes	Malle Gevallen	De familie van mijn vrouw	De vier Mullers	De Big van het Regiment	5	1897	1914	20	no films	0	Theatre
Jopie Koopman	Bleeke Bet	Malle Gevallen	Op Stap	De Big van het Regiment		4	1910	1933	1	no films	0	Revue
Lau Ezerman	Willem van Oranje	Bleeke Bet	Het Meisje met de Blauwe Hoed	Het leven is niet zoo kwaad		4	1892	1911	23	1913	7	Theatre - 1933 advertisement film for Persil

(continued)

(continued)

Actor	Film title 1	Film title 2	Film title 3	Film title 4	Film title 5	Films 1934–1935	Year of birth	Start career	Career before first Dutch sound film (years)	First silent film	Number of silent Dutch films	Career before film
Lies van Santen	Blokkade					1	not known	1934	0	no films	0	No earlier career - was discovered through a competion organised by the journal Cinema & Theater
Loesje Bouwmeester	De familie van mijn vrouw					1	1910	1932	3	no films	0	Theatre - Bouwmeester is a famous actors family
Lou Bandy	Het Meisje met de Blauwe Hoed	Het leven is niet zoo kwaad				2	1890	1926	8	no films	0	Revue
Lou den Hartogh	Blokkade					1	not known	1934	0	no films	0	No earlier career
Louis Borel	Malle Gevallen	De kribbebijter	De Suikerfreule	Fientje Peters, Poste restante		4	1905	1924	10	no films	0	Theatre
Louis Davids	De Jantjes	Op Stap				2	1883	1906	28	1906	11	Revue & Operette
Louis de Bree	Malle Gevallen	De kribbebijter	Het mysterie van de Mondscheinsonate	De Suikerfreule		4	1884	1907	27	no films	0	Theatre, Operette & Revue

(continued)

(continued)

Actor	Film title 1	Film title 2	Film title 3	Film title 4	Film title 5	Films 1934–1935	Year of birth	Start career	Career before first Dutch sound film (years)	First silent film	Number of silent Dutch films	Career before film
Louis de Vries	Blokkade					1	1871	1901	33	1909	0	Theatre - directed 1 silent film in 1909
Louis Gimberg	Malle Gevallen	De Suikerfreule				2	1880	1907	27	1913	2	Theatre
Louis Saalborn	Het mysterie van de Mondscheinsonate					1	1891	1908	27	no films	0	Theatre
Louise Kooiman	Willem van Oranje					1	1898	1919	15	no films	0	Theatre
Mary Dresselhuys	De Kribbebijter					1	1907	1929	6	no films	0	Theatre
Mary Smithuysen	De familie van mijn vrouw					1	1906	1926	9	no films	0	Theatre
Matthieu van Eysden	Het Meisje met de Blauwe Hoed	Op hoop van zegen	De Big van het Regiment			3	1896	1919	16	1922	3	Theatre & Operette
Max Croiset	Dood Water					1	1912	1933	1	no films	0	Theatre
Miep van den Berg	Op hoop van Zegen					1	1906	1919	15	no films	0	Theatre
Minny Erfman	De vier Mullers					1	1900	1917	18	1916	2	Theatre
Raoul de Bock	Het mysterie van de Mondscheinsonate					1	1926	1935	0	no films	0	No earlier career

(continued)

(continued)

Actor	Film title 1	Film title 2	Film title 3	Film title 4	Film title 5	Films 1934–1935	Year of birth	Start career	Career before first Dutch sound film (years)	First silent film	Number of silent Dutch films	Career before film
Rini van Ni	Het Meisje met de Blauwe Hoed	Het leven is niet zoo kwaad				2	not known	1934	0		0	No earlier career
Roland Varno	Malle Gevallen	Het Meisje met de Blauwe Hoed				2	1908	1928	6	1928	1	Film (abroad) - first Germany then US; 9 small roles (6 German films; 3 US films; 1 Dutch
Sien de la Mar-Klopper	De Big van het Regiment	De Kribbebijter				2	1881	1897	38	1914	1	Theatre & Operette
Silvain Poons	De Jantjes	Bleeke Bet	De familie van mijn vrouw	De Big van het Regiment		4	1896	1912	22	1914	4	Theatre, Operette & Revue
Sophie de Vries-de Boer	Op hoop van Zegen					1	1882	1894	40	no films	0	Theatre
Susie Klein	De Jantjes					1	1911	1928	6	no films	0	No earlier career - one small part in theatre in 1928
Theo de Maal	Dood Water					1	1902	1934	0	from 1920s	0	Film (abroad)

(continued)

(continued)

Actor	Film title 1	Film title 2	Film title 3	Film title 4	Film title 5	Films 1934–1935	Year of birth	Start career	Career before first Dutch sound film (years)	First silent film	Number of silent Dutch films	Career before film
Tilly Perin-Bouwmeester	De familie van mijn vrouw	De vier Mullers				2	1893	1916	19	1918	1	Theatre (gap between 1918–1932)
Tonny vd Berg	Het Meisje met de Blauwe Hoed	De Suikerfreule				2	not known	1934	0	no films	0	No earlier career
Truus van Aalten	Het Meisje met de Blauwe Hoed					1	1910	1927	7	1927	0	Film (abroad) - 1927 in Germany (27 films)
Wiesje van Tuinen	Het mysterie van de Mondscheinsonate					1	not known	1935	0	no films	0	No earlier career
Willem Hunsche	Op hoop van Zegen					1	1880	1903	31	1912	13	Theatre & silent film - was also in silent version of N18
Willem van der Veer	Het Meisje met de Blauwe Hoed	Op hoop van Zegen				2	1887	1903	31	1913	37	Theatre & silent film
Willy Castello	De Jantjes					1	1910	1927	7	1927	0	Film (abroad) - 5 small roles (3 US films; 2 French films)
Willy Haak	Willem van Oranje	Het Meisje met de Blauwe Hoed				2	1897	1919	15	1921	1	Theatre

(continued)

(continued)

Actor	Film title 1	Film title 2	Film title 3	Film title 4	Film title 5	Films 1934–1935	Year of birth	Start career	Career before first Dutch sound film (years)	First silent film	Number of silent Dutch films	Career before film
Wim Paauw	Het mysterie van de Mondscheinsonate					1	1909	1932	3	no films	0	Theatre

Source Honig, P.H. (1984). Acteurs- en kleinkunstenaars lexicon: 3200 namen uit honderd jaar Nederlands toneel. Diepenveen: Honig

References

Anon. The Endless Search for Screen Material. (1933, June 3). *Motion Picture Herald*, 110 (10), p. 28. https://archive.org/details/motionpictureher111unse

Bishoff, R. (1986). De zwijgende speelfilm. In K. Dibbets & F. Van der Maden (Eds.), *Geschiedenis van de Nederlandse film en bioscoop* (pp. 53–104). Het Wereldvenster.

Bordwell, D. (1989). A case for cognitivism. *Iris, 9*, 11–40.

Bordwell, D. (2007). *Poetics of cinema*. Routledge.

Bouber, H. (1920). *De Jantjes. Volksschets in 5 bedrijven*. Van Munster's Uitgevers–Maatschappij.

Delpher online newspaper archive. https://resolver.kb.nl/resolve?urn=ddd:110551744:mpeg21:p005

Donaldson, G. (1997). *Of joy and sorrow. A filmography of Dutch silent fiction*. Stichting Nederlands Filmmuseum.

Emmott, C., & Alexander, M. (2014). Schemata. In P. Hühn, J. C. Meister, J. Pier, & W. Schmid (Eds.), *Handbook of narratology* (pp. 756–764). De Gruyter.

Frijhoff, W. T. M. (2003). Toeëigening als vorm van culturele dynamiek. *Volkskunde, 104*(1), 3–17.

Garncarz, J. (2013). *Hollywood in Deutschland. Zur Internationalisierung der Kinokultur 1925–1990*. Stroemfeld/Nexus.

Garncarz, J. (2015). *Wechselende Vorlieben. Über die Filmpräferenzen der Europäer 1896–1939*. Stroemfeld/Nexus.

Hielkema, M. (1969). *Johan Kaart: Ik moet nog iets bekennen*. Semper Agendo N.V.

Honig, P. H. (1984). *Acteurs- en kleinkunstenaars lexicon: 3200 namen uit honderd jaar Nederlands toneel*. Honig.

Jong, A. M. (1920, December 4). Centraal Theater. Malle gevallen. *Het volk*, p. 4. https://resolver.kb.nl/resolve?urn=ddd:011081819:mpeg21:p004

Jurca, C., & Sedgwick, J. (2014). The film's the thing: Moviegoing in Philadelphia, 1935–36. *Film History, 26*(4), 58–83.

Koning, J. (1934, April 18). Een nieuw boek van mevrouw Szekeley-Lulofs. *Haagsche Courant*, b.5.p. 3. https://resolver.kb.nl/resolve?urn=MMKB04:000148166:mpeg21:p019

May, L. (2000). *The big tomorrow: Hollywood and the politics of the American way*. University of Chicago Press.

McDonald, K. I. (2006). *Reading a Japanese film. Cinema in context*. University of Hawai'i Press.

Miskell, P. (2016). International films and international globalisation of Hollywood entertainment, 1921–1951. *Media History, 22*(2), 174–200.

Nieuwe uitgaven. (1934, July 12). *Het Vaderland, Avondblad*, c. p. 1. https://resolver.kb.nl/resolve?urn=ddd:010015454:mpeg21:p009

Pafort-Overduin, C. (2012). *Hollandse films met een Hollands hart. Nationale identiteit en de Jordaanfilms, 1934–1936*. University of Utrecht.

Pafort-Overduin, C. (2018). Language and cultural nearness: Film programming strategies and audience preferences in big cities and small towns in the Netherlands 1934–1936. In D. Treveri Gennari, D. Hipkins, & C. O'Rawe (Eds.), *Rural cinema exhibition and audiences in a global context* (pp.283–302). Palgrave Macmillan.

Palmer, J. (1987). *The logic of the absurd. On film and television comedy*. St Edmunds Press.

Ross, T. (1986). De Nederlandse misdaadliteratuur. De moeizame weg naar volwassenheid. *Bzzlletin, 14* (137), 33–52. The journal is digitized by the Digital Library of Dutch Literature (DBNL): https://www.dbnl.org/tekst/_bzz001198501_01/_bzz001198501_01_0166.php

Sedgwick, J. (2000). *Filmgoing in 1930s Britain: A choice of pleasures*. Exeter University Press.

Sedgwick, J. (2020a). Constructing film histories: A bottom-up approach. *Academia Letters*. Article 86. https://doi.org/10.20935/AL86

Sedgwick, J. (2020b). From POPSTAT to Relpop: A methodological journey in investigating comparative film popularity. *TMG Journal for Media History, 23* (1–2), 1–9. https://doi.org/10.18146/tmg.776

Sedgwick, J., Pafort-Overduin, C., & Boter, J. (2012). Explanations for the restrained development of the Dutch cinema market in the 1930s, *Enterprise and Society, 13,* 634–671
Thompson, K. (1988). *Breaking the glass armor. Neoformalist film analysis.* Princeton University Press.
Van Gigch Jr, Mr.L. (1921, October 8). Theater successen. *De Telegraaf*, *Avondblad*, p. 58.
Van Wissen, L., Van Oort, T., Noordergraaf, J., & Kisjes, I. (2021). Cinema context as linked open data? Converting an online Dutch film culture dataset to RDF. *CEUR workshop proceedings, 2941.* http://ceur-ws.org/Vol-2941/paper10.pdf
Vos, J. (2011). *Johan Fabricius.* In J. Van Coillie, W. Van der Pennen, J. Staal, & H. Tromp (Eds.), *Lexicon van de jeugdliteratuur*. Martinus Nijhoff. https://www.dbnl.org/tekst/coil001lexi01_01/lvdj00307.php
Walch, F. (1996). *Roothaert: een biografie.* Baarn: De Prom.

Advertisements in Newspapers

(1921, February 5). *Algemeen Handelsblad*, p. 8. https://resolver.kb.nl/resolve?urn=ddd:010654606:mpeg21:p010
(1921, October 20). *Algemeen Handelsblad*, p. 8. https://resolver.kb.nl/resolve?urn=ddd:010655087:mpeg21:p008
(1922, April 4). *Algemeen Handelsblad,* p. 8. https://resolver.kb.nl/resolve?urn=ddd:010655215:mpeg21:p008
(1927, March 02). *Algemeen Handelsblad*, p. 7. https://resolver.kb.nl/resolve?urn=ddd:010657990:mpeg21:p007
(1932, April 25). *Algemeen Handelsblad*, p. 12. https://resolver.kb.nl/resolve?urn=ddd:010662530:mpeg21:p012
(1932, August 10). *Haagsche courant*, p. 8. https://resolver.kb.nl/resolve?urn=MMKB04:000146839:mpeg21:p007
(1918, May 27). *Het nieuws van den dag,* p. 8. https://resolver.kb.nl/resolve?urn=MMKB15:000638048:mpeg21:p00008
(1918, February 25). *De Telegraaf,* p. 3. https://resolver.kb.nl/resolve?urn=ddd:110549771:mpeg21:p003
(1919, September 27). *De Telegraaf*, p. 7. https://resolver.kb.nl/resolve?urn=ddd:110550798:mpeg21:p007
(1931, December 2). *De Telegraaf*, p. 11. https://resolver.kb.nl/resolve?urn=ddd:110571094:mpeg21:p011
(1934, August 10). *Het Vaderland*, p. 4. https://resolver.kb.nl/resolve?urn=ddd:010015504:mpeg21:p012

Films

Benno, A. (director). (1934). *Op hoop van zegen* [DVD].
Benno, A. & R. Oswald. (director). (1934). *Bleeke Bet* [DVD].
Gerron, K. (director). (1935). *Het mysterie van de Mondscheinsonate* [DVD].
Janson, V. (director). (1935). *Fientje Peters – Poste restante* [DVD].
Koster, H., & Winar, E. (director). (1935). *De kribbebijter* [DVD].
Meinert, R. (director). (1934). *Het meisje met den blauwen hoed* [DVD].
Meinert, R. (director). (1935). *De vier Mullers* [DVD].

Nosseck, M. (director). (1935). *De big van het regiment* [DVD].
Rutten, G. (director). (1934). *Dood Water* [DVD].
Speyer, J. (director). (1934a). *De Jantjes* [DVD].
Speyer, J. (director). (1934b). *Malle gevallen* [DVD].
Speyer, J. (director). (1935). *De familie van mijn vrouw* [DVD].
Teunissen, G. J. (director). (1934). *Willem van Oranje* [DVD].
Van Peski, H. (director). (1935a). *Suikerfreule* [DVD].
Van Peski, H. (director). (1935b). *Het leven is niet zo kwaad* [DVD].
Winar, E. (director). (1935). *Op stap* [DVD].

Clara Pafort Overduin is a lecturer and researcher in the Department of Media and Culture Studies & Institute for Cultural Inquiry (ICON), Utrecht University. She works on popular cinema in the Netherlands and has published several book chapters and articles on the popularity of national films in the 1930s—the subject of her Ph.D. With economic historian John Sedgwick and marketing economist Jaap Boter she published on the peculiarities of the structure and development of the Dutch film market in the 1930s. With Douglas Gomery she wrote the student handbook Movie History: A Survey. (Routledge, 2012). She strongly believes in sharing knowledge and expertise and tries to bring that into practice through the History of Moviegoing, Exhibition and Reception (HoMER) Network.

Unravelling Australia's 'Infamous "Contract" System': Evidence from Adelaide, 1942–1943

Dylan Walker and Mike Walsh

Abstract The conventional wisdom espoused by cultural nationalists in Australia is that Hollywood films dominated Australian screens by virtue of a powerful, inflexible block-booking system. Using a dataset of screenings from Adelaide, a second-tier capital city, this article seeks to replace such totalising generalisations with a more complex view of the diverse relations that constituted exhibition in Australia. Different exhibitors and distributors had a widely divergent set of tactical business arrangements, which conditioned the way films moved through the various phases of their release. Our study centres on the 1942–1943 financial year, for which we have specific box-office figures, thereby allowing us to check the accuracy of POPSTAT estimates.

In providing cinemas with a weight expressed as a potential revenue figure, the POPSTAT methodology provides us with the tools to answer specific questions. Most frequently, it is used to answer questions about the relative popularity of individual films and types of movies, for example, British films instead of Hollywood. We aim to pose slightly different questions about how audience preferences interact with various institutional relationships, particularly those concerning the policies of different distributors.

Notably, the POPSTAT methodology asks us to look at what films played on what screens and for how long. In his study of the British film industry in the 1930s, John Sedgwick noted that different films enjoyed very different exhibition patterns and explained this as part of rational economic activity and that exhibitors booked

D. Walker (✉)
Adelaide, SA, Australia
e-mail: sacinema@hotmail.com

M. Walsh
Flinders University, Adelaide, SA, Australia
e-mail: mike.walsh@flinders.edu.au

J. Sedgwick (ed.), *Towards a Comparative Economic History of Cinema, 1930–1970*, Frontiers in Economic History, https://doi.org/10.1007/978-3-031-05770-0_7

specific films in the expectation that audiences wanted to see them.[1] sar-Variations in the number and scale of exhibition engagements can be read as differences in the relative popularity of films.

This is not an uncontroversial assumption, at least in an Australian context, where block-booking and blind-bidding, which were illegal in other markets such as the United Kingdom, were a significant part of the relations between distribution and exhibition. Cultural nationalists have always been quick to invoke block-booking as the bogey that locked Australian films out of local cinemas. Diane Collins writes that 'the infamous "contract" system gave them (US distributors) what almost amounted to de facto control of exhibition'.[2] More recently, Stephen Gaunson has taken up a similar position, charging that block-booking anchored American film dominance both at home and abroad.[3]

Collins and Gaunson represent an alternative explanation to Sedgwick's popularity assumption, suggesting that cinema markets did not operate freely and that industrial fetters such as block-booking contracts might trump popularity in explaining the patterns of exhibition observed by POPSTATers.

While this is a polemic worth drawing, it, of course, oversimplifies the opposite positions of the argument. No one would assert that industrial manipulation or audience popularity offered adequate explanations of the market. When given two alternatives, our first impulse should be an attempt to accept both and to work out their interconnection. Even a cultural nationalist like Gaunson must acknowledge the popularity of Hollywood, providing a heavily Pavlovian explanation for it when he writes that 'Because block bookings had given Australians a staple diet of Hollywood product, it was Hollywood movies that filmgoers craved'.[4]

Except for Sedgwick's work on Sydney, we still know very little about the small-scale patterns of distribution and exhibition that were so important to how Australian audiences experienced the cinema.[5] In the 1980s, John Tulloch pointed to the need for a more complex narrative than the simple assumption of American distribution hegemony.[6] Most accounts of block-booking are over-stated, overly generalised or just plain wrong. Gaunson, for example, writes that:

> Under the plan, exhibitors were contracted to exclusively screen only films from the block packages: meaning no films from rival studios or independent films could be shown.[7]

As Sedgwick, Pokorny and Miskell point out, the balance of power between exhibition and distribution was radically different in the first-run compared to the subsequent suburban-run.[8] Approaches that ignore the differences between varying levels

[1] Sedgwick (2000).

[2] Collins (1987, p. 13).

[3] Gaunson (2012).

[4] Gaunson (2018, p. 215).

[5] Sedgwick (2011).

[6] John Tulloch (1982).

[7] Gaunson (2018, p. 213).

[8] Sedgwick et al. (2014).

of cinema presentation fail to grasp the diversity of the industrial practices that constituted film exhibition, obscuring the varieties of choices available to exhibitors and audiences. This chapter examines Adelaide's first-run and suburban exhibition for the 1942/3 financial year. Adelaide is the city where we live and have studied most intensely. The year has been chosen because of the availability of pricing and partial box-office information. At the outset, let us say that instead of the generalised pattern of Hollywood distribution dominance, our study will show a remarkable degree of diversity, with no two cinemas, or two distributors, operating in the same way.

1 General Context

Debates about the establishment and maintenance of Hollywood films' popularity are by no means unique to Australia. Still, they have a specific salience given how the United Kingdom attempted to use her Empire as a trade bloc to maintain her international trading position against the rising economic power of the United States in the years following World War 1. Hollywood cinema had achieved a dominant place on Australian screens by the late 1910s.[9] A Royal Commission in 1927–1928 had heard (and largely dismissed) charges that the major Hollywood distributors were acting as a cartel to suppress British and Australian films and damage Australian culture through effects ranging from juvenile delinquency to ugly slang. In the aftermath of the fall of Singapore and the change in Australia's defence policy from reliance on the United Kingdom to a dependence on the United States, popular cinema, more than ever, became a highly visible field in which these tensions could be played out.

At the outbreak of the Second World War, the exhibition industry in South Australia was concerned about how the war would impact cinema attendances. Having overcome the downturn of the Great Depression, Australian industry was re-establishing ground towards the end of the 1930s. By the onset of the Second World War, there was 131 permanent picture shows in South Australia, with attendances during the previous year estimated at nine million.[10] The Directors of D. Clifford Theatres reported, 'the serious turn of international affairs has effected (sic) the economic position, and clouded the future of the industry with some uncertainty'.[11] The South Australian Motion Picture Exhibitors Association's President shared this uncertainty, observing that 'the declaration of war has dampened general conditions'.[12] However, these fears were not realised. There was a growth in the

[9] Thompson (1985).

[10] South Australian Motion Picture Exhibitors Association (SAMPEA) President's Report of 18 October 1939, quoted in Paul Paech, *Cinema in Adelaide to 1945*, BA (Hons) Thesis, University of Adelaide, 1975.

[11] D. Clifford Theatres Ltd., *The Report of Directors for Half-Year ended 30 June 1939*, dated 20 September 1939, State Records of South Australia, GRS513/7/134/1922.

[12] SAMPEA, op. cit.

industry that saw new cinemas built and others renovated. According to Paul Paech, theatre employees demanded higher wages in October 1942 due to a 'prosperity wave in attendances'.[13]

2 The Diversity of the First-Run

In 1942/3, Adelaide's population was approximately 350,000, three to four times smaller than Australia's two largest cities, Sydney and Melbourne. Australia's third-largest city can be grouped with Brisbane (344,200) as a second-tier Australian city.[14] Adelaide's ten first-run Central Business District cinemas (CBD) were clustered close together.[15] The cinemas are listed in Table 1, along with screening practices and an indication of the variety of tariffs charged.

Films moved through second-tier cities in different ways to first-tier cities. While Adelaide had one-third to one-quarter of the population of Sydney and Melbourne and around half the number of first-release CBD cinemas, it still experienced the release of roughly the same number of films. Adelaide's first-run houses screened 397 new releases and 100 revival titles during the financial year (1 July to 30 June 1942/3). *Film Weekly* lists 362 new releases in Australia in the 1942 calendar year and 333 in 1943, suggesting that virtually all new releases travelled through Adelaide. Given the disparity of size, cinema numbers, and cinema control in each of Australia's principal cities, but the constancy of film throughput, we might expect different release patterns to emerge specific to each (Fig. 1).

In Australian capital cities, the standard first-release practice was to run a double bill or long single feature four times per day, six days per week. However, the surprising thing is the diversity represented within this basic structure. First-run releasing was anything but a standardised, unitary practice. Some cinemas ran films for extended seasons, while others were weekly change houses geared around weekly visits by customers who might book regular seats on a seasonal basis. Some changed programmes regularly on Fridays while others changed at other times or ran split weeks or shorter weeks. Some alternated between vaudeville and cinema, with film revival seasons in periods between live shows. Only one Adelaide cinema persevered with the tradition of live stage acts preceding the film presentation. Some cinemas were part of circuits, while a distributor directly owned one. These features bear closer analysis if we are to gain a more detailed sense of how the business of first-run film exhibition worked.

---

[13] Paul Paech, *Cinema in Adelaide to 1945*, BA (Hons) Thesis, University of Adelaide, 1975, p. 23.

[14] Commonwealth Bureau of Census and Statistics, Official Yearbook of the Commonwealth of Australia 1942/3, p. 272.

[15] We have excluded one newsreel theatrette. Nine of the cinemas were located on Hindley and Rundle Streets - which is the same street, changing names as it crosses King William Street, on the basis that no street name should go across that of a sovereign.

Table 1 Adelaide CBD cinemas 1942–1943

Cinema	Owners	(1) Seating capacity	(2) No. of weekly screenings	(3) Top price (d)	(4) Mid-range admission price (d)	(5) Box Office Potential (£)	(6) Cinema weight	(7) No. of seating tariffs	(8) No. of temporal tariffs
Civic	Greater Union	1,502	24	47	31	4,716	1.19	5	5
Liberty	Fullers Theatres	382	24	31	23	879	0.22	1	3
Majestic	Fullers Theatres	1,193	12	31	23	1,372	0.35	1	3
Mayfair	Greater Union	959	24	63	39	3,740	0.94	6	4
Metro	Metro-Goldwyn-Mayer	1,286	24	63	39	5,015	1.26	12	9
Regent	Hoyts'	2,262	24	63	37	8,309	2.10	9	4
Rex	Rex Theatres	1,171	24	39	27	3,162	0.80	5	3
Theatre Royal	Australian & NZ Theatres	1,500	24	31	23	3,450	0.87	3	1
Wests Theatre	Greater Union	1148	18	63	39	3,358	0.85	6	5
York	S.A. Theatres Ltd	1823	24	47	31	5,651	1.43	5	2

Source Film Weekly Yearbook, 1943 for seating capacity and ownership, National Archives of Australia for admission prices, and the Adelaide Advertiser (trove.nla.gov.au) for screening information

Notes CBD is the abbreviation for Central Business District. Prices reflect adult prices only and are expressed in pennies, of which there were 12 to a shilling and 20 shillings to a pound. The mid-price is derived by halving the difference between the top and lowest price for adult admission. In the case of most suburban cinemas where only two prices were set, the mid-price is unproblematic. However, in first-run cinemas such as the Regent, where multiple prices were established, including higher prices for the Saturday evening main show and even higher prices still on public holidays, the mid-price probably under-represents the potential revenue of the cinema, given the popularity of Saturday night and public holiday screenings

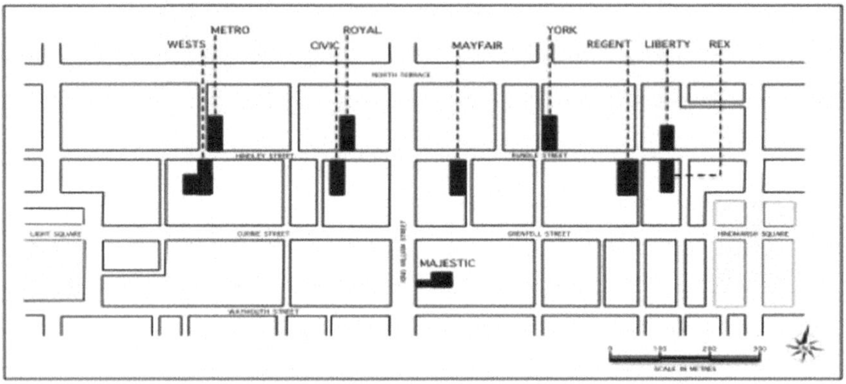

Fig. 1 Adelaide CBD cinemas map for 1942 (Courtesy of Dylan Walker)

Sedgwick's investigation of Sydney city and suburbs in 1934 notes the formation of a General Theatres Corporation, which temporarily brought major exhibitors Greater Union (GU) and Hoyts into a cartel as they sought to trade their way through the Depression. However, by the more prosperous 1940s, GU and Hoyts had re-emerged as separately profitable entities. GU had always enjoyed a more substantial presence in Adelaide, controlling four first-run screens to Hoyts's two. Theatrical impresario, Sir Benjamin Fuller, had a circuit of two theatres, both of which alternated between live theatre and film, while the Metro and Theatre Royal were independently programmed.

There were three principal classes of first-run cinemas[16]:

- Top of the line first-run, charging premium prices (up to 5 shillings 3 pence (5/3) or 63d (pence) on Saturday nights)—the Regent, Wests and the Metro.[17] As shown in Table 1, these cinemas practised multiple admission tariff regimes based spatial and temporal considerations. This was particularly so in the case of the Metro, which took price discrimination to a very high level.
- Second-tier first-release and move-over houses, charging lower maximum prices (3/11 or 47d on Saturday night). These are the York, Civic and Mayfair cinemas programmed by the GU and the Rex for Hoyts.
- Intermittent cinemas, vaudeville, and revival houses, charging lower prices still—the Majestic and the Theatre Royal.[18]

It is important to note that this first-run system catered for the differences in the popularity of films, which was reflected in the programming strategies of the various

[16] The Liberty cinema is not included in this classification.

[17] All pricing information is sourced from the National Archives of Australia, Series No. AP5/1, Control Symbol 40/926A, "Picture Theatre Prices", https://recordsearch.naa.gov.au/SearchNRetrieve/Interface/ViewImage.aspx?B=1331106.

[18] The Australia Pound comprised 20 shillings, with each shilling sub-dived into 12 pennies (d).

Table 2 Comparison of film programming at the Metro and Regent, 1942/3 Financial year

Metro
Films: 32 films (all MGM)
Average program: 2.4 weeks
Hoyts' Regent
93 films: 32 Fox (including 2 Gaumont British),
27 RKO,
20 UA,
12 Warner Bros.,
2 Columbia
Average program: 1.04 weeks

cinemas. The existence of move-over houses—GU's York and Hoyts' Rex—recognises that some first-release films will have exhausted their audience after a week. In contrast, others still yielded profitable grosses when run for a further week. It also assumes that first-release grosses were unpredictable and provided the necessary programming flexibility for varying success during a film's first week. GU further realised that some films would merit programming in larger houses while others could be moved more quickly through smaller, cheaper cinemas.

Accordingly, over time cinema exhibitors and film distributors had developed an adjustable environment that allowed audiences to see those films they most wanted to see and, in doing so, maximise box-office and rental revenues and consumer satisfaction. It is clear from Table 1 that considerable differences existed in the revenue potential of the respective cinemas. Based upon the seating capacity of cinemas, the number of daily screenings, and the mid-prices of admission, cinema weights are calculated, reflecting each cinema's revenue potential relative to the average. From this, we learn that the revenue-raising capacity of the Liberty cinema was just under ten times lower than the Regent.

Vertical integration played a vital role in the Hollywood system.[19] In Adelaide, the two main instances of vertical integration involved MGM and Fox, though they took very different forms. In 1930 Fox had bought control of Hoyts at the outset of the Depression. In 1939 MGM opened a cinema in Adelaide, as it did in many cities worldwide. In both cases, the possession of a dedicated first-run cinema became the lynchpin of very different distribution strategies. Table 2 highlights these differences.

MGM and Fox each released 32 of their in-house films at their vertically integrated exhibition outlet. However, this is where the similarity ends. MGM monopolised the Metro's programming, with all 32 of the films that screened there being MGM releases. It is worth noting that although Gaunson asserts that block-booking meant that cinemas could screen only the movies of a single distributor, the only cinema in the entire state to do this was the Metro. It ran 22 programmes over the year: 12 single feature programmes and ten double-bill programmes. The longest run was 40 days given over to *Mrs Miniver*, followed by 35 days for *Blossoms in the Dust*.

[19] See the Managing Risk…Chapter for a discussion of this.

A further two single feature programmes ran for three weeks (18 days)—*Babes on Broadway* and *Smilin' Through. Rio Rita* was also screened for three weeks, but this time as a lead feature on the double-bill programme. Other than one double bill of *The Feminine Touch* and *Girl in the News*, the remaining programmes were held over for a second week. The average programme length was 2.4 weeks.

On the other hand, the Regent predominantly ran weekly change programmes, with just two held over for a second week—*This Above All* as a single bill and *Weekend in Havana* as the main attraction on a double-bill programme. Part of the difference in turnover can be explained by the Regent's more extensive seating and revenue capacity (2262 seats) compared to the 1286-seater Metro. Hoyts' strategy in Adelaide was to keep capacity high by accentuating the scarcity of the film—'see it quickly, or it will be gone'. To supply the Regent's greater need for films, Hoyts contracted with RKO, United Artists and Warner Bros. for additional films.

Cinema size is an important feature—it is a crucial variable calculating POPSTAT methodology—but with it comes the burden of using that capacity, that is, keeping the cinema full. This is the likely explanation why the Regent, as the largest cinema in Adelaide, persevered with live stage shows—a costly staple of 1920s first-run and commonly understood as a trigger for the innovation of synchronised sound.[20] For competitive reasons, the Regent could not charge higher ticket prices than those of its direct rivals, the Metro and GU's flagship Wests, all of which charged 5/3 (63d—see note to Table 1 for an explanation of the Australian currency) maximum for seats in the lounge on Saturday nights. Patrons at the Regent were treated to a selection of weekly entertainments as a standard part of the evening bill. These included vaudeville acts, such as novelty dancers, contortionists, ventriloquists and even the winners of the Munitions Workers' Talent Quest. Live shows added to the programme's attractiveness and reinforced the factor of scarcity. A film might be seen later but a live act, once missed, might be missed forever.

The first-run exhibition involves keeping the programme scarce but not so scarce that demand went unsatisfied. Films were diffused across a series of linked first-release and move-over houses platforms. Hoyts' Regent and Rex cinemas operated in tandem, with 37 of Rex's 49 programmes (over 75%) coming from the Regent. The York had a more complex relationship with the Metro, with 13 of its 46 programmes containing films moved over from the Metro, including the main attractions mentioned above. The first two (*Mrs Miniver* and *Blossoms in the Dust*) were screened on single bill programmes for two weeks and one week, respectively. There is also a significant difference in the programming arrangements for these two move-over houses. The Rex took programmes immediately after finishing their one-week runs at the Regent, whereas the York always had four weeks between first-release and move-over.

The probable reason for this difference is that Hoyts controlled both the Regent and the Rex, whereas the Metro and the York had different ownership. Accordingly, MGM was interested in establishing a temporal window following Metro screenings

[20] Bakker, G (2012) How motion pictures industrialized entertainment, *Journal of Economic History*, 72(4):1036–1063.

to emphasise the time preference characteristics of the audience and encourage them to consume MGM films in the company cinema before subsequent distribution in non-in-house cinemas. (The one-month temporal zone became institutionalised in the form of the standardised exhibition contract due to the so-called Film War of 1934, fought between the General Theatres Corporation and the US distributors about the distribution of films between first and suburban cinemas. By 1942–1943, it would seem that only MGM ignored this practice, giving suburban premieres two weeks after the end of the first-run and before CBD move-over screenings at the York.)

Outside of the mainstream, a quite different programming strategy was pursued by the Liberty, controlled by theatrical entrepreneur Sir Benjamin Fuller. Opening as a cinema in January 1943, the Liberty registered the longest average run among Adelaide's first-run cinemas of 5.2 weeks for each programme, featuring five Warner Bros. films and one from Paramount. Five of its programmes were screened as single bill attractions. The nine-week season of Warner's *Yankee Doodle Dandy* was the longest run for any film in Adelaide. However, considering that the Liberty (advertised as 'Adelaide's new intimate theatre') contained only 382 seats—roughly one-seventh the capacity of the Regent—this is not quite as impressive as it would otherwise seem.

The evidence from the programming data is that every distributor had different relationships with the first-run exhibition circuits. These can be summarised as follows:

- MGM: first-releases at the Metro with move-overs and second-tier releases at the York. Some revival screenings were held in Hoyts' move-over cinema, the Rex.
- Paramount: A strong association with General Union and no screenings at cinemas run by Hoyts; 17 first-releases at Wests including *Reap the Wild West Wind* and *The Louisiana Purchase,* which screened as single bill attractions for five and three weeks respectively and 16 s-tier releases at York; and revivals at the Majestic and Theatre Royal.
- United Artists: Its most popular release was *Eagle Squadron,* which was screened for five weeks at Wests. However, most first-run releases were screened at the Regent with move-over to the Rex. Second-tier releases were screened at both the Rex and the York cinemas.
- Columbia: strong association with Greater Union's lower-tier weekly change houses, the Civic and the Mayfair.
- Universal was like Columbia in its strong association with the Civic and the Mayfair. Its three Top 20 films, all starring Abbott and Costello, were screened as lead attractions on double-bill programmes, each for four weeks.
- British Empire Films (BEF): owned by Greater Union, and its films were screened exclusively in the four cinemas programmed by the company.
- RKO: released primarily through Hoyts. None of the films produced by its studio wing made the Top 20 listing, although *Fantasia,* which it distributed for Walt Disney, was premiered at the York as a single bill attraction for 25 days.
- Fox: all of its new releases through the vertically linked Regent.

- Warner Bros. used a mixture of exhibition venues. Films were released through Hoyts' Regent, GU's York and Fuller's Liberty.

From the point of view of the exhibition circuits, Hoyts' programmes were built around Fox, with RKO and UA filling programming shortfalls. With double the number of cinemas, Greater Union gave the prime position to Paramount. It also provided the bulk of exhibition release berths for Columbia, Universal and its own vertically linked British Empire Films.

A word should be said about BEF, which Greater Union founded in the early 1930s to re-enter distribution using British films.[21] Ironically, by the 1940s, the bulk of the films BEF distributed was from second category American producers, Republic and Monogram, and heavily weighted towards westerns. Of the 63 films BEF released in Adelaide during the period, only ten were British compared to 32 Republic films and 19 Monograms—two Russian films were also distributed. Although BEF was ostensibly nationalist in its origin, the imperative of securing industrial supply can be seen here. The basis of the relationship between distribution and exhibition was the regularity of supply, which weighed against British film at this juncture of the Second World War. (The Top 20 films listed in Table 5 contain a single British film, *The 49*th *Parallel*. However, it is significant that four other films (*Mrs Miniver, Eagle Squadron, Dr Jekyll and Mr Hyde, How Green Was My Valley*) were fictional stories set in Britain, though made in the United States. While no Australian feature films were released during this period, local content was present through GU's Cinesound and Fox's Movietone newsreels and other shorts—not to mention the live acts at the Regent.

Along with Columbia and Universal, BEF distributed the largest number of new films, specialising in supplying Greater Union's lower-tier cinemas. Columbia had only one movie that ran longer than two weeks, while 37 of its 58 new releases were second features on double-bill programmes. The three distributors specialised in pumping enough new product through the system to mop up excess screen capacity and equalise film flows through larger and smaller cities.

Before moving to the suburbs, we might return to the initial question of the interconnection of popularity and industrial structure. A notable feature of Table 5 (found later in the chapter) is that the first 11 films in the POPSTAT Top 20 opened at the Metro, Regent or Wests—the highest-priced flagship cinemas in Adelaide. Some movies came into the market positioned to succeed by being programmed into high-ranked cinemas. But this does not explain subsequent variations in performance both in the first-run and then in the number of suburban bookings. The contractual relations between distribution and exhibition reflect what we might call an 'expectation of popularity', based on factors such as the production inputs (stars, budgets) and the performance of the films in earlier release markets (not only the United States and Britain but also Sydney and Melbourne). These expectations were constantly being

[21] During the period from 1913 to the mid-1920s Union Theatres' (GU's Pre-Depression forerunner) distribution arm, Australasian Films, dominated by buying the rights to Hollywood films they then distributed locally. This position was gradually eroded during the 1920s as the Hollywood studios established their own distribution subsidiaries in Australia.

tested and refined as films worked their way through the various phases of their release.

3 Distribution into the Suburbs

Film Weekly listed 53 suburban cinemas operating in Adelaide during the 1942–1943 season, 47 of which advertised regular programmes. These can be found in the Appendix. Programming data for these cinemas have been collected from the daily *Adelaide Advertiser*. Unfortunately, these records are patchy, with almost full sets of information available for only 26 cinemas. Our data is complete for June to December 1942 for all suburban Ozone and Clifford screening venues and independent suburban screening venues that were purpose-built cinemas. However, although incomplete, sufficient data exists for January to June 1943 to add to our knowledge of the sector.

A further difficulty emerges caused by the narrow time frame in which programming records have been collected. The consequence is that many films screened in the 1942–1943 season were released during the previous season and were coming to the end of their life cycle. At the other end, films such as *Mrs Miniver* and *Blossoms in the Dust* (Table 5) had not entered their suburban phase by the end of the 1942/43 financial year. Accordingly, the true popularity of films affected in either of these ways cannot be gauged, meaning that their revenues are necessarily underreported. Despite these caveats, the process of distribution in Adelaide captured by these data emerges strongly.

Two circuits dominated suburban exhibition: D. Clifford Theatres, branding many of their cinemas as 'Stars', and the Waterman family's circuit whose cinemas were branded as 'Ozone'. Altogether, D. Clifford Theatres controlled 17 suburban cinemas (including the 'Adelaide Star' located in the CBD, but which essentially operated as a suburban cinema) and, because of its larger-than-average cinemas, 43% of suburban seating capacity. Likewise, but on a smaller scale, Ozone Theatres ran nine suburban venues, supplying 26% of suburban seating capacity. The remainder comprised two smaller chains of four cinemas, one of three, two of two and six single cinema businesses. Outside of the city, in the enormous rural hinterland of South Australia, the two chains had a lower profile, operating between them only 10 of the 79 rural cinemas, the bulk of which were run as single independents.

Table 3 records that 885 films circulated in Adelaide and its suburbs during the financial year of 1942–1943, garnering 14,715 days of screening. These divided 35/65% between the CBD and suburbs. Of course, this statistic does not reflect the number of actual screenings. Whereas first-run cinemas in the CBD ran four programmes daily, six days per week, most suburban cinemas offered only nightly programmes apart from Saturdays when they offered evening and matinee screenings. Few screened six days per week, with several opening only on Saturdays. This factor, together with the higher admission prices, the greater preponderance of single

Table 3 POPSTAT derived Adelaide CBD and suburban film circulation statistics

Data	Value
Number of films screened	885
CBD Screening Days	4,764
CBD Potential Box Office (£)	2,047,106
Suburban Screening Days	9,951
Suburban Potential Box Office (£)	759,830
Total Screening Days	14,715
Total Potential Box-Office (£)	2,806,486

Source Adelaide Advertiser
Note See the *Notes* to Eq. 1 for an account of how the potential box-office is calculated

billing programmes and larger cinemas sizes of first-run cinemas, helps to explain the reversal in proportions shown by the Potential Box-Office columns in which the size of the CBD market is displayed to be approximately three times greater than that of the suburban market (75–25% share).

What is proposed is not a record of actual box-office but an index of the box-office potential of cinemas based upon POPSTAT methods.

$$\text{POPSTAT Index}_{it} = \sum_{j=0}^{n} (p * q)_j * l_{jt} * s_{jt} * bs_{jt} \tag{1}$$

The Potential Box Office for each *i*th film in period *t* is given by the product of the mid-price cost of admission and seating capacity ($p * q$) of the *j*th cinemas in which it is screened as well as its length of run (l), the number of screenings offered (s), and billing status (bs) of the film, where shared (two films) billings attract a 0.5 weighting. In contrast, a single bill programme is given the weight of 1.0.[22] (With 20 exceptions, all movies screened in suburban cinemas were on double-bill programmes.)

Depicted in Fig. 2, the Box-Office Index for the population of films circulating in Adelaide and suburbs during the 1942–1943 season gives rise to a familiar shaped, albeit extreme, frequency distribution of film revenues. From the associated statistics found in Table 4, it is evident that the distribution is highly unequal: one in which the most popular film is some 15 times the mean and 27 times greater than that earned by the median movie, with a coefficient of variation well above the value of 1. These statistics imply that many films were doing very little business during the period under analysis.

Table 5 lists the Top 20, 50th, 100th, 286th and 443rd films, the last two representing the Box-Office Index distribution's mean and median values. It also provides statistics about their circulation and information about their provenance and star and directorial inputs. In terms of earnings, the Top 20 most popular films generate close

[22] As indicated in the discussion around Table 1, several first-run cinemas practiced a high level of price discrimination. A mid-price procedure is used.

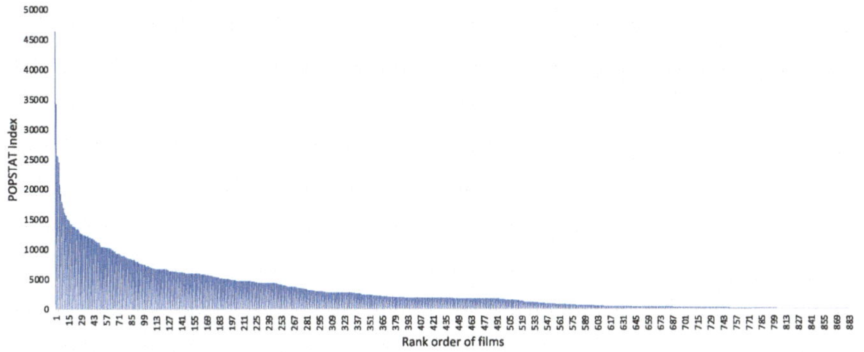

Fig. 2 Rank-size distribution of POPSTAT estimated Box-Office Index

Table 4 Descriptive statistics associated with Fig. 2

Statistics	Values
Mean	3,171
Standard error	140
Median	1,833
Mode	1,870
Standard deviation	4,169
Sample variance	17,378,853
Kurtosis	19.46
Skewness	3.24
Range	46,395
Minimum	15
Maximum	46,410
Sum	2,806,486
Count	885

Source Dataset

to 15% of the market, dwarfing films constituting the lower half of box-office distribution. MGM dominates the list of the most popular movies with four Top 5 films and eight of the Top 20.

Films in the lower half of the distribution were either screened just once in a CBD cinema, if at all, and then received a scattering of suburban bookings. Take, for instance, the median film *International Lady*. It was not screened in the CBD during our period but rather opened at the Capitol, in the suburb of St. Peters, in September 1942 on a 3-day double-bill programme, appearing at a further ten cinemas for mostly one-day bookings. Seven of these bookings were with the D. Clifford chain. Even with the block-booking system in which suburban exhibitors contracted to take several films from several distributors, there was no shortage of movies for exhibitors to choose between, as we have seen, causing a very thin tail to the statistical

Table 5 Top 20, 50th, 100th, Mean and Median Films Circulating in Adelaide (CBD and Suburbs, 1942–1943

(1) Rank	(2) Film title	(3) CBD POPSTAT Index	(4) Suburban POPSTAT Index	(5) Total POPSTAT Index	(6) CBD screening days	(7) Suburban screening days	(8) Total screening days	(9) Opening cinema	(10) Studio	(11) Distributor	(12) Star 1	(13) Star 2	(14) Director
1	Mrs. Miniver	46,410		46,410	54		54	Metro	MGM	MGM	Greer Garson	Walter Pidgeon	William Wyler
2	Blossoms in the Dust	34,281		34,281	41		41	Metro	MGM	MGM	Greer Garson	Walter Pidgeon	Mervyn Le Roy
3	Ziegfeld Girl	20,698	4,752	25,629	24	65	89	Metro	MGM	MGM	James Stewart	Judy Garland	Robert Z Leonard
4	Reap the Wild Wind	25,548		25,548	36		36	Wests	Paramount	Paramount	Ray Milland	John Wayne	Cecil B DeMille
5	Babes on Broadway	17,872	6,571	24,622	24	91	115	Metro	MGM	MGM	Mickey Rooney	Judy Garland	Busby Berkeley
6	Dive Bomber	15,145	5,416	20,801	18	77	95	Regent	Warner Bros	Warner Bros	Errol Flyn	Fred MacMurray	Micahel Curtiz
7	Fantasia	16,954	2,275	19,229	24	30	54	York	Walt Disney	RKO			Uncreditied
8	Eagle Squadron	11,193	6,553	17,925	30	96	126	Wests	Walter Wanger	United Artists	Robert Slack	Diana Barrymore	Aurhtur Lubin
9	49th Parallel	12,351	5,151	17,682	13	74	87	Regent	Ortus Films	TCF	Leslie Howard	Laurence Olivier	Michael Powell
10	They Died With Their Boots On	16,954		16,954	18		18	York	Warner Bros	Warner Bros	Errol Flyn	Olivia De Haviland	Raoul Walsh

(continued)

Table 5 (continued)

(1) Rank	(2) Film title	(3) CBD POPSTAT Index	(4) Suburban POPSTAT Index	(5) Total POPSTAT Index	(6) CBD screening days	(7) Suburban screening days	(8) Total screening days	(9) Opening cinema	(10) Studio	(11) Distributor	(12) Star 1	(13) Star 2	(14) Director
11	Dr. Jekyll and Mr. Hyde	12,856	3,101	16,137	18	41	59	Metro	MGM	MGM	Spencer Tracy	Lana Turner	Victor Flemming
12	Andy Hardy's Private Secretary	10,244	5,348	15,832	24	67	91	Metro	MGM	MGM	Louis Stone	Micky Rooney	George B Seitz
13	How Green Was My Valley	9,153	6,304	15,698	24	85	109	Regent	TCF	TCF	Walter Pidgeon	Maureen O'Hara	John Ford
14	Smilin' Through	15,046		15,046	18		18	Metro	MGM	MGM	Jeanette MacDonald	Brian Aherne	Frank Borzage
15	Hold That Ghost	9,312	5,522	15,014	24	75	99	Civic	Universal	Universal	Bud Abbott	Lou Costello	Arthur Lubin
16	San Antonio Rose	11,193	3,449	14,882	30	47	77	Wests	Universal	Universal	Jane Frazee	Robert Page	Charles Lamont
17	In the Navy	9,312	4,840	14,332	24	68	92	Civic	Universal	Universal	Bud Abbott	Lou Costello	Arthur Lubin
18	Louisiana Purchase	14,266		14,266	23		23	Wests	Paramount	Paramount	Bob Hope	Vera Zorina	Irving Cummings
19	Son of Fury	7,704	6,208	14,152	19	77	96	Regent	TCF	TCF	Tyrone Power	Gene Tierney	John Cromwell

(continued)

Table 5 (continued)

(1) Rank	(2) Film title	(3) CBD POPSTAT Index	(4) Suburban POPSTAT Index	(5) Total POPSTAT Index	(6) CBD screening days	(7) Suburban screening days	(8) Total screening days	(9) Opening cinema	(10) Studio	(11) Distributor	(12) Star 1	(13) Star 2	(14) Director
20	Caught in the Draft	8,954	5,737	13,758	24	68	92	Wests	Paramount	Paramount	Bob Hope	Dorothy Lamour	David Butler
50	On the Sunny Side	5,992	5,200	11,192	15	56	71	Regent	TCF	TCF	Roddy McDowall	Jane Darwell	Harold D Schuster
100	Parachute Nurse	4,656	2,823	7,480	12	30	42	Civic	Columbia	Columbia	Marguerite Chapman	William Wright	Charles Barton
286	Tanks a Million	2,826	346	3172	6	7	13	York	Hal Roach Studios	United Artists	William Tracy	James Gleason	Fred Guiol
443	International Lady		1,833	1,833		26	26	Capitol, St. Peters	Edward Small	United Artists	George Brent	Illona Massey	Tim Whelan
All Films		2,047,106.208	7,59,380	28,06,486	5,135	9.579	14,715						

Source Screening data from the Adelaide Advertiser, film data from Film Weekly Yearbook, 1943 and 1944
Note Cinemas were open six days a week

distribution of films in circulation. However, it is apparent in Table 5 that this is not the same as saying that specific films were not attractive to suburban audiences. Instead, it is the case that among the population of films in circulation, main attractions were comparatively rare; this was particularly problematic for small independent exhibitors, which were only given booking access to these films only after they had exhausted their stay in the Star and Ozone circuits (Fig. 3).

A strong performance in the CBD does not necessarily equate to an equally strong performance in the suburbs. Compare, for instance, the respective success of the 7th and 8th films in Table 5, suggesting that *Fantasia* had a more limited appeal in the suburbs: after a 24-day premiere the York cinema in the CBD, as a single bill attraction, its suburban circulation was, with one exception, confined to eight cinemas in the Ozone chain. In contrast, *Eagle Squadron* was screened by 43 different suburban cinemas, including both major suburban chains, following its premiere in the CBD at Wests, where it appeared on a strong 30-day double-bill programme with 16th ranked *San Antonio Rose.*

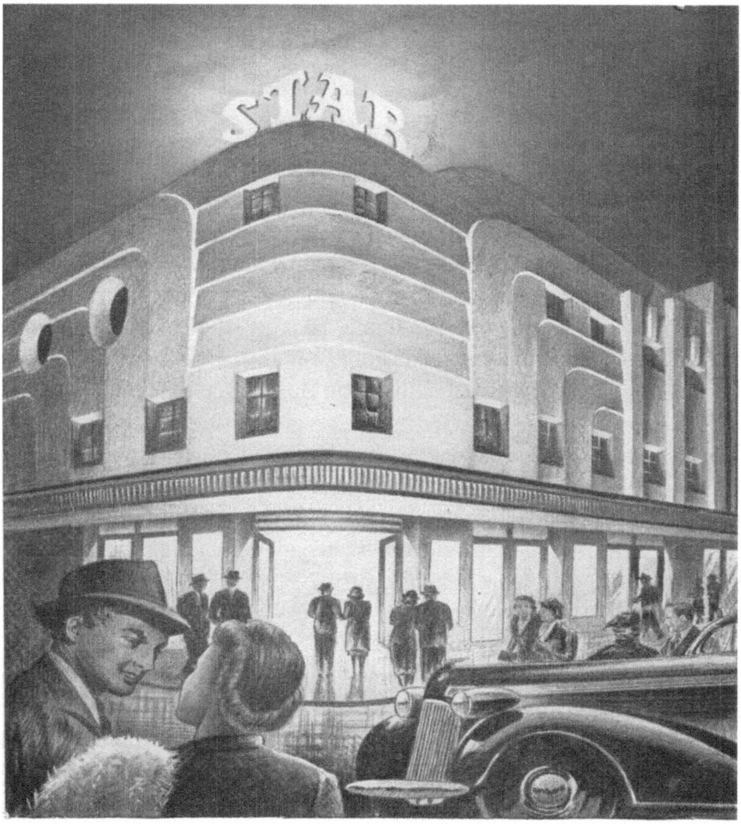

Fig. 3 The Goodwood Star opened on 8 October 1941 (Photograph from the original programme, courtesy of Dylan Walker)

Table 6 Top 10 Films in Suburban Release during 1942–1943

(1) Suburban rank	(2) Rank in all Adelaide cinemas	(3) Film title	(4) POPSTAT Box Office Index	(5) Suburban screening days
1	5	Babes on Broadway	6,751	91
2	8	Eagle Squadron	6,732	96
3	13	How Green Was My Valley	6,544	85
4	19	Son of Fury	6,448	77
5	35	Moon Over Miami	6,243	73
6	51	Flying Blind	6,217	51
7	27	Big Store, The	6,081	80
8	21	Honky Tonk	5,917	88
9	30	Aloma of the South Seas	5,707	75
10	15	Hold That Ghost	5,701	75

Source Dataset

An idea of the disparity between the two lists can be gauged from the Top 10 suburban releases listed in Table 6, showing that five of these numbers were ranked outside of the all-Adelaide Top 20 (Table 5). Just how widely these Top 10 films circulated in suburban release can be gauged by the number of screening days they accrued compared to the median for suburban release, which was just eight days. Another aspect of Table 6 is the much tighter packing of box-office data compared to Table 5, in which the Box-Office Index fell from over 46,000 to just under 17,000 between ranks 1–10. In contrast, the Suburban Box-Office Index fell by just 1,000, from 6,751.

Between them, the nine principal distributors supplied over 90% of the Adelaide market. Pertinent market share details are the subject of Table 7 and show a crowded market, in which the market shares of eight of the nine distributors are clustered between 6 and 12%. MGM is the clear market leader, garnering much higher mean box-office for each of its films, taking nearly 20% of the market. Compared with the other seven US distributors, both United Artists and Warner Bros. supply fewer films, while the low mean index figures for BEF suggest a supporting role.

As remarked upon earlier, one prominent observation from Table 7 is the considerable number of films in circulation, well beyond the annual outputs of the respective studios during the year in question. Finler (1988) counts the number of movies released by Hollywood studios in 1942 in the United States as follows: Columbia (59), 20th Century Fox (51), MGM (49), Paramount (44), RKO (39), United Artists (26), Universal (56) and Warner Bros. (34), aggregating to 358. Contrast this with the

Table 7 Market shares of the major nine distributors

Distributor	No. of films	POPSTAT Index	Mean POPSTAT per film	Proportion of market
BEF	81	182,684	2,255	0.07
Columbia	95	251,676	2,649	0.09
MGM	88	529,538	6,017	0.19
Paramount	93	336,661	3,620	0.12
RKO	84	274,993	3,274	0.10
TCF	79	331,483	4,196	0.12
United Artists	57	216,866	3,805	0.08
Universal	94	330,203	3,513	0.12
Warner Bros	54	156,429	2,897	0.06
Others	160	195,972	1,217	0.07
Total	885	2,806,505	3,168	1

Source Dataset

644 films circulating in Adelaide in the 1942–1943 season from these same studios.[23] Since, except for United Artists, the distribution wings of these studios handled in-house products, the difference can only be explained by them offering films from older vintages—some quite old. For instance, the Columbia 1934 'hit' *It Happened One Night* was screened twice—once at the Windsor in the suburb of Brighton and once at the Windsor in the suburb of St Morris, each for one performance as part of a double-bill programme. Likewise, MGM also distributed a 1934 'hit'—*The Barretts of Wimpole Street*—screened at four suburban cinemas for one or two days. Films of this vintage were rare, but many films occupying the lower half of the revenue distribution were re-released and date back to the 1930s. Part of the explanation for this will have been the burgeoning demand for films during these war years and the imperative of maintaining constancy of supply as small numbers of prints were shuttled around the country.

4 D. Clifford Theatres

The POPSTAT method is a tool for estimating box-office returns when the actual data is missing. Accordingly, when such information presents itself, it is expedient to test the reliability of the estimates. Chapter 3 does this concerning the accounts ledger of the Regent Cinema in Portsmouth in the mid-1930s. In the context of this chapter, a small number of financial records belonging to D. Clifford Theatres have been located in the State Records of South Australia and the National Archives of

[23] 886 films minus 81 BEF films minus 161 Others.

Table 8 D. Clifford theatres trading results, 1939–1940 to 1944–1945

Year	(1) Net income (£)	(2) Total takings (less tax)	(3) Cost of exhibiting	(4) Gross profit	(5) Gross profit of cost	(6) Nett profit (adjusted) (£)	(7) Nett profit of cost
1939–1940	148,184	106,989	63,265	43,724	0.69	23,769	0.38
1940–1941	160,754	125,893	71,077	54,816	0.77	33,139	0.47
1941–1942	184,800	141,797	75,965	65,832	0.87	42,531	0.56
1942–1943	191,772	149,127	85,319	63,808	0.75	41,582	0.49
1943–1944	190,472	150,648	85,992	64,656	0.75	41,888	0.49
1944–1945	203,996	153,913	94,185	59,728	0.63	43,948	0.47

Source National Archives of Australia, AP5/1, 42/1548
Note Gross and Net profit proportions (columns 5 and 7) are expressed in terms of Costs (column 3)

Australia. These provide the cinema historian with a closer insight into the economic history of suburban cinema exhibition.

Table 8 shows the trading results for the chain for the financial years ending from June 1940 to June 1946. The total takings for the financial year 1942/3 of £149,127 would be worth in the region of AUD 10.9 million in 2020.[24] The most successful financial year in terms of profit as a percentage of the cost was 1941–1942 when '… large number of troops, just returned from overseas, billeted in Adelaide early in 1942, resulted in greatly increased theatre attendances'.[25] According to the company's six-monthly report to shareholders, the second-best result, 1943–1944, was due to weather conditions favouring the entertainment industry.

Most important for our purpose is the financial records of the 17 cinemas comprising the chain.[26] These are presented in columns 2–5 in Table 9 for the 1942/3 financial year. Columns 1 and 5–8 present the information on which the POPSTAT Index is based. Column 8 is the product of columns 6 and 7. It is a proxy for each cinema's earning capacity (in £s) over 52 weeks. Note that the Index values for those three cinemas screening just once a week on Saturday night are very much lower than the others in the chain. Also, note that POPSTAT values are many times greater than actual box-office takings, reflecting how cinemas generally work to a fraction of their full earnings capacity. Column 9 suggests that the 14 cinemas screening multiple times during the week operate between 15 and 30% capacity. Most importantly, the two series correlate strongly. The correlation coefficient measuring the

[24] Using the Pre-Decimal Inflation Calculator on the Reserve Bank of Australia website https://www.rba.gov.au/calculator/annualPreDecimal.html.

[25] NAA AP5/1, 42/1548, Minute from Investigation Officer to Deputy Prices Commissioner, Adelaide, dated 17 November 1944.

[26] The accounts do not provide details of what 'Earnings' represent. Thus, it is not known whether the figures provided include retail sales of say confectionery, ices, and cigarettes.

Table 9 D. Clifford theatres—comparison of potential and actual nett takings for 1942/43 financial year

Cinema	(1) Seating capacity	(2) Total takings (less tax) (£)	(3) Film hire (£)	(4) Gross profit (£)	(5) Admission mid-price (d)	(6) POPSTAT Index per screening	(7) No. of screenings	(8) POPSTAT Index (cols. 6*7)	(9) Column 2 as a proportion of column 8
Adelaide Star	1,250	9,593	2,627	4,529	23	120	372	44,563	0.22
Goodwood Star	1,472	11,862	2,954	6,202	23	141	416	58,684	0.20
Hackney Star	300	806	232	372	23	29	52	1,495	0.54
Hindmarsh Star	1,150	13,240	2,908	8,202	19	91	370	33,685	0.39
Kingswood Vogue	1,481	9,046	2,228	4,455	23	142	371	52,656	0.17
North Adelaide Piccadilly	1,440	12,133	3,124	6,422	23	138	420	57,960	0.21
Norwood Star	1,642	9,699	3,019	4,240	23	157	372	58,537	0.17
Norwood Town Hall	1,100	1,394	254	706	19	87	52	4,528	0.31
Parkside Star	1,450	8,185	2,409	3,699	23	139	374	51,970	0.16
Port Adelaide Star	1,531	9,026	2,316	4,486	23	147	375	55,020	0.16
Semaphore Star	1,291	9,337	2,578	4,525	23	124	379	46,890	0.20
St. Peters Capitol	1,751	11,846	3,453	6,092	23	168	371	62,255	0.19

(continued)

Table 9 (continued)

Cinema	(1) Seating capacity	(2) Total takings (less tax) (£)	(3) Film hire (£)	(4) Gross profit (£)	(5) Admission mid-price (d)	(6) POPSTAT Index per screening	(7) No. of screenings	(8) POPSTAT Index (cols. 6*7)	(9) Column 2 as a proportion of column 8
St. Peters Town Hall	490	1,014	209	524	21	43	52	2,230	0.45
Thebarton Star	1,931	9,498	2,991	5,118	23	185	220	40,712	0.23
Torrensville Plaza	890	6,442	1,142	3,558	23	85	307	26,185	0.25
Unley Star	1,996	11,894	4,706	4,427	21	175	428	74,750	0.16
Woodville Star	1,402	7,657	2,608	3,941	23	134	204	27,409	0.28

Source National Archives of Australia, AP5/1, 42/1548

Note Mid-price admission is presented in pennies rather than shillings and pence. The number of annual screenings has been estimated from the records of cinemas for the six months 1 July to 31 December 1942. In this calculation, the number of screenings is double-counted in that each film in a double-bill programme is counted. However, the double counting is cancelled out because data represents programme data collected for the first half of the 1942–1943 season

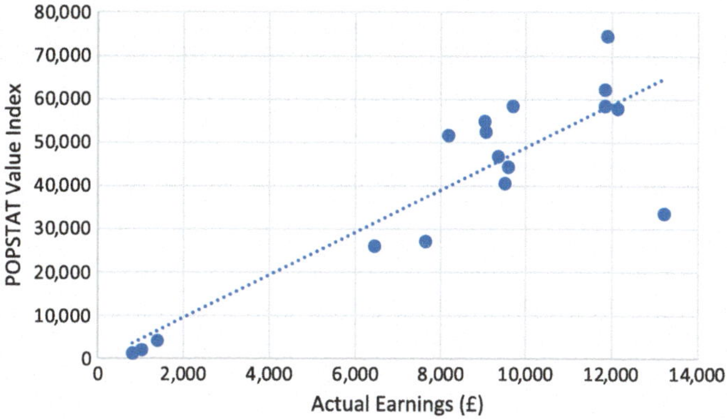

Fig. 4 Scatter to show the relationship between actual earnings and POPSTAT Index Values (*Source* Dataset)

strength of association is $r = 0.87$. A visual depiction of the variance is shown in Fig. 2, with the three Saturday night-only cinemas tucked up near the origin (Fig. 4).

5 The Circulation of 27 Films

As explained, the results in the previous section are based upon an incomplete dataset in which suburban cinema returns are comprehensive for the seven months, 1 July 1942 to 31 January 1943. Accordingly, the exhibition records of films in circulation are sometimes truncated, meaning the listings found in Tables 5 and 6 are not definitive, but importantly give a direction of travel. Further evidence about the pattern of distribution in Adelaide during World War 2 is provided through a sample of 27 films. Three are selected from each of the nine principal distributors released into a CBD cinema at the beginning of the 1942–1943 financial year and tracked through to their final suburban screening. In each case, the bulk of its suburban distribution has been captured. The films and their distributors are listed in Table 8, along with indicators describing their circulation.

Tracing the diffusion of these films through Star, Ozone and independent suburban cinemas, our investigation shows that the 27 films were on average screened 42.5 times in first-release and move-over, and another 65.2 times in suburban release. The Box-Office Index for the 27 films averaged 5,421 in CBD first-run and move-over cinemas and 3,871 in suburban release. In both cases, the suburban to CBD screenings and suburban to CBD Box-Office ratio is comparable to the whole population detailed in Tables 1 and 5.

Tracking the films from the first-release into the suburbs reveals the contractual links between distribution and suburban circuits. Contrary to the mythology of tyrannical block-booking, multi-sourcing was the norm: suburban exhibitors were not at the mercy of large product blocks from a single distributor. Both major exhibition circuits screened a spread of films from eight of the nine distributors, with RKO films not being screened in Star cinemas and Columbia films were not screened in Ozone cinemas. As shown in Table 8, the layover periods between city and suburban release were also flexible, with BEF's and Columbia's films tending to have longer windows of six and seven weeks.

Interestingly, while most of the 27 films did not journey to a second move-over cinema in the CBD, the MGM films that moved from the Metro to the York did so many weeks after being initially released into the suburbs. Ever the anomaly, MGM was party to a separate relationship linking it with first-run GU cinemas and the suburban Ozone circuits. Only two weeks after finishing at the Metro, MGM films would get a limited suburban release at the Ozone flagship cinemas in Port Adelaide and Semaphore before returning to the York cinema in the CBD. The York was programmed by General Union, though SA Theatres owned the building itself.[27] This example is valuable in suggesting that the opposition between distribution and exhibition and between city and suburban screenings was porous and that limited alliances frequently blurred these boundaries (Table 10).

Before the Ozone circuit got them, BEF's films went first to the Star circuit, which had exclusivity for 10–14 days. Columbia's films opened in the suburbs simultaneously at Star cinemas and the independent Colonel Light Gardens cinema before two to four weeks of exclusivity in the Star circuit. Universal's films were also exclusive to Star for 2–3 weeks. RKO went first to Ozone cinemas. Fox similarly went first to Ozone for 7–10 days of exclusivity. Paramount and Warner Bros. released simultaneously to Star and Ozone cinemas. There seems to be no pattern to how United Artists' films played the suburban circuits, indicating that they were more likely to have been sold separately rather than in blocks.

Two outliers among our figures warrant some comment. *A Tragedy at Midnight*, a BEF-released Republic programme film, played in first-release for a week at the Mayfair (as did the two other BEF films in our sample). It then played only one suburban booking before disappearing. Such is the fate of support films—sometimes they come in handy to plug schedules, but if not, they are entirely dispensable. Our other outlier is at the other end of the spectrum. Warner's *Meet John Doe*, a high-profile release by Frank Capra, played a week at the Regent and a move-over week at the Rex in CBD release, but then had only eight subsequent suburban bookings, all at independent cinemas. This seems an example of contractual arrangements militating against the success of a film in suburban release. The Star and Ozone circuits did not screen the film; one can only presume that Warners only made it available as a 'special'—outside of block-booking arrangements. Rather than being at the mercy of the distributors, the two suburban circuits had sufficient power to cooperate in enforcing a boycott.

[27] S.A. Theatres Limited was one of the associated companies owned and controlled by the Waterman Brothers who controlled the Ozone chain.

Table 10 Distribution details of 27 films—three per major distributor

Film	(1) Distributor	(2) Overall rank	(3) No. of cinemas	(4) No. of CBD screenings	(5) No. of suburban screenings	(6) Total No. of screenings	(7) POPSTAT Index	(8) Days between premiere and first suburban booking	(9) Days between premiere and move-over release	(10) Days between premiere and final suburban booking
Feminine Touch, The	MGM	56	26	49	77	126	10,399	14	47	241
Rage in Heaven	MGM	25	30	72	90	162	13,283	28	47	272
Honky Tonk	MGM	21	40	48	106	154	13,758	32	54	377
Tom, Dick and Harry	RKO	106	17	24	51	75	7,072	49		243
Little Foxes, The	RKO	85	20	48	54	102	8,478	49	7	209
Suspicion	RKO	74	25	48	70	118	9,070	7	64	176
Red River Valley	BEF	196	19	24	48	72	4,972	38		247
Tragedy at Midnight, A	BEF	376	2	24	2	26	2,038	78		78
Cowboy Serenade	BEF	258	14	24	31	55	3,889	42		199
49th Parallel	TCF	9	34	48	92	140	17,682	49	7	217
Belle Starr	TCF	49	28	48	81	129	11,202	84	42	164

(continued)

Table 10 (continued)

Film	(1) Distributor	(2) Overall rank	(3) No. of cinemas	(4) No. of CBD screenings	(5) No. of suburban screenings	(6) Total No. of screenings	(7) POPSTAT Index	(8) Days between premiere and first suburban booking	(9) Days between premiere and move-over release	(10) Days between premiere and final suburban booking
Remember the Day	TCF	42	32	48	91	139	11,811	49	7	168
You'll Never Get Rich	Columbia	77	31	48	81	129	8,932	57		185
Three Girls About Town	Columbia	190	24	24	54	78	5,086	50		213
Texas	Columbia	82	26	48	67	115	8,519	57		257
Black Sheep of Whitehall, The	United Artists	184	22	24	59	83	5,196	38		231
Lydia	United Artists	83	15	48	42	90	8,485	63	7	146
Ships with Wings	United Artists	46	24	64	80	144	11,384	70		117
Lady from Cheyenne, The	Universal	260	10	24	24	48	3,871	53		166
Bombay Clipper	Universal	135	27	24	77	101	6,253	38		192

(continued)

Table 10 (continued)

Film	(1) Distributor	(2) Overall rank	(3) No. of cinemas	(4) No. of CBD screenings	(5) No. of suburban screenings	(6) Total No. of screenings	(7) POPSTAT Index	(8) Days between premiere and first suburban booking	(9) Days between premiere and move-over release	(10) Days between premiere and final suburban booking
Mutiny in the Arctic	Universal	185	17	24	48	72	5,186	31		124
Aloma of the South Seas	Paramount	30	33	72	94	166	12,609	49		174
Nothing But the Truth	Paramount	63	33	48	92	140	10,111	42		167
No Hands on the Clock	Paramount	108	21	24	59	83	6,948	27		212
Dive Bomber	Warner Bros	6	40	72	81	153	20,801	49	7	302
Maltese Falcon, The	Warner Bros	47	36	48	95	143	11,276	39	7	269
Meet John Doe	Warner Bros	31	10	48	15	63	12,596	41	1	188

Source Dataset

6 Discussion and Conclusion

One theme of this book concerns the limits of the POPSTAT methodology, principally because it treats all films screened in one cinema as equivalents—they are accredited with generating the same POPSTAT Index value. This is wrong—different films perform differently at the same cinema. Consequently, it is a measure that discriminates against popular at the expense of unpopular films. Furthermore, the Index does not identify different sections of the audience—race, age, women, men, girls, boys and teens of either gender. Another problem is recognising the relative contribution of films on double-bill programmes. The use of POPSTAT methods in this chapter is no exception to these limits.

Further difficulties arise in this study because of the partial nature of the data collection over the year: while the dataset is comprehensive for the first six months of the 1942–1943 season, and for most of the CBD cinemas, for the remaining six months, this is not the case for suburban cinemas, many records of which end on 31 January 1943. Our primary interest here is with industrial structure rather than individual films. The decision was made to use what data we had when tracing the flow of movies in circulation to get the best possible understanding of their respective dynamics and the part played in this by those institutions (exhibitors and distributors) responsible for this.

No matter how crude POPSTAT may be as a measure, it facilitates researchers gathering large amounts of data about the history and processes of filmgoing, including audiences' tastes. Furthermore, evidence found in the financial reports of the D. Clifford suburban cinema chain shows that the actual box-office takings correlate strongly with the proxy POPSTAT Index values.

In many ways, reception studies should start here—not necessarily with the great and the good but rather the ordinary and prosaic. On Wednesday, 16 September 1942, our median film *International Lady* distributed by United Artists was on a three-day double-bill programme with the BEF-distributed *Law of the Jungle* (ranked 332nd). During our study, both films were distributed only in the suburbs. The audience for these two films made two choices—first to go to the cinema and second, to watch this pairing rather than other pairings in nearby cinemas. Both films received multiple screenings in the suburbs for 26 and 35 days, respectively. Watching them was part of the quotidian of suburban life in Adelaide at the time. The final point to emphasise is that Australian cinema is best discussed in terms of the variety of its practices and not in totalising generalisations about the dominance of Hollywood.

Appendix 1: Suburban Cinemas Used in the Study

Cinema	(1) Seating capacity	(2) Mid-admission price (d)	(3) Screening days	(4) Sum of screening sessions	(5) No. of films screened	(6) Potential Box Office revenue (£Aus)
Bowden Druids Hall Cameo	250	15	2	4	2	31
Capitol, St. Peters	1751	23	216	434	132	36,414
Col. Light Theatre	1756	23	190	385	167	32,395
Croydon Picture Theatre	1020	19	65	170	112	6,864
Edwardstown	250	15	3	6	3	47
Flinders Hall, Findon	300	15	21	23	13	218
Kilburn Progressive Hall / Cameo	300	15	2	4	2	38
Kilkenny Picture Palace	1020	18	65	116	112	4,437
Lyric, Hilton	500	18	15	17	11	319
Lyric, Lockleys	350	18	12	18	10	236
Melba, Dulwich	600	19	117	232	106	5,843
Milton Hall, Fullarton	250	19	12	19	12	188
Norwood Town Hall	1100	19	33	64	64	2,830
Ozone Alberton	1345	16.5	189	380	108	17,569
Ozone Enfield	1810	23	188	379	108	32,870
Ozone Glenelg	1920	23	186	411	104	37,812
Ozone Goodwood	1278	19	203	395	114	19,982
Ozone Marryatville	1264	23	182	373	106	22,591
Ozone Port Adelaide	1571	23	196	658	111	49,532
Ozone Prospect	1263	17.5	186	374	107	17,222

(continued)

(continued)

Cinema	(1) Seating capacity	(2) Mid-admission price (d)	(3) Screening days	(4) Sum of screening sessions	(5) No. of films screened	(6) Potential Box Office revenue (£Aus)
Ozone Semaphore	1193	23	196	422	110	24,152
Ozone Unley	991	23	201	399	114	18,947
Piccadilly, North Adelaide	1440	23	215	496	128	34,224
Plaza, Torrensville	890	23	203	357	138	15,225
Richmond Soldiers Memorial Hall	300	12.5	11	15	11	117
Roxy, Everard Park	995	21	156	285	117	12,780
Seacliff	280	23	4	4	4	35
Seaview, Glenelg	914	15	212	340	58	13,596
St. Peters Town Hall	490	21	33	64	64	1,503
Star, Adelaide	1250	23	216	436	128	26,115
Star, Goodwood	1472	23	212	484	128	34,138
Star, Hackney	300	23	32	63	63	748
Star, Hindmarsh	1150	19	210	433	136	23,860
Star, Norwood	1642	23	138	432	132	33,989
Star, Parkside	1450	23	279	439	138	30,501
Star, Port Adelaide	1531	23	223	444	132	26,907
Star, Semaphore	1291	19	217	449	137	27,757
Star, Thebarton	1931	23	88	257	136	23,779
Star, Unley	1996	23	220	500	135	47,821
Star, Woodville	1402	23	117	241	121	16,190
Strand, Glenelg	947	24	199	444	60	18,672

(continued)

(continued)

Cinema	(1) Seating capacity	(2) Mid-admission price (d)	(3) Screening days	(4) Sum of screening sessions	(5) No. of films screened	(6) Potential Box Office revenue (£Aus)
Unley City Hall	1300	21	6	12	6	683
Vogue, Kingswood	1481	23	215	434	137	30,799
Walkerville Talkies	400	19	9	14	9	222
Windsor, Brighton	390	19	68	188	125	2,902
Windsor, Parkside	500	19	5	9	5	178
Windsor, St Morris	640	19	134	241	122	6,105

Source Adelaide Advertiser

References

Collins, D. (1987). *Hollywood down under: Australians at the movies, 1896 to the present day.* Angus and Robertson.

Finler, J. (1988). *The Hollywood story.* Octopus Books.

Gaunson, S. (2012). Australian (inter)national cinema: The Royal Commission on the moving picture industry in Australia, 1926–28, Australasian Films Ltd. and the American monopoly. *Studies in Australasian Cinema, 6*(3), 291–300.

Gaunson, S. (2018). American cartel: Block bookings and the Paramount plan. In A. Danks, S. Gaunson, & P. Kunze (Eds.), *American–Australian cinema.* Palgrave Macmillan. https://doi.org/10.1007/978-3-319-66676-1_10

Sedgwick, J. (2000). *Filmgoing in 1930s Britain: A choice of pleasures.* Exeter University Press.

Sedgwick, J. (2011). Patterns in first-run and suburban filmgoing in Sydney in the mid-1930s. In R. Maltby, D. Biltereyst, & P. Meers (Eds.), *The new cinema history: Approaches and case studies* (pp. 140–158). Wiley-Blackwell.

Sedgwick, J., Pokorny, M., & Miskell, P. (2014). Hollywood in the world market—Evidence from Australia in the mid-1930s. *Business History, 56*, 689–723.

Thompson, K. (1985). *Exporting entertainment: America in the world film market 1907–1934.* BFI.

Tulloch, J. (1982). *Australian cinema: Industry, narrative and meaning.* Allen and Unwin.

Dylan Walker is an independent researcher interested in the history of film exhibition in South Australia. He holds a Ph.D. in Screen Studies from Flinders University in Adelaide, in which he researched film distribution and exhibition in rural South Australia from 1897 to the late 1930s.

He has published articles on rural cinema and his book, *Adelaide's Silent Nights* (1996), deals with the history of cinemas in Adelaide, South Australia, during the silent era.

Mike Walsh was an associate professor in Screen and Media at Flinders University in Adelaide, Australia, and supervisor of that university's Digital Media program in Hong Kong. He now holds Academic Adjunct status since his recent retirement. Michael is a programming consultant and writer for the Adelaide Film Festival. He has researched and published in various areas, including film distribution, Australian cinema history, and Asian cinema.

Film Exhibition, Distribution and Popularity in German-Occupied Belgium (1940–1944): Brussels, Antwerp and Liege

Roel Vande Winkel and John Sedgwick

Abstract This chapter investigates filmgoing and distribution in urban Belgium during the German occupation (1940–1944). It is based on all films screened in Brussels, Antwerp and Liege between 1 January 1941 and 31 December 1943—each city representing contrasting cultural and linguistic traditions. The research finds a clear cultural divide between film screenings in Flanders and Wallonia. The differences between the POPSTAT top 20 lists of the three cities are remarkable, particularly between Brussels-Antwerp and Liege-Antwerp. While subject to many edicts, filmgoing remained an essential activity for the Belgian people, irrespective of where they lived. The longevity of films in circulation represents a difference between the pre-and post-war system of distribution, occasioned by supply shortages. Films were required to work harder.

It is impossible to understand German film policy towards occupied Belgium without recognising the complex characteristics that constitute this small nation. Since its foundation in 1830–1831, Belgium has been divided by a linguistic and cultural border that separates the Dutch-speaking North (Flanders, the Dutch dialect spoken there is usually referred to as Flemish) from the French-speaking South (Wallonia). The Belgian capital Brussels is geographically located in Flanders and is Dutch-speaking. However, from the end of the eighteenth century, a slow process of Frenchification took place so that by the time of the German invasion on 10 May 1940, the city was predominantly French-speaking: higher education was only offered in French,

---

The original version of this chapter was revised: Captions of Figures 3, 4 were updated and unwanted first reference text was deleted. The correction to this chapter is available at https://doi.org/10.1007/978-3-031-05770-0_13

R. V. Winkel
KU Leuven and LUCA School of Arts, Schaerbeek, Belgium

J. Sedgwick (✉)
Oxford Brookes University, Oxford, UK
e-mail: sedgwicj52@gmail.com

J. Sedgwick (ed.), *Towards a Comparative Economic History of Cinema, 1930–1970*, Frontiers in Economic History, https://doi.org/10.1007/978-3-031-05770-0_8

the Belgian public administration primarily used French, and the bourgeoisie spoke French.[1] The consequence was that for French-speaking Belgians, it was sufficient to be monolingual, whereas Dutch speakers, by necessity, were more likely to be bilingual.[2]

1 Film Exhibition and Language Before and During the German Occupation

French was also the dominant language in the Belgian film business. In the 1930s, domestic film production was limited, with Belgian cinemas screening primarily imported films in subtitled or dubbed versions—sometimes both. Initially, many distributors subtitled films only in French. But from 1932 (approximately), giving in to pressure from Flemish film exhibitors, bilingual subtitles became the norm.[3] From then on, prints of films spoken in foreign languages usually carried two lines of subtitles, printed right above each other: one in French and one in Dutch. This procedure allowed distributors to make one print that could be distributed throughout.[4]

Foreign films were less commonly dubbed. The costs of making dialogue lists, hiring a director and actors/actresses, and editing and mixing the new soundtrack were prohibitive for all but the most popular films in the small Dutch-language market of Flanders and the Netherlands. In contrast, dubbing films into French was more feasible because of the size of the international French-speaking market, including Wallonia, France, Switzerland and cinemas in French colonies.

Consequently, many American, British and German productions exported to the international French-speaking market, were made available in French dubbed versions. These films were screened regularly in the larger Flemish cities of Antwerp and Ghent, where there were cinemas dedicated to French-language audiences. The (limited) available research and circumstantial evidence, such as film posters from the 1930s preserved in municipal archives, suggests showing American and other foreign films dubbed into French during that decade was commonplace.[5] For example, some cinemas—the Savoy in Ghent, targeted the Francophone audience in Flanders by screening French-spoken films without subtitles.[6] German movies, for

[1] In 1920, 59% of the inhabitants declared that they were francophone or francophone-bilingual. In 1930, it was 63% and in 1947 (shortly after World War II) 71%. In 1939, only 19% of the children went to Dutch-speaking schools. Witte and Craeybeckx (2010, p. 173).

[2] Witte and Craeybeckx (2010).

[3] Engelen and Vande Winkel (2018a, pp. 78–79).

[4] In 2021, this procedure is still applied, even though cinemas no longer screen physical prints but digital files.

[5] For instance, the city archives of Ghent and Leuven hold thousands of film posters that were submitted to municipal authorities (local police) to authorise for public display. For Ghent, visit https://beeldbank.stad.gent/. For Leuven, visit http://www.cinemaleuven.be/.

[6] Van de Vijver and Biltereyst (2010, pp. 75–76).

which a French dubbed version was available or filmed in alternate versions with a French cast, were sometimes also shown in that form in Flanders.[7]

Film distributors and film exhibitors were free to decide in which language they would present a film to the public and whether they wanted to subtitle such a print or not, a situation that would change during the German occupation.

Nazi Germany invaded Belgium on 10 May 1940. As the commander-in-chief of the Belgian army, the Belgian King capitulated on 28 May 1940. He did so against his government's will, which went into exile in London. The country remained occupied until the first days of September 1944, when the German troops withdrew from most parts of the country. Culturally and politically, Adolf Hitler and the entire National-Socialist apparatus felt closer to Flanders, which they considered a Germanic region. However, the social and linguistic structure of the country made it impossible to 'simply' divide Belgium and absorb Flanders into Germany. A decision about the political future of Belgium was postponed. Therefore, instead of installing a Civil Administration dominated by German National-Socialists to aggressively pursue the Nazification of the country as happened in the Netherlands, Hitler decided to impose a less ideologically driven Military Administration on Belgium, focused on economically exploiting the country's resources. That is, maximising Belgian's contribution to the German war effort while maintaining only a relatively small military presence on Belgium soil.[8]

In general, the Military Administration pursued a Flemish-friendly policy—the so-called *Flamenpolitik*—intending to promote rapprochement between Flanders and Germany while being careful not to alienate Francophone Belgians. Regarding the film business, the intention was to increase the exposure of *all* Belgians to the German language and German culture by promoting German films, which were preferably distributed in their original version, with Dutch and French subtitles. In line with the *Flamenpolitik*, cinemas located in Flanders were subsequently obliged to screen German films in their original version. Prints were subtitled in Dutch but usually (consistent with pre-war practices) also in French to ensure they could be distributed all over Belgium. The implication was that German films dubbed in French were no longer screened in Flanders. However, cinemas located in Wallonia were still allowed to screen such dubbings. Accordingly, where a German film was available in its original version or a dubbed version, film exhibitors in Wallonia were free to choose between them. This choice was also given to cinema owners in Brussels, where many exhibitors opted to screen French dubbed versions of German films because they knew their audience preferred this.

Introduced in the summer of 1940, German film policy compelled cinema owners throughout Belgium to screen a Belgian version of Ufa's Foreign Weekly Newsreel (*Auslandstonwoche*). These were spoken in Dutch or French, usually without subtitles—subtitling slowed down the production process.[9] Again, cinema owners in

[7] Engelen and Vande Winkel (2018b). For multiple-language versions, see Wahl (2009).

[8] For a brief introduction to the history of Belgium under the German occupation, see: Conway (2001).

[9] Vande Winkel (2003).

Brussels were given the choice of language. Most preferred French-spoken newsreels to Dutch-spoken ones, demonstrating that German film officials treated Brussels as part of the Francophone film market. Economically, this decision made sense because it corresponded, as will be shown, to the preferences of Brussels' cinemagoers. Politically, this decision was opposed by the Flemish-nationalist parties, which historically disliked the francophone character of 'their' capital and were disappointed that the 'New Order' installed by the Military Administration did not include significant attempts to make Brussels more Flemish.[10] Similar complaints were made concerning the city of Leuven, which, although located in Flanders, was given on account of the considerable Francophone academic community leeway to watch French-language versions of films.[11]

2 Research Questions and Context

The pragmatism of the Military Administration in acknowledging the agency of cinemagoers by giving film exhibitors a degree of flexibility in terms of language is typical of the German film policy *vis-à-vis* occupied Belgium. Nevertheless, the freedom of the film sector was limited. There was a substantial difference between the film offer before and after the German invasion. So, what were these differences? How did film exhibitors and cinemagoers respond to such changes? Is it possible to capture the choices made by audiences who frequented cinemas? Can we identify their preferences and interpret their choices?

This study is designed to investigate filmgoing and distribution in urban Belgium during the occupation. It is based on all films screened at least once in each of the three cities of Brussels, Antwerp and Liège between 1 January 1941 and 31 December 1943—each city representing contrasting cultural and linguistic traditions. As the Belgian capital, Brussels was home to several large and prestigious cinemas and, therefore, the city where most new releases premiered. Brussels was also (as explained in more detail below) the city where cinemagoers had the broadest possible films offer. Antwerp and Liège were the largest Flemish and Walloon cinema cities, respectively.

German film policy toward occupied Belgium was designed and implemented by the Military Administration's Propaganda Department (Propaganda-Abteilung Belgien, hereafter PAB). The PAB, which had close ties to Goebbels's propaganda ministry and the German film industry, drastically reformed the Belgian film sector. Double bills, which most cinemas had offered in large cities before the war, were forbidden.[12] Film programmes were required to include one feature film, one short film—ideally, a short documentary such as a German *Kulturfilm*, but short comedies were also accepted—and a newsreel. This three-pronged programme was made

[10] De Bruyn (1942a).

[11] De Bruyn (1941).

[12] Vande Winkel (2011, rev.).

compulsory in Nazi Germany in 1938 and was forcibly introduced in all the regions Germany conquered during the following years.[13] Cinemas that the PAB considered too small, unprofitable or unsuitable (for whatever reason) were closed. Some of the most prestigious and largest cinemas were secretly purchased by companies or individuals who claimed to represent independent businesses but acted on the German state's behalf. For instance, Alfred Greven, Goebbels' plenipotentiary for reorganising the film sector of Western Europe, acquired several prestigious Belgian cinemas.

In pre-war Belgium, some 4,000 films of various vintages (including silent films) were in circulation, distributed by 110 film distributors.[14] From the summer of 1940, all American and British movies, those referencing the First World War and those with Jewish directors or actors, were banned, drastically reducing the number of films in circulation.[15] During the second half of 1940 and early 1941, the number of films in circulation had fallen to just over 1,000, and distributors to 73. Meanwhile, Belgian film censorship was made redundant and eventually abolished. During these months, the German film industry was increasingly represented by the newly established Belgian branches of the German companies Ufa and Tobis, which in August 1940 distributed around 90 German films between them. According to the PAB, the remaining 71 companies combined offered approximately 950 films: 500 French productions, 350 German films and around 100 films of Italian, Belgian or other origins.

The market position of French films, already sizeable before the war, was strengthened by the disappearance of American and British competition. This situation was not what the PAB had intended, leading to a new regulation introduced in March 1941 forbidding the circulation of feature films released in Belgium before 1 June 1937.[16] There can be no doubt that this measure was taken about restricting the supply of French movies, again to foreground recent German releases. In addition, supply was cut further following a mandate that closed those distributors' businesses offering fewer than ten feature films.

According to the PAB, by March 1941, the number of films in circulation had dropped further to 568 titles.[17] Additional controls and regulations were introduced in January 1942, when those remaining distributors that wanted to make more prints of specific titles had to request permission from the PAB. This mechanism allowed it to stimulate or reduce the profitability of certain films.[18] At this time, the German Authorities introduced a classification system to register cinemas, in which they

13 Welch and Vande Winkel (2011, rev.).

14 Propaganda-Abteilung Belgien (1941, pp. 58–60).

15 Also, Jews were no longer allowed to own distribution companies or cinemas. It was not until 28 October 1940 that the occupying forces announced such anti-Jewish measures for all companies and enterprises established in Belgium. This suggests that, in terms of anti-Semitic policy, the film sector was targeted earlier than other economic sectors. See Roekens (2011).

16 The German reorganisation of film distribution occupied Belgium is described in detail in Vande Winkel (2017).

17 Vande Winkel (2017, p. 57).

18 Het corporatief leven (1942).

graded cinemas from the status of 1a—the most prestigious first-run cinemas—to 3b, through which they determined the maximum price of admission, ranging respectively from 6BF (Belgium Francs) to 3BF. They also were concerned to restrict the supply of French films to Dutch speaking Flanders. In February–March 1942, several distributors were informed that certain French films were no longer distributed in Flanders. In October 1942, the rules governing the distribution were tightened further, with an exception was made concerning the films of Continental Films, headed by Alfred Greven.[19]

Interestingly, films restricted to Flanders or Wallonia only were allowed in Brussels, making it the only Belgian city to have screened virtually every film in German-occupied Belgium. For instance, the German colour film *Das Bad auf der Tenne* (1943), set in 17th Century Flanders, was premiered at the prestigious Eldorado cinema in Brussels (2,352 seats) on a two-week run, after which it was exhibited only in Flemish cities.[20] In contrast, the French film *L'Assassinat du Père Noël* (1941), which also premiered at the Eldorado in Brussels, was screened only in Walloon cities.[21] During the last few weeks of the occupation, the scarcity of new films and new film prints resulted in cracks in this binary distribution policy when movies previously available only in one part of the country appeared in the other.

During the entire occupation period, only a small number of feature and short films were produced in Belgium. The Authorities paid lip service to the importance of 'Germanic' film production and, by extension, the European film sector. In practice, it showed no interest in structurally supporting Belgian or Flemish film production.

The occupying forces were principally concerned with extending the market for German films. Nevertheless, they needed to be pragmatic.[22] Cinemas were opened or closed throughout the occupation for various reasons, but there were usually at least 760 cinemas active, requiring a different film every week. Raw film stock was scarce and in high demand to make new prints of the (propagandistically important) weekly newsreel. Therefore, even films considered to have significant commercial and, or propagandistic potential were released with only a limited number of prints. Thus, to maintain supply, many hundreds of films released before the German invasion had to remain in circulation. Replacing them with newer and preferably German titles was difficult for various reasons. As the war progressed, the German film industry's capacity to produce new films declined. Several of the latest movies released had been made for German audiences only and deemed unsuitable for foreign markets such as Belgium. (In the film industry of the 'Third Reich', there was increasing frustration that so many films were produced without consideration of foreign markets and

[19] Vande Winkel (2017, p. 64), Eue and Lang (2017), Leteux (2017).

[20] Vande Winkel (2020).

[21] Vande Winkel (2020).

[22] The key measures imposed on film distributors by the PAB, the underlying motivations behind these measures and the consequences of their implementation for film distributors have been analysed extensively previously and are therefore summarized here are detailed in Vande Winkel (2017).

were therefore unexportable.)[23] These factors contributed to French films keeping a sizeable market share throughout the occupation.

As shown later in the chapter, film supply was boosted by importing films from regions occupied by Germany (Czechoslovakia) or having alliances with them (Italy, Hungary and a small number from Spain). These imports were dubbed into German and then distributed (with subtitles) to the Flemish part of Belgium. Again, in Wallonia and Brussels, exhibitors could choose between the German version or, if available, a dubbed French-language version.[24]

3 Method

The PAB was authorised to moderate the supply of films while promoting German films and maintaining industry profitability. They were also charged with giving exhibitors a limited degree of agency. The outcome of this policy is monitored using film programming data collected from Belgium newspaper advertisements for Brussels, Antwerp and Liège and analysed using POPSTAT methods.[25] We focus on the years 1941–1943, drawing from a dataset that contains information about film programming from mid-June 1940 until early September 1944.[26] There are various reasons for this. In 1940, the PAB was engaged in reorganising film distribution and exhibition, determining which cinemas could reopen, which distributors could resume their activities, and what films could be shown. It was not until the end of the year that the PAB signalled the end of the transitional period by communicating with Belgian film exhibitors and distributors through the bilingual trade journal *Cinema*—first published in December 1940. The situation towards the end of the occupation is more relevant to us. Still, it is harder to analyse because, by 1944, the shortage of paper curtailed the supply of newsprint, leading to the withdrawal of copy space available to cinema advertisements. Also, as the year progressed, cinemas were increasingly shut down to save electricity, out of fear of Allied bombardments and (in Wallonia in particular) as German retaliation against civil disorder.

Accordingly, during these three years (1941–1943), it can be considered that Belgian cinema functioned effectively under occupation regulations: the period in which the new cinema rules had taken root but before the significant disruption to supply that occurred in 1944. The choice of years further serves to allow the programming records of films in circulation in early 1941 to be traced back to their premiere in 1940, and those films premiered in late 1943 forwards into 1944.

[23] Vande Winkel (2021a).

[24] Vande Winkel (2017, p. 64).

[25] Information from various Dutch- and French-language newspapers (*Gazet van Antwerpen*, *Het Algemeen Nieuws*, *Het Laatste Nieuws*, *La Légia*, *Le Soir*, *Volk en Staat*) was used and compared. Most newspapers have been digitized by the Royal Library of Belgium. Access is restricted to academic institutions, see https://www.belgicapress.be/. For the POPSTAT method see Chap. 1. See also Sedgwick (2000, 2020a, 2020b).

[26] Vande Winkel (2020).

Table 1 Characteristics of the sample set of cinemas

City	(1) City population	(2) No. of cinemas	(3) Sample no. of cinemas	(4) Mean seating capacity	(5) No. of Category 1a cinemas	(6) Screening days	(7) Screening days per cinema
Brussels	9,33,430	102	83	809	7	92,721	1,117
Antwerp	5,21,993	49	47	854	6	34,419	732
Liege	2,42,580	17	16	937	0	20,094	1,256

Source Cinema; dataset
Note The count of Category 1a (first run) cinemas is based upon the 1942 classification. Populations are given for 1941: source: http://www.npdata.be/BuG/392-Bevolking/Bevolking.htm

Table 2 Cinema weights characteristics

City	(1) Cinema population	(2) Mean weight	(3) Median weight	(4) Maximum weight	(5) Minimum weight
Brussels	102	1	0.76	6.18	0.21
Antwerp	47	1	0.83	3.73	0.1
Liege	16	1	0.64	3.77	0.2

Source Dataset

The coverage across the three cities is uneven. As presented in Table 1, the Brussels dataset is built upon 83 of the 102 cinemas that were active in the city and suburbs—cinemas for which no data could be found were all located in the suburbs—while programming data is available for all 49 Antwerp cinemas and 16 out of the 17 Liège cinemas.[27] However, the records of Brussels and Liège cinemas are fuller. Based upon the 1095 days covered by this study, together with the screenings of films that were first screened in 1940 or last screened in 1944, Table 1 counts the programming records available on average for the sample set of cinemas in each of the three cities, with Antwerp much less well covered.

As evident in Table 2, the revenue earning capacity of the cinemas in the respective samples varies significantly. For instance, in Brussels, the 2,795-seater Normandie, 2,352-seater Eldorado, and 2,041-seater Agora, all classified as 1a cinemas, could earn revenues 6.39, 5.37, and 4.66 times the mean cinema revenue. The skewness in cinema weights is reflected in the median weight being 0.75. While the maximum

[27] Information about all the cinemas that were active in German-occupied Belgium, their address, seating capacity and other information has been compiled by Vande Winkel (2020) and made available on the website "Cinema in Occupied Belgium (1940–1944)". The most important sources that were used, are the 91 issues of the trade journal CINEMA that were published in German-occupied Belgium between December 1940 and August/September 1944, as well as the only 'year-book' published during the occupation: Cinema Jaarboek (1942).

Table 3 Characteristics of the POPSTAT Index of Films screened, 1941–1943

City	(1) Films	(2) Mean POPSTAT	(3) Median POPSTAT	(4) Maximum POPSTAT	(5) Standard deviation	(6) Coefficient of variation
Brussels	1101	92.91	67.74	553.05	89.31	0.96
Antwerp	744	46.84	37.91	196	40.74	0.87
Liege	897	23.91	18.99	126.08	20.82	0.87

Source Dataset
Note Films that appear in more than one year are counted once

Cinema Weights in Antwerp and Liege were much lower, median weights reflect similar inequality in the revenue potential of the respective sets of cinemas.

Applying these weights to the programming data enables POPSTAT Index calculations to be made for each film screened at least once during the three years 1941 to 1943 in each of the three cities. The statistical distribution of POPSTAT Index values is the subject of Table 3, from which the relative size of the three markets is evident, both in terms of the films screened and the three sets of POPSTAT Index values. Given this, the standardised variance, measured by the coefficient of variation (column 6), is of the same order for each, suggesting that the statistical distribution of popularity statistics is similar across the three cities, a conclusion supported by the similar median ratios to mean values.

4 The Size of the Market

The national origins of the films watched by audiences from the three cities show a binary divide between the two language groups. Before discussing this, however, Table 4 shows that although the number of films in circulation declines significantly in Brussels between 1941 and 1943—and to a lesser extent in Antwerp and Liege—it is more than compensated for by an increase in the number of screenings. On average, films worked harder, reflected by the velocity of circulation increasing appreciably in the two largest cities over the three years. That supply held up in French-speaking Liege demonstrates the availability and dominance of French production for the audience. Measured by their respective aggregate POPSTAT Index scores, the market for films in Brussels and Antwerp films increased by approximately a third over the three years. Given the limited leisure opportunities available and the severe dislocation to civil society occasioned by the occupation, cinema likely served as a haven for many. In contrast, the cinema market in Liege is much more stable, with screenings lower in 1943 than in 1941, although, as in the other two cities, mean POPSTAT values increase markedly. All three city markets reflect a very high variance in film popularity, indicating markets dominated by 'hit' films.

The main feature of Table 5 is the marked difference in the diet of films consumed by the audiences in the respective cities, reflecting a combination of cultural identity

Table 4 Annual circulation and POPSTAT data

	(1) Films in circulation	(2) No. of weekly screenings	(3) Mean velocity of circulation	(4) Total POPSTAT	(5) Maximum POPSTAT	(6) Mean POPSTAT	(7) Standard deviation	(8) Median POPSTAT	(9) Coefficient of variation
Brussels									
1941	609	2,577	4.23	21,326	229.03	35.02	35.44	23.28	1.01
1942	538	3,398	6.32	26,424	471.26	49.11	47.79	35.39	0.97
1943	494	3,730	7.55	27,018	443.63	54.69	63.5	30.64	1.16
Antwerp									
1941	329	856	2.6	6,796	100.65	20.66	19.21	12.51	0.93
1942	315	1,161	3.69	8,070	115.98	25.62	27.05	14.43	1.06
1943	298	1,502	5.04	9,831	180.15	32.99	35.26	19.02	1.07
Liege									
1941	376	770	2.05	4,503	75.14	11.91	10.49	9	0.88
1942	395	832	2.11	5,150	88.33	13.48	14.09	8.93	1.05
1943	343	709	2.07	5,177	74.26	15.09	14.92	9.77	0.99

Source Dataset
Note Table 4 counts separately films that appear in more than one year

Table 5 National characteristics of film preferences

	1941			1942			1943		
Country of origin	(1) Films in circulation	(2) Total POPSTAT	(3) Market share	(4) Films in circulation	(5) Total POPSTAT	(6) Market share	(7) Films in circulation	(8) Total POPSTAT	(9) Market share
Brussels									
Germany	200	9,739	0.46	231	10,720	0.41	229	9,962	0.37
France	334	9,639	0.45	250	13,572	0.52	198	12,761	0.47
Belgium	12	427	0.02	14	220	0.01	8	127	0
Austria	15	374	0.02	6	149	0.01	4	65	0
Italy	12	347	0.02	13	908	0.03	29	3,108	0.12
Germany-France	14	331	0.02	11	376	0.01	8	290	0.01
Others	22	469	0.02	13	309	0.01	18	704	0.03
Totals	609	21,326	1	538	26,254	1	494	27,018	1
Antwerp									
Germany	182	4,953	0.73	210	6,443	0.8	225	7,002	0.71
France	103	1,193	0.18	51	428	0.05	12	555	0.06
Belgium	6	264	0.04	11	134	0.02	10	205	0.02
Austria	16	80	0.01	11	202	0.03	6	39	0
Italy	4	36	0.01	12	572	0.07	25	1,283	0.13
Germany-France	4	50	0.01	5	52	0.01	3	124	0.01
Others	14	218	0.03	15	238	0.03	17	623	0.06
Totals	329	6,796	1	315	8,070	1	298	9,831	1

(continued)

Table 5 (continued)

Country of origin	1941			1942			1943		
	(1) Films in circulation	(2) Total POPSTAT	(3) Market share	(4) Films in circulation	(5) Total POPSTAT	(6) Market share	(7) Films in circulation	(8) Total POPSTAT	(9) Market share
Liege									
Germany	95	1,692	0.38	152	1,997	0.38	132	1,411	0.27
France	247	2,438	0.54	209	2,893	0.54	161	2,699	0.52
Belgium	2	61	0.01	1	2	0	4	12	0
Austria	9	77	0.02	3	11	0	4	18	0
Italy	7	82	0.02	14	290	0.05	24	667	0.13
Germany-France	5	57	0.01	4	39	0.01	8	224	0.04
Others	11	96	0.02	12	92	0.02	10	146	0.03
Totals	376	4,503	1	395	5,324	1	343	5,177	1

Source Dataset

and opportunity. In Brussels, German and French movies dominate, taking over a 90% share of the market when measured by POPSTAT in 1941 and 1942. In 1943, Italian films significantly impacted the market, taking market share from German and French films—these films were not projected in Italian but German and French dubbed versions. Although the supply of French films on the market declined over the years, its market share remained higher in 1943 than in 1941. In contrast, the growth in German film supply corresponds with an apparent decline in their popularity, with market share falling from 46 to 37% over the three years.

The experience in Dutch-speaking Antwerp and French-speaking Liege dramatically encapsulates cultural differences within Belgium society. In Antwerp in 1941, 182 German films were screened, increasing as the war progressed to 225 in 1943. In contrast, French films in circulation declined from 103 to just twelve by 1943—a direct consequence of the PAB's policy of reducing the availability of French cinema in Flanders. These twelve films, all new productions, were *Annette et la dame blonde* (1942), *Caprices* (1942), *Le club des soupirants* (1941), *Le dernier des six* (1941), *La fausse maîtresse* (1942), *Fièvres* (1942), *Les inconnus dans la maison* (1942), *Mam'zelle Bonaparte* (1942), *Le mariage de chiffon* (1942), *Péchés de jeunesse* (1941), *Premier rendez-vous* (1941) and *Simplet* (1942). Of these twelve titles, ten films had been produced by Continental and were distributed by the same company: Ufa/Tobis. The exceptions were *Fièvres* (1942) and *Le mariage de chiffon* (1942), distributed by Atlas-Films and Monopol-Film. By 1943, Ufa/Tobis had become the leading distributor of French-language films in Flanders. Economically, this made perfect sense, as the Continental films had been made with German money, and the proceeds went to the German treasury. But politically, it must have felt awkward because German film policy was not designed to promote or encourage the spread of the French language or French culture in Flanders. To solve this problem, Ufa/Tobis decided—or may have been ordered—not to release these French-spoken films in their original version in Flanders but to opt instead for French-language dubbings made for Germany and the German-controlled European market. This policy, however, led to protests: even the Flemish-nationalist film critic Jeanne de Bruyn made clear that she would rather watch a French film in French than in a German dubbing.[28]

In Liège, while the supply of French films declined similarly to Brussels, market share remained at over 50% of the market, with the demand for German films significantly lower than in Brussels.

5 Film Popularity

The statistics presented in Tables 4 and 5 double count those films in circulation across one or more calendar years—that is, films first screened in one year that continue their run into the following year and beyond are counted separately for each year

[28] De Bruyn (1942b).

in which they are screened.[29] When measuring individual film performance overall, the performance indicators of films are summed over multiple years. Based upon the criteria that films were screened at least once during 1941–1943, Table 6 provides circulation details of the Top 20 films screened in each of the three cities measured by their POPSTAT Index scores. The statistics of the Top 20 films reinforce the evidence of a cultural divide in Belgium, showing binary differences—Antwerp to Brussels, and Antwerp to Liege, with German films dominating in the Dutch-speaking city and French films in the two Francophile cities. A clear asymmetry in film diets is apparent. No fewer than 35 of the 60 films in the three listings appear in just one city. Antwerp audiences support a different diet of films to Brussels and Liege, with 17 of Antwerp's 20 most popular movies not featuring in the Top 20 listings of Brussels and Liège. While there is only one German film in the Top 20 in Liège (*Kora Terry*, dubbed into French), sixteen German movies feature Antwerp.

In Brussels, 15 of the Top 20 films are French, with German and Italian films securing two and three berths. The relatively poor performance of German cinema is reflected in both Top 50 and Top 100 listings summarised in Table 7. However, two German films appear on both Brussels and Antwerp Top 20 lists, the 1942 production *Die Goldene Stadt* (The Golden City), and *Kora Terry* (1940)—the first of these two was ranked 24th in Liege.

Conversely, no French films made the Top 20 listings in Antwerp. Indeed Table 7 shows that only two French films were listed in that city's Top 100. *Le Dernier des Six*, ranked 76th (33rd in Brussels) and *Les Inconnus dans la Maison*, ranked 87th (6th in Brussels), were both produced by Continental (based in Paris and marketed as a French enterprise but secretly owned by the German state) and distributed by the Ufa subsidiary in Brussels. Both films were released in Brussels eight months earlier than their subsequent appearance in Antwerp.

The top 20 lists of Brussels and Liège are more like one another. Apart from *Kora Terry*, they have nine French-language films in common. Some of these films were made before the German invasion of France, others more recently. None refer to ongoing political or military current affairs, with storylines set in former times or an unspecified recent past. Neither is there a reference to National Socialism, the World War, nor the German occupation of France. A set of films that contrast strongly with Antwerp in this respect.

6 Findings

Another striking feature of Table 6 is the long life of the most popular films in circulation, indicating that they were not removed from the market once released,

[29] The reader will be familiar with the method of tracking films backwards in time to the date and venue of first screening, and forwards to final screening. Accordingly, the statistics presented in the tables that follow date at their earliest from screenings held on 13 June 1940 and at the latest from 7 September 1944, with the qualification that each film in the population was screened at least once in the population of Brussels' cinemas between 1 January 1941 and 31 December 1943.

Table 6 Top 20 Films screened in Brussels, Antwerp and Liege

(1) Rank	(2) IMDB No	(3) Film Title	(4) Nationality	(5) Distributor	(6) POPSTAT Index values	(7) Date of first screening	(8) Premiere cinema	(9) Opening run (days)	(10) Number of cinemas	(11) Total screening days
Brussels										
1	33,193	Empreinte du Dieu, l'	France	Emka	553	26-03-1942	Métropole	36	47	388
2	34,800	Goldene Stadt, die	Germany	Ufa	444	05-03-1943	Eldorado	28	38	336
3	161,825	Monsieur Hector	France	Abel-Films	442	01-11-1940	Métropole	21	40	328
4	169,909	Fièvres	France	Atlas-Films	420	06-11-1942	Eldorado	21	49	377
5	35,158	Ore 9: Lezione di chimica	Italy	Fama-Films	413	05-02-1943	Métropole	28	32	259
6	34,893	Inconnus dans la maison, les	France	Ufa	407	18-09-1942	Eldorado	35	35	295
7	182,671	Acrobate, l'	France	Fama-Films	390	14-08-1942	Métropole	21	35	284
8	247,493	Mademoiselle Swing	France	Atlas-Films	381	20-11-1942	Métropole	21	43	325
9	195,586	Cartacalha, reine des gitans	France	Atlas-Films	377	10-07-1942	Eldorado	21	38	323
10	162,038	Voile bleu, le	France	Idéal Film	375	16-06-1944	Métropole	49	7	98
11	184,831	Premier bal	France	Idéal Film	368	09-10-1942	Métropole	21	36	281
12	170,002	Histoire de rire	France	Idéal Film	364	25-12-1942	Métropole	24	29	241

(continued)

Table 6 (continued)

(1) Rank	(2) IMDB No	(3) Film Title	(4) Nationality	(5) Distributor	(6) POPSTAT Index values	(7) Date of first screening	(8) Premiere cinema	(9) Opening run (days)	(10) Number of cinemas	(11) Total screening days
13	31,084	Battement de Coeur	France	A.C.C	360	15-11-1940	Queen's Hall	14	41	352
14	274,709	Pavillon brûle, le	France	Atlas-Films	360	04-10-1940	Métropole	21	34	268
15	193,894	Elles étaient douze femmes	France	Emka	359	30-10-1942	Galeries	64	34	348
16	32,677	Kora Terry	Germany	Ufa	341	21-02-1941	Eldorado	28	33	252
17	33,489	Corona di ferro, la	Italy	Atlas-Films	339	04-06-1943	Métropole	21	32	245
18	268,284	Enfer des anges, l'	France	Osso	334	24-01-1941	Métropole	21	28	238
19	34,063	Premier rendez-vous	France	Ufa	333	09-01-1942	Eldorado	21	36	281
20	160,639	Paris New-York	France	Filmsonor	326	22-11-1940	Métropole	21	31	231
Antwerp										
1	34,265	Tanz mit dem Kaiser	Germany	Ufa	196	11-09-1942	Eldorado	21	24	236
2	35,294	Schicksal	Germany	Tobis	189	14-01-1943	Rex	28	23	189
3	33,049	Sieben Jahre Pech	Germany	Ufa	183	13-11-1942	Eldorado	21	23	221

(continued)

Table 6 (continued)

(1) Rank	(2) IMDB No	(3) Film Title	(4) Nationality	(5) Distributor	(6) POPSTAT Index values	(7) Date of first screening	(8) Premiere cinema	(9) Opening run (days)	(10) Number of cinemas	(11) Total screening days
4	34,800	Goldene Stadt, die	Germany	Ufa	183	05-03-1943	Eldorado	35	24	196
5	154,669	Janssens en Peeters, dikke vrienden	Belgium	Vanderheyden	178	06-12-1940	Empire	21	14	119
6	34,823	Hab' mich lieb!	Germany	Ufa	172	14-05-1943	Eldorado	14	25	203
7	33,275	Wunschkonzert	Germany	Ufa	169	19-12-1941	Scala	28	16	139
8	158,468	Anuschka	Germany	Ufa	166	09-10-1942	Studio 48	14	22	198
9	35,559	Wiener Blut	Germany	Ufa	165	27-11-1942	Eldorado	27	22	202
10	34,815	Grosse Liebe, die	Germany	Ufa	163	24-12-1942	Eldorado	21	21	173
11	32,468	Figlia del corsaro verde, la	Italy	Vanderheyden	155	10-07-1942	Scala	14	19	147
12	32,677	Kora Terry	Germany	Ufa	152	21-02-1941	Scala	21	15	139
13	36,191	Münchhausen	Germany	Ufa	152	05-11-1943	Eldorado	21	18	160
14	33,207	Unser Fräulein Doktor	Germany	Ufa	151	01-05-1942	Scala	14	19	161
15	33,557	Dreimal Hochzeit	Germany	Ufa	150	31-12-1942	Scala	21	15	126
16	35,045	Maske in Blau	Germany	Tobis	150	24-12-1943	Rex	28	15	125

(continued)

Table 6 (continued)

(1) Rank	(2) IMDB No	(3) Film Title	(4) Nationality	(5) Distributor	(6) POPSTAT Index values	(7) Date of first screening	(8) Premiere cinema	(9) Opening run (days)	(10) Number of cinemas	(11) Total screening days
17	33,129	Sündige Dorf, das	Germany	Tobis	149	16-10-1942	Rex	28	16	139
18	31,949	Sogno di Butterfly, il	Germany-Italy	Fama-Films	148	26-02-1943	Scala	21	14	119
19	35,158	Ore 9, lezione di chimica	Italy	Fama-Films	148	04-12-1942	Scala	14	18	161
20	33,359	Auf Wiedersehen, Franziska	Germany	Ufa	146	21-01-1943	Eldorado	14	21	174
Liege										
1	161,825	Monsieur Hector	France	Abel-Films	126	01-11-1941	Liege-Palace	21	15	91
2	194,013	Homme qui cherche la vérité, l’	France	Atlas-Films	102	25-10-1940	Forum	14	11	68
3	32,888	Paradis perdu	France	Atlas-Films	99	20-09-1940	Forum	7	15	78
4	34,893	Inconnus dans la maison, les	France	Ufa	99	04-09-1942	Forum	21	7	49
5	35,075	Monsieur La Souris	France	Atlas-Films	98	04-02-1942	Forum	21	6	42
6	33,193	Empreinte du dieu, l’	France	Emka	98	04-04-1942	Liege-Palace	21	11	77

(continued)

Table 6 (continued)

(1) Rank	(2) IMDB No	(3) Film Title	(4) Nationality	(5) Distributor	(6) POPSTAT Index values	(7) Date of first screening	(8) Premiere cinema	(9) Opening run (days)	(10) Number of cinemas	(11) Total screening days
7	195,586	Cartacalha reine des gitans	France	Atlas-Films	93	08-05-1942	Forum	14	10	65
8	191,978	Duel, le	France	Idéal Film	92	12-06-1942	Forum	14	9	58
9	199,611	Huit hommes dans un château	France	Monopol-Film	91	28-05-1943	Forum	7	8	55
10	32,677	Kora Terry	Germany	Ufa	91	28-03-1941	Forum	14	10	67
11	217,482	Ferme aux loups, la	France	Ufa	89	14-01-1944	Forum	21	5	31
12	34,063	Premier rendez-vous, le	France	Ufa	86	19-12-1941	Liege-Palace	21	9	64
13	184,831	Premier bal	France	Idéal Film	85	22-05-1942	Liege-Palace	21	9	59
14	31,084	Battement de cœur	France	A.C.C	85	12/20/1940	Marivaux	21	14	93
15	169,909	Fièvres	France	Atlas-Films	84	20-11-1942	Liege-Palace	19	10	57
16	162,038	Voile bleu, le	France	Idéal Film	82	28-04-1944	Forum	14	3	21
17	31,158	Circonstances atténuantes	France	OIF	81	06-09-1940	Forum	7	11	78
18	34,643	Dernier atout	France	Monopol-Film	79	09-07-1943	Liege-Palace	3	10	56
19	199,507	Face au destin	France	GPA	79	13-12-1940	Forum	7	6	42
20	207,372	Caprices	France	Ufa	78	22-05-1942	Forum	14	9	54

Source Dataset

Table 7 National representation in the most popular films

	France	Germany	Italy	Others
Brussels				
Top 20 films	15	2	3	0
Top 50 films	37	9	3	1
Top 100 Films	62	27	9	2
Antwerp				
Top 20 films	0	16	2	2
Top 50 films	0	43	4	3
Top 100 films	2	81	11	6
Liege				
Top 20 films	19	1	0	0
Top 50 films	37	7	5	1
Top 100 films	63	20	13	4

Source Dataset

as would likely have been the case during peacetime but in perpetual circulation. Compare the 93 screening days that *Top Hat* generated in Philadelphia in 1935–1956 (see Chap. 2) with the 388 days given to the top-ranking French film *L'Empreinte du Dieu* (*Two Women*, 1941) in Brussels, a city in 1940 with about half Philadelphia's population of just under 2 million.[30]

While sampling differences may partly explain this difference, the French film's longevity in circulation is striking, and the contrast with Philadelphia is worth further examination. *Top Hat* opened at the 3,009-seater Stanley on 6 September 1935 and closed with a 2-day booking at the Oxford on 12 December of the same year, some 96 days later. In contrast, *L'Empreinte du Dieu* opened at the 2,795-seater Métropole on 26 March 1942 and was last screened at the Continental and Forum cinemas some 833 days later, on 6 July 1944—just before the liberation of the city from German rule on 3 September 1944.

L'Empreinte du Dieu is also interesting on a historiographical level. This French film, directed by Léonide Moguy, has fallen into oblivion. Brought into prominence through the POPSTAT methodology, it is hardly mentioned in literature on French cinema; it was never released on VHS tape, DVD, or in any other digital format. It is not remembered as an important film and is not considered part of the French film canon. Neither has it been mentioned in studies of Belgium cinema during the German occupation. Distributed by a minor Belgium distributor (Emka), which rarely advertised in the trade journal *CINEMA*, *L'Empreinte du Dieu* was based on

[30] This observation needs to be tempered by the limited nature of the Philadelphia sample, which is restricted to films screened in cinemas owned by the Warner Bros. organisation. The population of Philadelphia is given in the *International Motion Picture Almanac, 1937–38* (1938) as 1,960,961. According to IMDB, *L'Empreinte du Dieu* was released in the USA on 1 November 1940 as *Two Women.*

the novel of the same title by the French writer Maxence Van der Meersch, who won the prestigious 'Prix Goncourt' prize for it. The story was partly set in Belgium, with the exteriors partially filmed in Antwerp, Brussels, and Bruges in and around August 1939.[31] Given these facts, it seems highly plausible that the film would have succeeded in Flanders and certainly in Flemish cities where the Francophone middle class was undoubtedly familiar with the book. However, the film was not screened in the principal Flemish cities of Antwerp, Bruges and Ghent at all. Programming data suggest that Emka released a limited number of film prints circulated only in Brussels and French-speaking Belgium. (The PAB likely ordered Emka not to release the film in Flanders).

Another interesting example of this polarity of distribution can be seen in the performance of the Dutch-speaking Belgium film *Janssens en Peeters, Dikke Vrienden*, which ranked fifth in Antwerp. This comedy, set in Antwerp, and featuring well-known local comedians, was directed by Jan Vanderheyden, a director/distributor who acted as the figurehead leader of the Belgian film sector and helped the German propaganda services implement their policy.[32] It was one of the few Belgian feature films released during the occupation—all of them were directed by Vanderheyden or his companion Edith Kiel. As a Flemish film, it was not released in Francophone territory probably because francophone audiences had shown no interest in Flemish sound films before the occupation. In Brussels, the film appeared in just six cinemas between September 1941 and June 1943. On each occasion for a one-week run, another confirmation of Brussels, although geographically located in Flanders, functioning as a Francophone film market.

The top-ranking film in Antwerp was the German film *Tanz mit dem Kaiser* (*Dance with the Emperor*, 1941)—a film ranked 38th in Brussels and 99th in Liege. It opened at the Eldorado on 11 September 1942 and was screened consistently during the remainder of the year and the following year, ending with a final two-week screening in June 1944. This success can be attributed to Marika Rökk, the Hungarian-born actress/singer/dancer who had personally visited Antwerp and Brussels in February 1941, promoting her film *Kora Terry*—the only film that appeared in the top 20 of all three cities. *Kora Terry* was a lavishly produced musical with an erotic snake dance reminiscent of Pre-Code Hollywood cinema. *Tanz mit dem Kaiser* was not as risqué but, like *Kora Terry*, featured several songs sung by Marika Rökk recorded in German and French versions and played on German-controlled radio. The film's sheet music popularity ensured further publicity for the film. Altogether, *Tanz mit dem Kaiser* was screened for 266 days in Antwerp, contrasting starkly with *L'Empreinte du Dieu*, which was not screened there at all[33] (Fig. 1).

A film that was similarly popular among Brussels and Antwerp audiences, but less so in Liege, is *Die Goldene Stadt* (1943). Although released late in the study period, in March 1943, the film ended up as the second highest-ranked film in Brussels and fourth in Antwerp. It was one of the first colour feature films released in Belgium and

[31] On tourne (1939), L'empreinte (1939).

[32] Vande Winkel (2021b).

[33] Vande Winkel (2019).

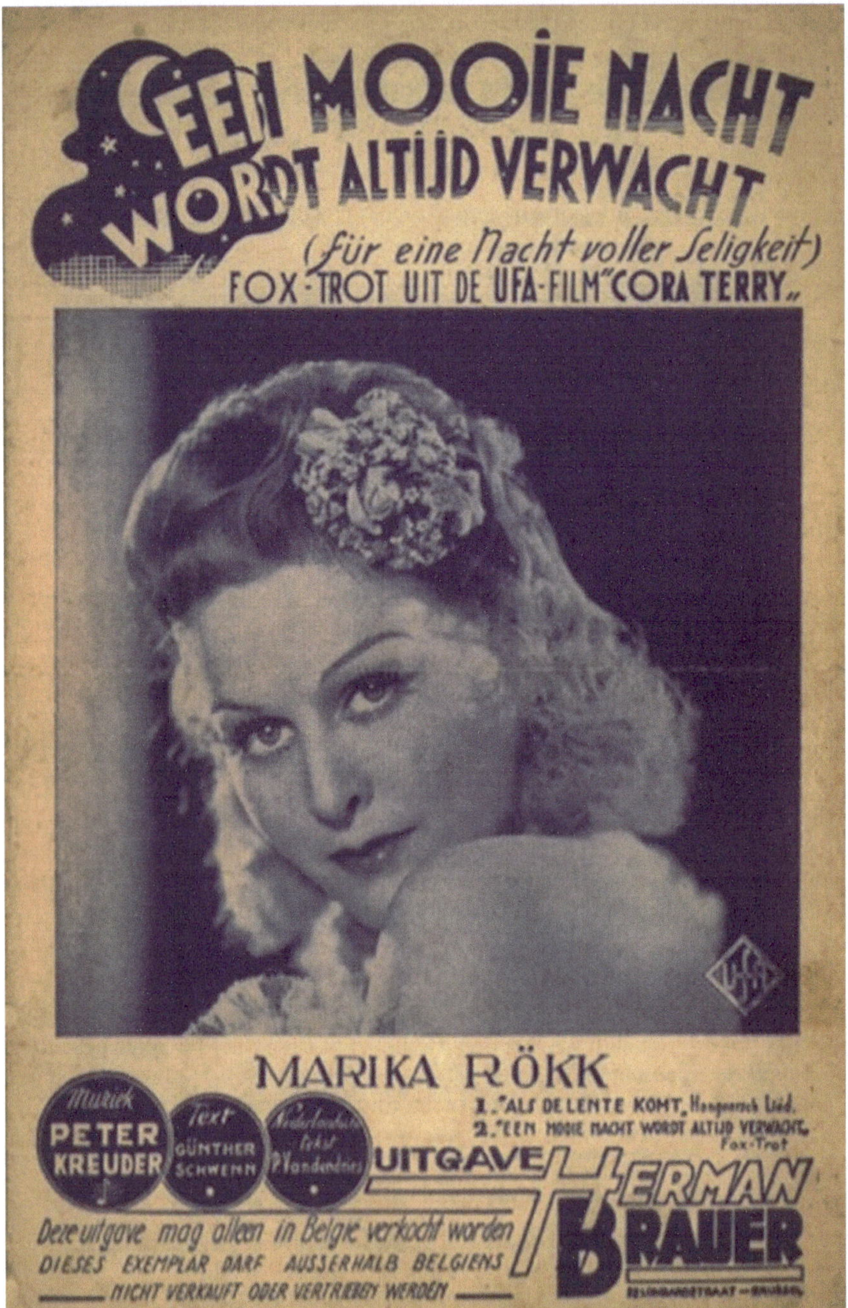

Fig. 1 Belgian sheet music for the song 'Für ein Nacht voller seligkeit' (For a Night Full of Bliss), sung by Marika Rökk in the film Kora Terry (1940) (*Source* Vande Winkel Private Collection)

starred the popular actress Kristina Söderbaum. It carried a controversial storyline about a young German woman whom a distant family member seduced. The fact that the suitor/seducer spoke German with a Czech accent and that the film carried anti-Czech sentiments was probably lost on most Belgian cinemagoers.

Nevertheless, it was not lost on anyone that Söderbaum's character eventually agreed to have sex with him. Rumours about the film, including a sex scene, contributed to its appeal. That Söderbaum's character, carrying a child out of wedlock, eventually kills herself, made the film even more controversial, particularly within Catholic circles. Several priests appear to have told their parishioners not to watch the movie, which inspired some of them to do that very thing.[34] *Die Goldene Stadt* was also heavily marketed by film distributor Ufa, which advertised it as groundbreaking and must-see. Ufa released the film simultaneously in three prints (highly unusual at the time) in Antwerp, Brussels, and Ghent—in Liege, it was the second most popular German film, ranked 24th in the city.[35]

Italian films made a marked impression in the Belgium market in 1943, securing over 10% market share in each city. The appetite for these films appears to have transcended the cultural division of the country. For instance, *Ore 9, Lezione di Chimica* (*Schoolgirl Diary*, 1941), a film starring Alida Valli, appears in Brussels and Antwerp Top 20 listings. The film's success was probably linked to the clever way it was marketed by the small distributor Fama-Film. Entitled *Boarding School Scandal* (French: Scandale au pensionnat; Flemish: Schandaal in de kostschool), the film dealt with tensions at a school where some adolescent female pupils were in love with the handsome male chemistry teacher. The unspoken promise of sex is likely to have contributed to the film's appeal. *Ore 9, Lezione di Chimica* offered a genre no longer made in Germany. The same can be said of other Italian movies featured in Table 6. *La figlia del Corsaro Verde* (*The Daughter of the Green Pirate*, Italy, 1940) was a swashbuckler and *La Corona di Ferro* (*The Iron Crown*, Italy, 1941) was an adventure film set in a mythical, medieval-like kingdom. In the absence of Hollywood, Italian films partially filled that gap. In the Antwerp Top 20 in Table 6, *Premiere der Butterfly* (The Dream of the Butterfly, 1939) was a German-Italian co-production shot simultaneously in German and Italian. Still, only the German version (dubbed in French) was released in occupied Belgium (Fig. 2).

Two cinemas dominated the screenings of the premieres of the most popular films in each of the three cities. In Brussels, these were the 2,795-seater Métropole and the 2,352-seater Eldorado, at which 18 of the 20 films were premiered on multiple-week programmes. (Both cinemas were located at the Place de Brouckère in the heart of Brussels, where the Eldorado is still in operation.) One of the two exceptions was the film *le Pavillon Brûle*, which had a different exhibition profile, running for 16 weeks at the 600-seater Galeries cinema. (This French film was distributed by a smaller company, Atlas-Films, which had difficulty accessing the most important cinemas.) In Antwerp, Table 6 shows that 15 of the Top 20 films screened were premiered

---

[34] Belgien (1944).

[35] Vande Winkel (2020).

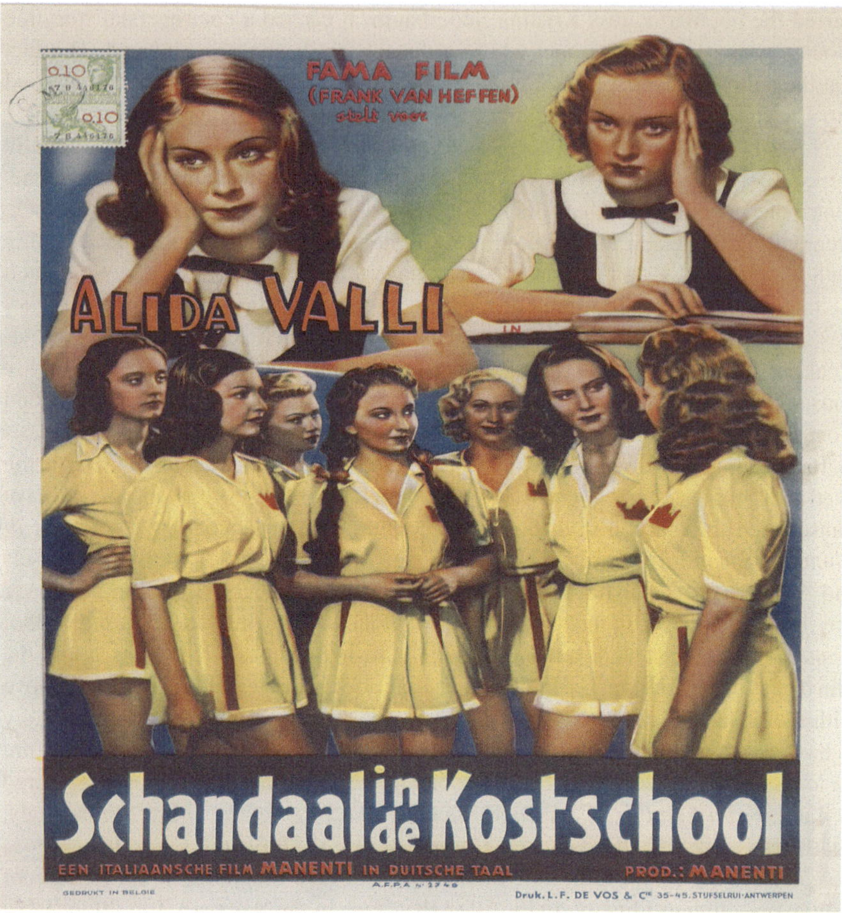

Fig. 2 Belgian poster for the film *Ore 9, Lezione di Chimica* (1941) (*Source* Vande Winkel Private Collection)

either at the 1,000-seater Eldorado or the 1,384-seater Scala. Finally, in Liege, the Liege-Palace and Forum cinemas premiered 19 of the Top 20 films.

The distribution of the most popular films in Antwerp was dominated by the Belgian branches of Ufa and Tobis, with 16 out of the most popular 20 movies.[36] The remainder, with two apiece, was distributed by two domestic production companies that played an essential role in the Belgian Film Guild: Jan Vanderheyden (with his company of the same name) and Frank Van Heffen (Fama-Films). By way of contrast, in Brussels, only four of the top 20 films were distributed by Ufa/Tobis: the German films *Kora Terry* and *Die Goldene Stadt*, as well as Continental's productions *Premier*

[36] In Nazi Germany in January 1942, all German film companies were merged into one large holding (Ufi). During that year the foreign offices of Tobis were absorbed by Ufa. See Vande Winkel (2017, pp. 58–59).

Rendez-vous (Her First Affair, France, 1941) and *Les inconnus Dans la Maison* (Strangers in the House, 1942). Eight other companies distributed the remaining sixteen films. A similar pattern can be identified in Liege: five films distributed by Ufa/Tobis (one German film and four Continental productions) and fifteen films distributed by eight other companies, including many, but not all, the same distributors found in the Brussels listing. In contrast, the smaller Belgian distribution companies that had survived the German downsizing measures were more successful in getting access to the Francophone film market than the Flemish market. Some firms owed their success to one or two hits, such as Emka (*Elles étaient douze femmes* [1940], *L'Empreinte du dieu* [1941]) and Abel-Films (*Monsieur Hector* [1940]). Others scored a series of 'hit' films, such as Atlas-Films (seven French productions and one Italian) and Idéal-Films (four French productions).

7 Discussion

In occupied Belgium, a clear cultural divide is evident between film screenings in Flanders and Wallonia. Did this division exist before the German occupation? The question is difficult to answer because of the absence of previous comparative research. Although the dataset used in the chapter covers a short period of film history (1940–1944), it is geographically wide-reaching, facilitating comparative analysis. Research by other film historians on cinema exhibition and film programming in Belgium before World War II is for a more extended period but limited to a single Flemish city—Antwerp or Ghent.[37] One consequence is that the comparative findings found in the chapter cannot be corroborated.

Nevertheless, it is plausible to assume a less strict separation between film programming in Flanders and Wallonia before the German occupation. Differences prevailed, of course—we know that the Belgian sound films of Jan Vanderheyden and Edith Kiel, filmed in the Flemish language from 1934 and very popular in Flanders, were not screened in French-speaking cinemas in the 1930s.[38] Thus, the observation made in the chapter that the film *Janssen and Peeters, Dikke vrienden*, was hardly screened in Brussels and not screened at all in Liege is consistent with this pre-war finding.

As mentioned at the beginning of this chapter, we know that, before the Second World War, some cinemas in Flanders targeted Francophone audiences by screening French-spoken films without subtitles. Before the Second World War, we also know that German films for which a French dubbed version was available were screened in that form in Flanders. None of this was allowed by the German occupiers. Therefore, we can conclude that the occupation period (1940–1944) broke with some pre-war traditions because of the dictates of the German authorities. After the liberation, American films (and English-language films from Great Britain and other countries)

[37] Van de Vijver and Biltereyst (2010), Engelen and Vande Winkel (2018a).

[38] Vande Winkel and Van Engeland (2014).

were allowed again in Belgium. After dubbing into French, they were screened in Wallonia, Brussels and parts of Flanders. German films, however, did not entirely disappear. Several Belgian companies acquired (or, in some cases, stole) the distribution rights to movies that had been popular during the war and re-released them. Films such as *Kora Terry* and *Die Goldene Stadt* were screened again in the late 1940s and early 1950s. The stars of such films as Marika Rökk and Zarah Leander remained popular, and their post-war films were also exhibited in Flemish cities such as Antwerp and Ghent (Figs. 3 and 4).

The differences between the Top 20 lists of the three cities (Table 6) are marked, particularly between Brussels-Antwerp and Liege-Antwerp. *Kora Terry* is the only film common to the three sections in Table 6. One historian describes it as '...a hearty cocktail of flamboyant costumes, sensual rhythms, exotic scenery (parts of the film were set in Algeria), and titillating romance, celebrating wickedness, sex and eroticism'.[39] Several books on Third Reich cinema mention that Goebbels did not like the film and objected to Rökk's portrayal of two different characters (twin sisters)—a claim mainly based on Rökk's memoirs not yet corroborated by further evidence.[40] The point is that the film cannot be described as ideologically supporting Nazi Germany, unlike films such as *Jud Süss* (1940) or *Stukas* (1941)—films that did not make the listings.

In contrast, German dramatic and romantic films in which the propaganda is more subtly interwoven into the storyline, such as *Wunschkonzert* (1940), *Auf wiederseh'n Franziska* (1941), *Die grosse Liebe* (1942), and *Die goldene Stadt* (1943) do appear in the top 20 lists. In the first three of these four films, we find direct references to the ongoing world war and to the sacrifices made by the German people to help the Wehrmacht achieve the final victory. This topic is quickly touched upon in the last scene of *Auf wiederseh'n Franziska* (1941) and is essential to the storylines of *Wunschkonzert* (1940) and *Die grosse Liebe* (1942). It must be noted that these three films made the Top 20 listing in Antwerp but not of the other two cities.

8 Conclusion

The POPSTAT method provides a novel account of filmgoing in Belgium during the occupation. While subject to many edicts, filmgoing remained an essential activity for the Belgium people, irrespective of where they lived. Deprived of Hollywood movies dubbed into French for the Walloon population or subtitled into Dutch for the Flemish, these respective populations turned to French and German films. With Francophone Belgium, the asymmetric distribution of films in occupied Belgium offered more French films (and French dubbings of German films). In comparison, Dutch-speaking audiences in Flanders screened non-dubbed German films and far fewer French films. This binary division of the film market makes establishing a national popularity chart

[39] Ascheid (2003, p. 94).

[40] Fox (2000, p. 125). See also Ascheid (2003, p. 93).

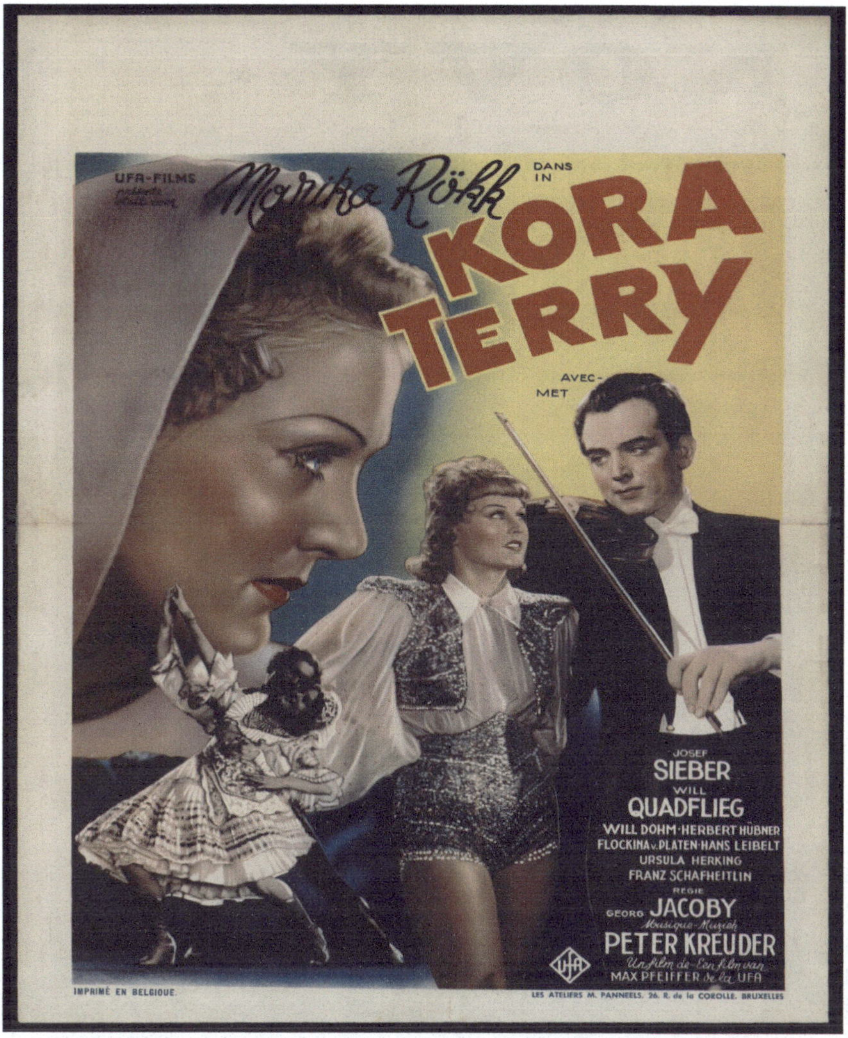

Fig. 3 Poster for *Kora Terry* (1940), screening at the Astrid cinema in Ghent, from 26 December 1941 until 1 January 1942 (*Source* Collectie Archief Gent, MA_ROM_XVI_AF_04304)

pointless. Instead, the approach taken here is to explore further these differences. The method unearths many surprises, not least the popularity in Brussels of *L'Empreinte du Dieu*, Italian cinema's widespread distribution and successes, particularly in 1943, and the Top 20 rating of *Kora Terry* in all three city markets. As noted, the most popular film screened in Brussels over the period was not screened in Antwerp or the other cities in Flanders. Indeed, of the 1030 films screened in Brussels over the period, a little more than half of them (575) were circulated in Antwerp, with nine of

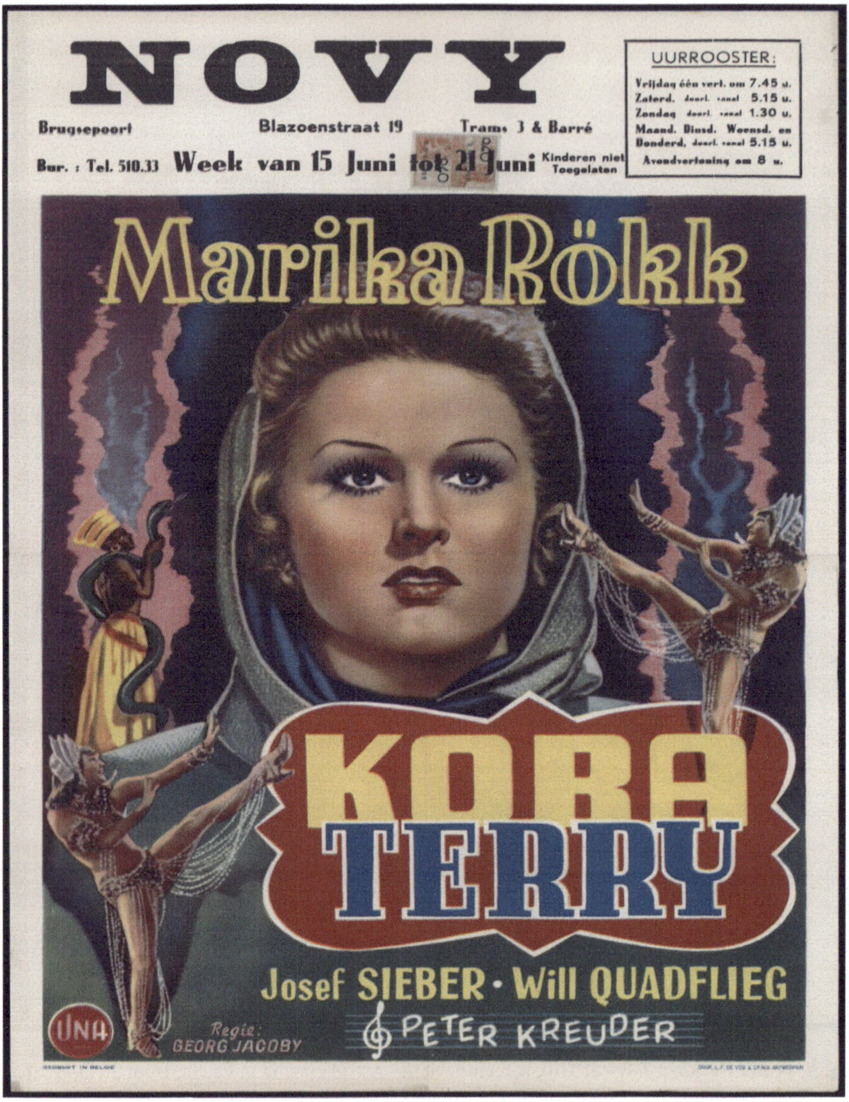

Fig. 4 Poster for the same film, *Kora Terry* (1940), screening at the Novy cinema in Ghent, from 15 until 21 June 1951 (*Source* Collectie Archief Gent, MA_ROM_XVI_AF_04094)

the Top 20 films screened in Brussels, featured in Table 6, not screened in Antwerp at all, eight of which were French and one, Italian.[41]

[41] These are: *L'Empreinte du Dieu, L'Acrobate, Mademoiselle Swing, Cartacalha Reine des Gitans, Premier Bal, Histoire de Rire, Le Pavillon Brûle, Elles étaient douze Femmes*, and *La Corona di Ferro.*

The longevity of films in circulation represents a difference from the pre-and post-war system of distribution, occasioned by supply shortages. Films were required to work harder, and audiences were likely more prepared to watch movies for a second or third time. However, this does not appear to have affected the distribution pattern in which films circulated through time and space outwards from box-office rich cinemas. Nor did it change the highly unequal statistics of popularity, if anything, making them more extreme, since if audiences were prepared to view films on more than one occasion, it would seem rational that they chose the movie they enjoyed the most. If this behaviour were shared across the population, it would make the most popular films even more popular. There was money to be made, costs met, profits generated and audiences to please, even in wartime.

References

Ascheid, A. (2003). *Hitler's heroines: Stardom and womanhood in Nazi Cinema*. Temple University Press.

Belgien: Konfessionelle Agitation gegen dt. Film. (1944). Bundesarchiv, R 58/193.

Cinema Jaarboek 1942 Annuaire du cinema. (1942). Belgische Syndicale Kamer van Filmverhuurders en Vereeniging der Cinemabestuurders van België - Association des Directeurs de Cinéma de Belgique et Chambre Syndicale des Distributeurs de Films.

Conway, M. (2001). Belgium. In I. C. Dear & M. R. D. Foot (Eds.), *The Oxford companion to World War II* (pp. 93–96). Oxford University Press.

De Bruyn, J. (1941, May 6). Een Franskiljonsche kinema te Leuven. *Volk en Staat*.

De Bruyn, J. (1942a, May 1). Onze taal in de bioskopen. *Volk en Staat*.

De Bruyn, J. (1942b, September 4). Nog altijd die afschuwelijke dubbing. *Volk en Staat*.

Engelen, L., & Vande Winkel, R. (2018a). *Cine Zoologie. Hoe film de Antwerpse dierentuin heeft gered*. Letterwerk.

Engelen, L., & Vande Winkel, R. (2018b). Het filmaanbod van Cine Zoologie (1930–1936): een casestudy naar filmverdeling en -programmatie in de jaren dertig. In *HistoriANT 6 - 2018. Jaarboek voor Antwerpse Geschiedenis* (pp. 83–103). Gompel & Svacina.

Eue, R., & Lang, F. (Eds.). (2017). *Schillernd grau. CONTINENTAL - Eine deutsche Filmproduktion im besetzten Frankreich 1941–1944*. Synema.

Fox, J. (2000). *Filming women in the Third Reich*. Berg.

Het corporatief leven. (1942, January 2). *CINEMA, 2*(3), 14.

International Motion Picture Almanac, 1937–38. (1938). Quigley Publishing Company.

L'empreinte du dieu als film. (1939, September 2). *Algemeen Handelsblad*.

Leteux, C. (2017). *Continental films. Cinéma français sous contrôle allemand*. La tour verte.

On tourne à Bruges. (1939, 13 August). *Journal de Bruges*.

Propaganda-Abteilung Belgien. (1941). *Jahresbericht der Propaganda-Abteilung Belgien beim Militärbefehlshaber in Belgien und Nordfrankreich (August 1941)*. https://www.cegesoma.be/en/reports-propaganda-abteilung-about-belgium

Roekens, A. (2011). *Gewillig België*. De Bezige Bij.

Sedgwick, J. (2000). *Popular filmgoing in 1930s Britain: A choice of pleasures*. Exeter University Press.

Sedgwick, J. (2020a). Constructing film histories: A bottom-up approach. *Academia Letters*, Article 86. https://doi.org/10.20935/AL86

Sedgwick, J. (2020b). From POPSTAT to Relpop: A methodological journey in investigating comparative film popularity. *TMG Journal for Media History, 23* (1–2): 1–9. https://doi.org/10.18146/tmg.776

Van de Vijver, L., & Biltereyst, D. (2010). Hollywood versus Lokaliteit. Het (on)gelijke aanbod van Amerikaanse en Europese film in de jaren dertig in Gent. *TMG Journal for Media History, 13*(2), 60–79. https://doi.org/10.18146/tmg.578

Vande Winkel, R. (2003). *Nazi newsreels and foreign propaganda in German-occupied territories. The Belgian version of Ufa's foreign weekly newsreel (ATW), 1940–1944.* Universiteit Gent.

Vande Winkel, R. (2011). German influence on Belgian Cinema, 1933–45: From low-profile presence to downright colonisation. In R. Vande Winkel & D. Welch (Eds.), *Cinema and the Swastika: The international expansion of Third Reich Cinema* (2nd ed., pp. 72–84). Palgrave Macmillan.

Vande Winkel, R. (2017). Film distribution in occupied Belgium (1940–1944): German film politics and its implementation by the 'corporate' organisations and the film guild. *TMG Journal for Media History, 20*(1), 46–77. https://doi.org/10.18146/2213-7653.201280

Vande Winkel, R. (2020). *Cinema in occupied Belgium (1940–1944).* First published 17 November 2020. Last update: 7 May 2021. https://www.cinema-in-occupied-belgium.be

Vande Winkel, R. (2021a). Jan Vanderheyden and Edith Kiel: 'Leading' the Belgian film sector while taking orders from the German Propaganda Service. In P. Skopal & R. Vande Winkel (Eds.), *Film Professionals in Nazi-occupied Europe: Mediation between the national-socialist cultural "new order" and local structures* (pp. 87–117). Palgrave Macmillan.

Vande Winkel, R. (2021b). Rekordeinnahmen und Kassengift. Die Ufa-Auslandsabteilungund der deutsche Filmexport im Zweiten Weltkrieg. In P. Stiasny, J. Kasten, & F. Lang (Eds.), *Ufa international. Ein deutscher Filmkonzern mit globalen Ambitionen* (pp. 126–143). Edition text + kritik.

Vande Winkel, R., & Van Engeland, D. (2014). *Edith Kiel & Jan Vanderheyden. Pioniers van de Vlaamse film.* Cinematek.

Wahl, C. (2009). *Sprachversionsfilme aus Babelsberg. Die internationale Strategie der Ufa 1929–1939.* Edition text + kritik.

Welch, D., & Vande Winkel, R. (2011). Europe's new Hollywood? The German film industry under Nazi rule, 1933–45. In R. Vande Winkel & D. Welch (Eds.), *Cinema and the Swastika. The international expansion of Third Reich cinema* (2nd ed., pp. 1–24). Palgrave Macmillan.

Winkel, V. (2019). Německé filmové hvězdy v okupované Belgii jako kulturní aktéři (1940–1944). *Iluminace, 30*(4), 51–60.

Witte, E., & Craeybeckx, J. (2010). *Political history of Belgium: From 1830 onwards.* Academic and Scientific Publishing.

Roel Vande Winkel is an associate professor in Film & TV Studies at KU Leuven and LUCA School of Arts, Belgium. He is associate editor of the *Historical Journal of Film, Radio and Television*. Recent books include *Film Professionals in Nazi-Occupied Europe* (2021, with Pavel Skopal), *Researching Newsreels. Local, National and Transnational Case Studies* (2018, with Ciara Chambers and Mats Jönsson), *Silencing Cinema: Film Censorship around the World* (2013, with Daniel Biltereyst) and *Cinema and the Swastika: The International Expansion of Third Reich Cinema* (2011 revised, with David Welch). His website www.cinema-in-occupied-belgiu m.be provides an overview of film programming and the organisation of the cinema sector during the Second World War in Belgium.

John Sedgwick is a visiting professor in the Faculty of Technology, Design and Environment, Oxford Brookes University. He researches the economic history of cinema and is particularly interested in the ontological characteristics of film as a commodity. He created the POPSTAT Index of Film Popularity as a proxy for box-office returns. This tool provides a means of reflecting audience preferences and monitoring the distribution process. His research has focused on American, Australian, British, Dutch, Italian and international markets during the 1930s and 1950/60s.

He has written a monograph, edited an anthology and published articles in *Business History, Cinema Journal, Economic History Review Explorations in Economic History Enterprise and Society Film History, Historical Journal of Film, Radio and Television, Journal of Applied Statistics, Journal of Cultural Economics, Journal of Economic History* and *Journal of Transnational Cinema.*

Five Italian Cities: Comparative Analysis of Cinema Types, Film Circulation and Relative Popularity in the Mid-1950s

Daniela Treveri Gennari and John Sedgwick

Abstract This chapter investigates cinema types, film distribution patterns and consumption in five regional capitals in Italy in the mid-1950s. It aims to develop a framework of comparative analysis, extending previous research of filmgoing in Italy, comparing Rome with the cities of Milan and Turin in the North and Naples, and Bari in the South. Evidence of regional differences in film preferences is presented.

With audiences peaking in 1955, the production side of the film industry, supported by state subsidies and screen quotas, had by the early 1950s recovered from the traumatic events of the last years of World War II.[1] Like many economies in the developed West at the time, filmgoing was the dominant paid-for-leisure activity of the population absorbing approximately 70% of all leisure expenditure, with domestic film production vying with Hollywood for market share.

This chapter investigates film distribution and consumption patterns in five regional capitals in January 1952.[2] It provides a cross-section of the distribution and exhibition sectors in operation, comprising films at various stages in their life cycles. We aim to develop a framework of comparative analysis by extending previous research on filmgoing in Rome during the mid-1950s to the cities of Milan and Turin in the North and Naples and Bari in the South. A particular concern is whether the different economic circumstances in the country affected distribution practices. For instance, cinema expenditure per head in Bari in 1957 was only two-thirds that of

[1] See Nicoli (2017, 2018) for an account of the Italian film industry's emergence from the Second World War and the complex financial arrangements put in place to support it by the Italian State. See Sedgwick and Nicoli (2018) for an account of filmgoing in Milan during the mid-1950s.

[2] The limited period is explained by constraints imposed by the data collection of hundreds of daily cinema programmes from 2 to 29 January 1954 in the five cities. The snapshot provides a cross-section of the distribution and exhibition sectors, comprising films at various stages in their life cycles.

D. T. Gennari · J. Sedgwick (✉)
Oxford Brookes University, Oxford, UK
e-mail: sedgwicj52@gmail.com

J. Sedgwick (ed.), *Towards a Comparative Economic History of Cinema, 1930–1970*, Frontiers in Economic History, https://doi.org/10.1007/978-3-031-05770-0_9

Rome and less than 60% that of Milan.[3] Did this lead to a qualitatively distinctive pattern of distribution in this city and the South in general?

The analysis is based on two types of data—programming records derived from listings in daily city-based newspapers and trade sourced box-office performance records. The film programme serves as a point on the journey of a film as a commodity from birth to death. It is explicit to time and place and bears the imprint of the building and owners, its history, capacity, degree of comfort, status, access to films and potential audience. Such micro-foundations form the networks through which films diffuse—city centre, suburb, town, countryside, province, regions and territories. The extent to which city networks resemble one another is a subject of this chapter.

Typically, popular films deliberately pass through a city's cinemas, moving through time from box-office rich to poor cinemas. In the upper tier of cinemas, prices are higher, the accoutrements better, and access to films sooner. Only the most popular movies will appear in such cinemas, an indicator of the audience's willingness to pay and the film's appeal. Accordingly, cinemas should not be treated as equivalents when assessing the popularity or the pattern of diffusion of films—a screening in one is not the equivalent of a screening in another. Using a methodology developed by the AHRC-funded *European Cinema Audiences* research project, cinemas in each of the five cities are classified according to their access to films and seating capacity. Those cinemas premiering the most popular movies are positioned above those with limited or no access to such films. Our findings provide a systematic catalogue of cinema types. They differ from the variable and inconsistent official classifications of cinemas and can be used more confidently to conduct comparative analysis.

Finally, the chapter will examine the comparative popularity of those films screened in January 1954, entailing the backward and forward tracking of these films from the date of release to the date of exit from the market. Data of first-run box-office takings were collected by the film industry trade association (AGIS) and published in the bi-weekly national *Bollettino dello Spettacolo.* Contextual support is provided by the annual collection of film industry data published by SIAE (the Italian Society of Authors and Publishers) in a series dating back to 1934 called *Annuario dello Spettacolo.*

1 General Context

By 1950 the film industry had re-taken its dominant position as a source of entertainment. As Table 1 shows, a combination of rising attendances and real admission prices led to a near four-fold growth in the box-office (measured in 1950 prices) between 1946 and 1955. Indeed, in common with much of continental Europe, cinema attendance peaked in 1955, some ten years later than Great Britain and the

[3] See Table 2.

Table 1 Assorted films industry statistics, 1950–1956

Year	(1) Consumer price deflator (1950 = 1)	(2) Films released	(3) Cinema box-office (millions of lire at 1950 prices)	(4) Box-office as a proportion of all paid-for leisure	(5) Ticket sales (millions)	(6) Mean admission prices (in lire at 1950 prices)	(7) Operating cinemas	(8) Population per cinema	(9) Admissions per capita
1950	1.00	368	63,404	0.69	662	95.8			
1951	1.10	456	66,723	0.70	706	94.6	8,678		
1952	1.14	481	73,156	0.70	748	97.8	8,953	5,253	15.9
1953	1.17	497	81,047	0.71	778	104.2	9,560	4,922	16.5
1954	1.20	500	87,837	0.71	801	109.7	9,946	4,752	16.9
1955	1.23	469	94,795	0.69	819	115.7	10,570	4,565	17.0
1956	1.29	462	89,784	0.68	790	113.6	10,629	4,578	16.2

Sources Adapted from Treveri Gennari and Sedgwick (2015, Table 1, 2015)
Notes Column 1, Istat. (The index series represents the prices experienced by the households of workers and other employees); Columns 2–8. *Annuario dello Spettacolo* 1957, SIAE: col. 2, Table 44; cols. 3, 5, 6 Table 24; col. 4, Table 1; 7, Table 31; 8, Table 33

United States.[4] Italy was exceptionally well endowed with cinemas in the 1950s. For instance, Browning and Sorrell counted 4,597 operating cinemas in Great Britain in 1951—some 53% of the Italian total.[5] Given that the Italian population was smaller—in 1951, 45.5 million compared to 48.8 million—this seems extraordinary. The explanation is likely to be the number of occasional cinemas in existence, including the Catholic Church's provision of cinematic entertainment through the network of parish cinemas.[6] There was no shortage of cinemas or films in Italy at the time.

The number of operational cinemas required a proportional number of films for screening. While Table 1 registered new releases between 1950 and 1956 ranging from 383 to 512, the same source, *Annuario dello Spettacolo,* recorded 5,638 films in circulation in 1954. Movies released in 1953 or 1954 made up a fifth of this total, rising to just under a third if 1952 releases are added. The box-office share of new releases is respectively 72.8 (1953–1954) and 85.8% (1952–1954), indicating that 14.2% of the box-office was shared between 3,863 films first released before 1952. Many of the movies in circulation date back to the 1930s, with 483 first released between 1934–1939, with 152 from 1933 or earlier. The market was bifurcated between upper-tier cinemas screening recent releases and lower-tier regular and occasional cinemas which screened films of older vintages for much shorter periods. In structural terms, the AGIS could not remove the vast supply of older movies from the market because lower-tier exhibitors could generate sufficient audiences from them.

The data presented in Table 2 reflect a North–South difference between Italian cities, with both *per capita* admissions and average admission prices lower in the South. However, it is apparent that when compared to national figures, filmgoing was established in all the major Italian cities, except for Reggio Calabria, where 13 visits *per capita* and (for the South) a high mean admission price suggest a particular local story. However, the growth in cinemas between 1952 and 1957 was higher in the South than in the North. During these years, the ratio of inhabitants per cinema in the three poorest provinces of Basilicata, Calabria, and Sicily fell from 9,585, 9,921, and 9,604 to 7,097, 7,851 and 6,697, while the national average dropped from 5,253 to 4,663. Table 2 indicates that filmgoing was an important social activity for urban Italians.

Ordered by expenditure *per capita* (column 8), Table 2 shows that Milan and Rome were the most significant urban markets (column 4), boasting significantly more cinemas, ticket sales, box-office and screening days than the other cities. Florentines went to the cinema the most frequently and Northern Italians more often than those from the South. In 1954, of the five cities that form the body of this study, mean admission prices were lower in Bari than the national average of Lire (L.)131. The

[4] Miskell and Nicoli (2016) show, inflation-adjusted revenues continued to hold up for the next fifteen years, even though attendances fell back, due to rising admission prices.

[5] Browning and Sorrell (1954).

[6] Fanchi (2006), Treveri Gennari (2009).

Table 2 Cinemagoing statistics for Italy's major cities in 1954

	(1) Population	(2) Cinemas	(3) Screening days	(4) Ticket sales	(5) Tickets per capita	(6) Ticket expenditure (L.)	(7) Mean admission price (L.)	(8) Expenditure *per capita* (L.)
Rome	17,23,099	231	67,443	6,45,53,920	37	10,50,52,16,637	162.7	6,097
Milan	12,88,571	194	50,312	4,42,56,380	34	9,20,80,01,392	208.1	7,146
Naples	10,42,316	111	36,672	2,81,98,310	27	4,23,03,42,196	150.0	4,059
Genova	6,85,787	136	36,561	2,41,50,920	35	4,02,08,37,889	166.5	5,863
Turin	7,47,153	119	32,959	2,33,43,470	31	4,42,50,15,074	189.6	5,923
Florence	3,90,484	73	21,202	1,60,38,310	41	2,57,23,94,518	160.4	6,588
Bologna	3,50,884	59	16,334	1,34,66,580	38	2,31,88,54,097	172.2	6,609
Palermo	5,06,706	56	21,169	1,30,48,280	26	1,90,50,10,493	146.0	3,760
Trieste	2,72,900	52	16,602	99,51,930	36	1,76,12,42,553	177.0	6,454
Venezia	3,23,138	72	18,407	97,80,760	30	1,60,86,44,632	164.5	4,978
Catania	3,10,291	36	14,351	91,56,880	30	1,31,75,28,549	143.9	4,246
Bari	2,80,899	29	10,331	87,26,820	31	1,09,92,40,391	126.0	3,913
Padova	1,71,258	30	8,077	54,51,690	32	92,52,73,724	169.7	5,403
Verona	1,82,927	47	10,547	52,86,640	29	85,07,36,621	160.9	4,651
Messina	2,25,389	31	8,257	51,59,280	23	72,56,84,620	140.7	3,220
Taranto	1,75,965	20	7,895	51,18,210	29	51,30,61,337	100.2	2,916
Cagliari	1,43,380	25	5,836	47,70,620	33	63,41,11,966	132.9	4,423
Brescia	1,45,686	35	6,631	46,81,620	32	72,49,93,100	154.9	4,976
Ferrara	1,37,080	28	6,897	44,08,370	32	60,35,75,147	136.9	4,403
La Spezia	1,14,955	22	6,124	43,46,170	38	52,33,44,251	120.4	4,553

(continued)

Table 2 (continued)

	(1) Population	(2) Cinemas	(3) Screening days	(4) Ticket sales	(5) Tickets per capita	(6) Ticket expenditure (L.)	(7) Mean admission price (L.)	(8) Expenditure *per capita* (L.)
Livorno	1,44,560	23	6,403	41,41,660	29	76,12,69,199	183.8	5,266
Modena	1,13,998	21	5,491	41,19,980	36	60,22,61,344	146.2	5,283
Parma	1,18,784	15	5,006	39,86,250	34	56,52,09,257	141.8	4,758
Bergamo	1,06,724	30	5,494	34,11,650	32	62,11,14,929	182.1	5,820
Foggia	1,04,579	12	3,612	25,28,220	24	34,83,42,380	137.8	3,331
Reggio Di Calabria	1,43,334	13	4,114	19,32,650	13	29,26,02,438	151.4	2,041

Source Annuario dello Spettacolo (1954), Tables 27, 35; *Sommario di statistiche storiche*, 1861–2010, Table 2.20, ISTAT

other four cities had appreciably higher prices but not attendance rates: filmgoers in Bari went to the cinema as often as they did in Turin and went more frequently than Neapolitans.

2 The Velocity of Film Circulation

From the film programmes listed (and, or advertised) in daily city-based newspapers, films are tracked between 2 and 29 January 1954 in the five cities. From these, a picture of film circulation emerges. Table 3 provides descriptive statistics of the data collection. Not surprisingly, the number of films screened in each municipality correlates positively with the number of cinemas. When this information is coupled with how few days the median film in each city was screened, it is apparent that large numbers of films were required to meet cinema programming requirements. For instance, in Rome, each of the 137 cinemas in the sample screened on average 12.8 distinct film programmes in January 1954, between them showing 730 films. Roman film exhibitors needed vintage films to feed the filmgoing appetite of their audiences when given the number of new movies released year onto the market (Table 1).

Comparing the maximum number of exhibition days garnered by those films most widely circulated in January 1954 in each of the cities with the median movie gives a good idea of the market dynamics. Films are at various stages in their life cycle: a few significant hits are released and play for extended runs at a single cinema; others are past that stage and are on broader release, being screened simultaneously in various cinemas; while other films were not released with any expectation of becoming 'hit'

Table 3 Comparative statistics for the five cities in January 1954

	Rome	Milan	Turin	Naples	Bari
City population	17,23,099	12,88,571	7,47,153	10,42,316	2,80,899
Cinemas in sample population	137	112	74	69	17
Cinemas open in 1954	231	194	119	111	29
Population for each sample cinema	12,577	11,505	10,097	15,106	16,523
Film programmes	1950	1183	708	700	192
Films	731	598	435	416	188
Population for each Film	2,357	2,155	1,718	2,506	1,494
Screening days	3,478	3,313	1,990	2,033	413
Median film exhibition (days)	2	3	3	2	2
Max film exhibition (days)	88	102	45	54	8
Films screened for 1-day	294	48	33	92	89

Sources Newspapers sources: L'Unita (Rome); Corriere della Sera (Milan); La Stampa (Turin); Il Mattino (Naples); La Gazzetta del Mezzogiorno (Bari); Cinemas open in January 1954: Annuario Dello Spettacolo (1954), Table 35 (Cinemas)

films get occasional screenings for a few days at a small number of cinemas. For example, in Milan in January 1954, the film *Moulin Rouge* aggregated 102 screening days at 21 different cinemas, while in the same month, 48 films were screened in the city for one day only. The statistics presented in Table 3 show that a considerable proportion of films on release did little business during the month, while some did a great deal. A further feature of the tables is that films circulating in the larger cities did more work. While 730 movies screened in Rome were billed on 1751 film programmes, in Bari, the 72 films which appeared that month appeared on only 79 programmes.

3 Cinema Classification

Under the organisational umbrella of the 'Unione Nazionale Distributori' (based upon a law of 16 June 1927 n.1121), film distribution and exhibition were State regulated. Cinemas in the major cities were organised into several categories, which served as distribution tiers—first, second and third run. Embodied in this structure is the idea of regulated clearance. Films circulated through a cinema hierarchy during their life cycle, with set intervals between each stage. Yet, the classifications are, in many cases, problematic.[7]

The bottom-up approach to film distribution highlights disparities between actual and designated practices. Developed by the *European Cinema Audiences* project, we propose a typology based upon the revenue potential of cinemas, on the premise that potential cinema earnings motivate distributors—the higher the potential earnings, the more eager they are to have their films screened. Applied to the five cities, differences between this typology and official city-based classifications of cinemas are apparent. More pertinent, however, is that the typology provides a way of classifying cinemas consistently across different cities. By sorting cinemas according to their programming status, the ECA typology allows us to conduct a comparative analysis of film distribution across cities.

For illustrative purposes, Table 4 lists the most frequently circulated films in the five cities in January 1954. These films had previously premiered and were in the process of diffusing widely among lower-order cinemas in the city, often for only a two- or three-day billing. From this, it is evident that among widely circulated movies, the period of clearance is a misnomer—films moved consecutively from cinema to cinema. There is an exponential pattern to the number of cinemas where they appeared and days screened, based on the size of the city, with Rome and Milan able to sustain much greater circulation velocity than Turin and Naples. The much smaller city of Bari differs from the other four in that it did not have a sufficiently large population to sustain popular movies for much more than a week in the largest cinemas.

[7] For instance, SIAE (from 1948) classified all venues that screened films, even for a day, but do not include open-air cinemas, which in 1953 constituted 14% of total film exhibition venues.

Table 4 The five most circulated films in January 1954, in Rome, Milan, Turin, Naples and Bari

(1) Rank	(2) Italian title	(3) Original title	(4) Exhibition days	(5) Number of cinemas	(6) Star 1	(7) Star 2
Rome (Pop 1,787,997)						
1	Il prigioniero di Zenda	The Prisoner of Zenda	88	21	Granger, S	Kerr, D
2	Il sergente Bum	South Sea woman	68	24	Lancaster, B	Mayo, V
3	Villa Borghese		63	18	Ferrero, A	De Filippo, E
4	Gli avventurieri di Plymouth	Plymouth Adventure	60	24	Tracy, S	Tierney, G
5	La vergine sotto il tetto	The moon is blue	57	23	Holden, W	Niven, D
Milan (Pop 1,328,372)						
1	Moulin Rouge		90	21	Ferrer, J	Gabor, Z
2	Anni facili		68	14	Taranto, N	Tonti, A
3	Lucrezia Borgia		62	15	Carol, M	Armendariz, P
4	L'avventuriero della Louisiana	The Mississippi gambler	60	15	Power, T	Laurie, P
5	La vedova allegra	The merry widow	59	13	Turner. L	Lamas, F
Turin (Pop 821,146)						
1	Il più grande spettacolc del mondc	The Greatest Show on Earth	45	11	Stewart, J	Heston, C
2	Prigioniero di Zenda	The Prisoner of Zenda	45	12	Granger, S	Kerr, D
3	Salomè	Salome	36	7	Hayworth, R	Granger, S
4	La vedova allegra	The Merry Widow	31	9	Turner, L	Lamas, F
5	La tunica	The Robe	27	1	Burton, R	Simmons, J
Naples (Pop 1,078,071)						
1	Lucrezia Borgia		54	11	Carol, M	Armendariz, P
2	Salomè	Salome	52	10	Hayworth, R	Laughton, C

(continued)

Table 4 (continued)

(1) Rank	(2) Italian title	(3) Original title	(4) Exhibition days	(5) Number of cinemas	(6) Star 1	(7) Star 2
3	Anni facili		50	10	Taranto, N	Mangini, A
4	…e Napoli canta		45	12	Rondinella, G	Lisi, V
5	Il prigioniero di Zenda	The Prisoner of Zenda	43	8	Granger, S	Kerr, D
Bari (Pop 293,744)						
1	Vortice		8	2	Pampanini, S	Girotti, M
2	La leggenda di Robin Hood	Robin Hood	7	1	Flynn, E	De Havilland, O
2	Pane, amore e fantasia		7	1	Lollobrigida, G	De Sica, V
2	Un turco napoletano		7	2	Totò	Barzizza, I
5	Frine, cortigiana d'Oriente		6	1	Kleus, E	Cressoy, P

Source Dataset

Extending the analysis to the 30 most screened films in each city makes it possible to understand better the hierarchy of cinemas through which films passed. All cinemas at which one of these films is screened are given weights based upon seating capacity and mean price of admission. Ticket price is an essential factor in analysing filmgoing. It provides information on how much consumers are willing to pay and what level of revenue exhibitors can hope to make.

Admission price information has been found for Rome and Milan cinemas in the evening newspapers *Momento Sera* and *La Notte*. Unfortunately, price information is not available for cinemas in Turin, Naples and Bari. In these cases, a price proxy is established based upon the diffusion trajectory of the 30 most screened films. Cinemas are given a score of 3 when they premiere films; 2 for the subsequent booking and 1 for further bookings. Scores are then averaged so that Cinema X premiering two Top 30 films during January 1954 will generate a proxy score of 3 (2*3/2).

In contrast, Cinema Y screening ten films towards the end of their circulation history will create a proxy of 1 (10*1/10). The mean score reflects the status of the cinema in the cinema hierarchy and, accordingly, is termed Cinema Status Index value (CSI). Cinema Weights are derived by expressing the CSI of each *j*th cinema in the population of cinemas as a proportion of the mean CSI of all (*n*) cinemas in that population.

$$\text{Cinema Weight}_J = \text{CSI}_j \div \sum_j^n \text{CSI} \div n \tag{1}$$

Four types of cinemas are demarcated: *elite*, *major*, *intermediate* and *minor*. Details of this are found in Table 5. Each city has its hierarchy based on the programming record of its cinemas. Because of this study's limited one-month period, occasional cinemas that opened during the summer months are not included in the January listings and thus do not attract weights.

Table 5 Cinema types in the five cities

Cinema types	Weighting range	Rome	Milan	Turin	Naples	Bari
Elite	3 and above	5	7	3	7	4
Major	1.25–2.99	23	20	20	26	4
Intermediate	0.55 to 1.24	39	40	20	17	4
Minor	Below 0.55	49	45	30	14	5
Total		116	112	73	64	17

Source Bollettino dello Spettacolo, La Gazzetta del Mezzogiorno, Corriere della, Sera, Il Mattino, L'unita, and La Stampa

Note The number of cinemas in the sample differs from Table 3 because only those listed in the newspapers on 26 or more days are included. The types for Rome and Milan are based on actual prices. Those for Turin, Naples and Bari derive from proxy prices, using the methodology characterised in Eq. 1

Located in city centres, *elite* cinemas are venues where films are premiered. In general, with higher seating capacities than the other cinemas, they also charge higher prices to audiences willing to pay more to see movies earlier in their cycle. *Elite* cinemas are few and constitute the apex of the distribution chain, attracting the most popular films and screening them until attendances fall below a predetermined threshold.

The next tier down comprises *major* cinemas. These cinemas either premiere less popular movies in the portfolio of the principal distributors or provide second-run venues for films premiered at elite venues. *Intermediate* and *minor* cinemas are generally smaller venues at the end of the circulation chain. They tend to have lower seating capacities and are cheap, attracting working-class audiences.

4 Four Case Studies

An analysis of four of the most popular films illustrates both the dynamic aspects of film distribution and the part played by cinemas. The films chosen are *Moulin Rouge* (GB, 1952), *Pane, amore e fantasia* (Italy, 1953), *Roman Holiday* (US, 1953) and *The Robe* (US, 1953). *Bollettino dello Spettacolo* shows each to have been a Top 10 film. From the dates of their premieres (section a, Table 6), these films were at different stages in their life cycles when screened during January 1954, as seen from the number of distinct bookings (section b, Table 6).

The earliest of the four films released was *Moulin Rouge.* By January 1954, the film was in its mature phase in Milan, circulating among 21 *intermediate* and *minor* cinemas during the month. Although released in Rome during the same week, *Moulin Rouge* was still only in its second run there, appearing in three *major* cinemas during the month—the Bernini, Delle Vittorie and Palestrina. In Bari, after an initial 15-day release at the end of November 1953, the film started its second run for seven days at the Palazzo at the end of January 1954. Meanwhile, it was also in its expansive distribution phase in Naples, appearing at nine *intermediate* and *minor* cinemas. The film opened in Turin with three six-day bookings between the 4th and 9th of January at the Capitol and Faro (*major*) and the Alexandra (*intermediate*). The film then appeared later in the month for four days at the *major* Colosseo and five days at the *intermediate* La Perla.

Premiered in Rome three weeks after *Moulin Rouge*, *The Robe* (*La Tunica*) was still in the first run during the month, screening in one *elite* cinema in each of the four largest cities for the duration—the Capitol in Rome and Milan, the Metropolitan in Naples and the Reposi in Turin. Opening in Bari 91 days after its Rome premiere, the film was not screened in January.

Although released a week after *The Robe* in Rome, *Roman Holiday* was already in its second run in Rome in January, appearing simultaneously for 14 days at the beginning of the month at two *major* cinemas—the Ariston and Fiamma—before moving to the *intermediate* Plaza for the last two weeks of the month. Table 6 shows that *Roman Holiday* premiered in Milan and Turin two weeks after Rome. In Milan,

Table 6 The premiere and circulation records of four Top 10 films

a. Premiere records

Film	Premiere date in Rome	Opened in Milan (Days)	Opened in Turin (Days)	Opened in Naples (Days)	Opened in Bari (Days)
The Robe	27–11-1953	−8	−25	n/k	−91
Pane, amore e fantasia	22–12-1953	−4	−37	n/k	−10
Moulin Rouge	04–11-1953	−1	−2	n/k	−7
Roman Holiday	05–12-1953	−18	−18	n/k	−18

b. Circulation records

Film	Bari	Milan	Naples	Rome	Turin	Total
The Robe		1	1	1	1	4
Pane, amore e fantasia	1	1	7	2	1	12
Moulin Rouge	1	21	9	3	5	39
Roman Holiday		2	3	3	2	10
Total	2	25	20	9	9	65

Source Bollettino dello Spettacolo, La Gazzetta del Mezzogiorno, Corriere della, Sera, Il Mattino, L'unità, and La Stampa

Note Premiere dates were not published for Naples. However, from the date of the published issues, Moulin Rouge was first screened in Naples in November 1953, while the other three films were first shown in the following month. The dates covered are from Saturday 2 to Friday 28 January 1954

it premiered in late December 1953 at the *major* cinema Astra and screened there for the first three weeks before transferring to the *elite* Del Verme at the end of the month. In Turin, it opened at the *elite* Corso where it was screened for the first two weeks before transferring to the *intermediate* Augustus for the remainder of the month. *Roman Holiday* was screened at three Neapolitan cinemas—in sequence, the *elite* Augusteo, where it was ending its first run, the *intermediate* Corona (for 19 days), and the *major* Modernissimo (for 16 days). Finally, the *Roman Holiday* opened in Bari at the *elite* Impero for a one-week run in the final week of December but was not screened again in the city for the next two months.

The last film in the quartet, *Pane, amore e fantasia,* opened in Rome in late December 1953. It was screened at two *elite* cinemas during January—the Barberini (for the whole month) and Metropolitan (the first two weeks). Appearing four days later in Milan, the film was screened at the *elite* Corso cinema for the duration of January. Premiered in Turin 37 days after it first appeared in Rome, *Pane, amore e fantasia* opened at the end of the month at the *elite* Lux cinema. In contrast, the film appeared on the screens of seven cinemas in Naples, ranging from the *elite* S. Lucia and Sala Roma at the beginning of the month to the *major* Ariston, where it had a two-week run. It then moved to a set of cinemas—Eden (*major*), Astoria (*minor*) and Elena (*intermediate*)—at the very end of the month. The film was screened for a week at the *elite* Margherita in Bari.

The programming details of these four films during January 1954 capture them at various junctures on a dynamic trajectory from box-office rich to box-office poor cinemas. Illuminated by our cinema typology, the logic followed is based on whether films meet threshold box-office criteria, indicating that those that do not are moved on. The process ends when there is nowhere else for them to go. The most telling statistics concern the limited distribution of *The Robe* and *Pane, amore e fantasia* during the initial stages of their release in Rome and Milan when contrasted to the explosion that best describes the circulation data of *Moulin Rouge* in Milan. Yet, within the general framework explained, details differ from city to city and film to film, generating questions and suggesting idiosyncratic processes at a local level. Why, for instance, was *Pane, amore e fantasia* released so late in Turin? Why was Turin behind Milan by a week or two in premiering two of the other four films? Or take the diffusion of *Roman Holiday* in Naples during its second run. Why was it screened at the *intermediate* 342-seat Corona before the *major* 700-seat Modernissimo? Is the same film's screening at the *major* Astra before its engagement at the *elite* Del Verme in Milan connected to the former's more central location?

5 Film Popularity

While the analysis of film programmes introduces indicators from which to gauge the pattern of movie circulation in each city, it only provides oblique evidence concerning the popularity of the films screened. While it is true that films that are intensively circulated are likely to have been popular in *elite* cinemas earlier in their life cycle, it is not possible to say confidently by how much. A film such as *Moulin Rouge*, so ubiquitous in Milan in January 1954 in intermediate and minor cinemas, might have been particularly attractive to working-class audiences.

Fortunately, a listing of first-run box-office takings in the most prominent Italian cities is available. Published every fortnight, the trade paper *Bollettino dello Spettacolo* provides an invaluable listing of the most popular films in circulation. A series of tables comprising the Top 20 films first screened in elite cinemas in the five cities from September 1953 to January 1954 can be found in the Appendix of this chapter. In the cases of Milan and Turin, information is also provided about audience size, and for Milan, second and third-run box-office is also reported.

The box-office characteristics of the cities are the subject of Table 7. The rate at which film revenue declines with rank diminishes throughout its length, indicating a concave relationship. The drop in revenue between first and tenth ranked films is particularly dramatic. The curve then smooths out, making minimal differences around the median film.

Films ranked 1st, 20th and 50th in Milan generate higher grosses than comparable films in Rome, with this position reversed for the 10th film. Also, in Table 7, Milan's first-run cinemas generate higher daily returns than their Roman counterparts, explained by higher ticket prices and *per capita* spending. Furthermore, *elite* cinemas in Milan shared 'hit' films more frequently than in Rome, with average

Table 7 Box-office by rank

City	(1) Rank No. 1 box-office (L.)	(2) Rank No. 10 box-office (L.)	(3) Rank No. 20 box-office (L.)	(4) Rank No. 50 box-office (L.)	(5) Top 20 mean daily earnings (L.)	(6) Top 50 mean daily earnings (L.)
Milan	6,93,25,940	2,14,19,030	1,47,65,700	71,67,130	10,01,793	9,16,129
Rome	6,16,94,000	2,47,04,000	1,42,34,000	65,30,000	7,06,360	5,85,760
Turin	3,81,62,040	1,42,56,220	92,94,280	45,00,400	7,07,549	5,99,725
Naples	4,15,65,000	96,47,000	60,98,000	24,85,000	5,66,291	4,78,371
Bari	1,10,05,020	36,79,300	26,99,650	18,15,000	4,80,819	3,94,305

Source Bollettini dello Spettacolo, September 1953 to June 1954

screening days for Top 20 movies lower in Milan (30) than in Rome (38)—see the Appendix. In making Top 20 films more accessible to audiences, *elite* exhibitors in Milan had a higher turnover, implying a higher threshold (limit) of earnings. Earnings that fell below this were replaced.

For reasons explained earlier around the discussion of film circulation, revenues generated in the much smaller city of Bari are the lowest by a considerable margin. Between the top two cities and Bari, film revenues in Turin were higher than in Naples, except for the extraordinary success of *The Robe* in Naples, which earned well over twice that of the second-ranked film *Moulin Rouge.*

Mean daily Top 20, and 50 box-office shows that earnings across the cities were more equivalent in elite cinemas, with those in Bari respectively a little under half that of Milan. These differences become even smaller once the much lower cinema admission prices and per capita spending are considered—see Table 2.

Gerben Bakker has explained the emergence of Hollywood and the demise of European film producers in the 1910s as the outcome of a quality race in which a larger domestic market and bigger budgets resulted in Hollywood producing films that, on average, promised audiences better film quality for the price of a ticket.[8] Once films became markedly differentiated, perceived quality became critical in the competitive environment. Audiences have only rarely been required to pay more to see films widely considered to be better—unlike most other products, admission prices to cinemas were (and remain) invariant irrespective of the perceived quality of the movie being screened. The consequence is that films were not rationed because they cost more to make, quite the opposite—see Chap. 1.

The market for films in Italy in the mid-1950s was no different. Table 8 comprises movies released in Rome between September 1953 and January 1954 and subsequently screened in the four other cities, with a June 1954 cut-off. These films are ranked not by absolute box-office but relative box-office—box-office divided by median box-office—and represent an index of popularity (RelPOP) independent of

[8] Bakker (2008).

the size of the city.[9]

$$\text{RelPOP}_i = \sum_{c=1}^{n} \frac{\text{BO}_i}{\text{BO}_m} \div n \tag{2}$$

where

i	the ith film in a truncated population of the most popular 101 films
c	the cth city in a population of five
Σ	Sum
BO	actual box-office
BO_m	median box-office

Accordingly, each of the five cities in this study is equivalent. Irrespective of the size of the population, per capita income and the number and types of cinemas, the RelPOP metric offers a way of making inter and intra-city comparisons of film popularity, which, in contrast with rank, better reflects the exponential nature of film revenues. From the metric, it is possible to say that Film X was more popular in city C^1 than in city C^2, even though C^1 may be smaller and generate lower actual revenues.

The films listed in Table 8 are ordered by their mean RelPOP Index values (column 9). They are predominantly Hollywood and Italian productions, suggesting a sizable following for home-produced movies. However, film popularity is not evenly spread. Of the 35 films that share the top 20 berths of the five cities (see the Appendix): nine films are common to all five cities; three films to four; six films to three; eight films to two; and nine films particular to just one city.

The Robe is the standout-out film, ranked first in the four largest cities and second in Bari. In relationship to the median movie, *The Robe* is a giant. However, this consistency of performance across the five city markets is not always typical. Thus, the film ranked second in three of the five cities was not *Moulin Rouge* but *Pane, amore e fantasia* in Rome and Milan and *The Robe* in Bari.

Ranging from 0.16 to 1.01, the coefficient of variation of these 20 films highlights films is featured in column 11 of Table 8. Films with comparable levels of popularity generate low coefficient values, while high coefficient values accompany those with varying levels of popularity. Thus, in contrast to *The Robe*, the Hollywood cowboy movie *Shane*, starring Alan Ladd, appears to have been exceptionally popular with the audiences of Turin and Milan, while in Bari, it was barely rated above the median film. In Naples, it was not much more successful.

The domestic comedies *Un Turco Napoletano* and *Una di Quelle*, both starring the Neapolitan comic actor Totò, also register high coefficient values but, in this case, were more popular in Naples than in the other four cities. In contrast, *Il Ritorno di Don Camillo*—a film foregrounding the ideological differences between a Communist

[9] See Sedgwick et al. (2018). To be included in the RelPOP Index, films needed to be screened in all five cities during the period.

Table 8 Relative box-office performance of Top 20 films, September 1953 to June 1954

(1) Popularity index rank	(2) Film title	(3) Original title (if different)	(4) Rome Box-office actual/median	(5) Milan Box-office actual/median	(6) Turin Box-office actual/median	(7) Naples Box-office actual/median	(8) Bari Box-office actual/median	(9) RelPOP Index	(10) Standard deviation	(11) Coefficient of variation
1	La Tunica	The Robe	10.07	19.12	12.05	17.02	5.66	12.78	5.41	0.42
2	Moulin Rouge		5.64	11.95	10.13	7.43	2.98	7.62	3.56	0.47
3	Pane, amore e fantasia		8.55	13.46	5.13	6.68	3.09	7.38	3.95	0.53
4	Quo Vadis?	Quo Vacis?	5.41	5.74	11.36	6.59	6.12	7.04	2.45	0.35
5	Il ritorno di Don Camillo		5.28	11.30	9.97	2.42	1.77	6.15	4.33	0.70
6	Vacanze romane	Roman Holiday	4.76	9.20	4.02	4.10	2.31	4.88	2.58	0.53
7	Il cavaliere della valle solitaria	Shane	4.22	5.74	9.58	2.54	1.52	4.72	3.16	0.67
8	Salome		4.19	5.72	5.19	4.17	2.68	4.39	1.17	0.27
9	Il prigioneiro di Zenda	Prisoner of Zenda	5.31	4.47	5.30	2.74	2.38	4.04	1.40	0.35
10	L'avventure di Peter Pan	Peter Pan	3.82	6.58	4.50	2.55	1.69	3.83	1.88	0.49
11	La Maschera di cera	House of Wax	3.95	3.52	3.48	5.34	1.09	3.48	1.53	0.44

(continued)

Table 8 (continued)

(1) Popularity index rank	(2) Film title	(3) Original title (if different)	(4) Rome Box-office actual/median	(5) Milan Box-office actual/median	(6) Turin Box-office actual/median	(7) Naples Box-office actual/median	(8) Bari Box-office actual/median	(9) RelPOP Index	(10) Standard deviation	(11) Coefficient of variation
12	Un turco napoletano		2.59	2.91	2.31	7.03	2.51	3.47	2.00	0.58
13	Il più comico spettacolo del mondo		1.68	5.03	3.68	3.95	2.24	3.32	1.35	0.41
14	I vitelloni		3.16	6.18	3.47	1.91	1.43	3.23	1.85	0.57
15	Il favoloso Andersen	Hans Christian Andersen	2.24	7.69	2.02	2.19	1.17	3.06	2.62	0.86
16	Le vacanze del signor Hulot	Les vacances de Monsieur Hulot	2.21	8.31	2.95	1.29	0.51	3.05	3.08	1.01
17	La vedova allegra	Merry Widow	2.54	4.15	2.98	3.15	1.99	2.96	0.80	0.27
18	Lucrezia Borgia		4.03	3.51	3.13	2.36	1.50	2.91	0.99	0.34
19	Anni facili		3.38	3.34	2.94	2.86	1.35	2.77	0.83	0.30
20	Quando le donne amano		2.30	5.55	3.20	1.43	0.93	2.68	1.82	0.68

Source Bollettino dello Spettacolo

mayor and Roman Catholic priest set in Lombardy—performed relatively poorly in the Southern cities of Naples and Bari compared to the North.

Other examples of relative differences in performance are apparent. For instance, in Milan, *I vitelloni, Hans Christian Anderson* and *Les vacances de Monsieur Hulot* are not as well received in the other cities. Indeed, the latter experienced the most variation. The film was exceptionally well received in Milan, marginally so in Rome and Turin but not popular in Naples and Bari. In Bari, it was screened for just four days. Less arresting from an analytical perspective, the popularity of the Italian film *Canzoni, canzoni, canzoni* and Hollywood films *Salome* and *The Merry Widow* is consistent across the cities.

Thus, several tendencies are evident among the most popular films of the season. Some movies dominate, others perform less well but consistently, and others perform significantly better in one or more city markets but not in all. Thus, while the earnings of films listed in Table 8 positively correlate with the RelPOP Index, ranging from 0.75 (Bari) to 0.92 (Rome), a careful study shows that certain films are out of sequence.

Comparisons between the cities are also fruitful. Table 9 presents a city-on-city correlation chart for the top 10 and 20 films listed in Table 8. Turin stands out regarding the Top 10, with moderate-to-low coefficient values compared to the other cities, especially Milan. The correlation between Bari and Milan is also low. In contrast, coefficient scores between Rome, Milan and Naples are high. In extending the analysis to the Top 20 films, these findings are moderated, with the higher coefficient values lowered and lower values raised.

Table 9 Inter-city correlation coefficient table

	Rome	Milan	Turin	Naples	Bari
Top 10 RelPOP correlation coefficients					
Rome	1	0.86	0.37	0.86	0.60
Milan		1	0.40	0.81	0.39
Turin			1	0.54	0.57
Naples				1	0.77
Bari					1
Top 20 RelPOP correlation coefficients					
Rome	1	0.78	0.69	0.75	0.69
Milan		1	0.60	0.66	0.48
Turin			1	0.57	0.71
Naples				1	0.78
Bari					1

6 Conclusion

From the cross-section of films on release in January 1954, it has been possible to understand the Italian film business in operation. Film programming data has been collected from the principal daily newspapers servicing the cities of Rome, Milan, Turin, Naples and Bari for that month. In conjunction with the box-office records of upper-tier cinemas reported in the trade journal *Bollettino dello Spettacolo*, a dynamic account of the film circulation and earnings is presented, in which life-cycle stages and intra-city differences in provision and taste are highlighted. Film circulation draws attention to the cinemas where films are screened and the sequence of when. A measure is applied, distinguishing between *elite*, *major*, *intermediate* and *minor* cinemas through which films are distributed.

The narrowness of the time frame is an inhibiting factor and handicaps the scope of the analysis. Nevertheless, the cross-section of exhibition programmes from five Italian cities draws attention to the type of films Italians went to see throughout the breadth of the cinema network and the stars that appeared in them. Furthermore, in conjunction with the box-office returns of first-run cinemas, it is possible to assess the popularity of those films screened in January 1954 and compare this across the cities. We find marked differences in the reception of some films by city audiences and overall differences in film tastes.

Appendix to the Chapter: Top 20 Films in the Five Cities, Released Between September 1953 and December 1954

Rome									
Rank	Film title	Release title if different from original	Nationality	Production Studio	Distributor	Opening cinemas	Exhibition Days	Box-office (£lire)	Day ratio (£Lire)
1	La Tunica	The Robe	US	TCF	Fox	1	63	6,16,94,000	9,79,270
2	Pane, amore e fantasia		Italian	Titanus	Titanus	2	62	5,24,10,000	8,45,323
3	Moulin Rouge		US	Romulus	Dear	4	50	3,45,36,000	6,90,720
4	Quo Vadis?		US	MGM	MGM	3	63	3,31,55,000	5,26,270
5	Il prigioneiro di Zenda	Prisoner of Zenda	US	MGM	MGM	4	38	3,25,59,000	8,56,816
6	Il ritorno di Don Camillo		Italian	Co-production	Dear	3	40	3,23,52,000	8,08,800
7	Vacanze romane	Roman Holiday	US	Paramount	Paramount	2	48	2,91,35,000	6,06,979
8	Il cavaliere della valle solitaria	Shane	US	Paramount	Paramount	4	38	2,58,31,000	6,79,763
9	Salome		US	Columbia	Ceiad	4	37	2,56,72,000	6,93,838
10	Lucrezia Borgia		French	Co-production	Dear	4	34	2,47,04,000	7,26,588
11	La Maschera di cera	House of Wax	US	WB	WB	4	32	2,42,27,000	7,57,094
12	L'avventure di Peter Pan	Peter Pan	US	Disney	RKO	2	16	2,34,21,000	14,63,813
13	Anni facili		Italian	Co-production	Paramount	4	37	2,06,85,000	5,59,054
14	I vitelloni		Italian	Co-production	Enic	2	32	1,93,37,000	6,04,281
15	Il Principe di Scozia	Master of Ballantrae	US	WB	WB	3	24	1,67,64,000	6,98,500

(continued)

(continued)

Rome

Rank	Film title	Release title if different from original	Nationality	Production Studio	Distributor	Opening cinemas	Exhibition Days	Box-office (£lire)	Day ratio (£Lire)
16	Canzoni, canzoni, canzoni		Italian	Co-production	Minerva	4	31	1,63,37,000	5,27,000
17	Un turco napoletano		Italian	Co-production	Lux	3	27	1,58,45,000	5,86,852
18	La vedova allegra	Merry Widow	US	MGM	MGM	4	32	1,55,84,000	4,87,000
19	L'avventuriero della Louisiana	Mississippi Gambler	US	Universal	Universal	4	26	1,44,24,000	5,54,769
20	Una di quelle	One of Those	Italian	Co-production	Paramount	4	30	1,42,34,000	4,74,467

Milan

Rank	Film	Release title if different from original	Nationality	Production Studio	Distributor	Opening cinemas	Exhibition Days	Audience	Box-office (£lire)	Mean admission Price	Day ratio (£Lire)
1	La Tunica	The Robe	US	TCF	Fox	1	63	98,805	6,93,25,940	702	11,00,412
2	Pane, amore e fantasia		Italian	Titanus	Titanus	1	38	95,243	4,87,98,050	512	12,84,159
3	Moulin Rouge		US	Romulus	Dear	3	26	77,764	4,33,11,550	557	16,65,829
4	Il ritorno di Don Camillo		Italian	Co-production	Dear	1	34	73,482	4,09,62,240	557	12,04,772

(continued)

(continued)

Milan											
Rank	Film	Release title if different from original	Nationality	Production Studio	Distributor	Opening cinemas	Exhibition Days	Audience	Box-office (£lire)	Mean admission Price	Day ratio (£Lire)
5	Vacanze romane	Roman Holiday	US	Paramount	Paramount	1	31	56,138	3,33,43,265	594	10,75,589
6	Le vacanze del signor Hulot	Les vacances de M.Hulot	US	Co-production	Alba	1	50	51,007	3,01,37,260	591	6,02,745
7	Il favoloso Andersen	Hans Christian Andersen	US	Goldwyn	RKO	1	15	45,897	2,78,77,310	607	18,58,487
8	L'avventure di Peter Pan	Peter Pan	US	Disney	RKO	1	43	45,003	2,38,36,140	530	5,54,329
9	I vitelloni		Italian	Co-production	Enic	1	23		2,24,10,890		9,74,387
10	Giulio Cesare	Julius Caesar	US	MGM	MGM	1	24		2,14,19,030		8,92,460
11	Il cavaliere della valle solitaria	Shane	US	Paramount	Paramount	1	32		2,07,89,429		6,49,670
12	Quo Vadis?		US	MGM	MGM	1	32		2,07,89,420		6,49,669
13	Salome		US	Columbia	Ceiad	2	14	31,928	2,07,46,725	650	14,81,909

(continued)

(continued)

Milan

Rank	Film	Release title if different from original	Nationality	Production Studio	Distributor	Opening cinemas	Exhibition Days	Audience	Box-office (£lire)	Mean admission Price	Day ratio (£Lire)
14	Quando le donne amano	Adorables créatures	French	Co-production	Ceiad	1	27	37,323	2,01,18,380	539	7,45,125
15	Il più comico spettacolo del mondo		Italian	Rosa Film	Paramount	1	13	16,615	1,82,32,845	1097	14,02,527
16	Lili		US	TCF	MGM	1	42		1,78,22,150		4,24,337
17	Il prigioneiro di Zenda	Prisoner of Zenda	US	WB	MGM	1	14		1,62,13,220		11,58,087
18	Il bruto e la bella	The Bad and the Beautiful	US	MGM	MGM	1	39		1,51,04,900		3,87,305
19	La vedova allegra	Merry Widow	US	MGM	MGM	1	16		1,50,35,010		9,39,688
20	Niagara		US	TCF	Fox	1	15	28,301	1,47,65,700	522	9,84,380

(continued)

(continued)

Turin											
Rank	Film	Release title if different from original	Nationality	Production Studio	Distributor	Opening cinemas	Exhibition Days	Audience	Box-office (£lire)	Mean admission Price	Day ratio (£Lire)
1	La Tunica	The Robe	US	TCF	Fox	1	41	82,037	3,81,62,040	465	9,30,781
2	Quo Vadis?		US	MGM	MGM	1	43	88,402	3,59,74,060	407	8,36,606
3	Moulin Rogue		US	Romulus	Dear	2	44	89,909	3,20,71,370	357	7,28,895
4	Il ritorno di Don Camillo		Italian	Co-production	Dear	2	45	95,264	3,15,80,816	332	7,01,796
5	Il cavaliere della valle solitaria	Shane	US	Paramount	Paramount	1	31	77,453	3,03,31,340	392	9,78,430
6	Vacanze romane	Roman Holiday	US	Paramount	Paramount	2	22	48,175	1,67,82,210	348	7,62,828
7	Il prigioneiro di Zenda	Prisoner of Zenda	US	MGM	MGM	2	23	42,600	1,64,35,600	386	7,14,591
8	Salome		US	Columbia	Ceiad	1	22	44,010	1,62,47,520	369	7,38,524
9	Pane, amore e fantasia		Italian	Titanus	Titanus	1	17	39,135	1,42,56,220	364	8,38,601
10	L'avventure di Peter Pan	Peter Pan	US	Disney	RKO	1	16	32,008	1,27,19,080	397	7,94,943

(continued)

(continued)

Turin

Rank	Film	Release title if different from original	Nationality	Production Studio	Distributor	Opening cinemas	Exhibition Days	Audience	Box-office (£lire)	Mean admission Price	Day ratio (£Lire)
11	Le vacanze del signor Hulot	Les vacances de M.Hulot	French	Co-production	Alba	1	21	36,736	1,16,53,793	317	5,54,943
12	Il più comico spettacolo del mondo		Italian	Rosa Film	Paramount	2	15	30,176	1,10,28,200	365	7,35,213
13	I vitelloni		Italian	Co-production	Enic	1	14	30,599	1,09,74,785	359	7,83,913
14	La Maschera di cera	House of Wax	US	WB	WB	1	13	27,499	1,07,44,130	391	8,26,472
15	La legione del Sahara	Desert Legion	US	Universal	Universal	1	26	28,949	1,01,40,600	350	3,90,023
16	Quando le donne amano	Adorables créatures	French	Co-production	Ceiad	1	15	28,703	99,04,590	345	6,60,306
17	Lucrezia Borgia		French	Co-production	Dear	1	14	31,877	94,28,495	296	6,73,464
18	La vedova allegra	Merry Widow	US	MGM	MGM	2	27	n/l	93,36,920	n/l	3,45,812
19	Anni facili		Italian	Co-production	Paramount	1	14	26,093	93,19,460	357	6,65,676

(continued)

(continued)

Turin

Rank	Film	Release title if different from original	Nationality	Production Studio	Distributor	Opening cinemas	Exhibition Days	Audience	Box-office (£lire)	Mean admission Price	Day ratio (£Lire)
20	Il pui grande spettacolo del mondo	The Greatest Show on Earth	US	Paramount	Paramount	1	19	31,503	92,94,280	295	4,89,173

Naples

Rank	Film	Release title if different from original	Nationality	Production Studio	Distributor	Opening cinemas	Exhibition Days	Box-office (£lire)	Day ratio (£Lire)
1	La Tunica	The Robe	US	TCF	Fox	1	37	4,15,65,000	11,23,378
2	Moulin Rouge		US	Romulus	Dear	2	25	1,81,49,000	7,25,960
3	Un turco napoletano		Italian	Co-production	Lux	2	38	1,71,78,000	4,52,053
4	Pane, amore e fantasia		Italian	Titanus	Titanus	3	17	1,63,05,000	9,59,118
5	Quo Vadis?		US	MGM	MGM	1	46	1,60,96,000	3,49,913
6	La Maschera di cera	House of Wax	US	WB	WB	1	15	1,30,50,000	8,70,000
7	Una di quelle		Italian	Co-production	Paramount	1	24	1,11,05,000	4,62,708
8	Salome		US	Columbia	Ceiad	2	13	1,01,91,000	7,83,923
9	Vacanze romane	Roman Holiday	US	Paramount	Paramount	2	27	1,00,10,000	3,70,741

(continued)

(continued)

Naples

Rank	Film	Release title if different from original	Nationality	Production Studio	Distributor	Opening cinemas	Exhibition Days	Box-office (£lire)	Day ratio (£Lire)
10	Il più comico spettacolo del mondo		Italian	Rosa Film	Paramount	2	14	96,47,000	6,89,071
11	Giulio Cesare	Julius Ceasar	US	MGM	MGM	3	22	76,96,000	3,49,818
12	La vedova allegra	Merry Widow	US	MGM	MGM	1	15	76,36,000	5,09,067
13	Lili		US	TCF	MGM	1	12	69,82,000	5,81,833
14	Anni facili		Italian	Co-production	Paramount	2	21	68,18,000	3,24,667
15	Canzoni, canzoni, canzoni		Italian	Co-production	Minerva	2	21	67,74,000	3,22,571
16	Un giorno In pretura		Italian	Excelsa Film	Minerva	1	11	66,82,000	6,07,455
17	Il prigioneiro di Zenda	Prisoner of Zenda	US	WB	MGM	1	11	62,29,000	5,66,273
18	L'avventure di Peter Pan	Peter Pan	US	Disney	RKO	1	26	62,09,000	2,38,808
19	Il cavaliere della valle solitaria	Shane	US	Paramount	Paramount	1	16	60,98,000	3,81,125
20	Il Principe di Scozia	Master of Ballantrae	US	WB	WB	2	9	59,16,000	6,57,333

(continued)

(continued)

Bari									
Rank	Film	Release title if different from original	Nationality	Production Studio	Distributor	Opening cinemas	Exhibition Days	Box-office (£lire)	Day ratio (£Lire)
1	Quo Vadis?		US	MGM	MGM	2	13	1,10,05,020	8,46,540
2	La Tunica	The Robe	US	TCF	Fox	1	17	1,01,65,290	5,97,958
3	Pane, amore e fantasia		Italian	Titanus	Titanus	1	9	55,43,910	6,15,990
4	Moulin Rouge		US	Romulus	Dear	1	15	53,46,620	3,56,441
5	Giuseppe Verdi		Italian	Co-production	PAT Film	1	9	48,51,040	5,39,004
6	Salome		US	Columbia	Ceiad	1	8	42,82,000	5,35,250
7	Un turco napoletano		US	Co-production	Lux	1	9	41,51,000	4,61,222
8	Il prigioneiro di Zenda	Prisoner of Zenda	Italian	MGM	MGM	1	8	40,27,000	5,03,375
9	Vacanze romane	Roman Holiday	US	Paramount	Paramount	1	8	38,59,000	4,82,375
10	Il più comico spettacolo del mondo		Italian	Rosa Film	Paramount	1	8	36,79,300	4,59,913
11	L'avventuriero della Louisiana	Mississippi Gambler	Italian	Universal	Universal	1	8	36,37,000	4,54,625
12	Cavalleria rusticana		US	Excelsa Film	Minerva	1	8	35,79,000	4,47,375
13	Un giorno in Pretura		Italian	Excelsa Film	Minerva	1	9	33,41,700	3,71,300

(continued)

(continued)

Bari

Rank	Film	Release title if different from original	Nationality	Production Studio	Distributor	Opening cinemas	Exhibition Days	Box-office (£lire)	Day ratio (£Lire)
14	Giulio Cesare		Italian	MGM	MGM	1	8	31,76,000	3,97,000
15	La vedova allegra	Merry Widow	Italian	MGM	MGM	1	10	30,91,000	3,09,100
16	Canzoni, canzoni, canzoni		US	Co-production	Minerva	1	8	30,42,341	3,80,293
17	Il ritorno di Don Camillo		Italian	Co-production	Dear	1	7	29,69,300	4,24,186
18	Aida	The Story of Three Loves	US	Oscar Film	Ceiad	1	7	27,92,320	3,98,903
19	L'avventure di Peter Pan	Peter Pan	US	Disney	RKO	1	4	27,92,320	6,98,080
20	La nave delle donne maledette		Italian	Excelsa Film	Minerva	1	8	26,99,650	3,37,456

Source Bollettino dello Spettacolo

Note All films were released in the first-run cinema of the five cities between September 1953 and January 1954, with box-office traced through to June 1954. The published box-office statistics associated with second and third-run cinemas in Milan are not reported

References

Bakker, G. (2008). *Entertainment industrialised: The emergence of the international film industry, 1890–1940*. Cambridge University Press.

Browning, H., & Sorrell, A. (1954). Cinema and cinema-going in Great Britain. *Journal of the Royal Statistical Society, 117*, 133–165.

Fanchi, M. (2006). Non censurare ma educare! L'esercizio cinematografico cattolico e il suo progetto culturale e sociale. In R. Eugeni & D. Viganò (Eds.), *Attraverso lo schermo. Cinema e cultura cattolica in Italia*. Ente dello Spettacolo.

Miskell, P., & Nicoli, M. (2016). From outsiders to insiders? Strategies and practices of American film distributors in postwar Italy. *Enterprise and Society, 17*(3), 546–590.

Nicoli, M. (2017). *The rise and fall of the Italian Film Industry*. Routledge.

Nicoli, M. (2018). Historia non facit saltus. The Italian movie industry from 1945 to 1965, working paper [online]. https://www.academia.edu/9042421/Movie_financing_in_Italy_after_WWII

Sedgwick, J., Miskell, P., & Nicoli, M. (2018). The market for films in postwar Italy: Evidence for both national and regional patterns of taste. *Enterprise & Society, 20*(1), 199–228. https://doi.org/10.1017/eso.20122

Sedgwick, J., & Nicoli, M. (2018). Popular filmgoing in mid-1950s Milan: Opening up the 'black box'. In D. Biltereyst, R. Maltby, & P. Meers (Eds.), *Routledge companion to new cinema history*. Routledge.

Treveri Gennari, D. (2009). *Post-war Italian cinema: American intervention, Vatican interests*. Routledge.

Treveri Gennari, D., & Sedgwick, J. (2015). Memories in context: The social and economic function of cinema in 1950s Rome. *Film History, 27*, 76–104.

Daniela Treveri Gennari is a professor of Cinema Studies at Oxford Brookes University interested in audiences, film programming and exhibition. She is currently leading the AHRC-funded *European Cinema Audiences* research project, exploring audience memories of cinemagoing, aspects of film popularity, exhibition strategies and cinema typologies in Europe. Recent publications, include: 'Challenges to Comparative Oral Histories of Cinema Audiences'. *TMG Journal for Media History* (2020) with Ercole and Van de Vijver, and *Italian Cinema Audiences. Histories and Memories of Cinema-going in Post-war Italy* (Bloomsbury 2020) with O'Rawe, Hipkins, Dibeltulo and Culhane.

John Sedgwick is a visiting professor in the Faculty of Technology, Design and Environment, Oxford Brookes University. He researches the economic history of cinema and is particularly interested in the ontological characteristics of film as a commodity. He created the POPSTAT Index of Film Popularity as a proxy for box-office returns. This tool provides a means of reflecting audience preferences and monitoring the distribution process. His research has focused on American, Australian, British, Dutch, Italian and international markets during the 1930s and 1950/60s. He has written a monograph, edited an anthology and published articles in *Business History, Cinema Journal, Economic History Review Explorations in Economic History Enterprise and Society Film History, Historical Journal of Film, Radio and Television, Journal of Applied Statistics, Journal of Cultural Economics, Journal of Economic History* and *Journal of Transnational Cinema*.

Cinemagoers Should '…learn from progressive movies, again and again'. Cinemagoing in Czechoslovakia, 1949–1952

Pavel Skopal, Terézia Porubčanská, and John Sedgwick

Abstract The chapter presents research findings on film popularity in Czechoslovakia during the period of late Stalinism. It also reflects upon methodological difficulties of using the POPSTAT Index in a central command economy. Nationally derived statistics set a context in which ideology and shortages were crucial features. These are supplemented by POPSTAT statistics for the city of Brno in 1952 based upon advertised film programmes. While national attendance figures corroborate these, they need to be carefully contextualised. This is because film programmes were required to meet ideological and commercial objectives.

Once it had come to power in Czechoslovakia in 1948, the ruling Communist Party (KSČ) sought to transform cinema's primary function from entertainment to education. As part of a policy termed 'cinefication',[1] filmgoing was encouraged as '…a political act of self-education'. Watching Soviet films was considered a manifestation of 'the inseparable friendship' with the Soviet Union.[2] Various administrative and institutional mechanisms were put in place to secure attendances at the screenings of ideologically appropriate movies. Thus, the position of district promotional officer was established, charged with educating cinemagoers and increasing attendances, while 82% of promotional expenses were dedicated to supporting 'progressive films'.[3] In addition, work enterprises and educational and social organisations patronised screenings. An example is the Union of Czechoslovak–Soviet friendship

[1] 'Cinefication' refers to screenings throughout the state. The term originates in the USSR in the 1920s when, along with 'electrification' or 'radiofication', it established a vocabulary intended to indicate the promises of revolutionary change through modern technologies.

[2] The Brno regional director Bohuslav Hammer at a meeting of cinema managers, 28 January 1949. Krajský filmový podnik, G 604, Moravský zemský archiv Brno (hereafter MZA, KFP, G604).

[3] Černík (1952, p. 60).

P. Skopal · T. Porubčanská
Department of Film Studies and Audiovisual Culture, Masaryk University, Brno, Czech Republic

J. Sedgwick (✉)
Faculty of Technology, Design and Environment, Oxford Brookes University, Oxford, UK
e-mail: sedgwicj52@gmail.com

J. Sedgwick (ed.), *Towards a Comparative Economic History of Cinema, 1930–1970*, Frontiers in Economic History, https://doi.org/10.1007/978-3-031-05770-0_10

sponsoring a 'week of revolutionary cinema' in Brno, promising full houses but screening to largely empty auditoria.[4]

Nevertheless, as Pavel Skopal has argued, the ideological imperative had to be balanced against the financial requirement of working within State budgets.[5] Showing films that nobody wished to see, or giving away tickets to encourage admissions, generated very little revenue. Indeed, the central contradiction governing the operation of the film industry was that it was required to cover its costs while promoting inherently unpopular films.

In the years leading to Stalin's death in 1953, Eastern Bloc countries were expected to replicate Soviet social, economic and ideological practices.[6] The consequence of this policy, according to Roman Krakovský, was that social space at all levels was state-dominated and that the collective, as defined by the state and its representatives, overrode private interest. In effect, ordinary people did not participate as individuals in the process by which the 'common good' was established.[7]

János Kornai depicts the classical one-party socialist system as 'the economy of shortage'—a market in which the demand for goods and services systematically exceeded the quantity supplied at a price determined centrally by the bureaucratic authorities.[8] The film industry was no exception. It was plagued by shortages, made worse by the ideological baggage of its mass-cultural status.

In this fraught environment, the idea of film popularity—filmgoers making choices leading to some films proving more popular than others—is far from straightforward. Nevertheless, this possibility is investigated in this chapter through the published statistics of film screenings, attendances and box-office drawn principally from the Yearbooks compiled and published by the film historian and journalist Jiří Havelka, in which data were collected for both the Slovakian and Czech parts of the country.[9] In addition, a second investigation is undertaken into filmgoing in the city of Brno through the programming records of local cinemas. This type of evidence makes it possible to identify what films filmgoers were attracted to by their ubiquity in Brno cinemas. The other side of this coin is that the state distributor identified popular movies and acted upon this knowledge, circulating them to cinemas in an orderly and consistent manner.

---

[4] Regional conference for district of Brno, 28 November 1950. MZA, KFP, G604, file 15.

[5] Skopal (2012, p. 81).

[6] Applebaum (2013). See Chapter 13 'Homo sovieticus'.

[7] Krakovský (2015), 'Building the Idea of The Common Good in People's Democracies: A Case Study of Communist Czechoslovakia in the 1950s' Cahiers du Monde russe, Vol. 56, No. 2/3, pp. 345–370.

[8] Kornai János (2008): From Socialism to Capitalism, Eight Essays, p. 3.

[9] Bringing together Czech film industry-based statistics and business records in the form of a trade journal, Jiří Havelka published his first book in 1935 covering the period 1929–1934. With the intention of providing a service to Czechoslovak film industry both for the domestic and international business, he produced Yearbooks from that time onward until the early 1970s. The data used in this Chapter are drawn from the Czech part of the country. Statistics for the Slovak part are published in separate tables.

1 General Context of Film Distribution in Post-War Czechoslovakia

Through the period of German occupation (1938–1945), Czechoslovakia did not experience the same collateral damage metered out to other Eastern European countries and the Soviet Union. Not subjected to major bombing, its cities remained, with some exceptions, intact and, consequently, so did its cinemas. One of the exceptions was Brno, with an arms factory, bombed twice by American aircraft (in August and November 1944) and by the Red Army (in April 1945) with the consequence that one-fifth of the city's buildings were damaged.[10] Although nine of Brno's cinemas were affected, six re-opened almost immediately after hostilities ended. Only one was destroyed and never re-opened.[11]

Based on three studios located in and around Prague and one in Zlín, film production in Czechoslovakia continued to produce films under the German Protectorate. Nationalised in June 1945, six movies started during the Protectorate were completed, while new film projects were launched and services provided for the Soviet film industry.[12] Thus, Czechoslovakia not only maintained its production capacity but had a dense network of cinemas in operation, albeit unevenly distributed in the two parts of the country. In 1946, 1,942 cinemas were operating in the Czech part of the country (hereafter referred to as the Czech lands), but only 263 in Slovakia. Most cinemas were small, with fewer than 300 seats, and only one-sixth had daily screenings.[13] By 1950, the number of permanent Czech cinemas had risen to 2,545.[14]

Intensive 'cinefication' was an integral aspect of the official 'Democratization of Culture' programme promoted by the immediate post-war regime. Following the KSČ engineered coup of February 1948, cinema became an element in the state planning process. At the same time, production was the subject of a heated debate between Ministerstvo informací a osvěty (Ministry of Information and Enlightenment, MIO) and Ministerstvo financí (Ministry of Finance) concerning its status as a cultural/industrial product.[15] A flavour of the disagreement can be found in the archives, with the MIO declaring that cinema was more than a business and that cinema production should be thought of in terms of the 'creation of cultural entities' and distribution, 'the spreading of enlightenment through films'.[16]

To realise the first Five-year Plan (1948–1953), the system of the socialist enterprise economy (socialistické podnikové hospodářství)—in which businesses were

---

[10] Kuča (2000, p. 177).

[11] See Václav Novák, *Historie brněnských kinematografů 1896-1981*. Unpublished manuscript. Archiv města Brna (Brno City Archives, hereafter AMB), f. T68.

[12] See Szczepanik (2016, pp. 64–65).

[13] Skopal (2014, p. 104).

[14] Havelka (1970, p. 220).

[15] Šmída (1954, p. 9).

[16] See letter from MIO to Ministry of Finance—reaction to a letter from 9 July 1952, and minutes from a meeting organized by MI, 18 July 1952. NA, MIO, dodatky, k. 127.

treated as independent enterprise workplaces—was replaced by complete centralisation.[17] Accordingly, Československý státní film (Czechoslovak State Film, ČSF) became an institution of state administration under the jurisdiction of the MIO.[18] At a local level, district offices of the ČSF were responsible for fulfilling an attendance plan for Soviet movies. For instance, in the city of Brno, the most attractive films were screened in the bigger cinemas in the city centre, while less popular 'progressive' (Soviet) films dominated the screens of smaller cinemas. Thus, in January–September 1953, the two largest premiere cinemas—the Moskva and Družba—exceeded overall attendance targets (125.7 and 103.5%, respectively), but not those set for Soviet movies (96.2 and 79.8%). It was the smaller cinemas that allowed the Authorities to meet this target.[19]

In the immediate Post-War period, coinciding with the displacement of the bulk of the German-speaking minority in the country, the most immediate film industry issue was how to replace German and German subtitled films.[20] Participating in the American MPEA scheme, potential shortages were overcome by importing films from Hollywood, Western Europe and the Soviet Union. In 1947, Hollywood and Western European movies took a leading market share regarding the number of screenings and attendances.[21]

However, these arrangements ended once the KSČ took control of the state. While MIO, in conjunction with the Culture and Publicity Department of the Central Committee of the Communist Party, continued to run the film industry through the now named Czechoslovak State Film, film policy took a new turn. A directive of the KSČ Central Committee issued in early 1948 set down a list of rules to govern film distribution during the early years of the communist regime, in which ideological and economic interests were made specific. These were:

- Film distribution must privilege Czechoslovak film production. Of the foreign movies allowed to circulate, distribution should accent friendship with USSR and support Soviet, Polish, Bulgarian and Yugoslav films.
- Film imports should support progressive tendencies and artistic values.
- Support should be given to small and independent West European and American production against MPEA producers.
- Imports should be rationed to preserve foreign currency reserves.

[17] Kaplan (2007, pp. 92–95).

[18] Šmída (1985, p. 154).

[19] District administration of the ČSF, report on fulfilling the attendance plan in the period January 1, 1953—September 30, 1953. AMB, B 1/30.

[20] Skopal (2014, p. 104).

[21] Hollywood and Western productions constituted more than 50% share of the screenings and 55.6% of the total attendance (Skopal, 2014, p. 104). See also Bláhová (2009). On the post-war film shortage in Czechoslovakia see Mareš (1991, 1994).

- For those MPEA films already contracted for, their circulation should be slowed, having them distributed during the 'dead season'—from mid-July to mid-September.[22]

Accordingly, following the Communist takeover of power in 1948, films that were ideologically unacceptable to the new regime—mainly from the capitalist West—were forbidden. (This did not preclude films from the West that were perceived as having a universal art value, such as the British film *Hamlet* (1948).[23] In conjunction with the Soviet film famine resulting from the masterpiece policy emanating from Joseph Stalin, the outcome was a chronic shortage in supply.[24] Only 76 films from Eastern Bloc countries premiered in 1949, leading Jiří Málek (head of Czechoslovak film distribution) to announce a shift from extensive to intensive distribution—meaning that cinemagoers should '...learn from progressive movies, again and again'. Consumers were being asked to repeat-consume films.[25] These policies were subsequently reinforced in April 1950 when the praesidium of the Central Committee of the KSČ passed a resolution 'On behalf of high ideological and artistic standards for Czechoslovak film' that scoped the primary cultural-political directive for cinema. It demanded a distribution policy that '... can recruit and raise viewers to our new films, as well as those of the Soviet Union and the People Democracies. It is a serious task for the party and mass organisations, state enlightenment care bodies, and school administrations to ensure mass attendance at Czechoslovak, Soviet, and other progressive films'.[26]

A short-lived experiment with discriminatory price practices occurred between 1951 and 1954. A few films, perceived as having low 'educational' but high 'entertainment' value, carried higher admission prices.[27] In 1951, the strategy was applied to two films, the Austrian ice revue *Frühling auf dem Eis* and the two-part Czech historical comedy *Císařův pekař—Pekařův císař* (*The Emperor's Baker—The Baker's Emperor*). Two other films were distributed similarly a year later—the Austrian musical *Das Kind der Donau* and the West German film *Der Tiger Akbar*. Finally, in 1953 and 1954, the Swedish film *One Summer of Happiness* and the French *Aux Yeux du Souvenir* were added. After this, the practice was stopped, replaced by a strategy of protracted programmes launched in 1953 that saw attractive movies screened in conjunction with a short film—commonly a documentary from the Soviet Union—thereby balancing the entertainment value of the feature film

[22] National Archives, Prague (herafter NA), Central Committee of the Communist Party of Czechoslovakia, culture and publicity department, file 660—Central film distribution, minutes from a meeting, 1946–1948.

[23] Filmová kartotéka (1949, pp. 3–4).

[24] On The Soviet film famine see Knight (2018).

[25] NA, f. 19/7 KSČ – Ústřední výbor 1945–1989, oddělení kulturně-propagační a ideologické, arch. j. 666. Jiří Málek's report on film distribution in 1949 and its results, addressed to meeting of Board for culture, 28 January 1949.

[26] *Rudé právo* (1950, pp. 1, 3).

[27] Rather than discriminating on the 'quality' of the seats, the highest price was applied to all the seats.

with the ideological significance of the documentary. Instead of all tickets being sold at the same high price (with the effect that only customers of the cheaper seats paid more), prices were raised by one crown above the standard price for all seats.[28] This practice also had the 'virtue' of increasing attendance figures for Soviet production, where mainly these documentaries were made.

2 Film Statistics

In 1950, Czechoslovaks went to the cinema as often as the French, East Germans and West Germans, with just under ten visits per head.[29] Dividing the country into two parts, the Czech lands and Slovakia, the Havelka Yearbooks indicate a split in attendances of 83/17 (per cent). From this point onwards, attention will be focused on the former.

Table 1 shows that in 1947 over 50% of Czech audiences attended films from the West. By 1952 this figure had fallen to just 6%,[30] with new releases tumbling from 207 in 1947 to 111 in 1951.[31] Not surprisingly, audiences readjusted to the new situation and restricted choice set of films by staying away, with Czech audience numbers falling from 129.7 to 98.8 million between 1948 and 1950. From this low point, recovery took place, eventually peaking in 1957 with 148.1 million.[32]

Table 1 also shows that attendances per screening after 1947 consistently favoured domestic production and films from the West. Even with the support that came with 'favoured status', the average number of viewers per screening for Soviet cinema in 1950 was 148, compared to 228 for films from non-socialist countries, a figure that declined further by 1952 to 126.[33]

Havelka's Yearbooks also collected data on individual films, from which we learn that films remained in circulation for lengthy periods from their first release accumulating revenues. Accordingly, the attendances attributed to the 778 feature films in circulation between 1949 and 1952 are aggregates for the period they were on release, with endpoints of 1945 and 1955. Thus, the attendance figure of a film released in 1947 and withdrawn in 1953 will be the sum of attendances for those years. Where films were not removed, attendances are aggregated until 1955.

From Table 2, an idea of supply difficulties is apparent in the vintage of feature films in circulation. Between 1949 and 1952, only 40% of the films in circulation were new releases, defined as films released between those years, thus excluding films first released earlier than 1949. Shortages of new films meant that movies stayed in circulation for longer, the diet of films consumed was older, and repeat viewing was

[28] Skopal (2014), Nesveda (1958, p. 80).

[29] Havelka (1970, 1972), Prommer (1999), Vincendeau (1995).

[30] Havelka (1972, p. 342).

[31] Havelka (1970, p. 202; 1972, p. 296).

[32] Havelka (1970, p. 228; 1973, p. 240).

[33] See Havelka (1970, p. 228; 1972, p. 342).

Table 1 Annual cinema attendances in the Czech lands, 1945–1955

			Czech films		Soviet films		Other people's Republics		All other countries		Total	
Year	(1) New film releases	(2) All feature-length films	(3) Number of screenings	(4) Attendance (millions)	(5) Number of screenings	(6) Attendance (millions)	(7) Number of screenings	(8) Attendance (millions)	(9) Number of screenings	(10) Attendance (millions)	(11) Number of screenings	(12) Attendance (millions)
1945	46	152	57,709	16.684	79,171	19.139	x	x	33,293	9.638	170,173	45.461
1946	146	202	136,602	37.295	167,167	32.344	x	x	160,116	40.375	463,885	110.014
1947	183	207	167,404	35.676	109,756	20.296	x	x	267,796	70.084	544,956	126.056
1948	88	104	173,329	38.528	150,252	29.446	4,729	1.040	240,991	60.709	569,201	129.723
1949	84	120	171,359	38.742	212,784	38.863	28,541	5.622	180,768	38.985	593,452	122.212
1950	67	143	156,409	30.911	275,707	40.685	22,360	4.444	99,482	22.713	553,958	98.753
1951	58	111	235,420	39.980	292,010	40.790	81,610	10.600	41,420	9.590	650,460	100.960
1952	73	119	258,100	46.670	295,590	37.540	101,710	15.050	28,960	6.790	684,360	106.050
1953	90	129	216,090	45.360	329,220	38.920	91,750	13.650	35,060	9.570	672,120	107.500
1954	100	138	260,370	49.950	277,500	39.050	54,470	8.510	93,810	22.280	686,150	119.790
1955	104	137	221,200	47.160	258,760	38.490	77,700	14.720	117,410	28.510	675,070	128.880

Source Havelka (1970, pp. 202, 228, 296, 342)
Note Here released refers to first screened in the Czech lands and not produced. Often a sizeable lag occurred between production and release

Table 2 Films in circulation in the Czech lands, 1949–1952

Country of origin	(1) All films in circulation	(2) All films attendance	(3) All films market share	(4) New films in circulation	(5) New films attendance	(6) New films market share	(7) Garncatz Index
Austria	2	4,335,400	0.01	2	4,335,400	0.01	
Belgium	1	422,400	0.00	0	0	0.00	
Bulgaria	3	1,097,500	0.00	3	1,097,500	0.00	
China	10	2,618,000	0.00	10	2,618,000	0.01	0.27
Czechoslovakia	168	288,688,700	0.36	89	132,987,100	0.43	1.54
Denmark	3	2,214,600	0.00	1	672,800	0.00	
Federal Republic of Germany	1	1,459,600	0.00	1	1,459,600	0.00	
France	66	46,488,500	0.06	21	17,751,500	0.06	0.87
German Democratic Republic	30	20,266,300	0.03	30	20,266,300	0.07	0.70
Great Britain	96	66,665,900	0.08	8	5,569,700	0.02	
Hungary	15	9,996,200	0.01	14	9,232,700	0.03	0.68
Italy	2	1,465,300	0.00	1	551,700	0.00	
Korea	2	519,200	0.00	2	519,200	0.00	
Mexico	4	1,201,500	0.00	0	0	0.00	
Netherlands	1	204,600	0.00	1	204,600	0.00	
Norway	2	269,500	0.00	2	269,500	0.00	
Poland	15	14,561,500	0.02	13	10,639,700	0.03	0.84
Romania	3	808,400	0.00	3	808,400	0.00	
Soviet Union	230	243,350,000	0.31	93	86,162,000	0.28	0.96
Sweden	7	3,196,400	0.00	4	2,087,800	0.01	
Switzerland	2	2,086,200	0.00	0	0	0.00	
USA	115	81,935,400	0.10	19	10,210,700	0.03	0.55
Total	778	793,851,100	1	317	307,444,200	1	
Eastern bloc countries	476	581,905,800	0.73	257	264,330,900	0.86	1.06
Westerm Countries	302	211,945,300	0.27	60	43,113,300	0.14	0.74

Source Havelka (1972)
Note All films in circulation during 1949–1952 are films that premiered between 1945 and 1952. New films in circulation during 1949–1952 are films that premiered during these years

Table 3 Descriptive statistics of the box-office generated in the Czech lands, 1949–1952

Statistics	All film attendance	New films attendance
Mean	1,021,687	969,856
Standard Error	28,525	45,487
Median	800,800	774,000
Standard Deviation	795,127	809,877
Coefficient of Variation	0.78	0.84
Kurtosis	2.08	2.33
Skewness	1.44	1.50
Range	4,212,200	3,994,900
Minimum	1,600	1,600
Maximum	4,213,800	3,996,500
Sum	793,851,100	307,444,200
Count	778	317

Source Havelka (1972)
Note Havelka does not provide attendance data for the Hollywood film *Action in the North Atlantic* (1943), distributed as *Konvoj do Murmaňska*

probably more common. The home country and the Soviet Union were the dominant suppliers, producing between them over 50% of the films in circulation and almost 60% of new movies. Czech films were popular with domestic audiences, taking a 43% share of the market for new films, compared to the 29% for the films of the Soviet Union.

Although 302 movies from the West are recorded in circulation, most were rented before the Communists took power and in the final stages of their licenced term. Between 1949 and 1952, only 60 were cleared for distribution, with France supplying just over a third.

Joseph Garncarz has developed an index to measure the performance of film clusters—in this case, national origins.[34] Measured by the market share (demand) to supply ratio, values rising above 1.0 indicate an increasingly strong reception and below 1.0 the opposite. Featured in column 7 of Table 2, the difference between the popularity of domestic productions and those of other nationalities is notable.

The descriptive statistics of attendance in the Czech lands for all and new feature films are presented in Table 3 and are remarkably similar. It might have been anticipated that attendances for new movies would exceed those of older films. However, the cumulative nature of attendances should be considered when interpreting the figures. They display the familiar characteristics of a long-right-tail distribution, with the mean well above the median, with the most popular film generating attendances

[34] Garncarz (2020).

many times that of the median film. However, the statistics depict a distribution less extreme than reported in other case studies found in the book, with the median film falling well into the second decile of the range. This result is likely to be the consequence of the relative shortage of new films entering the market, leading to films being recirculated and causing audiences to watch a wider range of movies. The result is to bulk up the central parts of the distribution at the expense of the extremes.

The most popular new feature-length films released between 1949 and 1952 are listed in Table 4. The decision taken here is to treat movies broken up into two parts (I and II) as a single entity, cumulating attendances from both parts. The exception is the Czech historical comedy *Císařův pekař—Pekařův císař*, which is registered separately-Havelka gives separate attendance numbers for both parts. In Brno, the movie was screened as one show, with a double admission price.[35] Not surprisingly, given their collective Garncarz Index value, Czech films dominate the Top 20, taking 11 berths. They also took 34 of the Top 50 berths and 55 of the Top 100. The films from the Soviet Union fared less well, taking seven, nine and 26 of these respective categories.

3 POPSTAT

The POPSTAT method details how films circulate within a locality/territory—what films were screened at what cinemas and for how long. These operational details capture the dynamics of how films were distributed and where they were screened. Applying this method to the industrial city of Brno, with a population of 273,000 in 1952, provides new evidence about film popularity to supplement that derived from the Havelka Yearbooks for the Czech lands.[36]

Of the 36 functioning cinemas, film programmes have been collected for 24 from the daily listings in the city's *Svobodné slovo* newspaper. Cinema weights derived from the sample cinemas' admission prices and seating capacity have been calculated and are presented in Table 5. We believe these correspond to the classification system used by the film authorities, based upon locality and seating capacity. First-class grouped all the big and modern cinemas in the regional capital cities where the films were premiered, while second-class comprised cinemas with good technical standards, mainly in the bigger cities. The final category consisted of third-class cinemas situated in smaller towns and the suburbs and districts of the cities. In each case, the ticket prices were determined by the Authorities. Typically, the cinema auditorium was divided into front and back stalls and balconies. Before 1953, first-class tickets were priced at 10, 15 and 20 Kčs (crowns) respectively; in the second-class 5, 10 and 15 Kčs; and in the third, two prices of 5 and 10 Kčs were charged. A

[35] There is some evidence from oral history sources that attendance for two-part movies presented in one screening were counted twice. But we do not have clear proof of the practice, nor are we are able to quantify how many screenings presented both parts of those movies in one show.

[36] Kuča (2000, p. 184).

Table 4 Top 20 films released in the Czech lands, 1949–1952

Rank	(1) Czech title	(2) Original title if different	(3) Country of origin	(4) Year of first release	(5) End year	(6) Attendance
1	Pyšná princezna		Czechoslovakia	1952	1955	3,996,500
2	Pád Berlina I., II	Padenie Berlina	Soviet Union	1950	1955	3,948,500
3	Rodinné trampoty oficiála Tříšky		Czechoslovakia	1949	1955	3,917,800
4	Divá Bára		Czechoslovakia	1949	1955	3,862,800
5	Pytlákova schovanka		Czechoslovakia	1949	1955	3,556,200
6	Muži v sedle	Smelye lyudi	Soviet Union	1951	1955	3,478,900
7	Vzbouření na vsi		Czechoslovakia	1949	1955	3,467,000
8	Hostinec U kamenného stolu		Czechoslovakia	1949	1955	3,326,200
9	Císařův pekař		Czechoslovakia	1951	1955	3,254,100
10	Mladá garda I., II	Molodaya gvardiya	Soviet Union	1949	1955	3,152,700
11	Jaro na ledě	Frühling auf dem Eis	Austria	1951	1955	3,077,800
12	Stalingradská bitva I., II	Stalingradskaya bitva I, II	Soviet Union	1949	1953	3,041,100
13	Věznice parmská I., II	La Chartreuse de Parme	France	1949	1955	2,910,000
14	Ve světlech manéže	Na arene tsirka	Soviet Union	1952	1955	2,908,200
15	Veselý souboj		Czechoslovakia	1951	1955	2,723,700
16	Setkání na Labi	Vstrecha na Elbe	Soviet Union	1949	1955	2,723,400
17	Temno		Czechoslovakia	1951	1955	2,669,700
18	Pára nad hrncem		Czechoslovakia	1950	1955	2,638,200
19	Příběh opravdového člověka	Povest o nastoyashchem cheloveke	Soviet Union	1949	1955	2,542,900
20	Pan Novák		Czechoslovakia	1949	1955	2,500,000

Source Havelka (1972)
Note Column 4 refers to when films were first released in Czechoslovakia

Table 5 Sample of Brno Cinemas operating in 1952

Cinema	(1) Location	(2) Seats	(3) Admission price (Kcs)	(4) Screenings per week	(5) Potential revenue (Kcs)	(6) Cinema weight
Cas	Central	364	1	21	9,173	0.36
Druzba	Central	799	4	21	67,116	2.60
Jadran	Suburban	700	4	8	22,400	0.87
Jalta	Central	661	4	21	55,524	2.15
Jas	Suburban	584	4	8	18,688	0.72
Letni kino Sport	Suburban	460	2	7	6,440	0.25
Letni kino Zimni stadion	District	3008	3	7	63,168	2.45
Lipa	District	598	4	8	19,136	0.74
Lucerna	District	318	4	8	10,176	0.39
Mir	District	524	4	8	16,768	0.65
Mladych	District	400	2	8	6,400	0.25
Morava	District	769	4	21	64,596	2.51
Moskva	Central	1012	4	22	89,056	3.45
Oko	Suburban	400	3	16	19,200	0.74
Praha	Central	400	4	21	33,600	1.30
Radost	District	517	2	21	21,714	0.84
Sibir	Suburban	441	3	15	19,845	0.77
Slovan	Suburban	510	3	9	13,770	0.53
Sport	Suburban	681	2	14	19,068	0.74
Studio	District	400	4	7	11,200	0.43
Svetozor	Suburban	300	2	14	8,400	0.33
Svoboda	District	300	2	14	8,400	0.33
Uderka	Central	237	2	21	9,954	0.39
Vlast	Suburban	272	2	9	4,896	0.19

Source Svobodné slovo (1952)
Note Post-devaluation 1953 Czechoslovak Crowns (Kčs) are used

further category of cinema called Čas or Čásek was being established in the cities, screening a continuous programme of newsreels, short documentaries and slapstick. In these cinemas, a single admission price of 5 Kčs was charged.[37]

In the face of a national economic and financial crisis, the nominal value of the currency was reset overnight on 31 May 1953. Savings were devalued by 50:1, while

[37] Čásek were a version of Čas cinemas – Čas screened 35 mm prints, while Čásek, 16 mm.

prices (including cinema admission prices) and salaries were devalued by 5:1.[38] For our purposes, the Havelka Yearbooks are expressed in new currency values.

The cinema weights in Table 5 reflect the new set of admission prices attributed to each of the cinemas in the Brno sample for routine screenings. In each, the top of the range price has been selected. Thus, eleven first-class cinemas charge an admission price of 4 Kčs; four cinemas belong to the second-class, 3 Kčs; and eight third-class cinemas, 2 Kčs. The cinema Čas has a single admission price of 1.2 Kčs.[39]

The range of cinema weights varies from 3.45 for the 1,012-seater Moskva to 0.19 for the 272-seater Vlast. Two of the cinemas—the Mladých and Studio—shared the same address but showed different programmes. The Letní Kino Sport and Letní Kino Zimní Stadion were open-air cinemas, only opening for the three summer months—from 6/7 June to 12 September. Another two cinemas, the Čas and Úderka, were dedicated to screening newsreels and information-type films. They have been included in the weighting process because, occasionally, they screened feature films: in 1952, the Čas cinema screened six films over 39 days, while the Úderka cinema screened more than 30 films over 119 days.

A POPSTAT Index series is created for each *ith* film screened in Brno during 1952 by multiplying the weight of the cinema at which it was screened by the days it was screened. Films were tracked forward until the end of January 1953. All programmes feature a single film attraction.

The descriptive statistics of the POPSTAT values are found in Table 6. It is instructive to compare the more extreme Brno statistical distribution with that generated by the official statistics found in Table 3. The Havelka-derived statistics represent the Czech part of the country, including rural populations for which film choice was restricted because of limited access to cinemas. Furthermore, they cover multiple years, giving films more opportunities to increase their audience. The Brno statistics, in comparison, provide an annual cross-section of filmgoing practice in a large urban environment, in which film consumers had a plentiful—if curtailed—choice, exaggerating the effect of some films being selected more often than others.

Table 7 shows that in Brno in 1952, a little over 20% of the movies screened were released in 1951–1952.[40] These films garnered 40% of screenings in Brno and took close to a 50% market share (measured by the POPSTAT Index), providing evidence of a preference for new films—something not possible to establish from the accumulated national attendance statistics found in the Havelka Yearbooks. Accordingly, 80% of film supply, 60% of screenings and 50% of market demand were generated by

[38] Accordingly, the devaluation lowered cinema admission prices from 20–4 Kčs, 15–3 Kčs, 10–2 Kčs and 5–1 Kčs (Havelka, 1972).

[39] The cinema classification implicit in Table 5 differs from the years of 1945-1948, when only five cinemas were regarded as first-class. While these continued to premiere new films, they were obliged to charge the same price as the six cinemas which newly entered the first-class category. The much flatter pricing structure was designed to encourage cinemagoing among the population.

[40] Here the distinction between released—first screened—and produced is significant, in that all films were subject to ideological scrutiny which took time, and film imports also required import licences to be granted, another time costing procedure. Source from Havelka, the years refer to the first screenings in Czechoslovakia—from the point when films started generating income.

Table 6 Descriptive statistics of POPSTAT Index Values, Brno, 1952

Statistic	Value
Mean	18.37
Standard Error	1.32
Median	8.38
Standard Deviation	25.82
Coefficient of Variation	1.41
Kurtosis	10.48
Skewness	2.99
Range	157.42
Minimum	0.25
Maximum	157.67
Sum	7016.09
Count	382

Source Svobodné slovo (1952)

Table 7 Vintage of films in circulation in Brno in 1952

(1) Vintage of films	(2) Number of films	(3) Proportion of films	(4) Screening days	(5) Proportion of screening days	(6) POPSTAT	(7) Proportion of POPSTAT
1925–1934	16	0.04	302	0.04	331	0.05
1935–1938	41	0.11	590	0.09	561	0.08
1939–1944	61	0.16	739	0.11	611	0.09
1945	10	0.03	127	0.02	120	0.02
1946	20	0.05	191	0.03	119	0.02
1947	32	0.08	423	0.06	320	0.05
1948	33	0.09	364	0.05	299	0.04
1949	49	0.13	640	0.10	563	0.08
1950	41	0.11	803	0.12	720	0.10
1951	51	0.13	1792	0.27	2131	0.30
1952	27	0.07	761	0.11	1243	0.18
Total	381	1	6732	1	7016	1

Source Dataset
Note The original release date of one film could not be traced

films first released before 1951. Films of earlier vintages kept urban cinemas supplied with films. These had quick turnovers, explaining the extreme statistics associated with the distribution of POPSTAT Index values. Many films had few screenings; a few had many.

Also of interest is the contribution made by (primarily Czech) films first released during the 1935–1938 and Protectorate period of 1939–1945. These vintage movies were often screened with a textual prelude that explained why they were once again in circulation. In this restricted market, audiences were attracted by newness but, in the case of re-run Czech movies, the opposite—familiarity and predictability.

The Top 20 films screened in Brno are reported in Table 8. Czech movies are well represented, taking eight of the berths, including the 1937 film *Tři vejce do skla* with Vlasta Burian, the biggest comedy star of the 1930s. However, most films popular with Brno audiences are from much more recent vintages. Four films from the Soviet Union, two from East Germany and two from Hungary indicate a market dominated by films from the Eastern Bloc, with four films from the West ranked 12, 15, 17 and 18th; a pattern similar to the Top 20 listing derived from the Havelka Yearbooks for the Czech lands, featured in Table 4.[41]

Comparing the popularity of films in Brno with the Havelka Yearbooks is problematic for several reasons. First, the collection periods are different. Second, movies released before 1952 had already been circulated in Brno, implying that their respective POPSTAT Index values do not capture their true popularity. The same is true for those films released in 1952 and still circulating in 1953 and later. The third problem is that the number of available prints will have restricted the availability of recently released movies in smaller towns and rural areas. Finally, some films were the subject of privileged distribution by the Authorities—a phenomenon influencing both Brno POPSTAT results and Havelka statistics, but unevenly.

An example of the latter is given by account Bohuslav Hammer, director of distribution for the Brno district, who received an order to screen the 10th ranked Soviet film *Kavalier zolotoy zvezdy* at the same time as the keenly anticipated top-ranked Czech historical comedy *Císařův pekař—Pekařův císař*. In the minutes of a meeting, Hammer is concerned that the Soviet film, following immediately after the screening of 'another Soviet film'—*Donetskie shakhtyory*—would perform very poorly.[42] The implication is that Soviet ideologically loaded movies were perceived as generic products with only a limited capacity to attract audiences. Hammer required a long distribution window between the screening of such films for them to be effectively exploited.

Thus, while the collection of programming data for Brno is not sufficiently extensive to make a confident assessment of film popularity, it nevertheless provides insight into the manner of film distribution. It also draws attention to those films that received many bookings in Brno but fared less well in the rest of the Czech lands.

[41] These results differ markedly from the top-ranking results established for Cracow in the next chapter, which was dominated by international films, particularly those from France.

[42] MZA, KFP, G604, file 77.

Table 8 POPSTAT Top 20 films in Brno, 1952

(1) Rank	(2) Original title	(3) Cczech title	(4) Year	(5) Country of origin	(6) Total screening days	(7) POPSTAT Index	(8) Czech admissions
1	Císařův pekař - Pekařův císař	Císařův pekař - Pekařův císař	1952	Czechoslovakia	103	157.67	4,460,400
2	Das kalte Herz	Chladné srdce	1950	East Germany	91	154.94	1,271,500
3	Na arene tsirka	Ve světlech manéže	1951	Soviet Union	98	153.38	2,908,200
4	Tři vejce do skla	Tři vejce do skla	1937	Czechoslovakia	81	146.64	1,330,600
5	Pysná princezna	Pyšná princezna	1952	Czechoslovakia	82	138.91	3,996,500
6	Zítra se bude tancit vsude	Zítra se bude tančit všude	1952	Czechoslovakia	57	133.40	2,375,900
7	Különös házasság	Podivné manželství	1951	Hungary	65	128.70	1,274,400
8	Akce B	Akce B	1951	Czechoslovakia	98	119.97	2,237,900
9	Mikolás Ales	Mikoláš Aleš	1951	Czechoslovakia	91	104.05	1,627,000
10	Kavalier zolotoy zvezdy	Rytíř zlaté hvězdy	1951	Soviet Union	62	97.85	1,156,300
11	Selskiy vrach	Venkovský lékař	1952	Soviet Union	46	90.56	1,261,700
12	The Heiress	Dědička	1949	US	57	83.38	615,600
13	Der Untertan	Poddaný	1951	East Germany	58	82.92	1,005,400
14	Velké dobrodruzství	Velké dobrodružství	1952	Czechoslovakia	53	80.63	1,880,700
15	Die Kuckucks	Kukačky	1949	Germany	49	77.52	919,900
16	Nezabyvaemyy 1919 god	Nezapomenutelný rok 1919	1951	Soviet Union	54	74.80	134,800

(continued)

Table 8 (continued)

(1) Rank	(2) Original title	(3) Cczech title	(4) Year	(5) Country of origin	(6) Total screening days	(7) POPSTAT Index	(8) Czech admissions
17	…Sans laisser d'adresse	Adresát neznámý	1951	France	40	73.41	686,600
18	La Chartreuse de Parme	Věznice parmská	1948	France/Italy	46	71.79	2,910,000
19	Štika v rybníce	Štika v rybníce	1951	Czechoslovakia	62	71.04	1,554,900
20	Déryné	Paní Déryová	1951	Hungary	41	70.25	789,300

Source Dataset, Havelka (1972)
Note Two films—*Císařův pekař -Pekařův císař*; and *La Chartreuse de Parme* were issued in two parts. But as we already mentioned, *Císařův pekař—Pekařův císař* was mostly screened in Brno cinemas in one show. Czech admissions are derived from the Havelka Yearbooks

The top-ranking film was the Czech two-part feature *Císařův pekař—Pekařův císař*. Between 29 February 1952 and 6 October, the movie passed through 12 cinemas and appeared on 103 daily programmes. As shown in Table 9, it opened the Moskva and Praha simultaneously for 28 and 21 days, generating almost 80% of its POPSTAT Index value from these bookings. It was screened simultaneously at the Sport during the final week of its exhibition at the Moskva. After a short two-week break, *Císařův pekař—Pekařův císař* then appeared in April 1952 at the Jadran, Mír, Lípa and Jas cinemas, each for a week booking. A two-month hiatus followed before the film was screened for a series of less than one-week bookings at the Vlast, Slovan, Letní Kino Sport and Studio cinemas.

Essentially *Císařův pekař—Pekařův císař* moved in an orderly fashion from box-office rich (cinemas with high weights) to box-office poor cinemas in a manner that was entirely in keeping with revenue maximising strategies found in the West. The likely explanation for this is that audiences wanted to see this film, and exhibitors wanted to show it. Table 9 suggests that this practice was common for the most popular movies, garnering the most significant proportion of their POPSTAT Index values in premiere cinemas.

A comparison of the Top 20 films in Brno based on the POPSTAT index with the attendance statistics found in Havelka highlights one significant anomaly: the 1951 Soviet civil war film *Nezabyvaemyy 1919 god*, featuring the character of Stalin. The movie was screened in November at the highly weighted Družba and Jalta cinemas, respectively, for 14 and 7 days. After this, it passed to the Jas, Radost and Jadran for four days apiece later in the month. However, according to the Havelka listings, the audiences were likely to have been very small, given the meagre numbers who watched the film in the Czech lands. The explanation for its wide diffusion in Brno is that November was the month of Czechoslovak–Soviet Friendship, in which cinemas screened Soviet films. Of the 525 screenings in Brno during that month, 341 were of Soviet cinema. Czech movies came next with 131, followed by Hungary (16) and Poland (12). Altogether, 70 Soviet films were screened during the month compared to 19 from the home country.

Nezabyvaemyy 1919 God, celebrated as a winner at the Karlovy Vary film festival, was at the centre of the Soviet offer for the month of Czechoslovak–Soviet Friendship.[43] Of course, POPSTAT works on the implausible basis that audience size is invariant to what film is being screened. This example is a classic case of a movie being favoured for reasons other than its popular appeal. Details on its distribution are revealing. The film received massive official support, including attendance contests between cities and ticket sales to factories and offices. Yet, despite these efforts, *Nezabyvaemyy 1919 God* was ranked 737 of 777 films in the Havelka listings, from which we learn that the authorities could not create hits when not sanctioned by cinemagoers.[44] In the Brno listings, *Nezabyvaemyy 1919 God* is preceded by movies that generated eight times and 14 times higher national attendances (*Die Kuckucks* and

---

[43] Filmový přehled (1952, p. 2).

[44] Kavka (1952, p. 13), Lidová demokracie (1952, p. 13).

Table 9 Premiere statistics of Top 20 films

(1) POPSTAT rank	(2) Original title	(3) Premiere cinema 1	(4) Days	(5) POPSTAT	(6) Premiere cinema 2	(7) Days	(8) POPSTAT	(9) Total premiere days	(10) Premiere POPSTAT	(11) Total POPSTAT	(12) Proportion of Premiere to Total POPSTAT
1	Císařův pekař - Pekařův císař	Moskva	28	96.73	Praha	21	27.37	49	124.10	157.67	0.79
2	Das kalte Herz	Druzba	48	124.97				48	124.97	154.94	0.81
3	Na arene tsirka	Moskva	24	82.91				24	82.91	153.38	0.54
4	Tři vejce do skla	Morava	49	122.78				49	122.78	146.64	0.84
5	Pysná princezna	Moskva	21	72.55				21	72.55	138.91	0.52
6	Zítra se bude tancit vsude	Moskva	21	72.55	Jalta	14	30.15	35	102.70	133.40	0.77
7	Különös házasság	Moskva	28	96.73				28	96.73	128.70	0.75
8	Akce B	Jalta	35	75.39				35	75.39	119.97	0.63
9	Mikolás Ales	Jalta	31	66.77				31	66.77	104.05	0.64
10	Kavalier zolotoy zvezdy	Moskva	21	72.55				21	72.55	97.85	0.74
11	Selskiy vrach	Moskva	21	72.55				21	72.55	90.56	0.80
12	The Heiress	Druzba	22	57.28				22	57.28	83.38	0.69
13	Der Untertan	Jalta	21	45.23				21	45.23	82.92	0.55
14	Velké dobrodruzství	Druzba	13	33.85				13	33.85	80.63	0.42
15	Die Kuckucks	Moskva	14	48.36				14	48.36	77.52	0.62

(continued)

Table 9 (continued)

(1) POPSTAT rank	(2) Original title	(3) Premiere cinema 1	(4) Days	(5) POPSTAT	(6) Premiere cinema 2	(7) Days	(8) POPSTAT	(9) Total premiere days	(10) Premiere POPSTAT	(11) Total POPSTAT	(12) Proportion of Premiere to Total POPSTAT
16	Nezabyvaemyy 1919 god	Lipa	3	2.23				3	2.23	74.80	0.03
17	…Sans laisser d'adresse	Druzba	24	62.49				24	62.49	73.41	0.85
18	La Chartreuse de Parme	Svoboda	3	0.98				3	0.98	71.79	0.01
19	Štika v rybníce	Druzba	17	44.26				17	44.26	71.04	0.62
20	Déryné	Moskva	14	48.36	Praha	7	9.12	21	57.49	70.25	0.82
40	Bolshoy kontsert	Druzba	7	18.22				7	18.22	46.82	0.39
60	Shangrao ji zhong ying	Jalta	14	30.15				14	30.15	32.77	0.92
80	Bylo to v máji	Jadran	3	2.61				3	2.61	25.87	0.10
100	Ruy Blas	Lipa	7	5.20				7	5.20	19.31	0.27

Velké dobrodružství, respectively), highlighting the distinctive nature of the distribution system in state-socialist Czechoslovakia and requiring caution when applying and interpreting of POPSTAT methods.

Other anomalies are evident in Table 8. The East German fairy story *Das kalte Herz* and the Hungarian drama *Különös házasság* perform much more strongly in the 1952 Brno POPSTAT Index than nationally. Behind these films is a narrative that requires development. What is clear from this discussion, based upon Tables 8 and 9, is that a geographical and temporal extension of the 1952 collection of data in Brno, supported by the rich data collected by Havelka, might yield unique insights into film preferences in Czechoslovakia during the years of late Stalinism.

4 Discussion

The official cultural policy that films should 'educate' required audiences to embrace Soviet movies, thereby combining economic and ideological goals. Unfortunately for the authorities, ideologically driven films from the USSR and 'people's democratic republics' following the norms of socialist realism did not fit Czech audiences' expectations and well-established preferences. Nevertheless, as the data we compiled from the Havelka yearbooks and cinema programming in Brno in 1952 indicate, a few Soviet movies and many Czechoslovak films with apparent reference to the values promoted by the new regime became arguably popular. Although these films were supported by promotional campaigns and sheltered from potential crowd-drawing competition from Hollywood and Western Europe, they drew large audiences attracted by combinations of attributes such as colour, spectacle, adventure, comedy or famous stars.

Further insight into this phenomenon of popularity coupled with ideological loyalty to the regime can be drawn from the mass gymnastic events known as 'Spartakiáda'.[45] In his work on this festivity, Peter Roubal identified a range of attitudes towards Spartakiads: from open resistance to enthusiastic acceptance. The most common reaction recognised by Roubal was, however, tactical. The author refers to the term 'Eigen-Sinn', which might be translated as 'obstinate wilfulness' or 'stubbornness', to describe the tactic by which 'people tolerate the strategy of the ruling power to the extent that is necessary, while pursuing their objectives as far as the ruling power allows'.[46] This perspective helps explain why two Soviet colour movies, one in the Brno Top 20 listing, *Na arene tsirka* (ranked 3rd in Table 8) and one from the Havelka Top 20 listing *Smelye ljudi* (ranked 6th in Table 4), were so

[45] These were organized every five years between 1955 and 1985 (see Roubal, 2020).

[46] Roubal (2020, p. 18). Roubal refers to the term eigensinn that was influentially coined by German historian Alf Lüdtke and applied to state-socialist societies by Thomas Lindenberger. The term in Lindenberger's use means "individuals' capacity to "make sense" of their behavior and their attitudes within relationships of authority in ways that are non "programmed" or anticipated by the ideological framework or the political function that the powers to be have invested in this relationship." See, e.g., Lindenberger (2010, p. 4).

highly attended. These films were promoted, respectively, as 'proof that it is the new order of society which allows circus art to develop fully',[47] and '...a celebration of the heroism of the Soviet man fighting for the happy future of his socialist homeland'.[48] Yet, while they were framed to transport audiences from the private sphere of consumption and autotelic pleasure towards the collective affirmation of socialist society, we suggest that viewers saw them in a different light.

An insight into the range of attitudes held by cinemagoers towards the limited film supply in the early 1950s can be had from the collection of letters cinemagoers addressed to various official bodies and collected by the Czechoslovak State Film. These represent a fragmentary and diverse sample of citizens' reactions ranging from clear opposition to the full confirmation of official cultural policy. Take the response to the premiere of the Austrian movie *Frühling auf dem Eis* in Czech cinemas. Some dislike was voiced from party organisations, local administration bodies or "workers correspondents", arguing that such 'film lemonades' should not be screened because of their detrimental effect on people's taste. Some letters even claimed that 'new people' rejected the movie, preferring Soviet productions. Other authors defended the distribution of *Frühling auf dem Eis* against the harsh press criticism and demanded more of this kind of fare that would provide 'rest after work'. An oppositional attitude is represented in a letter that rejected all Czechoslovak and Soviet movies extolling the virtues of socialism. Stridently the writer comments, 'I have seen neither Padenie Berlina nor Sekretnaja missija, Vstanou noví bojovníci, Zocelení, Karhanova parta, Smelye ljudi, Der Rat der Götter, or Kis Katalin házassága, and I do not regret it. But if I had not have seen *Frühling auf dem Eis*, I would be genuinely pissed off'.[49]

Although the letter's author paid a higher price for the *Frühling auf dem Eis*' ticket due to the distribution practices we described earlier, he still did not face the dilemma that authorities presented cinemagoers of the so-called extended programmes. One of the cinemagoers in this situation was novelist Čestmír Jeřábek who, while living in Brno, wrote in his diary on 1 July 1953: 'After a long time, we have seen a European movie this afternoon (a French one: *Fanfan la Tulip*). However, before this movie was screened, we had to chew through an extremely boring "educational" Russian movie about Soviet Moldavia, which seems to be a Schlaraffenland full of milk and honey'.[50] Jeřábek rather straightforwardly accepted the pragmatic deal offered by Czechoslovak State Cinema to cinemagoers, whereby Western entertainment had two prices, one literal (higher prices) and the other metaphorical (watching Soviet propaganda). This diary record provides an example of 'stubbornness'. It illustrates the value of the Eigen-Sinn concept in that it recognises agency on the part of audiences to mediate their way through the highly asymmetric contract between them and the authorities. In making his choice, Jeřábek saw the film that interested him while legitimising the regime and its cultural policy by watching a Soviet documentary.

---

[47] *Filmový přehled* (1952, p. 6).

[48] *Filmový přehled* (1952, p. 3).

[49] NFA, Filmová rada 1949–53, R9/AI/4P/9K.

[50] Jeřábek (2000, p. 223).

We contend that audiences in large numbers reacted similarly to Čestmír Jeřábek in that they found a way of selecting from films aspects that interested them while tolerating the more formal propagandist element. They were pragmatic and likely more interested in, say, films made in colour, or movies made in the well-established tradition of Czech film comedy, than in promotions of the new socialist society and its values.

5 Conclusion

The Brno dataset provides evidence that audiences played a sanctioning role. Clear patterns in film distribution emerge. Filmgoers made choices, and they were free to make them. The exceptions were obligatory screenings at education establishments and workplaces, which did not entail individuals making personal choices based on preferences. Of course, and this is critical, the choice set facing film consumers was heavily proscribed, ruling out the admission of recently released Hollywood and Western European films. This factor is one of the two main controls that the communist authorities imposed upon film distribution. The second was the favouritism shown to Soviet cinema, the consequence of which is that Soviet films attracted, on average, half the audience of films from the West per screening in 1952 — 234 for films from the West, compared to 127, with Czech movies falling between 180 (derived from Table 1).

These controls impacted a market where the supply of new Czech films appeared paralysed due to the constant flow of ineffective reorganisations—eight features only were produced in 1951, instead of the 22 films that were called for by the so-called 'thematic plan'.[51] After almost five years (February 1948 to December 1952) the communist party's aims of resolving their economic and ideological goals were no nearer to being realised. Only ersatz solutions were available. Audiences were exposed to ideologically prominent movies for as long as economically bearable. However, filmgoers were also supplied with more attractive and less 'valuable' movies whose ideological acceptability for the new regime was fixed either through discursive framing or burdening them with the film supplement of a Soviet documentary. The top-ranking lists presented in Tables 4 and 8 provide a vista on audience tactics. Audiences appropriate those movies that provided satisfying production values and entertainment (famous film stars of the 1930s and occupation era, comedy plots, adventure, spectacle) while often sceptically pushing the ideological wrappings of dialogue, storylines, promotion and film criticism to the background. In identifying the films that different audiences at different places went to see in various numbers, the chance of understanding audience motives is made more apparent.

[51] Szczepanik (2016, pp. 75–90).

References

Archives

Brno City Archives
Moravian Land Archives, Brno
National Archives, Prague
National Film Archives, Prague

Books and Articles

Books and Book Chapters

Applebaum, A. (2013). *Iron curtain: The crushing of Eastern Europe 1944–56*. Penguin.

Černík, A. (1952). *Výroční zpráva o čs. filmovnictví. Rok 1949*. Praha: Československý filmový ústav.

Garncarz, J. (2020). *Begeisterte Zuschauer: Über die Filmpräferenzen der Deutschen in der NS-Zeit*. Herbert von Halem

Havelka, J. (1970). *Čs. filmové hospodářství 1945–1950*. Československý filmový ústav.

Havelka, J. (1972). *Čs. filmové hospodářství 1951–1955, I.& II díl*. Československý filmový ústav.

Havelka, J. (1973). *Čs. filmové hospodářství 1956–1960*. Československý filmový ústav.

Jeřábek, Č. (2000). *V zajetí stalinismu. Z deníků 1948–1958*. Barrister & Principal.

Kaplan, K. (2007). *Proměny české společnosti 1948–1960. Část první*. Ústav pro soudobé dějiny AV ČR.

Kornai, J. (2008). *From socialism to capitalism: Eight essays*. Central European University Press.

Kuča, K. (2000). *Brno. Vývoj města, předměstí a připojených vesnic.*: Baset.

Nesveda, A. (1958). *Organisace a ekonomika distribuce filmů*. Československý film.

Prommer, E. (1999). *Kinobesuch im Lebenslauf: eine historische und medienbiographische Studie*. UVK Medien.

Roubal, P. (2020). *Spartakiads. The politics of physical culture in Communist Czechoslovakia*. Karolinum Press.

Skopal, P. (2012). The cinematic shapes of the socialist modernity program: ideological and economic parameters of cinema distribution in the Czech Lands, 1948–1970. In D. Biltereyst, R. Maltby, & P. Meers (Eds.), *Cinema, audiences and modernity. New perspectives on European cinema history* (pp. 81–98). Routledge.

Skopal, P. (2014). *Filmová kultura severního trojúhelníku: filmy, kina a diváci českých zemí, NDR a Polska 1945–1970*. Host.

Šmída, B. (1954). *Organizace a výroba uměleckého filmu*. Československý státní film.

Šmída, B. (1985). *Organizace československého filmového podnikání a filmové tvorby*. Státní pedgogické nakladatelství.

Szczepanik, P. (2016). *Továrna Barrandov. Svět filmařů a politická moc 1945–1970*. Národní filmový archív.

Vincendeau, G. (1995). *Encyclopedia of European Cinema*. Files on File.

Journals

Bláhová, J. (2009), Praha není žádný Minsk. Proces výběru hollywoodských filmů pro československý trh po druhé světové válce. *Iluminace, 21*(3), 5–40.

Knight, C. (2018). Nelli Morozova on censors, censorship and the Soviet Film Famine, 1948–52. *The Slavonic and East European Review, 96*(4), 704–730. https://doi.org/10.5699/slaveasteurorev2.96.4.0704

Krakovský, R. (2015). Building the idea of the common good in people's democracies. *Cahiers Du Monde Russe, 56*(2/3), 345–370. https://doi.org/10.4000/monderusse.8186

Lindenberger, T. (2010). The fragmented society: "Societal Activism" and authority in GDR state system. *Zeitgeschichte, 37*(1), 3–10.

Mareš, P. (1991). Všemi prostředky hájená kinematografie. Úvodem k edici dokumentu „Záznam na paměť". *Iluminace, 3*(2), 75–105.

Mareš, P. (1994). Politika a „Pohyblivé obrázky". Spor o dovoz amerických filmů do Československa po druhé světové válce. *Iluminace, 6*(1), 77–96.

Pištora, L. (1997). Filmoví návštěvníci a kina na území České republiky. Od roku 1945 do současnosti. *Iluminace, 9*(2), 63–106.

Podškubková, B., & Skopal, P. (2020). Klubisté sobě. Funkcionáři Filmového klubu v Uherském Brodě v letech 1976–1989. *Iluminace, 32*(3), 41–59.

Newspapers

-am- (1952, January 25). Ve světlech manéže. *Filmový přehled*, 4, p. 6.

Filmová kartotéka. (1949, November 11). 42, pp. 3–4.

Filmový přehled. (1952, November 14). 44, p. 2.

Kavka, M. (1952, December 12). 16.000 návštěvníků v krajském městě vidělo film "Nezapomenutelný rok 1919". *Jiskra,* p. 13.

Lidová demokracie. (1952, November 13). p. 13.

-lj- (1951, February 23). Muži v sedle. *Filmový přehled,* 8, p. 3.

Rudé arvo. (1950, April 19). 30(92), pp. 1–3.

Svobodné slovo (1952). Brno: Československá strana socialistická.

Pavel Skopal is an associate professor in the Department of Film Studies and Audiovisual Culture, Masaryk University, Brno, Czech Republic. In 2010–2012 he was a visiting researcher at the Konrad Wolf Film and Television University in Potsdam, Germany (on a research project supported by the Alexander von Humboldt Foundation). He coedited anthologies devoted to the Czechoslovak and East German film industries in the 1950s (Cinema in Service of the State, published by Berghahn Books in 2015, with Lars Karl) and to film industries of Nazi occupied countries (Film Professionals in Nazi-Occupied Europe, published by Palgrave Macmillan in 2021, with Roel Vande Winkel). He has published articles in numerous academic journals, including *Historical Journal of Film, Radio and Television, Studies in Eastern European Cinema, Convergences, Jump Cut, Iluminace and Participations.*

Terézia Porubčanská is a Ph.D. candidate at the University of Antwerp and Masaryk University in Brno, preparing her doctoral thesis on comparative research methods in New Cinema History with a case study of Brno, Antwerp and Ghent. She obtained master's degrees in Geography from the University of Pavol Jozef Safarik in Kosice, Slovakia, and Film Studies from the Masaryk

University in Brno, Czech Republic. She has been involved in a comparative research project, *European Cinema Audiences* researching Brno cinema culture in the 1950s.

John Sedgwick is a visiting professor in the Faculty of Technology, Design and Environment, Oxford Brookes University. He researches the economic history of cinema and is particularly interested in the ontological characteristics of film as a commodity. He created the POPSTAT Index of Film Popularity as a proxy for box-office returns. This tool provides a means of reflecting audience preferences and monitoring the distribution process. His research has focused on American, Australian, British, Dutch, Italian and international markets during the 1930s and 1950/60s. He has written a monograph, edited an anthology and published articles in *Business History*, *Cinema Journal*, *Economic History Review*, *Explorations in Economic History*, *Enterprise and Society*, *Film History*, *Historical Journal of Film, Radio and Television*, *Journal of Applied Statistics*, *Journal of Cultural Economics*, *Journal of Economic History* and *Journal of Transnational Cinema*.

'It Seems to Me that the Most Popular Films in the West Are Very Harmful to Us': Film Popularity in Poland During the years of 'High Stalinisation'

Konrad Klejsa and John Sedgwick

Abstract From a combination of archive materials, official statistics and programming data, this chapter examines the Polish film market during the years of 'High Stalinism'. We learn about the importance of cinema to Communist rule and the primacy of cultural links to the Soviet Union. For the authorities, filmgoing was an act of solidarity and ideological education. However, the shortage of new film releases in general and the small scale of the domestic film industry caused the authorities to import films from Western Europe, and these proved to be very popular with audiences. A POPSTAT analysis of Cracow and the proximate new industrial city of Nowa Huta shows familiar popularity, distribution and exhibition patterns. Some films popular with audiences are discussed.

A consequence of the vast destruction of physical capital in Poland during the Second World War was the small number of operational cinemas in the post-war years. According to the Bureau of War Reparations, Poland lost 38 per cent of its national assets during the conflict—massive compared to France (1.5 per cent) or Great Britain (0.8 per cent).[1] By the end of 1950, there were 1376 cinemas in operation.[2] This for a population of 25 million—some 10 million fewer than in 1939, attributable to murder (including 3 million Jews), death by other causes and changes in national boundaries.[3]

[1] Zamoyski (2017, p. 338).

[2] See Krzeczkowska (1969, pp. 305, 323).

[3] Applebaum (2013). See chapter "Introduction: 'Millions of People Every Day'—Cinema as Part of the Quotidian of Life" for a vivid description of the destruction of Eastern Europe during the war years.

J. Sedgwick (✉)
University of Lodz, Lodz, Poland

K. Klejsa
Oxford Brookes University, Oxford, UK
e-mail: konrad.klejsa@uni.lodz.pl

J. Sedgwick (ed.), *Towards a Comparative Economic History of Cinema, 1930–1970*, Frontiers in Economic History, https://doi.org/10.1007/978-3-031-05770-0_11

The years 1949–1954 in Poland witnessed creeping Sovietization. By the end of 1948, the Communist Party (called Polish United Workers' Party—Polska Zjednoczona Partia Robotnicza), entirely subordinate to its Soviet counterpart, attained absolute hegemony over the political sphere, bringing increased control and bureaucratic intervention in civil society. The state abolished both private and cooperative enterprises. Only individual peasant farms were allowed to operate (with the obligation of 'compulsory deliveries') since the prevalent opinion in the Party leadership was that Poland was not yet ready for the collectivisation in private agriculture. All economic decision-making was placed under central control; its symbol became the six-year plan, which focused on heavy industry. Trade unions were amalgamated into a single federation, subordinate to the state. At the same time, 'socialist competition' was introduced, splitting the working class into the aristocracy of udarniks (shock workers) and an impoverished majority. Those going on strike were denounced as class enemies. Forced labour camps were established in several regions.[4] The torture of political prisoners became routine, and terror unleashed against new targets, including the alleged enemy within the Party and the Catholic Church—one of the last forces independent of the state.[5] From 1949, when the Soviet Marshal Konstantin Rokosskowskii became Poland's minister of defence, the signs of direct Soviet intervention in Polish affairs became immediate and apparent.

Soviet influence embraced the cultural sphere as well. For example, in 1947, Soviet organisations exported 77,900 books to Poland. By 1950 this had grown to 1.3 million, and in 1952 to 2.3 million.[6] Until late 1947, Polish artists, scientists and intellectuals had enjoyed a relatively large margin of freedom, consuming newspapers, novels, films, and artworks from capitalist countries. In 1948 these freedoms started to recede and had vanished by the early 1950s. Culture was perceived as an ideological battlefront, and aesthetics that differed from the Soviet model of socialist realism were condemned as petty-bourgeois. As Patryk Babiracki maintains, the officials understood their mission to encompass three goals. The first was to secure maximum exposure to Soviet and Russian artistic and cultural production. The second was to ensure the explicit acknowledgement of the supremacy of Soviet culture. (Polish artists were expected to imitate the socialist realist method, while Polish communists were expected to praise and promote it). Finally, Soviet bureaucrats required Polish artists to sanction the new political context within works of art directed at the public. The outcome was a quasi-religious celebration of Stalin and the part paid by the agency of the Soviet Union in Poland's cultural transformation.[7]

In such circumstances, it is little wonder that the film industry in Poland took time to re-establish itself. In November 1945, the then provisional government,

[4] Kemp-Welch (2008, pp. 26-42).

[5] See Kersten (1999).

[6] Figures given in Babiracki (2015, p. 113).

[7] Babiracki (2015, p. 116).

already dominated by the communists, issued a decree nationalising all film industry sectors, bringing them under the canopy of a state organisation—Film Polski. After the accession to power of the Polish Communist Party in 1948, Film Polski was later (December 1951) restructured into the Central Office of Film (CUK—Centralny Urząd Kinematografii).[8] Under the auspices of the Ministry of Culture and the Arts, this monolith was charged with serving the ideological needs of the state.

Two categories of archive documents are called upon in this chapter. The first is correspondence between cinema institutions. The second category comprises minutes of high-ranking meetings. These documents shed light on the decision-making process, and sometimes they include information about the circulation of specific titles. For instance, in one of the minutes from late 1951, the members of the CUK Board name some pre-1950 films for which '...no audience mobilisation is needed, such as *The Unknown Singer* (1947), *The Red Stallion* (1947), *Ali Baba and the Forty Thieves* (1944) and *Lassie Come Home* (1943)'.[9] A year later, another minute signals a policy change: '...we have eliminated unnecessary films, so titles such as *The Red Stallion* and *The Unknown Singer* have been removed from our programme'.[10] The decision to withdraw 'unnecessary' films was not motivated economically but politically—they were removed from circulation despite their popularity.

In contrast to Western Europe, the diet of films presented to Poland audiences, as elsewhere in the Eastern Bloc, was confined mainly to a set of films made in the Soviet Union and other communist countries—films that, on average, were older and not replaced as quickly. Outside of this, only a relatively small number of selected films, mainly from Western Europe, were allowed to circulate.[11] Jerzy Lewiński, the head of one of the bureaus of Film Polski, put it bluntly during the meeting with the Minister of Culture and the Arts in 1950: 'At the moment, we should only show those foreign films that do not contain a clear hostile ideology (...) It seems to me that the most popular films are very harmful to us'.[12]

Consequently, the conception of film consumers in Poland differs from that in the West. In capitalist economies, audiences validate films put onto the market by either watching them or not. Profits are made by servicing public demand. In Poland, during the early years of communist rule, audiences were conceived not as agents of economic exchange but as subjects of cultural pedagogy. Under state socialism,

[8] The president of CUK was also a deputy Minister of Culture and the Arts. From 1948, Film Polski was led by Stanisław Albrecht, the brother of the secretary of the communist party's Central Committee, while film import policy was handled by Rita Radkiewicz, the wife of the Minister of Public Security. Before taking office, neither Albrecht nor Radkiewicz had anything to do with film culture.

[9] Board of Film Polski (1951a, 1951b, p. 40).

[10] Dytko (1952, p. 120).

[11] Dorota Ostrowska claims that Western films 'virtually disappeared during Poland's Stalinist period' (Ostrowska, 2017, p. 137)—which, as we will show, is not true. This mistake may have been caused by the fact that Ostrowska's chapter is based on the analysis of film reviews, and not cinema programming.

[12] Board of Film Polski (1950, p. 82).

as Dorota Ostrowska observes, '…cinema was envisioned as an essential sphere of cultural activity whose main function was didactic, meaning that while providing entertainment, the principal aim of cinema was to educate'.[13] In this spirit, Film Polski/CUK executives were not principally concerned with garnering audiences but rather ensuring they were offered a diet of films that balanced appropriate ideology and approved aesthetics with entertainment. Hence, rather than collect and analyse box-office returns, officials were tasked with demonstrating that the scope of film supply matched prevailing guidelines.

In such circumstances, where audiences are managed so assiduously, applying the POPSTAT method may appear irrelevant or inappropriate. Nevertheless, as will be shown for the city of Cracow from 1951 to 1953, the POPSTAT method yields a set of statistical outcomes indicating audiences formed preferences causing them to pay to watch one film but not another. The interpretation of POPSTAT results needs to be carefully balanced by countervailing evidence, particularly the pressure that all citizens were under to conform, including cinema employees and audiences. Reporting these results and interpreting them is the principal objective of this chapter.

1 Formal Structures

The main organisational features of the industry are depicted in Fig. 1, showing a hierarchy overseen by political and ideological agencies of the State.[14] Like Film Polski, the CUK commanded multiple separate enterprises, including the Film Rental Office (*Centrala Wynajmu Filmów*—CWF). Once a decision was made to purchase a film, CWF commissioned its copies and produced advertising materials, which subsequently were sent to District Offices (*Ekspozytury CWF*—ECWFs). While the ECWFs were entirely responsible for cinema programming in their respective areas, movie theatres were run by a separate entity within CUK.[15] These were known as District Boards of Cinema (*Okręgowe Zarządy Kin*—OZK), initially supervised by the Directorate of Cinemas (*Dyrekcja Kin*), later—in January 1952—renamed as Central Cinema Administration (*Centralny Zarząd Kin*—CZK).

While CZK was engaged with a massive nationwide plan of expanding the cinema chain, mainly in the countryside, OZKs were responsible for cinema infrastructure (properties and technical equipment) within a given territory, cinema employees and film tickets.

The Qualifying Committee (in June 1951 renamed Komisja Ocen Filmów—Commission for Film Assessment), comprising film critics and cultural bureaucrats,

[13] Ostrowska (2017, p. 139).

[14] In the Archive of Modern Records in Warsaw (Archiwum Akt Nowych) there is a huge collection of CUK files—circa 20,000 pages. Some of the folders are labelled 'Ordinances (of the particular year)'—these can contain more than 200 documents, some of them multi-page, totalling together to 300 to 400 pages.

[15] Until 1957, cinema managers were not involved at all in programme selection.

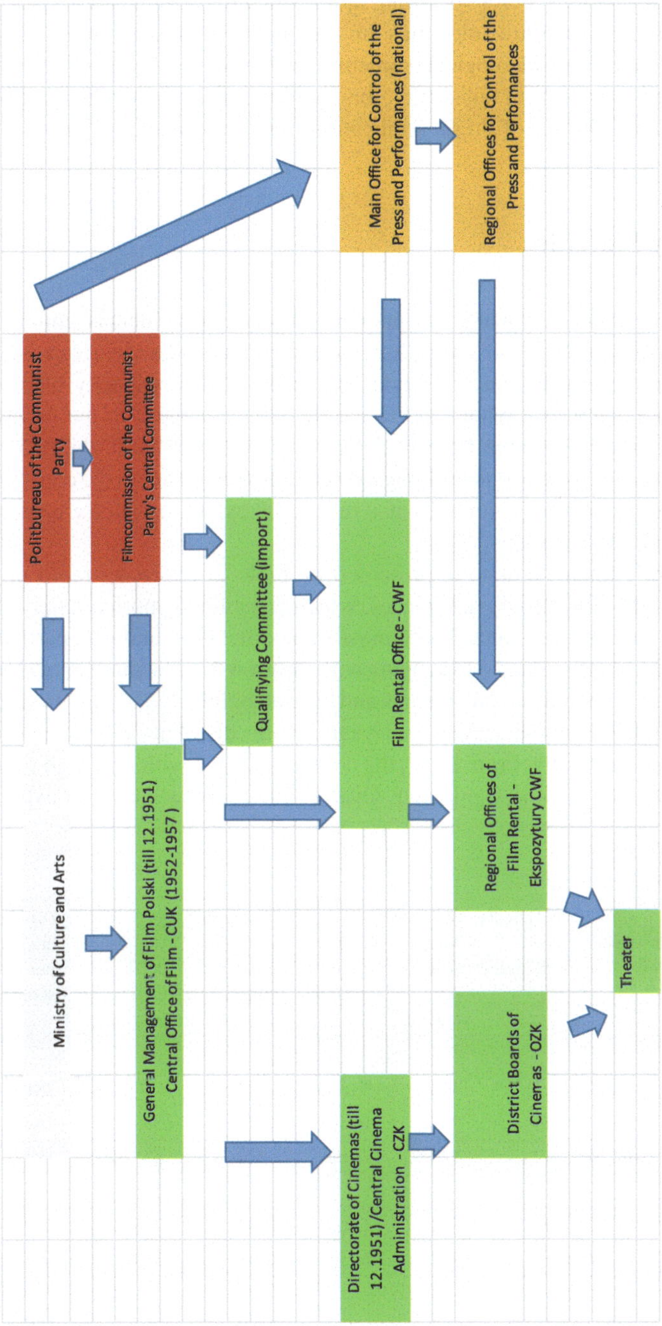

Fig. 1 Diagrammatic representation of the Authority Structure in Governing Polish Film Circulation in the early 1950s

watched imported films in closed screenings, usually with a dialogue sheet or even simultaneous translations, before deciding upon which to recommend for purchase. The minutes of the Committee meetings are lost, but it is known that the selection was guided by artistic and ideological (sometimes referred to as social) criteria. Even when a decision was made to buy a film, the distribution could be prevented by the Party or the General Office of Press, Publications and Performances Control.

2 Industry Statistics

As is evident in Table 1, Poland was poorly endowed with cinemas immediately after Second World War. From a very low base, cinemas and audiences rose, with the growth centring on the cities. The decline in the seating capacity of cinemas (column 4) for Poland as a whole, alongside the slight increase in the number of screenings per cinema (column 6), especially when contrasted with the two cities, suggests that much of the effort in building new cinemas took place in the countryside. Attendances per screening (column 8) also reflect the extent to which cinemagoing was an essential urban activity.

The industry's financial state is presented in Table 2, reflecting rapid growth. Taking 1950 as the benchmark, ticket sales, which constituted approximately 70 per cent of annual industry revenues, had almost trebled by 1956 and was particularly strong during the last three years. In keeping with the growth in the number of cinemas shown in Table 1, expenditure on cinemas and cinema building, and film production, more than doubled over the same seven years, while distribution costs and taxes paid also rose substantially. From 1952, the costs associated with imported films for this growing market became significant. Overall, the accounts show an expanding

Table 1 General cinema statistics

	(1) Permanent Cinemas	(2) Seats	(3) Seats per thousand	(4) Mean seats per cinema	(5) Number of screenings	(6) Mean screenings per cinema	(7) Attendances (000)	(8) Mean attendances per screening
Poland								
1945	409	170,130	7	416	130,856	320	36,718	281
1950	1376	340,380	14	247	516,141	375	123,165	239
1955	2672	462,862	17	173	998,939	374	183,162	183
Warsaw								
1950	10	8577	13	858	13,803	1380	7725	560
1955	26	13,306	13	512	27,755	1068	12,684	457
Cracow								
1950	8	5300	16	663	9500	1188	3762	396
1955	12	5900	14	492	14,000	1167	5600	400

Source: Krzeczkowska (1969, p. 270)

Table 2 The Financial Performance of the Polish Film Industry from 1946 to 1956 (all values in Zloty (zł), millions)[a]

	1946	1947	1948	1949	1950	1951	1952	1953	1954	1955	1956
Income											
Net Ticket Revenue	24.50	58.10	90.30	119.50	96.90	86.20	102.40	106.80	123.80	145.10	175.90
Film Fund[b]	x	x	x	x	91.50	178.00	217.20	224.70	257.10	303.10	359.90
Gross Ticket Revenue	24.5	58.1	90.3	119.5	188.4	264.2	319.6	331.5	380.9	448.2	535.8
Film Rental[c]	9.90	23.50	x	x	15.80	21.00	39.50	36.40	43.90	49.50	58.00
Film Production[d]	2.90	7.80	14.90	33.30	63.40	86.80	48.50	78.30	119.90	125.00	141.90
Total:	37.30	89.40	105.20	152.80	267.60	372.00	407.60	446.20	544.70	622.70	735.70
Costs[e]											
Cinema Costs	24.90	57.50	78.80	126.30	171.30	143.20	168.80	214.00	243.10	282.90	369.90
Tax	x	x	3.30	5.30	x	27.50	36.30	41.70	47.90	55.40	65.00
Distribution Costs[f]	6.20	14.80	x	x	13.30	67.60	54.40	57.60	72.50	83.80	120.10
Licence Fees of Imported Films	x	x	x	x	x	60.90	32.30	67.20	98.70	96.20	101.50

(continued)

Table 2 (continued)

	1946	1947	1948	1949	1950	1951	1952	1953	1954	1955	1956
Film Production[g]	3.20	5.00	14.70	32.60	58.10	57.20	43.00	72.30	103.70	119.20	138.40
Total:	34.30	77.30	96.80	164.20	242.70	366.40	334.80	452.80	565.90	637.50	794.90
Revenue minus Cost	3.00	12.10	8.40	11.40	24.90	5.60	72.80	6.60	21.20	14.80	59.20

Source: Basiński and Kupiec (1957, p. 64)
Notes: The figures in the table are derived from State-run enterprises. Outside this sector, a small number of theatres belonged to cooperative societies, large factories or the Soviet army. The symbol x indicates that the items of revenue or costs were not registered in the years in question
[a]These values are expressed in post-1949 values, after the devaluation of the Zloty in that year
[b]This was a special tax dedicated to supporting film production but also used for cinema refurbishment. In 1950 this constituted 50 per cent of the ticket price, rising in 1951 for the remaining years to 70 per cent
[c]Part of the income transferred to the Film Rental Office (also from not-state cinemas). From 1948 to 1949, Rental and Cinemas were managed within the same entity, called Central Board of Cinemas and Film Rental. Consequently, Film Rentals are included in the Net Ticket Revenue row
[d]Tickets revenue earned by Polish films at home and abroad
[e]It does not include the costs of the central bureaucracy
[f]Manufacture of copies and advertising/promotion materials
[g]Polish films (feature and documentary)

Table 3 National Origins of Films in Circulation, 1951–1955

Countries	1951	1952	1953	1954	1955	1956
Titles						
Poland	13	20	26	41	50	67
Soviet Union	214	231	253	348	311	209
People's Democracies	85	121	137	146	186	171
Capitalist Countries	42	45	34	55	88	133
Total	354	417	450	590	635	580
Copies						
Poland	693	1341	1764	2751	3145	3840
Soviet Union	4914	6114	7402	9605	9589	6993
People's Democracies	2020	3516	3312	5238	6904	5966
Capitalist Countries	426	627	1872	1752	2872	4562
Total	8053	11,598	14,350	19,346	22,510	21,361
Mean Copies per Film						
Poland	53.31	67.05	67.85	67.10	62.90	57.31
Soviet Union	22.96	26.47	29.26	27.60	30.83	33.46
People's Democracies	23.76	29.06	24.18	35.88	37.12	34.89
Capitalist Countries	10.14	13.93	55.06	31.85	32.64	34.30

Source Basiński and Kupiec (1957, p. 21)

industry broadly supporting itself, with revenues and costs rising in line with one another.

From 1950 to 1953, only 10 Polish feature films were released, with the bulk of movies seen by Polish audiences supplied by the Soviet Union and other People's Democracies behind the Iron Curtain.[16] Judged by the number of copies made, Table 3 shows that Polish films generally circulated widely. In contrast, the more plentiful supply of Soviet films required approximately half as many copies to fulfil circulation requirements. Unfortunately, the table does not distinguish between new releases and older films. As will become apparent later in the chapter, films of older vintages make up a considerable element in the overall supply, papering over the comparative scarcity of new film releases. This situation is reflected in the minutes of a CUK Board Meeting that took place in November 1952:

> We are seeing a shrinkage in our ability to import titles year by year. While until 1950 the most important group of films, namely that from the USSR, was supplemented with old titles, in 1951 and 1952 the number of these old films seriously decreased. These shortages cannot be covered by supplies from the People's Democracies. According to our data, China produces many films, but only a few titles receive export licenses. Also, the percentage of progressive

[16] Three of these films—*Zakazane piosenki*, *Skarb* and *Czarci żleb*—were screened as late as the 1960s.

> Western films is decreasing year by year. Finally, if some of these films are released here, Western distributors cause many difficulties for us regarding foreign exchange.[17]

The supply of foreign films was highly dependent on the political situation. Following an agreement concluded in April 1947 with the Motion Pictures Export Association (Hollywood's International Trade Department), films from capitalist countries were predominant among new titles entering distribution in early 1948. However, after a slowdown that began in mid-1949, the practice was halted in May 1950, from which time onwards, there was a complete ban on new American films, only partially lifted in 1954. In contrast, new films from Western Europe, principally from France and Italy, were increasingly allowed into Poland from 1953, reflected in Table 2 by the rise in import licence costs and Table 3 by the increased number of films in circulation.

Given that Film Polski/CUK was a monopolist supplier and importer, the availability of performance data of individual titles should not present a problem. However, the authorities did not publish statistics on the operational performance of specific foreign movies, being more concerned with establishing the extent to which targets had been met. Accordingly, their reports are built around the monitoring of averages and proportions—for instance: the average number of viewers for each average screening; the average number of screenings for each average cinema in a particular province; the share of screenings in a given region, as a proportion of the total number of screenings in Poland; the share of discounted tickets in a given province as a proportion of the total number of discounted tickets in Poland; the average number of viewers at closed screenings; the average number of viewers in the countryside, in cities and so on. Of the four categories of film listed in Table 3, film performance (measured by attendances) records for individual titles have only been found for the home country.

One of the most striking features of the films presented in Table 4 is the length of time films remained in circulation. Of the eight Polish movies released in 1947 (*Jasne łany* was withdrawn from the exhibition soon after its release), all were in continuous circulation during the seven years covered by the table and, after their first year in circulation, broadly maintained their popularity over the period. This is a surprising finding in that movies tend to decline sharply in popularity in a matter of months, as audiences are attracted to new films. In this respect, the performance of the first post-war feature film, *Zakazane Piosenki*, is extraordinary. Between 1947 and 1950, annual mean attendances average approximately 1.25 million per year. By 1951, these have fallen to half of that, after which they grow substantially during 1952 and 1953. The same pattern is observed with *Za Wami Pójdą Inni*, and *Stalowe Serca*. These unexpected results are likely to be the consequence of the expansion of the 16 mm cinema chain, especially in rural areas, attracting audiences that had little chance to watch the films earlier in their circulation history.

[17] Dytko (1952, p. 119).

Table 4 Polish Film Releases, 1947–1953

Film	1947–1950	1951	1952	1953	Total
Zakazane piosenki	6616.8	627.7	956.9	1029.4	9230.8
Skarb	4581.6	725.9	800.4	680.6	6788.5
Ostatni etap	4858.7	350.6	731.4	555.8	6496.5
Czarci żleb	4115.1	743.4	703.1	661.1	6222.7
Ulica Graniczna	4173.1	361.9	796.1	720.6	6051.7
Żołnierze zwycięstwa				3737.3	3737.3
Za wami pójdą inni	2385.8	231.7	421.0	425.5	3464.0
Miasto nieujarzmione		2235.6	637.1	487.1	3359.8
Warszawska premiera		2508.5	457.3	352.2	3318.0
Stalowe serca	2239.8	191.4	319.9	400.9	3152.0
Dom na pustkowiu	1782.8	392.0	474.8	456.1	3105.7
Pierwszy start		2189.3	493.3	415.0	3097.6
Załoga			2368.8	611.0	2979.8
Młodość Chopina			2182.1	492.4	2674.5
Sprawa do załatwienia				2119.3	2119.3
Pierwsze dni			1509.8	437.3	1947.1
Trzy opowieści				929.1	929.1
Gromada			644.2	226.2	870.4
Dwie brygady		313.6	115.3	157.1	586.0

Source Kulik (1957, p. 93)
Note Żołnierz zwycięstwa was issued in two parts in 1953. The attendance figure shown here is the aggregate value

3 Politics, Propaganda and Programming

In Poland, film executives were charged with fostering cinema as a vehicle to carry ideological messages. Here is how Mieczysław Dytko, the Director of CWF Centrala Wynajmu Filmów—the distribution arm of Film Polski/CUK—defined the goals facing the company:

> Centrala Wynajmu Filmów is an enterprise established to distribute highly ideological, socially and artistically valuable films which serve to develop the awareness of the Polish working masses and raise their cultural level – films which, while providing proper entertainment, will at the same time mobilise the nation to carry out the tasks set by the State and the Party to fight for peace and carry out the Six-Year Plan...By expanding cinema services, we strengthen and deepen the friendship of the Polish people with the Soviet Union and strengthen the unity of the world camp of the defenders of peace. With the help of films and cinema, let us strengthen people's power everywhere and at every turn, establishing trust in

> the Party and the Government in millions of viewers. With the use of cinemas, let us fight against the frauds, rumours and slanders of reactionary, imperialist propaganda, deepening the political consciousness of the broadest masses.[18]

There is no ambiguity in this message. Neither is there in an interview with Film Polski/CUF director Stanislaw Albrecht that appeared in the Polish magazine *Film* concerning his impressions of the Cannes Film Festival: 'There was a confrontation between two types of filmmaking. The art of declining capitalism—decadent, formalistic, and often even hostile to humanity—was opposed by the art of truth of life and humanism, the art of fighting for the peace and happiness of humanity. The latter was represented primarily by the cinematography of the Soviet Union and the People's Democracies'.[19] Sentiments manifested in the annual 'Festival' of Soviet Cinema (from late October to mid-November) when only Soviet films were shown at cinemas.[20]

Cinemas during the early 1950s were given a twofold task: to attract a target number of viewers and ensure that certain films received a specific number of screenings. These goals were often in conflict since cinema managers had to give certain privileged films more screenings than audiences were prepared to support. An official from the CUK sums up the dichotomy as follows:

> '…the political-program aspect creates contradictions between the distributor and the cinema manager… (when the) ideological and artistic maturity of a film and its attractiveness are concepts that do not coincide. …Thus, for example, it can be stated that the top, from the ideological and artistic point of view, achievements of Soviet cinematography, such as *The Great Citizen*, *Lenin in October*, and *The Man with the Gun,* achieved insignificant results in terms of viewers, compared to many films of little value, or even worthless ones, such as the Hungarian production *Flames*, the Czech *Mr Habětín Is Leaving*, or Western films, such as the Austrian *Verlorene Melodie*. The simple fact is that in all such cases, the local management, on whom the burden of managing audiences falls, strives to limit the screening of productions that threaten the execution of plans.'[21]

Due to the import policy, almost all new films from the People's Democracies were accepted, while few were from Western countries. In late 1952, the CWF director reported: 'This year, we evaluated 113 films, rejecting 27 and accepting 86; the rejected films accounted for 24 per cent of the total, with 23.5 per cent of these originating from the People's Democracies and 53.5 per cent from Western countries'.[22] (It is worth noting how statistical jargon hid the exact numbers. The remainder of the films rejected were likely produced in the Soviet Union).[23] The movies from capitalist countries were subject to a high level of scrutiny, as CWF administrators were

[18] Film Rental Office (1951, p. 68).

[19] Albrecht (1951, p. 5).

[20] Other public holidays—International Worker's Day (1 May), and the National Day of Rebirth of Poland (July 22)—had less stringent restrictions but required that any publicity relating to films from the West were removed from cinema waiting rooms and showcases.

[21] Albrecht (1954, pp. 27–28).

[22] Dytko (1952, p. 120).

[23] Most likely, the plots of these rejected films might have had something to do with the Ukraine. Given the partitioning of Poland under the German-Soviet Pact of 1939, resulting in the incorporation

Table 5 Earnings of Foreign Films (millions of zlotys)

	1951	1952	1953	1954	1955	1956
People's Democracies						
Bulgaria	1933	3850	5439	2691	987	2428
China	x	3688	3302	5587	6155	2442
Czechoslovakia	31,376	27,748	37,240	29,176	33,213	32,061
North Korea	x	x	931	205	1017	1641
GDR	17,409	24,300	16,582	11,402	20,925	27,946
Roumania	1393	856	3845	1328	1229	5211
Hungary	9849	12,750	17,654	11,535	15,350	30,648
USSR	102,718	107,164	139,906	154,252	143,106	125,441
Total	164,678	180,356	224,899	216,176	221,982	227,818
Selected Capitalist Countries						
Great Britiain	10,764	6450	323	7676	20,465	31,750
France	23,501	32,129	29,543	35,243	62,126	106,934
Italian	4366	14,538	20,013	23,678	28,561	31,581
Total	39,352	58,054	54,380	84,294	134,539	244,095
Total (all countries)	204,030	238,410	279,279	300,470	356,521	471,913

Source Basiński and Kupiec (1957, p. 25)

obliged to report to the Party's Film Commission which films from the West were in circulation—and why. This kind of establishment-type thinking can be learned from an internal report on British films in which the author summarises the plot of the *Scott of the Antarctic*:

> A story of the failed expedition of the Englishmen Scott in 1908. The rich and influential part of English society does not agree to finance the expedition, because they do not see any material profit in it. There is no tendency to exploit the story for the advantage of Great Britain; therefore, the film may be released. We own only three copies.[24]

The aggregate earnings of foreign films are presented in Table 5. Given their relative ubiquity and privileged status, movies from the Soviet Union, many of which dated back to the 1930s, secured the largest market share.[25] A sense of this privilege can be had from a circular of May 1951 that obliged local authorities to '...arrange the

of formerly Polish land (including the city of Lviv, for centuries one of the most vibrant centres of Polish culture) into the Ukrainian Republic of USSR, this constituted a delicate subject. The Soviet biopic *Chmielnicki* (1941), about a rebel political leader of the XVII century, is an example of such a film: this title is mentioned several times in the minutes of the meetings of the Film Polski officials as a movie which is inappropriate for Polish viewers—in Polish history textbooks printed before 1939, Chmielnicki was considered a traitor, whereas in the Marxist-Leninist view of history he was praised as a hero of class struggle).

[24] Radkiewicz (1950, pp. 47–48).

[25] The annual Soviet Film Festival that ran from mid-October to mid-November films. A further illustration of the favour shown the USSR is the attention given by the state-controlled monopoly that

programme of cinemas in cities with more than two cinemas in such a way that at least one screens a Soviet film'.[26] While the number of Soviet films in circulation increased up to 1955 (Table 3), declining dramatically in 1956, their share of import revenue fell steadily to 40 per cent by 1955—falling even further to just over a quarter in 1956. Similarly, during these years, the market share of the films from the People's Republics (including the Soviet Union) declined from 80 to just under 50 per cent.[27]

In contrast, films from the West contributed only five per cent of copies and eight per cent of titles in circulation (Table 3) yet generated 20 per cent of all foreign film revenues, leading the CWF director to report in 1952: '…a paradoxical situation has arisen in that only films of a high artistic form, and interesting subject materials, are accepted (by the Qualifying Committee), confusing some viewers, who might judge the entirety of Western production based on these few selected films'.[28] This hard-line policy was relaxed during the post-Stalin 'Thaw', causing a shift within programming policy. In 1956, the share of film revenues generated by the films from the West (France in particular) rose to just over 50 per cent (Table 5). Given the expansion of the market (Table 2), this statistic suggests a change in audience preferences.

4 Cracow, 1951–1953

Judged by the extent to which the Authorities intervened in the film market during the years of 'High Stalinism', it is easy to question the validity of official statistics.[29] Indeed, caution must be exercised in interpreting the dominant position of Soviet films found in official publications. Above all, they tell us little about how the market worked. What films were popular with audiences? What diffusion mechanisms allowed audience preferences to be met? In the micro-study of filmgoing in the Polish university city of Cracow that follows, a cross-sectional investigation of film distribution and circulation patterns during the three years 1951–53 is conducted. It is based on the programming records of the eight cinemas that serviced the population of Cracow (estimated population of 343,638 in 1950) and listed in the local

determined the décor of cinemas on anniversaries of events associated with communism. Examples are the 27th anniversary of Lenin's death celebrated on 19–23 January 1951, and the 33rd anniversary of the founding of the Soviet Army between 19 and 24 February 1951, during which promotional materials not related to Soviet films could not be displayed in cinemas. In bureaucratic language, these initiatives were referred to as 'special events'. An annual report reads: 'During 1952, we held 29 special events in our area, representing 32.6 per cent of all viewers attracted in 1952; screenings connected with special events represent 27.0 per cent of all screenings in 1952'. Central Office of Film (1953, p. 67).

[26] Film Rental Office (1951, p. 77).

[27] 1956 proved to be the apex of the post-Stalinist thaw.

[28] Dytko (1952, p. 121).

[29] Zajiček (1983, pp. 117–118).

Table 6 Cracow Cinemas, 1951–1953

Cinema	(1) Category	(2) Seats	(3) Prices (zl)	(4) Concessionary Prices (zl)	(5) Mid-Price (zl)	(6) Revenue Potential (zl)	(7) Cinema Weight
Uciecha	1	1100	4.5	2.3	3.4	3713	1.92
Wanda	1	800	4.5	2.3	3.4	2700	1.40
Warszawa	1	725	4.5	2.3	3.4	2447	1.27
Apollo	2	750	3.6	1.8	2.7	2025	1.05
Wolność	2	645	3.6	1.8	2.7	1742	0.90
Sztuka	2	480	3.6	1.8	2.7	1296	0.67
Młoda Gwardia	3	480	2.7	1.4	2.0	972	0.50
Chemik	3	270	2.7	1.4	2.0	547	0.28

Sources Price information comes from the Board of Film Polski (1950, p. 39). Data confirmed by the collection of cinema tickets in possession of Museum of Film Culture in Łodź

No official data on the number of seats in Cracow cinemas for the period in question has been found. The seating information comes from three sources: (1) an industry calendar from 1938 (Rotsztat-Miastecki, 1938); (2) information on theatre buildings from 1954 (District Board of Cinema in Cracow, 1954, pp. 1–3). If there was no account in the 1954 records, we chose the numbers from 1938. Finally, we cross-checked the numbers with the statistical yearbook (Krzeczkowska, 1969), which included the total number of seats for Cracow in 1955

Note The Młoda Gwardia cinema was formerly known as the Gdańsk; the Uciecha was closed for renovation between December 1951 and February 1952; the Apollo cinema was closed for renovation in September and October 1953. The table does not include Nowa Huta cinemas

daily newspaper *Dziennik Polski* for three years.[30] This study is supplemented by the partial programming records of the adjoining new model industrial settlement of Nowa Huta, whose construction started in 1949, and centred around the massive Lenin steelworks. Inhabited primarily by peasants migrating from other parts of Poland searching for work and accommodation, Nowa Huta officially became a part of Cracow in 1951.

Cracow is, of course, just a single city with a small population of cinemas—reflecting the scarcity of film entertainment in Poland at the time (see Table 1). However, in terms of its social composition and cultural eminence, it was not typical of urban life in Poland at the time. Accordingly, we cannot claim that our findings are representative of the nation. Nevertheless, they provide a different kind of evidence to that of the official statistics published by the Film Industry, evidence which throws light on choice sets encountered by filmgoers and, through their circulation history, the films most preferred by audiences in Cracow.

The cinemas and their characteristics are listed in Table 6. Following the procedure established in the chapter "Managing Risk", cinema weights are calculated, reflecting

[30] By 1955, the population had risen to 428,231, including the rapidly expanding industrial district of Nowa Huta.

Table 7 Descriptive Statistics of POPSTAT, Cracow 1951–1953

Statistic	POPSTAT Index Value
Mean	50.63
Standard error	2.62
Median	31.07
Mode	8.78
Standard deviation	58.74
Coefficient of variation	1.16
Sample variance	3450
Kurtosis	8.51
Skewness	2.42
Range	452.15
Minimum	0.27
Maximum	452.42
Sum	25,517
Count	504

Source Dataset

the respective earnings potential of individual cinemas relative to the mean earning potential of all cinemas in the population.[31] Unlike many programming investigations in Western Europe, cinema admission price information is available. What proved to be more challenging to establish was the seating capacity of the cinemas—see the footnote to Table 6.

Officially, cinemas were classified in one of three groupings, which in Table 6 reflect the relative earning capacities and weights of the eight cinemas in the dataset. Thus, for example, the earning power of the Wanda cinema (category 1) was over four times greater than that of the Chemik (category 3). By applying these weights to each *ith* film appearing at each *jth* cinema, a POPSTAT Index value is obtained for films screened at least once in Cracow during the three years.[32]

The summary statistics of the POPSTAT series are listed in Table 7. Between 1951 and 1953, 504 feature-length films were screened in Cracow, including documentaries and animations.[33] The statistics that emerge from the population of films display a familiar pattern, comprising a long right tail distribution, in which the median film falls into the first decile band and is nearly 15 times smaller than the most popular film. Thus, in relation to the median film, the most popular movies

[31] See Sedgwick (2000, 2020).

[32] For the POPSTAT method, see the earlier Chapter "Managing Risk in the Film Business". A measure of veracity of the POPSTAT Index for Cracow is given by the correlation between those Polish films for which we have attendance figures (Table 4) that were circulating between 1951-3, and their Cracow POPSTAT Index values. Coefficient values of 0.76 (POPSTAT) and 0.77 (screenings) were obtained.

[33] A few films were screened in two parts. However, the newspaper listings rarely indicated which part was being screened. For this reason, all two-part films are treated singularly.

are extraordinary and suggest a distribution pattern like the West, even given the exhortations, restrictions and controls that characterised film distribution. Indeed, Table 8 shows that all Top 20 films opened at one of the three 'category 1' cinemas, the Uciecha, Wanda and Warszawa, indicating a clear cinema hierarchy in which the most successful films are premiered in the most expensive cinemas.

Among Cracow audiences, the POPSTAT rankings presented in Table 8 show how popular films from Western Europe were—particularly those made in France and Italy, countries with strongly supported Communist Parties. These films occupy 11 of the Top 20 berths, with the 1933 production of *Les Misérables* positioned as the top film—an extraordinary occurrence, given the film's vintage.[34] Presumably, the Authorities allowed the film a licence because of its subject material—the revolutionary challenge to an established order.

The inclusion in the listing of *In nome della legge* and *Non c'è pace tra gli ulivi* suggests that the resemblance between Italian neorealist cinema and Soviet socialist realism was appreciated by both the Authorities and the filmgoing public.[35] However, the audience preferred another Italian film, *Wilhelm Tell*—a costume drama rarely mentioned in film history books. Another curiosity is the American film *Red Stallion*, ranked just outside the Top 20. One of only seven vintage American films in circulation,[36] and certainly not a 'hit' film during the year of its release in the U.S. (1947). Made by the minor studio Ben Stoloff Productions, *The Red Stallion* failed to make Variety's long 'Top Grossing' list published annually.[37]

For the most part, screening days correspond strongly with the rank order of films, apart from the Soviet movie *Smełyje lyudi*, which was screened for 43 of its 85 screening days in the two' category 3' cinemas—the Chemik and Młoda Gwardia. Given the small number of extant cinemas, the actual number of screening days accumulated by films in the Top 20 list is surprisingly high. All popular movies received intensive (almost saturation) bookings in Cracow over the years following their release. Undoubtedly, the principal reason for this was the shortage of supply. Not enough films were being made in Poland or by fellow People's Republics, compared to the number of films in circulation in Western Europe. Most films in Table 8 are of recent vintage, but further down the popularity charts comes increasing evidence of movies that are five or more years old. Altogether, of over 8000 daily screenings over

---

[34] An internal document shows that films from the West that critiqued the ruling elites were particularly favoured. For instance, British films awarded an import licence included *Fame is the Spur*, *Great Expectations*, *Hamlet*, *Henry V*, *Nicolas Nickleby*, and *Scott of the Antarctic*. The only British-made film with a contemporary subject was *Give Us this Day*, directed by the Hollywood blacklisted Edward Dmytryk, who along with Edward G. Robinson (*Dr Ehrlich's Magic Bullet*) and Paul Muni (*Life of Emil Zola*) were esteemed by virtue of their blacklisting by HUAC. (Radkiewicz, 1950, pp. 47–48).

[35] Klejsa and Miller-Klejsa (2021).

[36] The other US films in circulation were: *Dr Ehrlich's Magic Bullet* (1940); *Gulliver's Travels* (1939); *Lassie Come Home* (1943); *The Life of Emile Zola* (1937); *Madame Curie* (1943) and *Of Mice and Men* (1939).

[37] Sedgwick (2002) uses the *Variety* listings to build up a picture of the changing nature of film popularity in the United States between 1946 and 65. In 1947, 75 films were listed as Top Grossers. *Red Stallion* was not among them.

Table 8 Top 20 Films Screened in Cracow, 1951 to 1953

Rank	(1) Polish Film Title	(2) Original Film Title	(3) Country of Origin	(4) Year of Production	(5) Date of First Screening in Cracow	(6) Opening Cinema	(7) Screening Days	(8) POPSTAT
1	Nędznicy	Misérables, Les	France	1933	5/5/1952	Warszawa	109	452.42
2	Fanfan Tulipan	Fanfan la Tulipe	France/Italy	1951	1/1/1953	Wanda	88	388.08
3	Wilhelm Tell	Guglielmo Tell	Italy	1949	8/19/1952	Wanda	78	310.09
4	Żołnierze zwycięstwa	Żołnierz zwycięstwa	Poland	1953	5/13/1953	Warszawa	91	299.22
5	Zagubione melodie	Verlorene Melodie	Austria	1952	7/16/1953	Warszawa	67	291.68
6	Ditta	Ditte menneskebarn	Denmark	1946	9/3/1952	Uciecha	56	266.32
7	Cesarski piekarz	Císařův pekař—Pekařův císař	Czechoslovakia	1951	4/11/1953	Uciecha	59	257.35
8	Sprawa do załatwienia	Sprawa do załatwienia	Poland	1953	9/5/1953	Warszawa	54	242.66
9	Pod niebem Sycylii	In nome della legge	Italy	1949	7/14/1952	Uciecha	60	225.85
10	Warszawska premiera	Warszawska premiera	Poland	1950	3/6/1951	Wanda	64	222.63
11	Wesołe kumoszki z Windsoru	Lustigen Weiber von Windsor, Die	GDR	1950	7/11/1951	Uciecha	62	220.03
12	Nie ma pokoju pod oliwkami	Non c'è pace tra gli ulivi	Italy	1949	2/2/1953	Uciecha	49	214.44
13	Śmiali ludzie	Smiełyje ludi	USSR	1950	1/1/1951	Uciecha	85	212.61
14	Upadek Berlina	Padienije Berlina	USSR	1949	1/10/1951	Wanda	73	208.33

(continued)

Table 8 (continued)

Rank	(1) Polish Film Title	(2) Original Film Title	(3) Country of Origin	(4) Year of Production	(5) Date of First Screening in Cracow	(6) Opening Cinema	(7) Screening Days	(8) POPSTAT
15	Skandal w Clochemerle	Clochermerle	France	1947	12/14/1951	Warszawa	61	203.63
16	Dumna królewna	Pyšná princezna	Czechoslovakia	1952	6/3/1953	Wanda	71	198.81
17	Zabawna historia	Félicie Nanteuil/Histoire comique	France	1942	6/6/1951	Uciecha	54	198.72
18	Cywil na stadionie	Civil a pályán	Hungary	1951	10/22/1952	Uciecha	48	198.58
19	Bez adresu	Sans laisser d'adresse	France	1950	3/10/1952	Warszawa	53	192.70
20	Jednodniowi milionerzy	Millionnaires d'un jour	France	1949	2/8/1952	Warszawa	62	191.46

Source Dataset
Note The films *Nędznicy* (*Les Misérables*), *Żołnierz zwycięstwa* and *Upadek Berlina* (*Padienije Berlina*) were screened in two parts but treated in this table as a single film

the three years, 81 per cent of these are attributable to films produced within three years of screening, with the remainder drawn from the immediate post and pre-war years.

The official statistics reporting import penetration in the Polish market (Table 3) corroborate the POPSTAT-derived evidence produced in Table 9. Eastern Bloc countries dominate supply, particularly the Soviet Union, with 207 films in circulation in Cracow between 1951 and 53, seven of which were joint national productions—over three times the number supplied by Czechoslovakia, the next largest national supplier. However, irrespective of the hopes of the establishment that Soviet films would be well received, Table 9 shows that these films, on average, were screened much less frequently than those admitted from Western Europe. The market share of demand (column 5) to supply (column 6)—the Garncarz Utilization Index—for Soviet films was well below one.[38] Compared with the values for France and Italy, Soviet films appear relatively unpopular with Cracow audiences.[39]

In contrast, the films of France and Italy record Garncarz Index values well above one. These films are much less common and, in a university city, perhaps had more of an exotic or learned appeal. When taken in conjunction with the Top 20 listing in Table 8, the popular appeal of certain films from these national origins is inescapable.

A factor in this account is the vintage of Soviet films. Claire Knight draws attention to Stalin's 'masterpiece policy' that emerged during the last years of the dictator's life, which took an industry already struggling for resources in the immediate post-war era into an existential fight for survival. In the quest for 'masterpieces', Soviet production halved between 1948 and 1949, as senior personnel in government and industry competed to absolve themselves from approving projects that might not be of 'masterpiece' calibre.[40] From 1945 the annual count of new releases was 24, 18, 24, 22 (in 1948), 12, 13, 9, 10 (in 1952). This mattered in Poland because the shortfall in new productions could only be made up by an increasing reliance on films of vintage—films already consumed previously by many of the cinemagoing public or imports from elsewhere. Films from the West benefited in comparison because, among other attributes, they had novelty value.

5 Nowa Huta

On the eastern margins of Cracow, the first buildings in Nowa Huta were erected in 1949. It was intended as a model industrial community centred around the vast Lenin steelworks, which began operations in 1954. In State-sponsored propaganda, Nowa

[38] For an explanation of the Utilisation Index see chapter "'It Seems to Me that the Most Popular Films in the West Are Very Harmful to Us': Film Popularity in Poland During the years of 'High Stalinisation". Also see Garncarz (2021, pp. 77–82).

[39] Part of this is connected to the relative ubiquity of Soviet cinema—the larger the share of supply, the greater the tendency towards an Index value of one.

[40] Knight (2018, pp. 704–30).

Table 9 National Characteristics of Cracow's Film Popularity Listings, 1951–1953

Country of Origin	(1) Films in circulation	(2) Screening Days	(3) Screening Days per Film	(4) Aggegate POPSTAT Index Score	(5) Market Share Demand (POPSTAT) (per cent)	(6) Market Share Supply (Screenings) (per cent)	(7) Garncarz's Utility Index
Argentina	1	19	19	68.55	0.27	0.22	1.24
Austria	2	85	43	375.11	1.47	0.97	1.52
Bułgaria	6	110	18	382.43	1.50	1.25	1.20
China	8	62	8	163.23	0.64	0.70	0.91
Czechoslovakia	65	1212	19	3288.65	12.89	13.77	0.94
Denmark	3	84	28	317.40	1.24	0.95	1.30
Finland	2	61	31	175.46	0.69	0.69	0.99
France	28	752	27	2604.01	10.21	8.54	1.19
France/Italy	3	175	58	653.13	2.56	1.99	1.29
GB	7	212	30	730.97	2.86	2.41	1.19
GDR	29	610	21	2016.38	7.90	6.93	1.14
Netherlands	1	28	28	109.53	0.43	0.32	1.35
Hungary	29	472	16	1478.02	5.79	5.36	1.08
India	1	13	13	25.38	0.10	0.15	0.67
Italy	13	424	33	1584.25	6.21	4.82	1.29
North Korea	1	17	17	41.41	0.16	0.19	0.84
Poland	34	734	22	2149.34	8.42	8.34	1.01
Romania	5	75	15	181.14	0.71	0.85	0.83
USA	7	117	17	384.45	1.51	1.33	1.13

(continued)

Table 9 (continued)

Country of Origin	(1) Films in circulation	(2) Screening Days	(3) Screening Days per Film	(4) Aggegate POPSTAT Index Score	(5) Market Share Demand (POPSTAT) (per cent)	(6) Market Share Supply (Screenings) (per cent)	(7) Garncarz's Utility Index
USSR	200	3140	16	7772.10	30.46	35.67	0.85
USSR/China	2	8	4	16.34	0.06	0.09	0.70
USSR/Czechoslovakia	1	1	1	3.68	0.01	0.01	1.27
USSR/GDR	2	10	5	30.12	0.12	0.11	1.04
USSR/Hungary	2	36	18	50.47	0.20	0.41	0.48
Not identified	52	345	7	915.45	3.59	3.92	0.92
Total	504	8802		25,517.00	100	100	

Source Dataset
Note There is a discrepancy with Table 3. The former comprises feature films only, whereas some Polish and People's Republics mid-length documentaries and animations (approximately 45 min in length) are included in the Cracow dataset

Huta was portrayed as a pedagogical project—both practical (as a giant vocational school offering training for all young people looking for work) and, more abstractly, as a site of personal formation and transformation.[41] Little wonder that cinema was given a significant role in that process.

During this investigation, the 304-seater Nowa Huta (changing its name to Stal in April 1953) was in continuous operation. Between April and October 1951, daily screenings also took place in a worker's hostel known as the Robotnik. In early 1953, three new cinemas opened—the Swit (April 1953), Zryw (May 1953) and Związkowiec (October 1953). While information about the number of daily screenings—also found in the *Dziennik Polski*—is available, it has not proved possible to discover the seating capacities of these cinemas. With such a patchwork of information, it is difficult to conduct a convincing account of film popularity in the suburb using the POPSTAT method. Consequently, comparisons with the circulation of films in Cracow are limited to screenings from the five cinemas, necessarily giving greater weight to the movies screened in 1953 relative to 1951 and 1952.

Table 10 lists the 20 films most circulated in Nowa Huta. While the sample needs to be handled carefully, the table differs from the Cracow listing in Table 8 (column 7) on three accounts. The first is technical. Table 10 is measured in screenings, whereas Table 8 is in screening days. The second is the absence of Western European titles from the Nowa Huta list, except for *Les Misérables.* Accordingly, *Fanfan la Tulipe*, rated second in Cracow, received only 25 screenings over ten days in three cinemas in Nowa Huta, while *Guglielmo Tell* and *Verlorene Melodie* were screened on just nine occasions over three days in a single cinema. The much greater presence in the listing of films from Eastern Bloc countries is the third, especially those of Polish and Soviet origin. These films tended to be older than the most popular films shown in Cracow. The outstandingly successful film in Nowa Huta was the biopic *Żołnierz zwycięstwa*, securing almost twice the number of screenings as second-ranked *Les Misérables.*[42]

Because audiences were served by just one cinema for much of the period, what can be said about film popularity is limited. Coupled with the quota requirements of Soviet films, any inferences drawn from the screening data should be tentative and corroborated by archival evidence. Although a positive correlation coefficient of 0.65 can be established between the screenings of Nowa Huta's Top 20 films in Cracow, this falls to 0.4 for the Top 100, demonstrating a weak association between the two. Among the Top 20 films, several outliers are apparent—the Russian film *Lubow Jarowaja* and Polish film *Dwie brygady* are movies that circulated widely in Nowa Huta in 1953 but much less so in Cracow.

It is not clear what can be made of this difference. For instance, *Dwie brygady* is a typical socialist realist 'produkcyjniak' narrative about the factory workers. Suppose we accept without reservation the premise that screenings and popularity are correlated. In that case, the data in Table 10 suggests that audiences in Nowa Huta appreciated the film much more than those in Cracow. This indicates that

[41] Lebow (2013, p. 54).

[42] Kulik (1957, pp. 92–93).

Table 10 The 20 most frequently screened films in Nowa Huta

(1) Rank	(2) Polish Title	(3) Original Title if not Polish	(4) Country of origin	(5) Year of Production	(6) Year first screened in Poland	(7) Screenings in Nowa Huta	(8) Screenings in Cracow
1	Żołnierz zwycięstwa		Poland	1953	1953	87	263
2	Nędznicy	Misérables, Les	France	1933	1934	46	320
3	Orzeł Kaukazu	Gieorgij Saakadze/Giorgi Saakadze	USSR	1943	1950	43	74
4	Trzy opowieści		Poland	1953	1953	42	74
5	Bitwa Stalingradzka	Stalingradskaja bitwa I-II	USSR	1948	1949	40	58
6	Lubow Jarowaja	Lubow Jarowaja	USSR	1953	1953	36	15
7	Upadek Berlina	Padienije Berlina	USSR	1949	1950	36	217
8	Pierwsze dni		Poland	1951	1952	35	102
9	Przełom	Razłom	USSR	1952	1953	34	58
10	Biały kieł	Biełyj Kłyk	USSR	1946	1947	32	90
11	Skarb		Poland	1948	1949	32	96
12	Niezapomniany rok 1919	Niezabywajemyj 1919 god	USSR	1951	1952	31	75
13	Krążownik Wareg	Krejser "Wariag"	USSR	1946	1947	30	33

(continued)

Table 10 (continued)

(1) Rank	(2) Polish Title	(3) Original Title if not Polish	(4) Country of origin	(5) Year of Production	(6) Year first screened in Poland	(7) Screenings in Nowa Huta	(8) Screenings in Cracow
14	Maksymek	Maksimka/Maksimko	USSR	1952	1953	30	42
15	Ulica Graniczna		Poland	1948	1949	29	63
16	Antoni Iwanowicz gniewa się	Anton Iwanowicz sierditsia	USSR	1941	1945	27	61
17	Czekaj na mnie	Żdi mienia	USSR	1943	1946	27	84
18	Dwie brygady		Poland	1950	1950	27	4
19	Mongolia w ogniu	Jego zowut Suche-Bator	USSR	1942	1951	27	59
20	Pomysłowy sprzedawca	Állami áruház	Hungary	1952	1953	27	105

Source Dataset

Note Żołnierz zwycięstwa, Nedznicy, Upadek Berlina, Orzel Kaukazu were released in two parts. When listed in the newspaper, these parts were not identified; accordingly, they are treated in this table and subsequent analysis as a single film, which of course, they were

audiences associate with movies that depict aspects of their lives. However, caution is required. Implicit in the POPSTAT method is the concept that consumers have choice sets—hardly the case in Nowa Huta for much of the period.

Furthermore, it must be reiterated that cinema managers could not select films they thought local audiences might enjoy. Instead, they were entirely dependent on the Film Rental Office. Since Nowa Huta was an ideologically driven project, it is reasonable to think that cinema programming was shaped in a similarly ideological manner—that an industrial working-class audience was keen to watch films about their social class and workplace experience. Finally, we may also consider the film text itself—*Dwie brygady*, like any other *produkcyjniaks*, shows a romantic view of working-class life, at odds with the harsh realities of actual labour.

6 Discussion—Some Examples

A possible explanation for the presence of some films in the Top 20 listing is that they were forced on the public artificially, leading them to be screened in largely empty auditoria, as audiences stayed away. An example of this practice was the fourth-ranking Polish film *Żołnierz Zwycięstwa*, a biopic screened in two parts about a wartime Polish general and communist martyr set against the background of the history of the communist movement. It was 'One of the Most Important Movies of the Year'. According to official statistics, the film was dominant among Polish films in circulation in 1953 (Table 4).[43] However, archival evidence exists (for internal use of CUK) that audiences hated it, partly explained by it including sequences in which the characters of Lenin and Stalin spoke in Russian without translation. The same document reports that between 50 and 90 per cent of seats were occupied.[44] The apparent paradox is resolved by the likelihood that workers, billeted soldiers and schoolchildren were given time and free tickets to attend a film screening. In this way, the favoured film could show appropriate attendance statistics and meet administrative targets.

However, not all films carried the same ideological baggage as *Żołnierz Zwycięstwa*. While not underestimating the part played by the cinema authorities in promoting selected movies, the bulk of films in distribution did not receive this level of 'official' attention. (If this were the norm, filmgoing would have been an act of coercion). Instead, while those foreign films that dominated Cracow's cinemas' attendance were carefully selected not to cause ideological offence, their popularity was determined by audiences, who went to see them because they both could and wanted to.

One of the most successful foreign films—*Verlorene Melodie*—illustrates the complex cultural meanings associated with films during these years among different

[43] Confusingly, the newspaper listings make it impossible to distinguish between the two parts for POPSTAT purposes. In Table 8 *Żołnierz Zwycięstwa* is presented as a single film, as are all films.

[44] Main Office for Control of Press (1953, pp. 272–273).

societal groups. Released in Poland in 1953, the film plot centres on a young composer who dreams of following the famous Viennese composers of classical music but is compelled to work in a bar/nightclub as a jazz pianist (indeed, in one of the scenes, the ghost of the late Johann Strauss appears as if to taunt him). The condemnation of jazz plays a crucial role in understanding the film's reception in Poland since antipathy to jazz was a vital element in Stalinist cultural propaganda. It was treated as a symbol of 'rotten imperialism' and banned from the radio.[45]

Yet the film's success, far from exonerating the CUP, can be perversely explained, at least partly, by the fact that it was a rare opportunity for Polish audiences to listen to jazz, albeit in snatches. It can be conjectured that *Verlorene Melodie* attracted audiences who either liked or were at least interested in listening to jazz—a sort of 'negotiated reading' pleasure is taken in meanings opposite to those intended. Premiered in Poland in July 1953, a few months after Stalin's death in March, when hopes for a more normal life began to emerge, it is worth quoting extensively from a film review in the 'Film' magazine. Its author was:

> ...a bit embarrassed when after its premiere in Warsaw's Moscow cinema, the audience applauded... Director Edward von Borsody has set himself a much bigger task. Contrary to appearances, it is not the sympathetic pair of characters - Greta and Franz - that the director is most interested in. He does not care about Greta and Franz at all. Let them love each other, let them ten times tremble for their happiness and regain each other. The protagonists' adventures are a pretext to tackle much more important issues in the film, to show the conflict resulting from the clash of two worlds of cultural ideas. Using the counterpoint method, the director juxtaposes light Viennese music, originating from the rich Straussian tradition, with atonal jazz music imported from the USA, along with chewing gum, neckties and hatred for creative freedom.
>
> A satire on musical barbarism? That's the apparent front in the battle. Yes, but director von Borsody explains the deeper meaning of the struggle. It is not just about an abstract dispute over melody. After all, we know the mobilising power of music. Melodies can be dangerous to social orders when they express people's feelings. Let us just mention the 'La Marseillaise'. American' culture', by confusing people with jazz, plays a specific preventive, anti-humanistic role. The tendency is clear: with American barbarism, it is necessary to fight everywhere, and so also in light music. And so, the colourful musical comedy, to a certain extent, takes on the characteristics of a militant film.[46]

Another explanation for its success was that *Verlorene Melodie* was particularly well received in regions inhabited by indigenous German speakers (Silesia and Mazury). For these audiences, the film was one of the few 'normal' German-language genre films, different in this respect from ideologically driven films made in East Germany—films from West Germany were not released in Poland at that time. A third explanation may be that former areas under the Austro-Hungarian Empire, such as Cracow, had a strong cultural affinity with Viennese taste in classical music, leading them to read the film more literally.

Not all films perform similarly in the national and Cracow markets. Consider the second and third most attended films from 1951 to 1953 listed in Table 4, both released

[45] Despite the German dialogue, *Verlorene Melodie* was not released in West Germany, although it was premiered in East Germany.

[46] (Grzelecki 1953, p. 7).

in 1950. *Warszawska premiera* is popular in both. A light musical costume film set in the mid-nineteenth century, *Warszawska premiera* centres on staging a music play—the 'Halka'—an important part of Polish heritage. In contrast, the equally popular *Miasto nieujarzmione*, judged from national listings, performs poorly in Cracow, ranked 100. Kulik (1957) shows that this film received broader distribution in rural and industrial districts, distributed in 16 mm format.[47] Telling a similar story to Roman Polański's 2002 film *The Pianist*, *Miasto nieujarzmione*, based on the same source, was a disguised depiction of the Warsaw Uprising in 1944 including the role played by communist partisans as well as the Red Army. The highly sensitive subject material caused the film to be countlessly re-edited, leading to the removal of Czesław Miłosz, the author of the original screenplay and future Nobel prize winner, from the credits. Among Cracow's highly educated audience, the highly tailored *Miasto nieujarzmione* received limited distribution, opening at the category 2 Apollo (Table 6). It can be conjectured that audiences living away from the metropolitan centres of Poland were more tolerant of the heroic depiction of agencies close to the Communist authorities.[48]

7 Conclusion

During the late Stalinist period, the programmes of Polish cinemas were dominated by films from the countries of the Eastern Bloc, particularly the Soviet Union. Regularly, cinema managers received instructions from CZK headquarters that certain Soviet films carrying strong ideological messages must draw full-capacity audiences. Cinema managers fulfilled this obligation in various ways—one of which was for workers' factory councils to order workers to attend screenings. Another way was to attribute tickets bought for another screening to the Soviet film in question.[49] Archival documents give the strong impression that political considerations were more important than economic. In the minutes of the meetings of the CUK Board, it is possible to find multiple entries supporting this contention:

1. 'You cannot adopt a rule that a good film displaces a weak film; we have strict criteria in that regard. This approach is incorrect; we do not consider the audience's consciousness, since to do so would underestimate the value of the film;'[50]
2. 'In cinemas that enjoy capacity attendance, for the first morning and last screenings in the evening, we should schedule films that attract viewers, while documentaries should be planned for the afternoon screenings. This entails irrational copy management, blocking two attractive films for two non-fiction films. But

[47] Kulik (1957, pp. 92–3).

[48] In the 50 s it was the Party's ambition to bring cinema to rural workers. Based upon a diet of Polish and Soviet films, hundreds of new cinemas were built in the countryside.

[49] Central Office of Film (1953, pp. 181–184).

[50] Board of Central Office of Film (1952, p. 115). 'Good' is understood to box-office performance.

this issue can be considered; if it produces results in Moscow, it can produce results here as well;'[51]

3. '...arrange the cinema program so that more popular films are scheduled for the second half of the month, due to the tendency, especially in working-class communities, to cut family budgets at that time.'[52]

However, as shown in this chapter, the task of achieving these ideological ambitions was hampered by supply shortages meaning that films were kept in circulation for extended runs over many years. A likely consequence was that audiences saw their favourite movies more frequently than would have been the case in the West, where poorly supported films were removed from circulation and replaced quickly.

As pervasive as the bureaucratic imperative may have been, substantial evidence is produced to show that under the canopy of bureaucratic control, a functioning market was operating in which film consumers indeed did make choices. First, the demand for films was expanding (Table 2), with ticket sales almost trebling from (zl) 188.4 to 535.8 million between 1950 and 1956, with the costs associated with cinema building and refurbishment doubling. Secondly, a substantial change in preferences occurred during these years away from Soviet films towards domestic productions and movies from the West (Tables 3, 4 and 5).

Except for Polish films, the archives have failed to reveal data on the performance of individual films in the Polish market during the years of 'High Stalinism'. Accordingly, the approach taken in the chapter of supplementing official cinema statistics with programming data from Cracow 1951–1953 provides another source and type of evidence, showing that audiences played an essential part in determining what was screened. Even in a market in which choice was so constricted, some films circulated more than others, and this was primarily demand-led.

The POPSTAT approach shows that over half of the most popular 20 films screened in Cracow between 1951 and 1953 were of Western origin (Table 8). The market share of movies based on their nationality (Table 9) is corroborated partially by the import statistics produced in Table 2 and the earnings of foreign films in Table 5. Furthermore, national attendances of the 19 Polish movies released between 1951 and 1953 (Table 4) correlate positively with their POPSTAT Index values ($r = 0.77$), even though Cracow was hardly representative of the country.

Undoubtedly hindered by the 'masterpiece policy', Soviet cinema performed poorly in Poland. Although dominating supply with mostly old films, POPSTAT results show that they were poorly received on average, securing two Top 20 and no Top 10 berths. This failure is yet another example of the observation that despite the political Stalinisation of Poland, Soviet soft power turned out to be too weak to win the hearts and minds of most Poles. As Babiracki states, 'If the canonisation of the Soviet presence in Poland was the expected norm, Polish participants notoriously failed to deliver'.[53]

---

[51] Board of Film Polski (1951a, 1951b, p. 113).

[52] Film Rental Office (1951, p. 84).

[53] Babiracki (2015, p. 122).

Polish audiences, for their part, could only choose from the film set with which they were presented. We suppose they made their choices based on anticipated pleasure, for which they were prepared to pay. This would help explain the hierarchical pattern of distribution that emerges from the POPSTAT investigation into filmgoing in Cracow during the period of 'High Stalinisation', in which widely circulated films were screened initially in Category 1 cinemas and then moved to lower-order cinemas. This practice indicates that sections of the audience were prepared to pay higher prices to sit in more comfortable cinemas to watch films of their choice early in their life cycle. It is a practice that repeats itself with the most popular movies during their subsequent re-release.

Although no archive evidence has been found to frame the financial imperatives facing cinema and distribution managers, it is evident that as much as the Authorities wanted to shape the future communist citizen, they were mindful of pleasing them in the here and now. In the context of the university city of Cracow, this meant making the most popular films readily available. From this base, it is possible to go forward and investigate the qualities of the most popular movies even when set against the backdrop of a highly doctored choice set.

Acknowledgements Konrad Klejsa's research on film distribution was made possible through a grant from the National Science Centre, Poland (2016/22/E/HS2/00135).

References

Archival Sources

Board of Film Polski. (1950, January 28). *Minutes of the meeting of the board*. Collection 'Ministry of Culture and the Arts', files 'General Management of Film Polski', no. 141. Archive of Modern Records, Warsaw, Poland.

Radkiewicz, R. (1950, September 30). *Evaluation of American, British, and French films – An internal report*. Collection 'Central Committee of the Polish United Workers Party', files 'Subcommittee of Culture', no. 32. Archive of Modern Records, Warsaw, Poland.

Board of Film Polski. (1951a, March 5). *Minutes of the meeting of the board*. Collection 'Ministry of Culture and the Arts', files 'General Management of Film Polski', no 135. Archive of Modern Records, Warsaw, Poland.

Board of Film Polski. (1951b, October 1). *Minutes of the meeting of the board*. Collection 'Ministry of Culture and the Arts', files 'General Management of Film Polski', no 137. Archive of Modern Records, Warsaw, Poland.

Film Rental Office. (1951, May 19). *Programming and reporting rules*. Collection 'Ministry of Culture and the Arts', files 'General Board of Polish Film', no 152. Archive of Modern Records, Warsaw, Poland.

Dytko M. (1952, November 20). *Politics of film distribution*. Collection 'Ministry of Culture and the Arts', files 'Central Office of Film', no 6. Archive of Modern Records, Warsaw, Poland.

Main Office for Control of Press, Publication and Performance (1953, July 29). *Internal report on the public reception of the film 'Żołnierz zwycięstwa' – Appendix no. 1 to the instructional letter D/9*. Collection': Regional Office for Control of Press, Publication and Performance' no. 27. State Archive, Rzeszów, Poland.

Central Office of Film. (1953, no daily date). *Analysis of the performance of OZK in Bydgoszcz in 1953*, Collection 'Ministry of Culture and the Arts', files 'Central Office of Film', no. 172. Archive of Modern Records, Warsaw, Poland.

Central Office of Film. (1953, December 15). *Report on the improprieties in ticket sales in Robotnik cinema in Lublin*. Collection 'Ministry of Culture and the Arts', files 'Central Office of Film', no 75, Archive of Modern Records, Warsaw, Poland.

District Board of Cinema in Cracow. (1954, March 11). *Minutes of the meeting of the OZK-Krakow*. Collection: 'OZK Krakow', file 9/5. State Archive, Cracow, Poland.

Albrecht St. (1954, March 22). [Letter to the Prime Minister]. Collection 'Ministry of Culture and the Arts', files 'Central Office of Film Affairs', no 3. Archive of Modern Records, Warsaw, Poland.

Trade Source

Rotsztat-Miastecki, I. (Ed.). (1938). *Kalendarz Wiadomości Filmowych*. Warszawa: Towarzystwo Filmowe 'Wytwórnia Doświadczalna'.

Book and Articles

Applebaum, A. (2013). *Iron curtain: The crushing of Eastern Europe 1944–1956*. Penguin.

Babiracki, P. (2015). *Soviet Soft Power in Poland: Culture and the making of Stalin's New Empire, 1943–1957*. University of North Carolina Press.

Basiński, E., & Kupiec, A. (Eds.). (1957). *Kinematografia polska w cyfrach*. Naczelny Zarząd Kinematografii.

Garncarz, J. (2021). *Begeisterte Zuschauer: Die Macht des Kinopublikums in der NS-Diktatur*. Köln: Halem.

Grzelecki, S. (1953, August 2). Zagubione melodie. *Film*, p. 8.

Kemp-Welch, A. (2008). *Poland under Communism: A Cold War History*. Cambridge University Press.

Kersten, K. (1999). The Terror, 1949–1954. In Kemp-Welch, A. (Ed.). *Stalinism in Poland, 1944–1956*. International Council for Central and East European Studies & Palgrave Macmillan. https://doi.org/10.1007/978-1-349-27680-6_5

Klejsa, K., & Miller-Klejsa, A. (2021). Almost as good as Soviet cinema: Reception of Italian neorealism in Poland: 1946–56. *Journal of Italian Cinema & Media Studies, 9*(3), 367–84.

Knight, C. I. (2018). Nelli Morozova on Censors, Censorship and the Soviet Film Famine, 1948–52. *Slavonic and East European Review, 96*(4), 704–730.

Krzeczkowska, E. (Ed.). (1969). *Rocznik statystyczny kultury, 1945–1967*. Warszawa: Główny Urząd Statystyczny – Zarząd Wydawnictw, 1969.

Kulik, A. (1957). Badania nad odbiorczością filmu w Polsce. *Kwartalnik Filmowy, 2–3*, 73–80.

Lebow, K. A. (2013). *Unfinished Utopia: Nowa Huta, Stalinism, and Polish Society*. Cornell University Press.

Ostrowska, D. (2017). Humanist Screens': Foreign popular cinema in Socialist Poland (1945–56). In Ostrowska, D., Pitassio, F. & Varga, Z. (Eds.), *Popular Cinemas in Central and Eastern Europe: Film Cultures and Histories* (pp. 136–155). I.B. Tauris.

Sedgwick, J. (2000). *Filmgoing in 1930s Britain: A choice of pleasures*. Exeter University Press.

Sedgwick, J. (2020). Constructing Film Histories: a bottom-up approach, *Academia Letters*, Article86, https://doi.org/10.20935/AL86
Zajiček, E. (1983). *Polska produkcja filmowa. Problemy rentowności*. PWN.
Zamoyski, A. (2017). *Poland: A history*. Hippocrene Books.

Americanisation in Reverse? Hollywood Films, International Influences, and US Audiences, 1946–1965

Peter Miskell

Abstract This chapter focuses attention on the USA in the post-war decades. The period witnessed a dramatic decline in total cinema admissions and a shift in the composition and behaviour of audiences. These changes helped trigger a wider industrial upheaval which has been much discussed in academic literature. The chapter argues that an important feature of Hollywood's response to these changes involved the production of films with a distinctively international character. As international markets became increasingly important for US filmmakers, a key challenge for the industry was the creation of hit films that could appeal to international and domestic audiences alike. By combining evidence from new and existing datasets, I show how internationally themed pictures became increasingly prominent at the US box-office as the period progressed.

This chapter examines the US film industry from the end of the Second World War to the mid-1960s. The subject has been extensively studied, and readers may be forgiven for thinking that there is little left that is new to be said on the matter. It is well understood, for example, that US cinema admissions peaked in 1946 and underwent a dramatic decline during the 1950s.[1] This can be attributed to the diffusion of television and broader social developments such as increasing consumer affluence, alternative leisure pursuits, suburbanisation and the hollowing out of city centres.[2] We know that the 1948 anti-trust decision (the so-called Paramount Decree) forced the vertically integrated US film companies to sell off their chains of cinemas in the subsequent decades.[3] Scholars have pointed not just to declining audiences but changing audience demographics, with adolescents and young adults constituting

[1] Waterman (2005).

[2] Wasko (2012), Hall (2012).

[3] Conant (1976).

P. Miskell (✉)
Henley Business School, University of Reading, Reading, UK
e-mail: p.m.miskell@henley.ac.uk

J. Sedgwick (ed.), *Towards a Comparative Economic History of Cinema, 1930–1970*, Frontiers in Economic History, https://doi.org/10.1007/978-3-031-05770-0_12

an increasing share of moviegoers. These changes affected the nature of the entertainment being screened. The major studios released fewer films, but as the period progressed, these were increasingly likely to be big-budget productions with special characteristics to differentiate them from TV content. Typical themes shifted from family entertainment to pictures with more adult themes, and from romantic dramas intended for middle-aged housewives to war films or thrillers targeted more at young men. Richard Maltby even suggests that the 'shift in the gender of Hollywood's principal target viewer was the real marker of the change from Classical to post-Classical Hollywood'.[4]

The following pages will not present a revisionist history to challenge or overhaul this prior research. Instead, the chapter explores some of these themes in closer detail through a statistical analysis of new and existing datasets. Specifically, it will examine the data collected by John Sedgwick for his 2002 paper on 'Product differentiation at the movies', in conjunction with a new dataset utilising a methodology developed in 2016.[5] The Sedgwick dataset charts the box-office reception in the USA of the top 60 film releases in the twenty years from 1946 to 1965. It also contains information about other characteristics of these films, such as whether they were released in widescreen, 3D, or Cinemascope formats. To this, a new measure of the 'international orientation' of each film in the dataset is added. In his original 2002 paper, Sedgwick demonstrated that even as cinema attendances declined, a minority of films continued to reach very large audiences. It was the mid-budget pictures (previously the industry staple that underpinned the Hollywood studio system) that fell by the wayside. This meant that in the two decades after 1945, an increasing share of US box-office revenues was captured by just a small number of each season's hit films. Of the rental income generated by the top 60 film releases each year, the share captured by the top 10 pictures doubled from 25 per cent in 1946 to 51 per cent in 1965.[6] This chapter brings to light new evidence that helps us identify some of the features that differentiate these hit films from their competitors in the marketplace.

Two major questions will be addressed in this analysis. The first concerns the strategies that leading film producers adopted to differentiate their products from other films in circulation. I will examine the well-known case of widescreen and 3D technologies in this regard but also explore whether the presence of international themes or talent was a distinguishing feature of the most popular films. This line of enquiry allows for a novel argument to be developed about Hollywood as a potential agent of 'reverse-Americanisation'. There is considerable scholarship critiquing and complicating the popular idea that Hollywood entertainment served as a vehicle for the international spread of American ideas, tastes, and fashions—that it helped turn European, Asian, or Latin American audiences into 'temporary American citizens'.[7] But this study allows us to examine Hollywood's role from the opposite perspective.

[4] Maltby (2003, p. 22).

[5] Sedgwick (2002).

[6] Sedgwick (2002, p. 685).

[7] Glancy (2006), Stokes and Maltby (2004).

Were these US companies the mechanism by which European stars, stories, and characters were brought to the attention of mainstream American audiences?

The second question to be addressed here relates to the issue of uncertainty. William Goldman's famous aphorism about Hollywood—that 'nobody knows anything'—was coined in the 1980s but could equally be applied to the period under consideration here.[8] Sedgwick convincingly demonstrated that the risk management strategies successfully adopted by film companies in the inter-war decades became unsustainable in this period.[9] The trend of hit films capturing a greater share of box-office revenues may have been readily observable, but predicting which films would become each season's hits remained elusive.[10] While this chapter identifies certain film characteristics that were positively correlated with box-office revenue, we need to stay extremely cautious when making claims about the predictive power of these observations.

1 Context/Literature

The post-war decades are widely regarded as a period of upheaval for the US film industry. They marked the demise of the so-called 'studio-era', characterised by a few vertically integrated firms producing, distributing and screening a high volume of output for a large audience of regular filmgoers. In its place arose a new industrial arrangement, with the same major distribution companies at its core, but the films were made by a plethora of small independent producers and released to the public via separate chains of movie theatres. The process has come to be seen as a classic example of the transition from Fordist mass production to flexible specialisation, with Hollywood now widely regarded less as a factory town than as an archetypal industrial cluster.[11]

In many accounts, the critical event that triggered this process of industrial upheaval was the decision of the US Supreme Court in 1948, which required the dominant vertically integrated film companies (the so-called 'majors') to divest their cinema chains. This was undoubtedly an important decision. Several of these companies originated as film exhibitors and could plausibly be understood primarily as cinema chains with production facilities attached, rather than the other way around.[12] However, the notion that the wholescale disintegration of the industry can be traced to this single anti trust decision is disputed by some eminent scholars. No less a figure than Janet Staiger has argued that 'the 1948 consent decree was only one factor, and merely a reinforcing one, in a general transition away from a regular output and mass

[8] Goldman (1984).

[9] Sedgwick (2002).

[10] Caves (2000), De Vany (2004).

[11] Storper and Chistopherson (1987), Storper (1989), Scott (2005).

[12] Gomery (1986).

production of films to fewer releases and higher-priced product'.[13] Ten years earlier, Sedgwick made a similar argument: as demand for mid-budget movies collapsed in the face of competition from television, audiences became a great deal more selective about what they would pay to watch at movie theatres.[14] With industry revenues increasingly dominated by the box-office takings of just a few hit films, the studios scaled back in-house production, relying more heavily on independent producers' output, often based outside the USA.[15]

Central to Sedgwick's (2002) paper was the observation that in their quest for hits, film producers (be they major Studios or independents) were under increasing pressure to find ways of differentiating their pictures from the norm. Or, as Darryl Zanuck put it, that a picture 'must have at least an *idea* that will lift it out of the commonplace'.[16]

One well-known way in which producers sought to do this was by investing in new technologies that differentiated the movie-going experience from that of television viewing.[17] While David Bordwell concluded that such developments 'offered only trended changes in the classical style', others have emphasised the impact on audiences.[18] John Belton has argued that the introduction of various widescreen film exhibition practices in the 1950s represented '…a dramatic shift in the film industry's notion of the product it was supplying to the public'. Rather than providing 'entertainment' to relatively passive audiences, the industry's function shifted to providing a much more active and engaging form of 'recreation'.[19] This was evident not just in the array of audio-visual innovations to which audiences were increasing exposed (Technicolor, CinemaScope, 3D, stereo sound), but also in the revival of distribution practices such as 'roadshowing'—a practice in which certain 'event' films were presented to the public in a manner that resembled live theatre: an exclusive booking in a high-profile venue; a matinee and evening performance; raised ticket prices; advanced booking; and often an intermission.[20]

Aside from these technological innovations in film exhibition and shifting patterns of distribution, were there any other differentiation strategies that the industry employed? One potential candidate for our attention is the international orientation of the films themselves. Was it the case that the 'foreignness' of a film's setting or characters, or its key creative team, could provide the distinguishing feature that lifted it 'out of the commonplace'?

The post-war market for foreign films in the United States does feature in standard textbook accounts of the industry in this period. Maltby, for example, points out that many small urban cinemas needed to turn to imports to address the critical product

[13] Staiger (2012, p. 331).

[14] Sedgwick (2002).

[15] See also Miskell (2020).

[16] Quoted in Sedgwick (2002, p. 678).

[17] Casper (2007).

[18] Bordwell et al. (1985, p. 364).

[19] Belton (2012, pp. 355–356).

[20] Hall (2012).

shortage that occurred as the major studios scaled back production.[21] The emergence of 'art-house' cinemas, often screening foreign films, was further evidence of the fragmentation and segmentation of film audiences in this period. But is there any evidence of foreign influences proving influential within what we might call the Hollywood mainstream? Or, more specifically, was it an advantage for a film to have a strong international orientation if it was to become one of the all-important hits that dominated the industry?

The hypothesis may sound counter intuitive. Why on earth would American audiences prefer to watch films based on foreign stories or characters rather than ones derived from their own cultural and social milieu? Economists have pointed to a 'cultural discount' when trading media products such as TV shows and (to a lesser extent) films. The more culturally 'distant' such content is from audiences, the less they are likely to engage with it, and thus imported entertainment typically needs to be sold at a discount to find a market (Hoskins et al., 1997). Following this logic, a hit-making strategy based on the idea of imbuing films with a strong international flavour would appear implausible.

Yet there were very sound economic reasons why Hollywood needed to prioritise the production of precisely these types of films. While cinema audiences were in freefall in the United States, they held up far better in many other parts of the world. In Italy, for example, film attendance peaked in 1955 (a decade later than in the US), and even in 1965, more cinema tickets were being sold than had been the case in 1950.[22] The reopening of international markets after 1945, allied with the relative resilience of film-going as a social activity in many of these countries, meant that US distributors became increasingly reliant on overseas revenues. International markets have, of course, always been important for US film distributors.[23] But whereas foreign markets accounted for something close to 30 per cent of all revenues in 1945, this proportion had grown close to 45 per cent by the early 1960s.[24]

In earlier studies, I have demonstrated that films with a distinctly international orientation formed a critical component of the product portfolios of US distributors. Such films appealed strongly to Hollywood's international audiences without apparently alienating domestic consumers.[25] As international markets became increasingly important in the 1950s and 1960s, it was almost inevitable that these internationally themed pictures would continue to feature prominently in distribution portfolios. Jonathan Stubbs, for example, argues that Hollywood's longstanding fascination with England reached a peak in the mid-1960s.[26] But if Hollywood's 'international films' were a strategic necessity, how did domestic US audiences respond to them?

---

21 Maltby (2003).

22 Miskell and Nicoli (2016).

23 Thompson (1985), Miskell (2020).

24 Miskell and Li (2014).

25 Miskell (2016), Miskell and Li (2014).

26 Stubbs (2019).

Did the international orientation of these pictures create a negative 'cultural discount' as far as local audiences were concerned, or did it provide the type of differentiation that could lift films 'out of the commonplace'?

2 Data and Sources

This chapter brings together information held in two distinct datasets. Sedgwick created the first in preparing his 2002 *Journal of Economic History* article, which charted the increasingly unequal distribution of film revenues between 1946 and 1965.[27] There are two specific elements of that data that have been utilised here. The first is the data on the income generated by the most popular films in the American market annually from 1946 to 1965. The source of this information was the trade journal *Variety*, which regularly published a list of the most popular films released in the prior year in one of its January editions. The published data refers to the rental income each film generated for its distributor rather than the raw box-office takings (which were split between distributors and exhibitors). *Variety* included different numbers of films in each year's lists, ranging from 61 to 130. Accordingly, only the top 60 films from each year have been studied here. The other information from Sedgwick's dataset included in this analysis is a simple dummy variable to identify whether a film was released in a widescreen format. Widescreen films include a variety of formats, including CinemaScope, 3D, Vista Vision, Panavision, Technirama and Todd-AO.

Information from the second dataset has been added to the film popularity and release format data to measure each film's international orientation. The international orientation measure was constructed using the same methodology described in Miskell (2016). The metric consists of eight components. Four relate to each film's scenario (setting, character 1, character 2, and source text), with American nationalities scoring 0 and foreign nationalities scoring 2. A score of 1 is awarded in cases where nationality is mixed or, no nationality applies. The remaining four components refer to the nationality of the key creative team (actor 1, actor 2, director, and screenwriter). Scores are awarded on the same basis, with scores of 1 applied where foreign-born talent have been resident in the US for ten years or more at the time of the film's release.

The primary source for the above information was the catalogue of the American Film Institute (AFI). The catalogue provides plot summaries of each film, used to identify settings and the nationalities of leading characters. The two leading characters (and thus actors) for each film were identified by the order in which they are listed in the catalogue's cast list. The catalogue also provides information on the 'source text' on which the screenplay was based. This has been used to determine the national origin of the stories or texts. Information relating to the key creative personnel involved in each film was drawn from the internet movie database (IMDB).

[27] Sedgwick (2002).

Table 1 How the 'international orientation' score is constructed—some examples

Film	'Scenario'	'Artistic Resources'	International Orientation
Mary Poppins	Setting—UK (2)	Dir—R. Stevenson (1)	Scenario (8)
	Char 1—Mary Poppins (2)	Wr—B. Walsh (0)	Art Res (2)
	Char 2—Bert (2)	Act 1—J. Andrews (1)	
	Text—P. Travers (2)	Act 2—D. Van Dyke (0)	Total = 10
Trapeze	Setting—France (2)	Dir—Carol Reed (2)	Scenario (4)
	Char 1—Mike Ribble (0)	Wr—J.R. Webb (0)	Art Res (2)
	Char 2—Tino Orsini (0)	Act 1—B. Lancaster (0)	
	Text—M. Catto (2)	Act 2—T. Curtis (0)	Total = 6
Best Years of Our Lives	Setting—USA (0)	Dir—W. Wyler (1)	Scenario (0)
	Char 1—Al Stevenson (0)	Wr—R.E. Sherwood (0)	Art Res (1)
	Char 2—Milly Stevenson (0)	Act 1—F. March (0)	
	Text—M. Kantor (0)	Act 2—M. Loy (0)	Total = 1

Source Miskell and Li (2014)

In most cases, this provided the birthplace of lead actors, directors, and screenwriters, but other biographical sources were sought out where this was not available. The filmographies of this talent often made it possible to determine how long they had been based in the USA. American nationality was assumed in the few cases where it was impossible to identify the national origin of key actors, characters, directors, or writers.

Table 1 provides some worked examples applied to three well-known Hollywood films from our period. With this data on film income, release format, and international orientation, it is possible to undertake some statistical analysis to identify characteristics associated with the increasingly important hit films.

3 Widescreen Technology and Film Popularity

Let us start our analysis by simply charting the prevalence of widescreen films among the top 60 and top10 releases each year. Figure 1 illustrates the surge in the use of widescreen film formats in the mid-1950s.

Unlike the introduction of sound film in the late 1920s, the adoption of widescreen technology did not replace more traditional modes of film exhibition. Widescreen

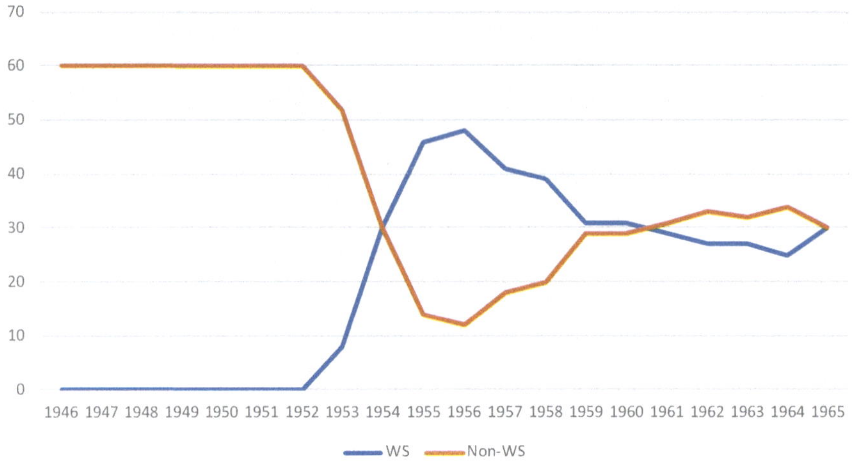

Fig. 1 The prevalence of widescreen formats among top 60 films, 1946–1965 (*Source* Sedgwick [2002] dataset)

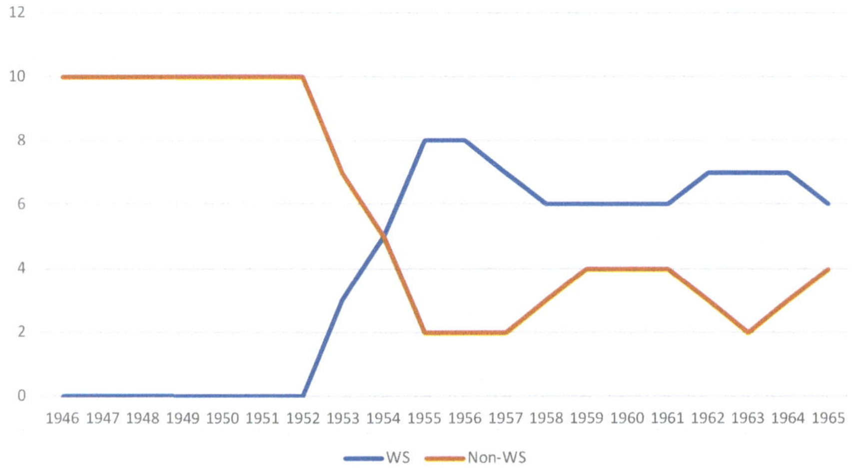

Fig. 2 The prevalence of widescreen formats among top 10 films, 1946–1965 (*Source* Sedgwick [2002] dataset)

remained important throughout this study, but its use was by no means completely ubiquitous. From the end of the 1950s to the mid-1960s, widescreen films consistently accounted for around half of the most popular film releases identified each year by *Variety*.

Focusing attention on just the top ten film releases each year, which, as we know, captured a growing share of overall revenues during this period, Fig. 2 takes on a somewhat different appearance.

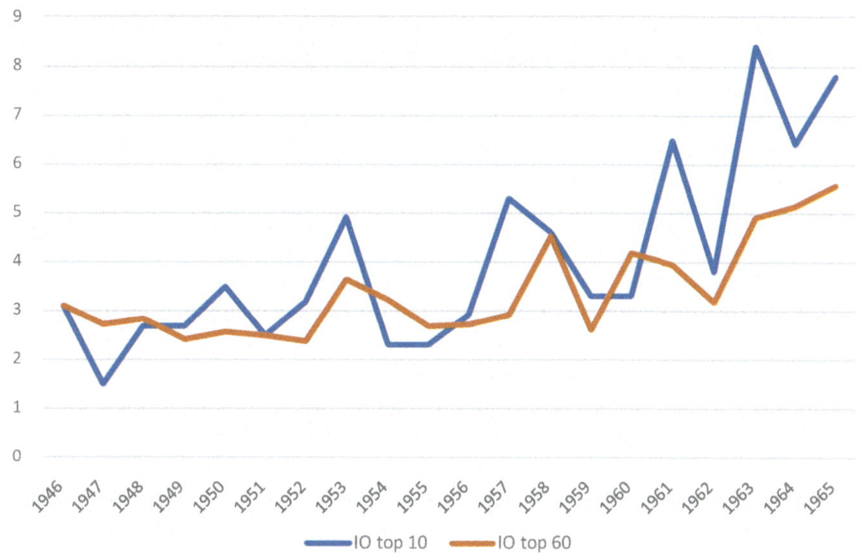

Fig. 3 Average IO scores for top 60 and top 10 films, 1946–1965 (*Source* Sedgwick [2002] dataset; Miskell [2021] dataset)

Once again, we see a surge in the prevalence of widescreen format releases in the early-to-mid-1950s, illustrating the success of such films in attracting very large audience shares. As Cole Porter observed in 1954: … 'if you want the crowds to come around, you've got to have glorious Technicolor, breath-taking CinemaScope, and stereophonic sound'.[28] What is perhaps more striking about Fig. 2, however, is that the balance of widescreen to non-widescreen films among the top 10 hits each year remained firmly tilted in favour of the former throughout our period. Widescreen movies typically constituted just under half of those in our dataset for the first half of the 1960s, but they consistently made up most of each season's biggest hits.

4 International Orientation and Film Popularity

Turning our attention to the international orientation of the films in the dataset, Fig. 3 provides some tentative evidence that it was not only the use of widescreen release formats that helped lift films 'out of the commonplace'. The use of international stories, setting and characters may have helped achieve a similar effect.

Unlike the data for widescreen films, we do not have a binary identification of films as 'international' or 'domestic'. Instead, as described above, each movie in our dataset has been allocated an international orientation score on a scale of 0–16. Figure 3 depicts the average international orientation scores for all the films

[28] Quoted in Belton (2012, p. 356).

in our dataset each year. Two points are worth highlighting. First, the international orientation of all films in the dataset (i.e., the top 60 releases each year) followed an upward trajectory throughout the period. From an average score of just under 3 in the late 1940s, by the end of the period, the average international score was above 5. We also see that the trend towards more internationally oriented films was particularly evident towards the end of the period, in the 1960s. Second, for most of the years under consideration here, the top 10 hit films were more 'international' in their orientation than those in the rest of the dataset. Movies with a relatively high international orientation score were not only represented among each year's major hits but disproportionately so. Again, this is most obviously apparent in the period 1960–1965. The importance of international orientation in relation to film popularity appears to have increased as the period progressed.

This leads to one further observation regarding the international orientation of the most popular films during this period, which is illustrated in Fig. 4: namely, that the increasing tendency for hit films to be internationally themed appears to track quite closely the share of revenue captured by top ten films relative to others in the dataset. As the inequality in the distribution of revenues between films increased, the prevalence of movies with a strong international orientation among the most successful hits also became more pronounced. In Fig. 4, this relationship is illustrated by comparing the average international orientation of each year's top 10 hits (measured on the left-hand axis) with the Gini-coefficient measure of inequality in the revenues earned by each year's films (on the right-hand axis). The correlation between these two sets of data is 0.69.

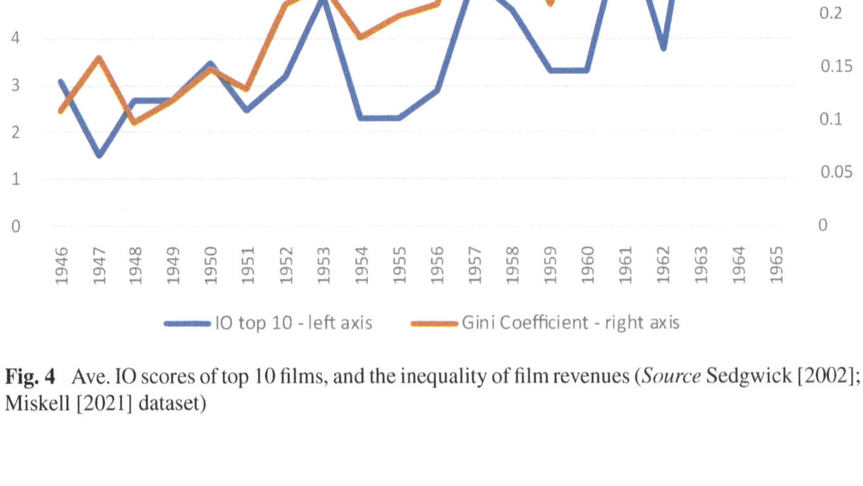

Fig. 4 Ave. IO scores of top 10 films, and the inequality of film revenues (*Source* Sedgwick [2002]; Miskell [2021] dataset)

5 International Orientation of Widescreen Films

So far, we have seen that both widescreen and internationally themed films have been disproportionately represented among the most popular hit films released each year. An obvious question to ask, therefore, is whether widescreen movies were themselves more likely to be internationally oriented than others in the dataset. If film producers and distributors saw widescreen technologies as an important method of product differentiation, is there any evidence to suggest that they may have similarly regarded international orientation? Or, to put it more directly, were film projects with a strong international orientation more likely to be singled out for widescreen treatment than those based on American themes and employing American creative teams?

Figure 5 answers this question in the affirmative. Almost without fail during the period studied here, popular films produced and released utilising widescreen formats were more likely than others to be international in their orientation.

Figure 6 shows the same data for completeness but only for the top 10 films. This doesn't tell us much about film companies' intentions or expectations when deciding whether to give these projects the green light. What it does show, however, is that of the films which were to become each season's top 10 hits, those developed using widescreen technologies were typically more likely to be internationally oriented than those which were released in the traditional format.

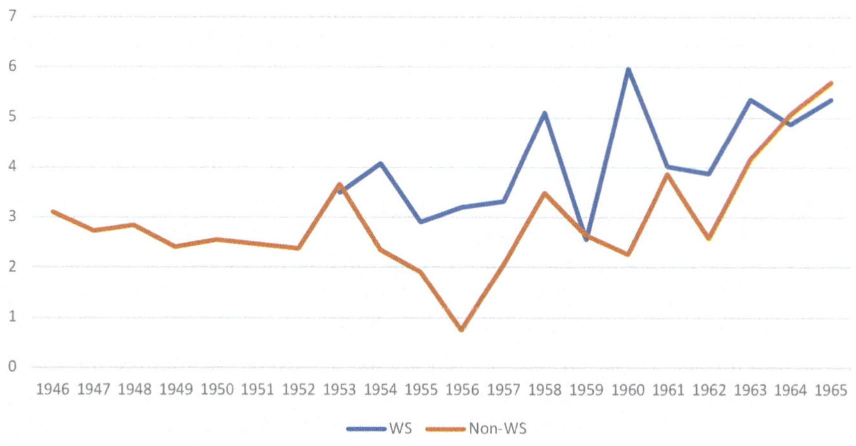

Fig. 5 Ave. IO scores for top 60 films, by format, 1946–1965

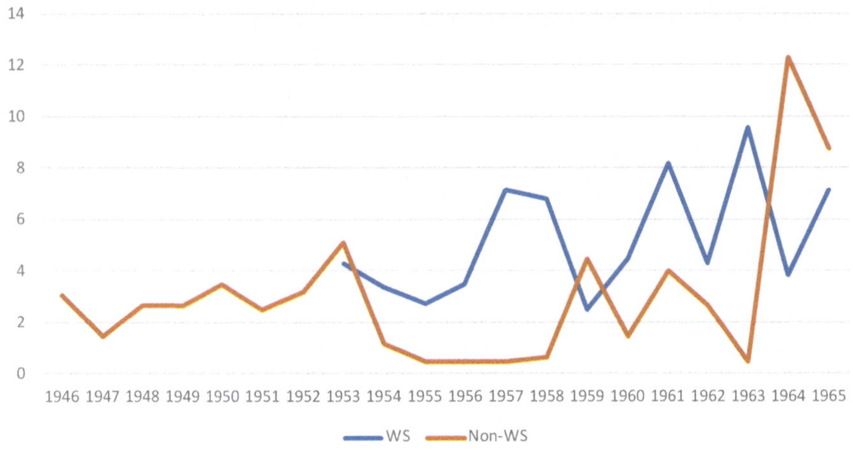

Fig. 6 Ave. IO scores for top 10 films, by format, 1946–1965

6 Predicting Hits?

Thus far, the analysis has been informal and descriptive. The charts above do appear to demonstrate a positive relationship between widescreen technologies and international orientation on the one hand and film popularity on the other. The evidence presented thus far shows, that both widescreen films and those based on international themes and teams were disproportionately represented among each year's all-important top 10 hits. The preceding analysis does not allow us to draw any firm conclusions about the statistical significance of these relationships. The following section will do precisely this.

Constructing a simple multiple regression model is the most direct way to formally measure the impact of widescreen technology and international orientation on film popularity. In this case, we use film revenue as our dependent variable, drawn from the film rental data reported by *Variety* and adjusted for inflation.

Three 'independent' variables have been included in the model. The first is a simple dummy variable indicating whether each film in the data was released in a widescreen format (I have not sought to differentiate between the multiple variations of widescreen technology). Once again, this information is drawn from the *Variety* dataset collected by John Sedgwick. The second variable used to predict film revenue is the international orientation score. As discussed above, this is based on a scale of 0–16, where a score of 0 denotes a film based entirely on American settings, characters, and creative personnel. In contrast, a score of 16 indicates a wholly non-American scenario and creative team. The construction of the international orientation scores was undertaken specifically for this project. It constitutes an original dataset, albeit one based on a methodology developed previously by this author, described above.[29]

[29] Miskell (2016).

Table 2 Regression output, 1953–1965 (dependent variable = film rental income at 1958 prices)

	Co-efficient
Widescreen	0.712**
International orientation	0.164***
US film	1.287*
R squared	0.04
No. observations	780

*** $p < 0.001$, ** $p < 0.01$, * $p < 0.05$

The third and final independent variable included is another dummy to indicate whether an American production company made each film. This enables us to differentiate between pictures with a high international orientation score simply because they were foreign films and Hollywood productions based on international stories employing international stars.

Table 2 presents the results of this analysis for the period 1953–1965. The first and most obvious point to observe is that all three variables are positively associated with film earnings and that these relationships are statistically significant. Thus, each year, among the top 60 films: those released in widescreen formats tended to earn more revenues than traditional releases; US films were stronger box-office performers than foreign ones; a higher international orientation score was associated with higher film revenues. American audiences, it would appear, preferred Hollywood pictures to those from other countries and particularly appreciated Hollywood films based on international stories and characters and or featuring international creative teams.

There are, inevitably, several caveats that need to be made at this point. The first is that the data does not represent a random sample of all films released in the US market in these decades. We are looking at the top 60 movies each year regarding revenues earned for their distributors: thus, *all* the films included in this analysis proved popular at the box-office. A dataset that fully included the 'long right tail' of film releases that struggled to find an audience may generate different results. Therefore, what we learn from Table 2 is not necessarily that these were the key factors that helped films become popular. Instead, among the most popular movies released each year, these factors help predict which would become the biggest hits. Given the increasing inequality in revenue distribution between the top 10 films and the rest during our period, this is potentially important information.

A second and more critical caveat is that while all three of the factors considered here are statistically significant at the five per cent level (and in the case of the international orientation at the 0.1 per cent level)—their predictive power is very weak. Were it the case that a Hollywood film released using widescreen technology and based on international themes could be reliably expected to become a 'hit', then we might reasonably have expected the market to become saturated quickly with such films. However, this did not happen. There certainly was a boom in the prevalence of widescreen film releases in the 1950s, but this settled back in the 1960s (see Fig. 1). We know that the *average* international orientation of films did increase through the period. Still, many popular film releases were based on purely American

Table 3 Regression outputs by period (dependent variable = film rental income at 1958 prices)

	1953–1959	1960–1965
Widescreen	0.516	1.001*
International orientation	0.085*	0.229***
US film	0.377	2.056**
R squared	0.02	0.06
No. observations	420	360

*** $p < 0.001$, ** $p < 0.01$, * $p < 0.05$

stories and made by domestic creative teams. This is reflected in the relatively low coefficient values in Table 2, including the *R* squared statistic that tells us how much of the variance in film revenues within our data can be explained by the three factors included in the model. In this case, the answer is just 4 per cent. So, while our three factors did make a statistically measurable difference, it was a very small one.

Predicting hits in the film business is exceptionally difficult for this period. It may seem strange to have a series of factors, each of which has a relationship with film revenues that is statistically significant, yet for the overall predictive power of the model to be so weak. In this case, however, a very low R squared number should come as no surprise. This is an industry that academic economists have characterised as stable yet shaped by 'extreme uncertainty'.[30] After 2000, there is some evidence that the industry developed a successful hit-making strategy based on the development of long-running film franchises, which has led to a noticeable shift in the typical content of big-budget Hollywood movies (Pokorny et al., 2019). However, no such formula was in evidence in the immediate post-war decades. If the factors we have discussed here resulted in just a four per cent increase in the likelihood of a film becoming a hit, it seems reasonable to maintain that this was indeed an industry in which 'nobody knows anything'.

Before concluding this discussion, there is one other piece of analysis to share. This involves running the same multi-factor regression analysis described but for two distinct sub-periods. From the trends discussed and represented in figures 1–6, we know that the final six years of the period (1960–1965) were noticeably different from the mid-1950s in several respects. While the 1950s saw the market flooded with widescreen films, the 1960s witnessed a much more even balance between widescreen and traditional formats. The 1960s was also when the increase in the typical international orientation of Hollywood films was most pronounced. Finally, during the closing years of the period, the inequality in revenues among the top 60 film releases reached its peak.

Table 3 provides the regression results showing the effect on revenues of the three film characteristics for the periods 1953–1959 and 1960–1965. Perhaps the most striking observation from these results is how much weaker the relationships were in the 1950s compared with the first half of the 1960s. While we can see positive correlations between all three variables and film revenues in the 1950s, only

[30] De Vany (2004, pp. 1–6).

the international orientation measure was statistically significant (at the 5 per cent level). International themes or stars did tend to feature in the most popular films of the period, although the impact of this measure was very modest. As far as technological innovation was concerned, several highly successful widescreen films were released in this period, but the various widescreen formats became so prevalent that this factor (in itself) was rendered ineffective as a method of product differentiation. A similar explanation might be offered concerning Hollywood films more generally. As the industry experienced a period of dramatic change in audience viewing habits, and as filmmakers scrambled to respond to these changes, it was not necessarily the case that US-based producers held an advantage in their ability to generate hits.

However, as we move into the 1960s, the picture changes quite noticeably. If the 1950s look like a period of transition in which the US film industry was struggling to come to terms with the new demands of its domestic audiences, the 1960s appears as one in which the industry was beginning to find its feet. The number of widescreen films appearing among the major releases of each year may have fallen back from its 1950s peak, but these films were now much more likely to be among each season's biggest hits. US filmmakers were, once again, much more likely to be responsible for the biggest hits than foreign producers. But if the popularity of foreign films diminished in the 1960s, the appeal of films with international settings, characters and stars most certainly did not. The list of the five most popular movies released in the US market in 1965 illustrates the point rather neatly: (1) *Sound of Music*; (2) *Mary Poppins*; (3) *My Fair Lady*; (4) *Goldfinger*; and (5) *Those Magnificent Men in their Flying Machines*. The filmmaking business remained fraught with uncertainty, and even in the 1960s, the predictive power of the three variables outlined here to explain film revenues was only six per cent. We appear to be not observing the emergence of reliable formula for hit-making in the post-war decades but rather a process by which the major studios were learning to adapt to a new risk environment for filmmaking. They not only learned to deploy new technologies more effectively but also to integrate international content (which had long been essential for their overseas markets) into film projects that could win over cinema audiences in the US itself.

7 Conclusion

In earlier research, I introduced the 'international orientation' measure of film content to explain how the major American producer-distributors sought to appeal to international audiences. Following a transition period in the late 1920s where audience demand was disrupted by the introduction of sound technology, US firms built into their annual film portfolios a distinct category of pictures (with high international orientation scores) that generated disproportionately large revenues from outside the USA. Think of the films starring Greta Garbo. This chapter has examined another significant disruption to the US film industry, affecting domestic US audiences. Perhaps unsurprisingly, we have found evidence that it took the industry time to adapt to this disruption, but rather more unexpectedly, we have also seen that the international orientation of films had a significant role in the industry's management of this transition.

As the weekly or twice-weekly habit of visiting the local neighbourhood cinema was eroded by television, suburbanisation, and a combination of other factors, the market for staple mid-budget Hollywood films collapsed. Film-going continued, but audiences became much more selective, with just a few hit films capturing an increasing proportion of box-office revenues. Predicting which films would become each season's hits was notoriously difficult. Still, industry executives also knew they had to invest their biggest pictures with some point of differentiation, something to lift them 'out of the commonplace'. The use of new technologies associated with widescreen or 3D film releases was a well-known way the industry sought to do this. Yet, as the preceding analysis has shown, the surge in the number of widescreen films in the 1950s did little to improve the prospects of the individual movies released in one of these formats. In terms of its statistical significance, international orientation appeared to be somewhat more effective as a product differentiation strategy. By the 1960s, widescreen formats were being targeted more effectively, but the strength of the relationship between international orientation and film revenues had also increased. It did appear that far from being put off by pictures based on foreign content or featuring foreign stars; such films attracted US audiences.

Does this constitute evidence of Americanisation in reverse? There are two reasons to be cautious about making this claim. The first is that although the relationship between film revenues and international orientation was statistically significant, the predictive power of the international orientation measure is very weak. The presence of Audrey Hepburn or Sean Connery may have added to a film's pulling power, but plenty of other international stars made little or no impression on US audiences. The second reason for caution is that even if internationally themed films were often popular, this did not mean they were influential in shaping US audiences' ideas, values, or beliefs. Most of these films were made by US production companies who had no interest in reshaping the worldview of the typical filmgoer. International settings, characters, or stars provided a point of differentiation rather than a point of departure. They allowed for conventional narrative devices to be deployed in new ways. As one recent study of hit-making in the creative industries put it: 'people crave new products, ideas and stories, provided they are just like the products, ideas and stories they already know'.[31] Hollywood's 'international films' show how film producers have sought to generate what Thompson refers to as 'optimally new' content.

But if claims of 'Americanisation in reverse' are perhaps a step too far, the internationalisation of Hollywood film remains a noteworthy feature of the period. These were decades when international markets became as important as the domestic for major US distributors. Even if US audiences had remained impervious to internationally themed films, they would likely have featured more prominently in production schedules. In the 1920s and 1930s, Hollywood's international films helped sustain the

[31] Thompson (2017, p. 284).

studios' revenues from international markets. By the 1950 and 1960s, internationally themed films were no longer a small element within wider product portfolios; they were increasingly becoming Hollywood's core product. The task facing US distributors in this period was not simply selling American films to international markets, but increasingly how to make the internationally themed pictures that did so well in foreign markets appeal to domestic audiences. On the evidence that we have reviewed here, it seems that they accomplished this task remarkably successfully.

References

Belton, J. (2012). Glorious Technicolor, breathtaking cinemascope and stereophonic sound. In S. Neale (Ed.), *The Classical Hollywood Reader* (pp. 355–369). Routledge.
Bordwell, D., Staiger, J., & Thompson, K. (1985). *The Classical Hollywood Cinema: Film Style and Mode of Production to 1960*. Routledge.
Casper, D. (2007). *Postwar Hollywood, 1946–1962*. Blackwell Publishing.
Caves, R. (2000). *Creative industries: Contracts between art and commerce*. Harvard University Press.
Conant, M. (1976). The impact of the *Paramount* Decrees. In T. Balio (Ed.), *The American Film Industry* (pp. 346–370). University of Wisconsin Press.
De Vany, A. (2004). *Hollywood economics: How extreme uncertainty shapes the film industry*. Routledge.
Glancy, M. (2006). Temporary American citizens? British audiences, Hollywood films and the threat of Americanization in the 1920s. *Historical Journal of Film, Radio and Television, 26*(4), 461–484.
Goldman, W. (1984). *Adventures in the screen trade: A personal view of Hollywood and screenwriting*. Warner Books.
Gomery, D. (1986). *The Hollywood Studio System*. British Film Institute.
Hall, S. (2012). Ozoners, roadshows and blitz exhibitionism: Postwar developments in distribution and exhibition. In S. Neale (Ed.), *The Classical Hollywood Reader* (pp. 343–354). Routledge.
Hoskins, C., McFadyen, S., & Finn, A. (1997). *Global television and film: An introduction to the economics of the business*. Oxford University Press.
Maltby, R. (2003). *Hollywood cinema*. Blackwell Publishing.
Miskell, P. (2016). International films and international markets: The globalisation of Hollywood entertainment, 1921–1951. *Media History, 22*(2), 174–200.
Miskell, P. (2020). Entertainment and the film industry. In T. S. Lopes, C. Lubinski, & H. J. S. Tworek (Eds.), *The Routledge companion to the makers of global business* (pp. 377–391). Abingdon.
Miskell, P., & Li, Y. (2014). Hollywood studios, independent producers and international markets: globalisation and the US film industry c. 1950–1965. *Henley Business School Working Paper, IBH-2014–07*.
Miskell, P., & Nicoli, M. (2016). From outsiders to insiders? Strategies and practices of American film distributors in post-war Italy. *Enterprise and Society, 17*(3), 546–590.
Pokorny, M., Miskell, P., & Sedgwick, J. (2019). Managing uncertainty in creative industries: Film sequels and Hollywood's profitability, 1988–2015. *Competition and Change, 23*(1), 23–46.
Scott, A. (2005). *On Hollywood: The place, the industry*. Princeton University Press.
Sedgwick, J. (2002). Product differentiation at the movies: Hollywood, 1946 to 1965. *The Journal of Economic History, 62*(3), 676–705.
Staiger, J. (2012). Individualism versus collectivism: The shift to independent production in the US film industry. In S. Neale (Ed.), *The Classical Hollywood Reader* (pp. 331–342). Routledge.

Stokes, M., & Maltby, R. (2004). *Hollywood Abroad: Audiences and cultural exchange*. British Film Institute.
Storper, M. (1989). The transition to flexible specialisation in the US film industry: External economies, the division of labour and the crossing of industrial divides. *Cambridge Journal of Economics, 13*(2), 273–305.
Storper, M., & Christopherson, S. (1987). Flexible specialisation and regional industrial agglomerations: The case of the US picture industry. *Annals of the Association of American Geographers, 77*(1), 104–117.
Stubbs, J. (2019). *Hollywood and the Invention of England: Projecting the English Past in American Cinema, 1930–2017*. Bloomsbury Academic.
Thompson, K. (1985). *Exporting Entertainment: America in the World Film Market*. British Film Institute.
Thompson, D. (2017). *Hit makers: How things become popular*. Allen Lane.
Wasko, J. (2012). Hollywood and television in the 1950s: The roots of diversification. In S. Neale (Ed.), *The Classical Hollywood Reader* (pp. 370–388). Routledge.
Waterman, D. (2005). *Hollywood's road to riches*. Harvard University Press.

Correction to: Film Exhibition, Distribution and Popularity in German-Occupied Belgium (1940–1944): Brussels, Antwerp and Liege

Roel Vande Winkel and John Sedgwick

Correction to:
Chapter "Film Exhibition, Distribution and Popularity in German-Occupied Belgium (1940–1944): Brussels, Antwerp and Liege": J. Sedgwick (ed.), *Towards a Comparative Economic History of Cinema, 1930–1970*, Frontiers in Economic History, https://doi.org/10.1007/978-3-031-05770-0_8

The original version of the book was inadvertently published with the author comments in the captions of Figures 3, 4 and in the first reference text in Chapter 8, which have now been corrected. The book has been updated with the changes.

The updated original version of this chapter can be found at https://doi.org/10.1007/978-3-031-05770-0_8

J. Sedgwick (ed.), *Towards a Comparative Economic History of Cinema, 1930–1970*, Frontiers in Economic History, https://doi.org/10.1007/978-3-031-05770-0_13

The manufacturer's authorised representative in the EU is Springer Nature Customer Service Centre GmbH, Europaplatz 3, 69115 Heidelberg, Germany. If you have any concerns regarding our products, please contact ProductSafety@springernature.com

Printed and bound by CPI Group (UK) Ltd, Croydon, CR0 4YY
30/09/2026
02225462-0013